Lecture Notes in Artificial Intelligence 6547

Edited by R. Goebel, J. Siekmann, and W. Wahlster

Subseries of Lecture Notes in Computer Science

Salvador Abreu Dietmar Seipel (Eds.)

Applications of Declarative Programming and Knowledge Management

18th International Conference, INAP 2009
Évora, Portugal, November 3-5, 2009
Revised Selected Papers

Springer

Series Editors

Randy Goebel, University of Alberta, Edmonton, Canada
Jörg Siekmann, University of Saarland, Saarbrücken, Germany
Wolfgang Wahlster, DFKI and University of Saarland, Saarbrücken, Germany

Volume Editors

Salvador Abreu
Departamento de Informática, Universidade de Évora
Lago dos Colegais, 2, 7004-516 Évora, Portugal
E-mail: spa@di.uevora.pt

Dietmar Seipel
Universität Würzburg, Fakultät für Informatik
Am Hubland, 97074 Würzburg, Germany
E-mail: dietmar.seipel@uni-wuerzburg.de

ISSN 0302-9743 e-ISSN 1611-3349
ISBN 978-3-642-20588-0 ISBN 978-3-642-20589-7 (eBook)
DOI 10.1007/978-3-642-20589-7
Springer Heidelberg Dordrecht London New York

Library of Congress Control Number: 2011925389

CR Subject Classification (1998): I.2.4, I.2, D.1.6

LNCS Sublibrary: SL 7 – Artificial Intelligence

Typesetting: Camera-ready by author, data conversion by Scientific Publishing Services, Chennai, India

Printed on acid-free paper

Springer is part of Springer Science+Business Media (www.springer.com)

Preface

This volume contains a selection of papers, revised and extended, which were presented at the 18th International Conference on Applications of Declarative Programming and Knowledge Management, INAP 2009, which was held in Évora, Portugal, during November 3–5, 2009.

Declarative programming is an advanced paradigm for modeling and solving complex problems. It has become more and more attractive, e.g., in the database domain, for natural language processing, for modeling and processing combinatorial problems, and for establishing knowledge–based systems for the Web.

The INAP series of conferences provide a forum for intensive discussions on applications of important technologies around logic programming, constraint problem solving, and closely related advanced software. The conferences comprehensively cover the impact of programmable logic solvers in the Internet society, its underlying technologies, and leading-edge applications in industry, commerce, government, and societal services.

The topics of the selected papers of this year's conference concentrated on three currently important fields: foundations and extensions of logic programming, databases and query languages, declarative programming with logic languages, and applications thereof.

During the last couple of years, a lot of research has been conducted on the usage of declarative programming for *querying databases* and *Web-based knowledge structuring and querying*. Reasoning about knowledge wrapped in rules, databases, or the Web leads to the exploration of interesting and hitherto implicit knowledge. Declarative techniques for the transformation, deduction, induction, visualization, or querying of knowledge have the advantage of high transparency and better maintainability compared with more traditional procedural approaches.

Another area of active research is the *extension* of the *logic programming paradigm* and its integration with other programming concepts. The successful extension of logic programming with constraints has already been mentioned. Other extensions aim to increase the expressivity of logic languages by including new logical constructs like contextual operators, temporal annotations, or tabling. The integration of logic programming with other programming paradigms has been mainly investigated for the case of functional programming. This combination is beneficial from a software engineering point of view: well–known functional programming techniques for improving the structure and quality of the developed software, e.g., types, modules, higher–order operators, or lazy evaluation, can also be used for logic programming in an integrated language.

The INAP 2009 conference was organized at the University of Évora, Portugal, by the following institutions: the University of Évora, the Society for Logic Programming (GLP e.V.), and the Portuguese A.I. Society (APPIA.) The conference took place over three days, with invited presentations by Terrance Swift and António Porto, which are part of this volume. We would like to thank all authors who submitted papers and all conference participants for the intense and fruitful discussions throughout the conference. We are grateful to the members of the Program Committee and the external referees for their timely expertise in carefully reviewing the papers, and we would like to acknowledge the University of Évora for hosting the conference.

January 2011

Dietmar Seipel
Salvador Abreu

Organization

Program Chairs

Salvador Abreu	University of Évora, Portugal
Dietmar Seipel	University of Würzburg, Germany

Program Committee

Salvador Abreu	University of Évora, Portugal (Co-chair)
Sergio A. Alvarez	Boston College, USA
Philippe Codognet	JFLI/CNRS, Japan
Daniel Diaz	University of Paris-I (Sorbonne), France
Ulrich Geske	University of Potsdam, Germany
Gopal Gupta	University of Texas at Dallas, USA
Petra Hofstedt	Technical University of Berlin, Germany
Ulrich Neumerkel	Technical University of Vienna, Austria
Vitor Nogueira	University of Évora, Portugal
Enrico Pontelli	New Mexico State University, USA
Irene Rodrigues	University of Évora, Portugal
Carolina Ruiz	Worcester Polytechnic Institute, USA
Vitor Santos Costa	University of Porto, Portugal
Dietmar Seipel	University of Würzburg, Germany (Co-chair)
Terrance Swift	CENTRIA, Portugal
Hans Tompits	Technical University of Vienna, Austria
Masanobu Umeda	Kyushu Institute of Technology, Japan
Armin Wolf	Fraunhofer FIRST, Germany
Osamu Yoshie	Waseda University, Japan

Local Organization

Vitor Nogueira	University of Évora, Portugal
Vasco Pedro	University of Évora, Portugal
Pedro Salgueiro	University of Évora, Portugal

External Referees

Dirk Kleeblatt	Florian Lorenzen
Johannes Oetsch	Paulo Quaresma
Judith Rohloff	Christian Schneiker
Ludwig Krippahl	Tran Cao Son

Table of Contents

Invited Talks

Foundations and Extensions of Logic Programming

Databases and Query Languages

Applications

Design Patterns for Tabled Logic Programming

Terrance Swift

Centro de Inteligência Artificial, Universidade Nova de Lisboa

Abstract. The use of design patterns is common in many areas of software engineering and programming. While they are informal, patterns provide a repository of solutions to common problems, as well as a survey of the features of a given language or software system. This paper uses design patterns to survey features and applications of Tabled Logic Programming (TLP). Patterns for commonly available features are presented, such as those of various recursion types that arise when tabling is used with definite programs, of automatic tabling and of tabling with DCGs. In addition, various patterns capture well-developed uses of tabled negation for non-monotonic reasoning. A final set of patterns describes the approaches of answer subsumption and tabled constraints, features that have fewer applications to date due to the fact that robust implementations of them have only recently become available.

1 Introduction

The past few years have brought an increasing amount of research into Tabled Logic Programming (TLP), so that TLP is now available in several Prolog systems including XSB, YAP, B Prolog, Mercury, ALS, and Ciao. A leading reason for this interest is the demonstrated ability of TLP to solve practical problems. TLP has been used in XSB to implement systems for program analysis, model checking, agent frameworks, semantic web applications, natural language processing, medical informatics, and software engineering. TLP has been used in YAP for machine learning and bioinformatics applications; TLP has also been used with B Prolog to implement probabilistic reasoning in the PRISM system and with XSB and YAP to implement other types of probabilistic inference. In some of these applications, TLP is used simply as a means to compute transitive closure. In other applications, the uses of TLP are more elaborate: tabling is used to evaluate large sets of mutually recursive predicates, to provide full well-founded negation, to provide a basis for quantitative reasoning, or is combined with logical constraints. A bibliography of such applications is available in [24].

This paper attempts to survey approaches to TLP by making use of the organizing principle of software design patterns (cf. [3]). Software design patterns were originally applied to object-oriented programs, but they have since been applied to a variety of areas including workflow systems, stream databases, and enterprise architectures. However, within logic programming the use of design patters is uncommon, perhaps because of their lack of formality. While software design patterns do not provide a formal basis for program synthesis or development, they can provide a useful framework to highlight programming idioms and to associate these idioms with their uses. Even a partial framework can benefit users by providing a survey of "tricks of the trade"; it can benefit

S. Abreu and D. Seipel (Eds.): INAP 2009, LNAI 6547, pp. 1–19, 2011.

engine implementors by indicating the types of operations that need to be efficient or robust and by providing guidance for a common suite of benchmarks; the framework can benefit compiler writers by indicating analysis problems that are characteristic of TLP. Towards that end, this paper makes the first known attempt at using design patterns to classify TLP programming idioms. While the tabling features we describe are in principle general, the patterns listed arise mainly from uses of XSB; other patterns would emerge from uses of tabling systems with features not found in XSB; in particular the combination of tabling and parallelism in YAP has lead to interesting approaches to model checking and machine learning; programming patterns used in such systems may not be covered here.

This paper assumes a general knowledge of how tabling from a programmer's perspective, and at times a basic understanding of the well-founded semantics. In certain patterns, however, we discuss the use of call variance or call subsumption. Most tabling systems implement only call variance in which answer resolution is used for a tabled subgoal S only if there is a table for a subgoal S_T that is a variant of S (i.e. S and S_T are the same up to variable renaming). Call subsumption on the other hand allows S_T to be used if it *subsumes* S (i.e. if $S = S_T\theta$). Accordingly, if numerous subsuming or even unifying calls are made to a tabled predicate, call subsumption can be much more efficient than call variance.

Section 2 details patterns that use various forms of tabling over definite programs; Section 3 covers patterns that emerge when tabled negation is also used. Section 4 discusses patterns used when tabling is used for quantitative or paraconsistent reasoning, for reasoning with constraints, or for grounding a program.

2 Tabling for Definite Programs

Pattern 1. *Tabling to save recomputation*

Perhaps the most obvious use for tabling is to factor out subcomputations that are reused within a larger computation. For instance, consider a predicate p/n whose computation is expensive – perhaps due to the complexity of p/n or because p/n is defined in an external database or on a web site. If information in p/n were expected to be repeatedly used by a program, it might well need to be cached. To achieve this, p/n might be loaded during program initialization and asserted as Prolog facts or clauses, but such a solution is not always satisfactory. For instance, if p/n were large, it would be more efficient to load only those parts of it that were used. In such a case, a better solution would be to lazily cache the answers to queries of p/n.

Of course, one could write a simple caching system that used asserted code, but without substantial work such an approach would be less declarative, less efficient, and more cumbersome than a solution that used tabling. Furthermore, tabling can efficiently handle subsuming calls to such caches when call subsumption is used, and tables can be incrementally updated if the cache is based on dynamic data (cf. Pattern 12). Applications such as the semantic web and machine learning benefit from TLP's ability to save recomputation, but as shown below, tabling provides much richer benefits for these and other areas.

Pattern 2. *Left linear recursion*
Left linear recursion arises when tabling is used to program transitive closure over a binary relation, as in the rule

```
:- table reach/2.
reach(X,Y):- reach(X,Z),edge(Z,Y).
reach(X,Y):- edge(X,Y).
```

The first rule is linear because it has a single occurrence of a (tabled) recursive predicate in its body, and is left-linear because the occurrence is the leftmost literal in the body. If `edge/2` is a finite relation, `reach/2` will terminate, with cost linear in the size of `edge/2`. While the underlying `edge/2` relationship is commonly thought of as a graph, binary relations are ubiquitous in computer science. Similar relations also form the basis of process logics (when modeled as transition systems or nets) and of temporal and modal logics (when modeled as binary Kripke structures). The following example shows how this simple pattern forms the basis of an evaluation of Workflow nets. This use of tabling to emulate Workflow nets is representative of tablings use to evaluate Petri Nets, CCS, the π-calculus and other process logics.

Example 1 (Workflow Nets). Representations of workflows are often based on an extension of Petri nets, called Workflow nets. Such nets can formally and graphically represent control and data flows, such as loops, I/O preconditions, if/then clauses and many other synchronization dependencies between workflow units. Reachability is a central problem for analysis of such nets, to which problems such as liveness, deadlock-freedom, and the existence of home states can be reduced. Workflow nets consist of a set of *places* that can contain various kinds of tokens, and the configuration of a net is determined by the tokens in each of its places. Transitions move a net from one configuration to another. As in Petri nets, the definition of a transition T includes a list of places with input arcs to T ($\bullet T$) and output arcs from T ($T\bullet$). In addition, transitions in Workflow nets are extended with guard conditions and after effects. These conditions and effects can may affect places that are not included in the input and output of a transition: they can dynamically create sub-instances, check for the presence or absence of tokens in given places (which allows merging of dynamically created paths through the net), and delete tokens from places if a transition is taken (which allows cancellation).

To model a Workflow net using TLP, a token is represented as a term that identifies a given instance, perhaps along with other information, e.g. `order_instance(7)`. The state of a place $p1$ is maintained as an ordered list within the term $p1/1$. Transitions for Workflow net have the abstract form

```
trans(InConf,OutConf,dyn(Conditions,Effects),Name).
```

Figure 1 shows a program for determining reachability in a Workflow net [1]. For efficiency the reachability program assumes that the `InConf` and `OutConf` lists in all transitions and configurations are ordered: XSB's trie indexing of transitions makes use of this ordering. The potential of a given transition to fire in a given state, or its *concession* is checked by the predicate `hasTransition/2` in Figure 1 which recurses

[1] All process net code in this paper is available via `xsb.sourceforge.net` in the module `mttests`.

```
% Prolog representation of the Producer-Consumer net
:- index(trans/3,trie).
trans([p1(X)],[],dyn([],[insert(p2(o(X,I)),p1_gen(I))),split).
trans([p2(X)],[p3(X)],dyn([finished_p2(X)],[]),process).
trans([p3(o(X,_)],[p4(X)],dyn([doesnt_contain(p2(o(X,_))),
                              [delete(p3(o(X,_)))])),merge).

:- table reachable/2.
reachable(InConf,NewConf):-
   reachable(InConf,Conf),
   hasTransition(Conf,NewConf).
reachable(InConf,NewConf):-
   hasTransition(InConf,NewConf).

hasTransition(Conf,NewConf):-
   get_trans_for_conf(Conf,AllTrans),
   member(Trans,AllTrans),
   apply_trans_to_conf(Trans,Conf,NewConf).

get_trans_for_conf(Conf,Flattrans):-
   get_trans_for_conf_1(Conf,Conf,Trans),
   flatten(Trans,Flattrans).

get_trans_for_conf_1([],_Conf,[]).
get_trans_for_conf_1([H|T],Conf,[Trans1|RT]):-
   findall(trans([H|In],Out,Dyn,T),
           trans([H|In],Out,Dyn,T),Trns),
   check_concession(Trns,Conf,Trans1),
   get_trans_for_conf_1(T,Conf,RT).

check_concession([],_,[]).
check_concession([trans(In,Out,Dyn,Name)|T],Input,
                 [trans(In,Out,Dyn,Name)|T1]):-
   state_subset(In,Input),
   check_dynamic_constraints(Dyn,Input),!,
   check_concession(T,Input,T1).
check_concession([_Trans|T],Input,T1):-
   check_concession(T,Input,T1).

apply_trans_to_conf(trans(In,Out_Name),Conf,NewConf):-
   ord_subtract(Conf,In,Diff),
   flatten([Out|Diff],Temp),
   apply_dynamic_effects(Effects,Temp,Temp1),
   sort(Temp1,NewConf).
```

Fig. 1. TLP Program for analyzing Workflow Nets

through the places in the current configuration (`Conf`) to find sets of transitions that might have concession. This recursion (in `get_trans_for_conf_1/3`) allows trie indexed calls to transitions to be made based on each place in the input configuration. The predicate `check_concession/2` filters each set of possible transitions to include only those that actually have concession in `Conf`. This is done by checking that the input states for the transition are covered by the current configuration, and then evaluating the guard conditions for the transition. The resulting list contains all applicable transitions. Each transition is applied upon backtracking through the list, when its after effect will also be applied.

The transitions in Figure 1 represent the combination of two workflow patterns from [18]: multiple instance creation followed a synchronized merge, shown graphically in Figure 2. When a given token instance `X` reaches place `p1`, multiple subinstances of `X` are created and placed in `p2`, handled by an after effect in transition `split`. When each sub-instance is finished with process represented by `p2` it moves to `p3` via transition `process`. Once all sub-instances of `X` have reached `p3` (as determined by a condition in transition `merge`), they are deleted by an after effect and the reconstituted instance `X` is moved to `p4`. The full code for this Workflow net evaluator is approximately twice the size of that in Figure 1, and can emulate nearly all common workflow control patterns in [18]. It has been used to analyze health care workflows based on clinical care guidelines.

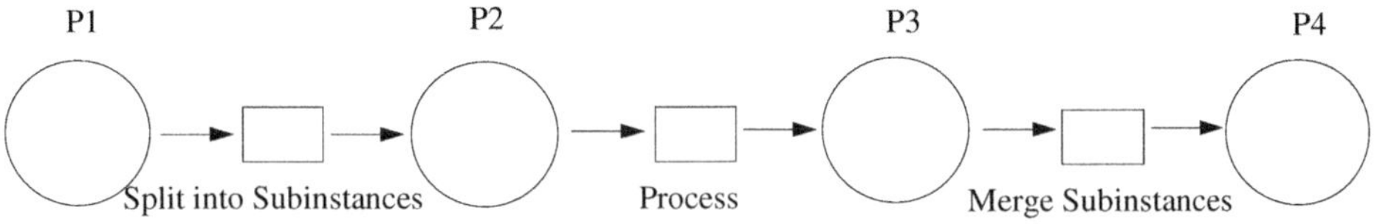

Fig. 2. Instance Creation with Synchronizing Merge

Pattern 3. *Single-predicate recursion*

Even if only a single recursive predicate is tabled, the position of a tabled literal within the body of a clause can affect efficiency, as shown by the following sub-patterns.

Pattern 3a *Non-Left linear recursion.* The `reach/2` predicate could also be written in a non-left linear form as

```
:- table reach/2.
reach(X,Y):- edge(X,Z),reach(Z,Y).
reach(X,Y):- edge(X,Y).
```

While both forms are logically equivalent, the left linear form is more efficient for many purposes (assuming Prolog's literal selection strategy). Consider a query to `reach/2` with the first argument bound and the second free. Left linear recursion would create a single table, containing every reachable vertex in the graph as an answer. In the non-left (here, right) linear recursive form, the binding of head `reach(X,Y)` differs from that of the body occurrence `reach(Z,Y)`. As a result, this form would contain a separate table for each binding $Z\theta$ in `reach(Z,Y)`, while each of these tables would contain the vertices reachable from $Z\theta$. In the worst case, the cost would be quadratic in the size of the graph rather than linear. This may not be as large a disadvantage if reachability of all pairs were desired. However a query $reach(-,-)$ to the left linear form would create a single table rather than multiple tables (although both queries would create the same total number of answers) and with call subsumption the left-linear form would generally be more efficient.

While transitive closure is most efficiently modeled using left recursion, some properties of a relation cannot always be efficiently transformed. For instance, a positional property of a directed acyclic graph can be modeled using the `same_generation/2` predicat

```
same_generation(X,X).
same_generation(X,Y):-
    parent(X,Z),same_generation(Z,Z1),parent(Y,Z1).
```

If a (partially) bound query were made to `same_generation/2`, then transforming `same_generation(Z,Z1)` to be the left-most body literal would cause a completely unbound call will be made to `same_generation/2`. In this case all of the underlying `parent/2` relation would be traversed, rather than just that portion relevant to the query.

Pattern 3b *Non-linear recursion.* It would also be possible to write the `reach/2` predicate using non-linear recursion – here, double recursion

```
:- table reach/2.
reach(X,Y):- reach(X,Z),reach(Z,Y).
reach(X,Y):- edge(X,Y).
```

For `reach/2` double recursion is less efficient even than the right-linear form, as each solution to a `reach/2` subquery must be returned to two places rather than one. Non-linear recursion is not needed for the simple example of transitive closure because of the uniformity of the structure being searched – the single `edge/2` predicate. However, as shown in the next pattern, non-linear recursions can be useful when combinations of different relations need to be searched.

Pattern 4. *Mutual recursion*

Mutual recursion is necessary when properties of several relations need to be determined at once, or when properties of non-binary relations are desired. One example of different relations needing to be simultaneously evaluated arises in the implementation of a temporal logic query evaluation mechanism for model checking (cf. [15]), which uses tabled mutual recursion between a predicate that evaluates properties that are true for a given temporal world W and a predicate that evaluates properties false for W. More complex situations arise below when tabling is used to parse grammars based on interdependent and possibly non-binary categories (e.g. noun phrases, verb phrases etc.).

Pattern 4a *Chart Parsers.* Prolog DCGs provide a useful means for parsing many grammars, but DCGs suffer from two potentially serious disadvantages. First, to ensure termination, a programmer may have to execute left-recursion and left-factoring.

Such transformations may not only complicate a grammar, but may give rise to incorrect parses – by changing left-associative operators into right-associative operators for instance. Second, executing a DCG in Prolog performs recursive descent parsing which can be exponential on many grammars that can be parsed in polynomial time by Earley parsing [7] or chart parsing.

Both of these disadvantages can be addressed by tabling, but care must be taken when tabling a DCG. A DCG is represented in Prolog as a difference list, so tabled evaluation of a DCG under such a representation would need to copy the list into and out of the table each time a tabled grammar production is called. If this were to occur at every prefix position, the total cost of copying would be quadratic in the size of the input string. Fortunately, this problem is easily handled by altering DCG expansion to use a labeled binary relation rather than a difference list. Full details of this transformation, introduced in [27], can be found in the XSB manual. The main idea is to express a string such as *john finds a unicorn* as a set of facts

```
word(0,john,1).  word(1,finds,2).  word(2,a,3).
word(3,unicorn,4).
```

rather than the Prolog form: `[john,finds,a,unicorn]`.

Example 2 (The Proper Treatment of Quantification (PTQ) Grammar). English (and other natural languages) treat quantification ambiguously. For instance, the statement *every man loves a woman* may mean either

$$\forall M \exists W[man(M) \wedge woman(W) \wedge loves(M,W)]; \text{ or}$$
$$\exists W \forall M[man(M) \wedge woman(W) \wedge loves(M,W)]$$

The PTQ grammar was an approach by the logician Robert Montague to assign a logical semantics to English [25]. While the grammar is quite complex, it has been programmed using tabling in a few hundred lines of code (along with a database of words). The PTQ

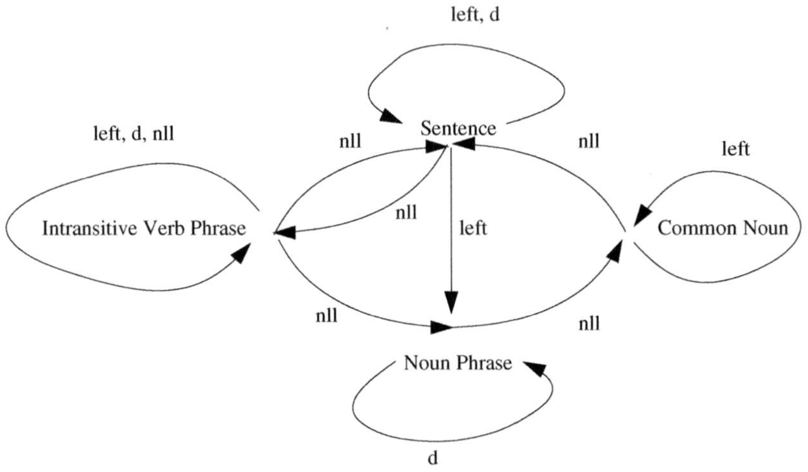

Fig. 3. Table Dependency Graph for PTQ Parser

grammar offers an excellent illustration of how parsing may require complex recursive forms involving several tabled predicates. For instance, the production `s/5`, which is tabled, has the following double recursion (slightly simplified for presentation):

```
s(T,Sa,Sb) --> s(S1,Sa,Sb1),[and],s(S2,Sa1,Sb2).
```

Figure 3 shows the dependencies among tabled predicates in the PTQ parser (dependencies with non-tabled predicates are omitted) [2]. In addition, Figure 3 shows the types of each dependency: `left` for left-linear, `nll` for non-left linear, and `d` for double, indicating the complex natures of the self- and mutual- recursions in this parser.

Pattern 5. *Tabling to evaluate sub-models*
As implemented in Prolog systems, TLP is generally used to query a program. However, many applications require computation of the entire model of a sub-program. For instance, if tabling is used to analyze a program, global properties of the program need to be determined; similarly, when sending the residual of a sub-program to an ASP solver (as in Pattern 11) the entire sub-program may need to be reduced.

Example 3 (The OWL Wine Ontology [24]). An example of evaluating a sub-model arises when querying the OWL wine ontology (`www.w3.org/TR/owl-guide`). When translated by KAON-2 [10], the wine ontology produces a definite program with about 1000 clauses. A small fragment of the translated code has the form:

```
pinotblanc(X) :- q24(X).
pinotblanc(X) :- pinotblanc(Y),kaon2equal(X, Y).
pinotblanc(X) :- wine(X),madefromgrape(X, Y),ot_nom21(Y).
madefromgrape(Y, X) :- madeintowine(X, Y).
madefromgrape(X, X) :- riesling(X),kaon2namedobjects(X).
madefromgrape(X, X) :- wine(X),kaon2namedobjects(X).
% 18 other clauses

wine(X) :- q14(X).
wine(X) :- texaswine(X).
% 24 other clauses
wine(X) :- q24(X).
% 31 other other clauses

q24(X) :- pinotblanc(X).
q24(X) :- muscadet(X).
q24(X) :- q24(Y),kaon2equal(X,Y).
```

The generated program is highly recursive: for instance, `pinotblanc (yellowTail)` depends on `pinotblanc(X)` which depends on `wine(X)` and on `wine(yellowTail)`. In fact, nearly every concept depends on nearly every other concept (more or less) due to `wine(X)` atoms occurring in body literals. Furthermore, mixed instantiations are often present in loops, due to the propagation of bindings in rules. When XSB evaluates the query `pinotblanc(yellowTail)` using call variance it runs out of memory on a laptop machine. When using call subsumption to evaluate the query, XSB's time is comparable with specialized semantic web software, and is much faster than comparable ASP systems [9].

[2] The predicate sentence in Figure 3 corresponds to *s* in [25], noun to *cn*, noun-phrase to *te* and intransitive verb phrase to *iv*. Parser code is available via `xsb.sourceforge.net` in the module `xsbtests`.

Pattern 6. *Automatic Tabling of Generated Code*

Example 3 differs in another way from previous examples. Both the workflow emulator of Example 1 and the PTQ parser of Example 2 were carefully written programs, while the Wine ontology was automatically generated. To use tabling on generated programs, the tabling declarations must also be automatically generated. In XSB this can be done by adding the declaration `auto_table` to a file or module. When XSB automatically tables, it chooses enough tables to break all loops in the predicate dependency graph of a file or module. XSB's current auto-table mechanism has proven useful for datalog programs, but it does not distinguish recursion over binary relations from recursion over Prolog terms, and thus would also declare a predicate such as `append/3` to be tabled. Future work will enable auto-tabling to make use of basic termination analysis [20].

3 Tabling with Negation

In addition to positive loops, tabling can be used to evaluate negative loops according to the well-founded semantics (WFS), or to preprocess such programs so they can be evaluated via the stable model semantics. As an example of WFS consider one of Russel's paradoxes *The village barber shaves every man in the village iff that man does not shave himself.* This can be expressed in a logic program (using default negation) as

```
shaves(barber,Person):-
   villager(Person),
   tnot shaves(Person,Person).
shaves(doctor,doctor).

villager(barber).     villager(mayor).     villager(doctor).
```

For Russel, the barber shaves the mayor, does not shave the doctor, and it is undefined whether he shaves himself – which is exactly the meaning given by the 3-valued WFS (the predicate `tnot/1` is XSB's operator for tabled negation). The ability to evaluate using WFS is important for logic programs for several reasons. First, it gives a semantics to *all* programs, allowing inconsistencies and paraconsistencies to be represented, and perhaps repaired (if additional mechanisms are used). Second, WFS has a low polynomial complexity, and is more scalable than less skeptical stable models semantics. Thirdly, and perhaps controversially, the ability to representation of unknown or undefined truth values may critical to representing common-sense reasoning (cf. [22] which argues for a 3-valued semantics with default negation as a basis for formalizing human reasoning).

Pattern 7. *Well-founded negation for knowledge amalgamation*

Most representations of knowledge strive to be consistent, and usually describe a single model. From this point of view, a loop through negation (that is not otherwise resolved) is likely to be a mistake. However, when amalgamating knowledge, loops through negation can arise due to the use of default negation in different sources.

Example 4 (Amalgamation of Psychiatric Knowledge). A concrete example is evident when logic programming is used to model knowledge about the domain of psychiatry.

Figure 4 presents the actual criteria used in judging whether a patient can be diagnosed with Alzheimer's Dementia according to DSM-IV [1], the standard manual of mental disorders used in the U.S. Of interest is the last clause in Figure 4, termed an *exclusion criterion*, which represents the fact that there is no conclusive test (other than autopsy) to conclusively diagnose Alzheimer's. When DSM-IV was modeled as a logic program for teaching purposes, it turned out that exclusion criteria for different disorders

1. The development of multiple cognitive defects manifested by both
   (a) memory impairment (impaired ability to learn new information or to recall previously learned information)
   (b) one (or more) of the following cognitive disturbances
      i. aphasia (language disturbance)
      ii. apraxia (impaired ability to carry out motor activities despite intact motor function)
      iii. agnosia (failure to recognize or identify objects despite intact sensory functions)
      iv. disturbance in executive functioning (i.e., planning, organizing, sequencing, abstracting)
2. The cognitive deficits in criteria A1 and A2 each cause significant impairment in social or occupational functioning and represent a significant decline from a previous level of functioning.
3. The course is characterized by gradual onset and continuing cognitive decline.
4. The cognitive deficits in Criteria A1 and A2 are not due to any of the following
   (a) other central nervous system conditions that cause progressive deficits in memory and cognition (e.g. cerebrovascular disease, Parkinson's disease, Huntington's disease, subdural hematoma, normal-pressure hydrocephalus, brain tumor)
   (b) systemic conditions that are known to cause dementia (e.g. hypothyroidism, vitamin B_{12} or folic acid deficiency, niacin deficiency, hypercalcemia, neurosyphilis, HIV infection)
   (c) substance-induced conditions
5. The deficits do not occur exclusively during the course of a delirium
6. *The disturbance is not better accounted for by another Axis I disorder (e.g., Major Depressive Disorder, Schizophrenia)*

Fig. 4. Diagnostic Criteria for Dementia of the Alzheimers Type

caused loops through negation. There was a possibility for a particular patient to face the situation

```
'Alzheimers Dementia':- not_better 'Major Depressive Disorder'.
'Major Depressive Disorder':- not_better 'Alzheimers Dementia'.
```

if she fulfilled all other relevant criteria (the predicate `not_better/1` was implemented using XSB's `tnot/1`). Several other instances of conflicting exclusion rules created practical ambiguities. The conflicts arose because DSM-IV was created by different committees: for dementias, for mood disorders, and so on.

We argue that when negative loops arise through amalgamation of knowledge such as this they should be flagged as undefined; in this example, psychiatrists were trying to define an unambiguous manual of disorders, and accordingly are better represented using WFS than the stable model semantics. Such a case may be contrasted with that of an agent who must weigh all applicable scenarios in order to make a decision, where the stable model semantics would be more useful than WFS.

Situations similar to that of Example 4 may be expected to arise when knowledge is amalgamated in semantic web projects, so that evaluation using WFS is likely to prove important for querying many semantic web bases

Pattern 8. *Tabling to implement preferences*

Within logic programming, non-monotonic reasoning is commonly programmed using ASP systems. However, negation can be highly useful for implementing preferences among well-founded derivations. Under this framework, an atom A cannot be derived if another atom A_{pref} is derived that is preferred to A. In the simplest form this would mean that each rule `A :- Body` would be transformed to

```
A :- Body, tnot(unpreferred(A))
```

where `unpreferred(A)` is true if some other derivable atom is preferred to A. The following example illustrates a sophisticated approach to defeasibility whose implementation relies on this basic idea..

Example 5 (Defeasibility in Silk). The commercial rule language Silk is an extension of the object logic Flora-2 and is implemented using XSB. One of the distinguishing features of Silk is its support for defeasible rules through the formalism *Logic Programming with Defaults and Argumentation (LPDA)* [26]. A defeasible rule R may fire only in certain circumstances – roughly if R is not defeated by another rule. Using Prolog rules rather than Silk rules for illustration, a defeasible rule has the form:

```
ruleName@Head :- Body
```

and is compiled into the form

```
Head :- Body, tnot '_$defeated'(ruleName,Head).
```

I.e. the rule is true if clause `ruleName` with head bindings `Head` is not defeated. The definition of `'_$defeated'/2` itself is given as [3].

```
'_$defeated'(ruleName,Head) :-
     overrides(handle(ruleName1,Head1),handle(ruleName,Head)),
     opposes(handle(ruleName1,Head1),handle(ruleName,Head)),
     Head1.
```

Here, `handle/2` can be thought of as a meta-predicate that associates a rule name and atom with a given clause. In Silk, the overriding of rule `ruleName` by rule `ruleName1` does not necessarily mean that `ruleName1` will never fire if `ruleName` fires: rather it means `ruleName1` will never fire if `ruleName` fires and `ruleName` and `ruleName1` *are in opposition* – i.e. lead to a contradiction.

[3] Minor syntactic changes are made to LPDA syntax so that it conforms with Prolog syntax. LPDA also allows more elaborate definitions of `_$defeated/2` than is given here.

Silk, like many other forms of defeasibility and preferences in logic programming specifies defeasibility of rules.

Pattern 8a *Preference logic grammars.* Preference logic grammars [8,5] declaratively resolve ambiguity in grammars. For instance in most programming languages the string *if A then if B then C else D* is parsed as *(if A then (if B then C else D))* rather than as *(if A then (if B then C) else D)*. This potential ambiguity is easily handled in a formal language as part of the grammar. However when parsing is used for natural language analysis or information retrieval, handling ambiguity can seriously complicate a parser. Preferences form a simple and effective solution. Preference statements *outside* the grammar indicate that one parse tree is to be preferred to another. Such statements may of course use partially instantiated parse trees, or may refer to various levels of a sub-parse. The preference statements are then compiled into the grammar using tabled negation as above. This approach has been used commercially, where a large grammar for data standardization was reduced by about 80% using preferences [5]

Pattern 8b *Tabled negation for inheritance systems.* While traditional logic programs do not use of inheritance systems, inheritance is becoming more widely used when logic programs are mixed with ontologies, or extended to object logics (e.g. Flora-2). When making a query to an inheritance system, one generally does not want all properties inherited by an object or all superclasses of a class. In the case of monotonic inheritance systems such as ontologies (where there is no over-riding) properties inherited from more specific classes are usually desired rather than those from more general classes, as the specific properties are more informative. For non-monotonic inheritance systems that allow over-riding, such as object hierarchies, only non-overridden properties are desired. Tabled negation has been used to implement both types of inheritance systems: the key idea being that an object inherits a property P if no other inherited property is more specific than P, or overrides P.

Example 6 (Querying CDF Ontologies). Consider a fragment of a commercial ontology used by XSB, Inc on a project to help the US Government find sources for medical supplies. Figure 3 shows this in a simplified form of the syntax of XSBs Coherent Description Framework library which was used on the project. The fragment describes the fact that absorbable sutures are made from a certain set of materials (`absSutMaterial`), can only be made from those materials and have at most one such material. It also indicates that the object `DemaTechPGA` has the particular material `polyglyconicAcid`. Clearly, any queries about the material `DemaTechPGA` should indicate that it is made out of `polyglyconicAcid`. On the other hand, queries about some other suture object whose specific material is not known should indicate that it is made of some `absSutMaterial` – i.e. the name for the set of possible materials from which it is made. No query should return `material` the name for the set of all known materials.

Although no explicit preferences need to be declared, returning the most specific answer from an inheritance hierarchy is implemented using tabled negation in a manner similar to compiled preferences, where the most specific answers are preferred.

```
hasAttr(absSutPart,hasMaterial,absSutMaterial)
maxAttr(absSutPart,hasMaterial,material,1)

isa(material,domainTypes)
  isa(absSutMaterial,material)
    isa(catgut,absSutMaterial)                  % obsolete in US
    isa(vicryl,absSutMaterial)
    isa(vicryl_rapide,absSutMaterial)
    isa(monocryl,absSutMaterial)
    isa(polyglyconicAcid,absSutMaterial)
    :

object_hasAttr(DemaTechPGA,hasMaterial,polyglyconicAcid)
```

Fig. 5. Fragement of a Medical Parts Ontology

4 Answer Subsumption, Constraints, and Other Extensions

Pattern 9. *Answer subsumption for paraconsistent and quantitative reasoning*

Pattern 9a *Answer subsumption for multi-valued logics.* As mentioned, preferences allow a programmer to specify a partial order among answers to a query. However for certain domains, it is useful to specify the additional structure of an upper semi-lattice. For instance, a range of paraconsistent logics can be modeled by assigning a bilattice relation to answers.

Example 7 (A Multi-Valued Logic). Using the lattice $\mathcal{FOUR}$ (Figure 6) a given atom `p(a)` may have the truth value `bottom` until it is shown to be explicitly `true` or `false`. If `p(a)` is shown to be both explicitly `true` and `false`, it receives the value `top`. Tabling can be extended to evaluate `p/1` according to $\mathcal{FOUR}$ in the following

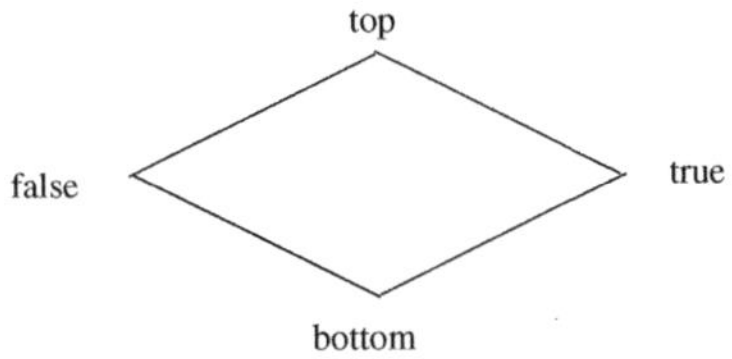

Fig. 6. The Lattice $\mathcal{FOUR}$ for Multi-valued Logics

manner. First, an extra argument may be added to `p/2` to represent its truth value. Next, the declaration

```
:- table p(_,four/3 - bottom).
```

indicates tabling uses the following code to maintain the second argument:

```
four(Val,Val,Val):- !.
four(bottom,Two,bottom):- !.
four(One,bottom,One):- !.
four(One,Two,top):- (One = top ; Two = top),!.
four(_,_,top).
```

If the table contains an answer `p(a,One)` and a new answer `p(a,Two)` is derived, `One` and `Two` are joined, and if `Val` is different than `One`, `p(a,One)` is replaced with `p(a,Val)`. If there are no answers `p(a,_)` in the table, `p(a,Two)` is simply added.

Pattern 9b *Answer subsumption for analysis.* Answer subsumption can model abstraction functions as well, making it useful for analysis as shown in the following example.

Example 8 (Reachability in Infinite Nets). The tabling used in Example 1 only ensures termination of reachability if it can be ensured that there are a finite number of reachable configurations, which is not true in general. The lack of finiteness is also a problem of Place/Transition (PT) Nets which are simpler than Workflow nets. Unlike Workflow nets, PT nets have no guard conditions or after effects, and do not distinguish between tokens. However, PT nets do allow a place to hold more than one token, leading to a potentially infinite number of configurations. Despite this, reachability is decidable and can be determined using an abstraction method called ω-sequences, (see e.g. [6]). The main idea in determining ω sequences is to define a partial order $\geq_\omega$ on configurations as follows. If configurations C_1 and C_2 are both reachable, C_1 and C_2 have tokens in the same set PL of places, C_1 has at least as many tokens in each place, and there exists a non-empty $PL_{sub} \subseteq PL$, such that for each $pl \in Pl_{sub}$ C_1 has strictly more tokens than C_2, then $C_1 >_\omega C_2$. When evaluating reachability, if C_2 is reached first, and then C_1 was subsequently reached, C_1 is abstracted by marking each place in PL_{sub} with the special token ω which is taken to be greater than any integer. If C_1 was reached first and then C_2, C_2 is treated as having already been seen.

From the viewpoint of TLP, ω-abstractions can be seen as an example of answer subsumption, although unlike Example 7 the combination operation is not commutative. To compute reachability with ω abstractions, when each solution S to `reachable/2` is obtained, the solution S is compared to answers in the table. If some answer in the table is greater than or equal to S in $\geq_\omega$ then S is not added to the table; however if S is greater than some set $\mathcal{S}_A$ of answers, the answers $\mathcal{S}_A$ are removed from the table and the ω abstraction of S with respect to $\mathcal{S}_A$ is added.

While the preceding example discussed abstraction in a process logic, the same ideas apply to abstract interpretation for program analysis and to analysis over other potentially infinite structures.

Pattern 9c *Answer subsumption for tabled aggregation.* Aggregate functions such as min, max, count, and sum can be represented as upper semi-lattices, and efficiently evaluated. As one use case, tabled aggregation using answer subsumption has been used in analysis of social networks (Example 9).

Pattern 9d *Answer subsumption for quantitative reasoning.* In many types of quantitative reasoning the results of different derivations need to be combined, leading to another area of application. Answer subsumption has been used to implement Generalized Annotated Programs where it takes the join of different annotations [23]; and recently has formed part of an efficient implementation of probabilistic logic [17], where it sums probabilities of derivations.

Pattern 10. *Tabling with constrained variables*
So far tabling has been presented as an extension of Prolog, but tabling extends constraint logic programming (CLP) in many of the same ways. In Version 1(beta) of XSB, variables in tabled subgoals and answers can be constrained via special-purpose libraries such as CLP(R) or CLP(FD) or through general-purpose CHR modules.

Whether tabling will help a CLP problem depends on the type of problem at hand. Some CLP programs use Prolog to set up complex constraints which are then sent to a solver, e.g. to solve a combinatorial problem such as Sudoku. Such problems may not have a form of recursion whose termination is problematic, or even redundant computations that benefit from factoring by tabling. However, tabling can help in cases where constrained variables in atoms represent complex sets – for instance temporal intervals in scheduling, sets of possible call or success patterns in program analysis, or a complex system state in a process logic. As one instance, nets like those of Example 1 have been extended to use constraints so that the tokens can incorporate temporal or spatial information, and so that transitions can synchronize and modify such information.

Tabling with constrained variables has been used to analyze security protocols in [19]. In this approach, a security context is taken to include information about a user and her allowed potential roles with respect to a resource of a given type. Constraints are ideal to represent security contexts. In many situations a user may have multiple potential roles with respect to a given resource. In addition, roles and resource types may be hierarchical, so that exceptions may be represented via inequality constraints. Furthermore, many roles may be time-sensitive (e.g. a session may only persist for a period of time) so that temporal information is needed as well. Under this framework, [19] analyzes properties of Security-Enhanced Linux such as access to raw disk data for various user roles (perhaps without passing through a given class of intervening security contexts), the potential of daemons to create and run modified executables, and the existence of permissions for given roles that are neither explicitly allowed nor prohibited.

While the use of constrained variables is a straightforward extension of tabling from a semantic viewpoint, its applications have been relatively unexplored (though [2] provides an early exception). This is largely because until recently no systems supported mature implementations of both tabling and constraint packages. Tabling with constraints seems promising to implement and perhaps extend constraint-based grammars [21], particularly given tabling's support for chart parsing (Pattern 4a) and preference logic grammars (Pattern 8). The ability of answer subsumption to combine information from different constrained answers is another mechanism that appears useful for program and process analysis.

Pattern 11. *Tabling to ground a program*

Closely related to Pattern 5 (*tabling to evaluate sub-models*) is the use of tabling to preprocess a program to ground it for an Answer Set Programming (ASP) solver. We start with an application in which the tabled grounding does not even make use of negation.

Example 9 (Social Network Analysis). One problem in Social Network Analysis [28] is to determine the coherent subgroups of a network. The definition of a coherent subgroup may depend on whether the application being studied is one of public health, organizational behavior, marketing, etc., and may depend on the possible properties of a vertex ("male","female","lives-in-city") or of an edge ("father-of","exchanges-needles-with"). ASP holds potential for determining coherent subgroups as such subgroups can be defined by via a changing set of constraints: such as maximum and minimum subgroup size, whether the subgroups partition the network, the existence or balance of vertex or edge properties within a subgroup, etc. ASP can concisely and declaratively represent such constraints, so that an analyst can potentially configure a coherent subgroup definition from a menu or other user interface.

One particularly important attribute for subgroups is their *coherence* which is a function defined on the minimum distance between all vertices in the subgroup (the metric for distance may be defined on different edge types, or their combination). The following simplified code can be used by a grounder such as `lparse` or `clasp` to determine the minimum distance between all pairs of vertices in a network.

```
vertex(X):- edge(X,Y).

distance(X,Y,1):- edge(X,Y).
distance(X,Y,C+1):-
      vertex(X), C = 1..NumberOfVertices,
      distance(X,Z,C),edge(Z,Y), not smallerDistance(X,Y,C).

smallerDistance(X,Y,C):-
      distance(X,Y,C1),C1 <= C,
      C = 1..NumberOfVertices,C1 =1..NumberOfVertices.
```

The current generation of grounders scales poorly on such examples, as the number of clauses is $\mathcal{O}(NumberOfVertices^4)$. Such a distance predicate could be written using answer subsumption for tabled aggregation (cf. Pattern 9c) as:

```
:- table distance(X,Y,min/3-maxDist/1).
distance(X,Y,1):- edge(X,Y).
distance(X,Z,N):-   distance(X,Y,N1),edge(Y,Z),N is N1 + 1.
```

Experiments show that for this problem tabling scales to networks several orders of magnitude larger than can be grounded by current grounders. The resulting distance predicate or coherence measure is sent to an ASP solver either through an intermediary file or pipe, or directly through XSB's XASP interface.

In Example 9 top-down grounding is more efficient than bottom-up grounding because most clauses produced by bottom-up grounding have a false head and so are unnecessary. Top-down grounding can also be efficient if it is known that not all of a program needs to be sent to an ASP solver. However, there are also many cases where bottom-up grounding is faster than top-down grounding, e.g. in cases where bottom-up grounding produces fewer clauses with false heads than in Example 9 or in cases where cardinality or other constraints can be given directly to a bottom-up grounder.

Pattern 11a *Using a residual program for grounding.* In ASP, even loops through negation are used to represent choices while odd loops represent constraints. Tabling over

WFS may be thought of as a transformation that reduces a program with respect to its well-founded model, producing a *residual* program that may be sent to an ASP solver. As illustration, consider the program $P_{nonstrat}$

```
p(X):- reach(X,Y),tnot q(Y).          q(X):- reach(X,Y),tnot p(Y).

edge(1,2).          edge(3,4).          edge(4,3).
```

where `reach/2` is defined as in Pattern 2. `p(1)` is true in the well-founded model of $P_{nonstrat}$, `p(2)` false, and `p(3)` and `p(4)` both undefined. In general, any $p(v_1)$ is undefined if v_1 is reachable from itself. SLG resolution, upon which XSB is based, represents an undefined atom such as `p(3)` as a conditional answer: a clause whose body is partially reduced by the well-founded model, such as `p(3) :- tnot q(4).` Thus, when tabled negation is used, answers may be clauses with bodies and not just facts, and the clauses can be sent to an ASP solver using XASP or an intermediary file. In a sparse graph, where the number of pairs of reachable vertices is much less than the square of the number of vertices, top-down grounding will be more efficient than bottom-up, as the residual will contain conditional answers for `p/1` and `q/1` only when a vertex is self-reachable (in addition to answers for which `p/1` or `q/1` is true).

There is an obvious danger in top-down grounding, since the residual program contains clauses only for subgoals that are encountered during an evaluation: so it is actually a residual sub-program. This can easily be addressed by issuing multiple queries to ground the full program, by mixing top-down and bottom-up grounding, or by using analysis to ensure that partial grounding does not present a semantic problem: i.e. the partial stable model or layered stable model [13] is adequate.

This pattern has been extensively explored by Luis Pereira and his colleagues in the context of autonomous agents. An application of monitoring agents for Elder Care [11] is in this volume, other applications include modeling ethical choices of agents [12], and probabilistic decision making for agents [14].

Pattern 12. *Incremental tabling based on dynamic data*

Tabling has been used in various kinds of reactive systems, from collaborative agents such as those noted above, to GUI controllers. Within such systems, tables that depend on dynamic data must be efficiently refreshed when the data changes. The approach of incremental tabling allows tables to be incrementally computed or abolished whenever a change is made to a given dynamic predicate. A particularly interesting application of tabling based on dynamic data is a deductive spreadsheet [16]. Cells in the spreadsheet are defined by rules that are computed using tabled predicates. When dynamic data changes, tables that depend on the data also change and their changes may also propagate to new tables. As described in [16] the use of incremental update routines was critical to providing reasonable response time for the spreadsheet.

5 Discussion

This paper has used design patterns as an organizational principle to bring together a number of different aspects of TLP that have proven useful over the past decade or more. The 12 patterns and 10 sub-patterns identified here differ in kind. For instance, the recursion patterns (2-4) are defined syntactically, while the negation patterns (7-8) are based on uses of non-monotonic reasoning; the answer subsumption pattern (9) groups widely different applications using a computational feature. Despite this heterogeneity, if a design pattern is taken to be a "general reusable solution to a commonly occurring problem in software design" (Wikipedia) the patterns described here may help determine if TLP is of use for a given problem, and may help features such as answer subsumption or the use of residual programs become more widely used.

Of course, reusable solutions to commonly occurring problems depend on what problems commonly occur. Further research in TLP is likely to enable new applications, and with them new types of patterns. For instance, research into how search strategies can make TLP useful for semi-decidable problems (e.g. by adding features such as iterative deepening) would be especially intriguing given TLPs ability to model quantitative logics and logics of paraconsistency. As another example automatic tabling, perhaps combined with adaptive indexing [4] brings to TLP some of the features of a declarative query language. The addition of multi-threading to these features gives rise to the possibility of using TLP as a foundation for deductive rule bases or semantic web bases. No doubt such applications will bring their own challenges, whose solutions will precipitate new patterns.

References

1. Diagnostic and Statistical Manual of Mental Disorders. American Psychiatric Association, Washington, DC, 4th edition, Prepared by the Task Force on DSM-IV and Other Committees and Work Groups of the American Psychiatric Association (1994)
2. Codognet, P., Filé, G.: Computations, abstractions and constraints in logic programs. In: ICCL, pp. 155–164 (1992)
3. Coplien, J., Schmidt, D.: Pattern Languages of Program Design. Addison-Wesley, Reading (1995)
4. Santos Costa, V., Sagonas, K., Lopes, R.: Demand-driven indexing of prolog clauses. In: Dahl, V., Niemelä, I. (eds.) ICLP 2007. LNCS, vol. 4670, pp. 395–409. Springer, Heidelberg (2007)
5. Cui, B., Swift, T.: Preference logic grammars: Fixed-point semantics and application to data standardization. Artificial Intelligence 138, 117–147 (2002)
6. Desel, J., Reisig, W.: Place/transition Petri nets. In: Reisig, W., Rozenberg, G. (eds.) APN 1998. LNCS, vol. 1491, pp. 122–174. Springer, Heidelberg (1998)
7. Earley, J.: An efficient context-free parsing algorithm. CACM 13(2), 94–102 (1970)
8. Jayaraman, B., Govindarajan, K., Mantha, S.: Preference logic grammars. Computer Languages 24, 179–196 (1998)
9. Liang, S., Fodor, P., Wan, H., Kifer, M.: OpenRuleBench: An analysis of the performance of rule engines. In: WWW: Semantic Data Track, pp. 601–608 (2009)
10. Motik, B.: Reasoning in Description Logics using Resolution and Deductive Databases. PhD thesis (2006)
11. Pereira, L.M., Han, A.: Elder care via intention recognition and evolution prospection. In: INAP (2010)
12. Pereira, L.M., Lopes, G.: Prospective storytelling agents. In: Carro, M., Peña, R. (eds.) PADL 2010. LNCS, vol. 5937, pp. 294–296. Springer, Heidelberg (2010)

13. Pereira, L.M., Pinto, A.M.: Layered models top-down querying of normal logic programs. In: Gill, A., Swift, T. (eds.) PADL 2009. LNCS, vol. 5418, pp. 254–268. Springer, Heidelberg (2008)
14. Pereira, L.M., Ramli, C.: Modelling probabilistic causation in decision making. In: KES-IDT (2009)
15. Ramakrishna, Y.S., Ramakrishnan, C.R., Ramakrishnan, I.V., Smolka, S., Swift, T., Warren, D.S.: Efficient model checking using tabled resolution. In: Grumberg, O. (ed.) CAV 1997. LNCS, vol. 1254, pp. 143–154. Springer, Heidelberg (1997)
16. Ramakrishnan, C.R., Ramakrishnan, I.V., Warren, D.S.: XcelLog: A deductive spreadsheet system. Knowledge Engineering Review 22(3), 269–279 (2007)
17. Riguzzi, F., Swift, T.: Tabling and answer subsumption for reasoning on logic programs with annotated disjunctions (2010), `www.cs.sunysb.edu/~tswift/papers`
18. Russell, N., ter Hofstede1, A., van der Aalst1, W.M.P., Mulyar, N.: Workflow control-flow patterns: A revised view. Technical report, BPM Center Report BPM-06-22, BPMcenter.org (2006)
19. Sarna-Starosta, B.: Constraint-based Analysis of Security Protocols. PhD thesis, SUNY Stony Brook (2005)
20. De Schreye, D., Decorte, S.: Termination of logic programs: The never-ending story. JLP 19, 199–260 (1994)
21. Shieber, S.: Constraint-based Grammar Formailsms. MIT Press, Cambridge (1992)
22. Stenning, K., van Lambalgen, M.: Human Reasoning and Cognitive Science. MIT Press, Cambridge (2008)
23. Swift, T.: Tabling for non-monotonic programming. AMAI 25(3-4), 201–240 (1999)
24. Swift, T., Warren, D.S.: XSB: Extending the power of Prolog using tabling (2010), `www.cs.sunysb.edu/~tswift`
25. Thomason, R. (ed.): Formal Philosophy. Selected Papers by Richard Montague. Yale, New Haven (1974)
26. Wan, H., Grosof, B., Kifer, M., Fodor, P., Liang, S.: Logic programming with defaults and argumentation theories. In: Hill, P.M., Warren, D.S. (eds.) ICLP 2009. LNCS, vol. 5649, pp. 432–448. Springer, Heidelberg (2009)
27. Warren, D.S.: Programming the PTQ grammar in XSB. In: Ramakrishnan, R. (ed.) Applications of Logic Databases, pp. 217–234 (1995)
28. Wasserman, S., Faust, K.: Social Network Analysis. Cambridge University Press, Cambridge (1994)

An Alternative High-Level Approach to Interaction with Databases

António Porto

LIACC / DCC, Faculdade de Ciências
Universidade do Porto
ap@dcc.fc.up.pt

Abstract. Most applications rely on relational databases for persistence, interacting through SQL embedded in the host programming language. Such code being error-prone and hard to maintain, many proposals have been made to raise its level, mostly in the direction of deductive and/or object-oriented databases. We have put forward an alternative approach, inspired by natural language, that packs a lot of power in very concise and readable code, while relying on standard database technology. This is achieved using the flexible term syntax and deductive capabilities of logic programming, both to compile a database scheme from a high-level description, and to interpret high-level queries and commands.

In this paper we review the basic ideas of the novel approach and concentrate on the interaction language of queries and commands, formalizing its semantics on the basis of characterizing canonical database schemes. These rely on uniform notions of concept, attribute and reference, rather than the dichotomous entity-relationship model. Query and command expressions are variable-free terms, reading very naturally when appropriate nouns (rather than verbs) are chosen for all concept and attribute names. Attribute inheritance and chaining avoid many explicit joins, which are automatically derived as inner or outer joins.

Scheme-derived multi-valued global parameters can flexibly be used for implicit current values. The abstraction power is further raised by having manifold attributes, whose values may actually vary along a parametric domain, the main examples being the handling of temporal validity and multi-lingual data. Commands can also be very high-level, with simple statements possibly resulting in large transactions.

1 Introduction

About a decade ago we launched a large project to implement a full-blown academic management system for our institution. We had a vision of what a proper information system should be, that raised a corresponding need of proper software technology to be achievable, namely a concept-oriented architecture, declarative sub-languages, generic programming capabilities, and a high-level interaction-persistence link. So we ended up with the double challenge of re-engineering the academic processes through a proper information system and building proper software support for implementing the system.

S. Abreu and D. Seipel (Eds.): INAP 2009, LNAI 6547, pp. 20–39, 2011.

We successfully met our goals using logic programming to develop the software [1], with some scientific achievements along the way. Paramount among these was a novel high-level approach for interacting with databases, offering a language for defining the scheme and another for queries and commands, inspired by natural language noun phrases. Having reported a first overview of the approach [2], in this paper we give a more detailed account of the interaction language of queries and commands, presenting a formal semantics that rigorously anchors the illustrating examples, stemming from a new characterization of a canonical database scheme.

In the quest for better, more maintainable code for database access, we are unaware of other approaches quite similar in spirit to our own. In deductive databases (see e.g. [3,4]) database tables are viewed as predicates in logic programs, with joins expressed through variable sharing. We rely instead on a few fixed query and command predicates, whose "input" arguments are ground terms structurally derived from simple natural language principles and lifted from the atomic terminology introduced for concepts and attributes in a given scheme definition. Deductive object-oriented approaches, such as F-logic [5], are closer in spirit to our own by using the equivalent of our concepts (classes), attributes (methods) and references (types), but differ essentially on their view that data storage is object-oriented whereas we keep it relational (more flexible) while allowing object-orientation in our queries and commands. Accordingly, we use a different language for defining a scheme than for querying a corresponding database, and precompile the scheme into unit clauses used for the interpretation of queries and commands. An explicit logic programming representation of a scheme has been advocated before [6], but to encode basic set-theoretic constructions supporting the low-level relational calculus as a query language. In deductive and/or object-oriented databases logic variables are used to denote individuals inside query expressions, but we avoid them altogether (much as natural language does); in this respect we are closer to using concept languages (see e.g. [7]), also known as description logics [8]. Another major difference is our conservative stance of keeping the power of deductive rules outside of the semantics of the persistent storage. This apparent shortcoming was actually not an issue in building our large real-world application, and, importantly, it allows the use of stable, well-established logic programming and relational database technologies. Finally, a distinguishing methodological standpoint is that we attach great importance to the choice of concept and attribute names, given its impact on how natural (thus readily understandable) conceptual expressions become.

Our framework has two major components, a compiler for a scheme definition language NACS (NAtural Conceptual Scheme) and an interpreter for a query and command language NADI (NAtural Database Interaction) using the compiled scheme. In this paper we focus on the latter; a taste of the former is found in [2]. For presenting the semantics of queries we do need a scheme's abstract characterization, that we present in a preliminary section. In essence we rely on the notions of concept, attribute and reference (sets, functions and set inclusion), with attributes being lexical (yielding atomic values) or non-lexical (with a lexical tuple signature), identity or dependent (part of the primary key or not), and having a simple unambiguous semantics under a definition of canonical scheme. The next section presents the syntax and semantics for queries. Syntax exploits the flexible usage of prefix and infix operator syntax in Prolog, with e.g. a/c\$(b<x) reading as "the a of the c whose b is less than x". Semantics is expressed in terms of tuples of values from a database. A highlight of NADI's abstraction power is the use of manifold attributes for dealing with temporal and multilingual data. Commands are overviewed next, and we conclude with a summary of achievements and future work.

1.1 Notational Conventions

Object-language expressions are in fixed-length teletype font, with standard term notation including the use of prefix and infix operators.

In the meta-language we extensively use sequences (tuples), with two structural notations: parenthesized comma-separated elements $(e_1, \ldots, e_n)$, and simple concatenation, with Roman and Greek letters ranging over respectively elements and sequences, say $e\sigma$ for the sequence with first element e and remaining (possibly empty) sub-sequence σ. The symbol ε denotes the empty sequence. The notation σ_i is used to refer to the ith element in the sequence σ, with indexes starting at 1. We use $\{\!\{\sigma\}\!\}$ for the set of elements in the sequence σ.

The subscript $_{\mathsf{fin}}$ signals restriction to finite sets, and S^+ denotes the finite non-empty sequences of elements of S.

We refer to the domains of functions with *dom*. Currying is assumed for functions, with the notation f_x for $f(x)$ and f_x^y for $f(x, y)$, e.g. for a function $f : A \to B \rightharpoonup C$ (total on A, partial on B) we have $dom(f) \subseteq A \times B$ and $a \in A \Rightarrow dom(f_a) \subseteq B$.

In any formal statement we implicitly assume universal quantification of the free meta-variables in the appropriate domains (as with a above).

2 The Scheme

As announced, we do not present here our own concrete language NACS for defining a database scheme. Nevertheless we must convey the structure of its outcome, i.e. the formal characterization of a scheme and a corresponding database.

After an initial brief summary of our modelling viewpoint we formalize a scheme as an abstract syntactic structure lifted from a vocabulary of names, and provide a corresponding database semantics lifted from the domains of the data types. We first give a scheme definition that is too broad, but which allows the definition of auxiliary notions (including sub-concepts) that finally help in defining a canonical scheme, on which to base the semantics of queries.

2.1 The Modelling Viewpoint

We consider irrelevant, and detrimental to our simplicity goal, the traditional distinction between entities and relationships made in most approaches to database modelling. We find it much more convenient to have a uniform view of *concepts* encompassing all our usual carving up of the world into types of entities, relationships, situations, events, etc. for which we have nouns in natural language such as student, course edition, enrollment, registration, etc.

These concepts are all amenable to a simple semantics of sets of individual "things" (henceforth called *individuals*) with an inner structure given by a set of local *attributes* mapping each individual in a concept to a tuple of individuals in other concepts, with the data types as the base concepts.

Attributes also correspond to nouns in natural language, usable to form attribute chains such as "the name of the lecturer of the course" that will find a direct counterpart in our query language. The *lexical* attributes are those with atomic values, and any attribute has a signature as a (possibly unary) tuple of lexical attributes. Every concept has an *identity* tuple of lexical attributes, e.g. the (student, course, year, period type, period number) of an enrollment. The classical entity-relationship distinction is the linguistically unimportant one between concepts with unary and non-unary lexical identity.

The concepts and lexical attributes map directly into tables and fields of a relational database, with the lexical identity attributes constituting the primary key and attributes with concept images yielding foreign keys.

We can contrast our modelling viewpoint with the OWL language [9] proposed for the Semantic Web [10]. We give importance to attributes with their functional nature and noun-phrase terminology, whereas in OWL they are particular properties that in general are relations, and mostly adapt verbal terminology with ensuing variant forms and the need to relate them, e.g. as inverse. For example we may have a `course_edition` concept with attributes (among others) `course` and `lecturer`, whereas in OWL we would have a `teaches` property relating lecturers and course editions and the inverse `isTaughtBy`.

2.2 The Scheme Structure

The basic concepts are the *data types* $\mathcal{T}$ that are usual in relational databases, including $\{\,\texttt{int}, \texttt{num}, \texttt{date}, \texttt{time}\,\} \cup \{\,\texttt{str}(n) \mid n \text{ is a positive numeral}\,\}$, with predefined interpretations as the sets of (respectively) integers, numbers, dates, time points and strings of at most n characters; included in $\mathcal{T}$ are also a few other size-parametric data types for large textual and binary objects, that we will not illustrate in this paper.

A conceptual scheme is an abstract syntactic structure built from the set of data types $\mathcal{T}$ and a set of names $\mathcal{N}$ disjoint from $\mathcal{T}$ that includes the special names `*` and `{}`, respectively "all" and "self".

Definition 1. *A* conceptual scheme *is a 4-tuple* $\langle C, A, T, R\rangle$ *with a* concept *set* $C \subset_{\text{fin}} \mathcal{N}$ *and mappings for* attribute signature $A : C \to \mathcal{N} \rightharpoonup \mathcal{N}^+$, lexical type $T : C \to \mathcal{N} \rightharpoonup \mathcal{T}$ *and* conceptual reference $R : C \rightharpoonup \mathcal{N} \rightharpoonup \wp_{\text{fin}}(C)$, *satisfying the following conditions:*

1. *the* lexical attributes *are* $L_c = dom(T_c) = \{\, a \mid A^a_c = a \,\} \subset_{\text{fin}} \mathcal{N}$*;*
2. $(A^a_c)_i \in L_c$*, and* $(A^a_c)_i \neq (A^a_c)_j$ *if* $i \neq j$*;*

3. $\{\{\},*\} \subseteq dom(A_c)$, *with the* whole A^*_c *being a permutation of* $L(c)$ *and the* identity $A^{\{\}}_c$ *a prefix thereof;*
4. $dom(R_c) \subseteq dom(A_c)\backslash\{*\}$;
5. $c' \in R^a_c \Rightarrow \tau^{\{\}}_{c'} = \tau^a_c$, *with the* tuple type $\tau : dom(A) \rightarrow \mathcal{T}^+$ *defined by* $(\tau^a_c)_i = T_c((A^a_c)_i)$;
6. $c' \in R^{\{\}}_c \Rightarrow A^{\{\}}_{c'} = A^{\{\}}_c$.

We can see that each concept c has a non-empty finite set of lexical attributes (those with atomic data types) that are totally ordered in the whole signature A^*_c, a prefix of which is the identity signature $A^{\{\}}_c$, meant to uniquely identify individuals of c, as will be apparent in the forthcoming definition of database semantics. For convenience a concept may also have non-lexical attributes, standing for their signature's tuple of lexical ones. As an example, consider the concept `course_edition` whose lexical attributes are those of its identity (`course`, `year`, `period_type`, `period_number`) and the (dependent) `lecturer`, along with a non-lexical `period` with signature (`period_type`, `period_number`). An attribute a of c may reference other concepts R^a_c, its lexical tuple A^a_c having the same tuple type as the identity of every referred concept. In the latter example we could have $R^{\texttt{lecturer}}_{\texttt{course\_edition}} = \{\texttt{person}\}$ with $\tau^{\texttt{lecturer}}_{\texttt{course\_edition}} = \tau^{\{\}}_{\texttt{person}} = \texttt{int}$.

The scheme definition language has features not reflected in this simple scheme structure, namely virtual concepts and sub-attribute inheritance, that contribute to the abstraction power of the interaction language. We can also define attributes as having null values; this can be captured simply by having in $\mathcal{T}$ extended versions $*t$ of each primitive data type t, whose domains incorporate the special null value `[]`, i.e. $[\![*t]\!] = [\![t]\!] \uplus \{\texttt{[]}\}$.

Database semantics. A conceptual scheme can be given a semantics in terms of its possible *databases*, a notion lifted from the semantic domains of values $[\![\tau]\!]$ for the data types $\tau \in \mathcal{T}$, with $[\![\tau_1 \cdots \tau_n]\!] = [\![\tau_1]\!] \times \cdots \times [\![\tau_n]\!]$ for tuple types.

Definition 2. *A* database Δ *for a scheme* $\langle C, A, T, R\rangle$ *is a mapping of* C *where:*

1. $\Delta_c \subseteq_{\text{fin}} [\![\tau^*_c]\!]$;
   the attribute projections $\pi^a_c : \Delta_c \rightarrow [\![\tau^a_c]\!]$ *are defined by* $(\pi^a_c(t))_i = t_j$ *if* $(A^a_c)_i = (A^*_c)_j$;
2. $t, t' \in \Delta_c,\ t \neq t' \ \Rightarrow\ \pi^{\{\}}_c(t) \neq \pi^{\{\}}_c(t')$;
3. $t \in \Delta_c,\ c' \in R^a_c \ \Rightarrow\ \exists t' \in \Delta_{c'} \,.\, \pi^a_c(t) = \pi^{\{\}}_{c'}(t')$.

Each member of Δ_c is the syntactic characterization of an individual of the concept c as a tuple of values, of the prescribed data types, for the concept's *whole* tuple A^*_c of lexical attributes. Condition 1 ensures type correctness. The role of the self attribute `{}` as *identity*, corresponding to the chosen *primary key* in database parlance, is enforced by condition 2. Finally any conceptual reference, corresponding to a database *foreign key*, is satisfied by condition 3.

Non-lexical attributes other than `*` or `{}` are not strictly needed for defining a scheme and database, as we could define R directly on lexical tuples. But they are essential abstractions for writing concise scheme definitions and also queries and commands, where they can be global parameters (see later).

Canonical scheme. In practice we want to tighten the given definition of a scheme, to ensure reasonable syntactic and semantic restrictions that simplify, without sacrificing expressiveness, the handling of queries and commands. For this purpose we define first a few auxiliary notions.

Definition 3. *Given a conceptual scheme* $\langle C, A, T, R\rangle$,

1. ${}^{I}\!A_c = \{\, a \mid \{\!\{A^a_c\}\!\} \subseteq \{\!\{A^{\{\}}_c\}\!\}\,\}$ *are the* identity *attributes of* c*;*
2. ${}^{D}\!A_c = dom(A_c)\backslash({}^{I}\!A_c \uplus \{*\})$ *are the* dependent *attributes of* c*;*
3. *the transitive closure of* $\{\,(c, c') \mid c' \in R^{\{\}}_c\,\}$ *is the* sub-concept *relation* $\sqsubset$.

As an example, consider $\texttt{user} \sqsubset \texttt{person} \sqsubset \texttt{agent}$ with ${}^{I}\!A_{\texttt{user}} = {}^{I}\!A_{\texttt{person}} = {}^{I}\!A_{\texttt{agent}} = \{\texttt{\{\}}, \texttt{id\_code}\}$, ${}^{D}\!A_{\texttt{user}} = \{\texttt{user\_id}\}$, ${}^{D}\!A_{\texttt{person}} = \{\texttt{sex}\}$ and ${}^{D}\!A_{\texttt{agent}} = \{\texttt{name}, \texttt{common\_name}\}$.

The sub-concept relation, in our formalization a particular case of conceptual reference, is actually a very important notion when modelling a real-world domain. It must give rise to a proper hierarchy, with implicit inheritance of attributes reflected in the interaction language. Hierarchically related concepts share their identity attributes, being distinguishable through their dependent attributes. In the interaction language attributes should be usable across hierarchy paths in an unambiguous way. Such concerns are addressed as follows.

Definition 4. *A conceptual scheme* $\langle C, A, T, R\rangle$ *is* canonical *if*

1. $\sqsubset$ *is a strict partial order, i.e.* $c \not\sqsubset c$*;*
2. *every concept* $c \in C$ *has a unique* root $\overline{c} \in C$ *such that* $c \sqsubseteq c' \Rightarrow c' \sqsubseteq \overline{c}$, *where* $\sqsubseteq$ *is the reflexive closure of* $\sqsubset$*;*
3. $c_1, c_2 \in R^a_c \;\Rightarrow\; \overline{c_1} = \overline{c_2}$*;*
4. *hierarchically related concepts share identity but not dependent attributes, i.e.* $c_1 \neq c_2,\ \overline{c_1} = \overline{c_2} \;\Rightarrow\; {}^{I}\!A_{c_1} = {}^{I}\!A_{c_2},\ {}^{D}\!A_{c_1} \cap {}^{D}\!A_{c_2} = \emptyset$.

The first condition is not surprising. In NACS it is automatically enforced, because one can only refer to previously defined concepts when defining a new one, thereby avoiding referential loops.

The condition on unique roots may not seem essential, but it is quite natural to assume, as ideally the sub-concept relation is viewed as set inclusion for individuals of the same sort, and we naturally consider the root concept of the whole sort. The third condition makes the natural demand that an attribute value may be of only one sort.

The uniqueness of attributes among hierarchically related concepts is very important for unambiguously giving meaning to attributive expressions in the NADI interaction language. This uniqueness is quite natural in modelling, since attribute names should be nouns in natural language that reflect a (possibly partial) *functional* property of individuals of the same sort. In the previous example the `id_code` of a `user`, `person` or `agent` uniquely refers to their (shared) identity code, the `name` of a `person` is uniquely defined (through `agent`), and the `user_id` of a `person` also uniquely defined (if the `person` is a `user`). The same dependent attribute in two database tables sharing identity would open the door to the inconsistency of multiple attribute values for the same individual.

So we extend and classify the attributes applicable to a concept, as follows.

Definition 5. *For any concept c in a canonical conceptual scheme:*
1. ${}^{H}\!A_c = \bigcup_{c' \sqsubseteq \overline{c}} {}^{D}\!A_{c'}$ *are the* hierarchical *attributes;*
2. ${}^{P}\!A_c = \{\, a \in {}^{H}\!A_c \mid c \sqsubseteq c' \Rightarrow a \notin {}^{D}\!A_{c'} \,\}$ *are the* partial *attributes.*
3. ${}^{T}\!A_c = {}^{I}\!A_c \uplus ({}^{H}\!A_c \backslash {}^{P}\!A_c)$ *are the* total *attributes;*
4. ${}^{N}\!A_c = {}^{H}\!A_c \backslash {}^{D}\!A_c$ *are the* non-local *attributes;*
5. ${}^{L}\!A_c = {}^{I}\!A_c \uplus {}^{D}\!A_c$ *are the* local *attributes;*
6. ${}^{A}\!A_c = {}^{I}\!A_c \uplus {}^{H}\!A_c = {}^{T}\!A_c \uplus {}^{P}\!A_c = {}^{L}\!A_c \uplus {}^{N}\!A_c$ *are the* applicable *attributes.*

To illustrate this terminology using our running example, for the concept `person` the hierarchical attributes include `name` which is total and non-local (being locally defined above in `agent`), `sex` which is total but local, being a dependent attribute of `person` itself, and `user_id` which is partial (necessarily non-local) for being local in the sub-concept `user`.

Total/partial attributes intuitively correspond to total/partial functions on the concept domain. We can locate any hierarchical attribute in the hierarchy.

Proposition 1. *In a canonical scheme, for every concept c there is a unique* location *mapping* $\lambda_c : {}^{H}\!A_c \to \{\, c' \mid c' \sqsubseteq \overline{c} \,\}$ *such that* $a \in {}^{H}\!A_c \Rightarrow a \in {}^{D}\!A_{\lambda^a_c}$.

Proof. By definition 5.1, for any $a \in {}^{H}\!A_c$ there is at least one $c' \sqsubseteq \overline{c}$ such that $a \in {}^{D}\!A_{c'}$. For any other $c'' \sqsubseteq \overline{c}$ we must have $\overline{c''} = \overline{c} = \overline{c'}$, and from condition 4 of the canonicity definition 4 we conclude that ${}^{D}\!A_{c''} \cap {}^{D}\!A_{c'} = \emptyset$, so $a \notin {}^{D}\!A_{c''}$. Therefore $\lambda^a_c = c'$.

3 Queries

In our interaction language NADI a query is expressed in a term, defining a database view yielding a (possibly empty) sequence of base value tuples. Two ways are available for retrieving such answers: either one at a time, through the backtrack-able call (`Query <? Tuple`), or all at once with the determinate (`Query <?> Tuple_list`). The term representation of tuples is simply

<tuple> ::= <value> | <value>,<tuple> [1]

We first introduce by examples the main features of NADI queries, followed by a formal semantic account of their core functionality.

3.1 Illustration of the Main Features

All conceptual expressions in NADI are built using a variety of infix and prefix operators, taking advantage of the flexible precedence definition mechanism (a standard feature of Prolog) to minimize the use of parenthesis.

As an example, the query for "the name and sex of the students enrolled in courses of the CS department in 2008/09" can be represented by a term whose main operators, besides the usual conjunction and equality, are the left-associative '/' ("of the") and the stand-alone '$' ("for which"):

[1] We can avoid lists because <value>s are of base types and not themselves lists.

```
( name, sex ) / student /
enrollment $ ( acronym/department/course = 'CS', year = 2009 )
```

The query consists of a *projection* `(name,sex)/student` of a *concept* `enrollment` under *constraints*. The form of the expression is close to its natural language counterpart, certainly much closer than the corresponding SQL statement

```
select distinct a1.name, p1.sex
from   enrollment e1, course c1, organization o1,
       student s1, agent a1, person p1,
where  e1.course = c1.code
   and c1.department = o1.code  and o1.acronym = 'CS'
   and e1.year = 2009           and e1.student = s1.code
   and s1.person = a1.code      and s1.person = p1.code
```

where many more concepts have to be made explicit, along with aliases and join equations. Attribute chains like "the acronym of the department of the course" are explicit in our conceptual expression and effective towards its readability, whereas they are scattered and therefore hidden in the SQL syntax.

The default ordering of answers is database-dependent. We can specify ascending or descending order on given projection attributes by prefixing them with `*>` or `*<`, respectively. Prefixing an intermediate projection attribute with `?` puts its identity in the projection tuple. In our example, the alternative projection `( *<sex, *>name ) / ?student` would ask for the descending sex, ascending name and identity code of the students.

By default the SQL `distinct` qualifier is applied to the selection, yielding distinct tuples, i.e. a set of answers. This can be overridden with the `??` prefix, e.g. `??grade / enrollment $ ( course_edition=CE )` retrieves the multiset of grades for a particular course edition (for computing a histogram, say).

A very useful feature in most applications is to have parameters under global assignment, whose current values are reflected in the queries through the linguistic equivalent of using the definite article. For example, the query for the students enrolled in *the* course edition (assumed to be contextually assigned) is `student/enrollment$(@course_edition)`. Its processing performs the call `course_edition=@CE` to retrieve the current value, and then uses the constraint `course_edition=CE`. Usage is very flexible for scheme-defined parameters, e.g. `course_edition=@CE` succeeds with `CE=(123,2009,s,1)` after the assignments `year@=2009`, `course@=123` and `period@=(s,2)`, and conversely `year=@Y` succeeds with `Y=2008` after `course_edition@=(95,2008,s,1)`.

Constraints under `$` can be grouped inside nested conjunctions and disjunctions. A common individual constraint is <attribute-chain> <op> <value>, with <attribute-chain> ::= <attribute> | <attribute-chain>/<attribute-chain> and appropriate <op>s (`=`, `\=`, `>`, etc.) and <value>s (`@`<parameter> is a value). The common case of identity valuation, `{}=V`, can be written simply as `{V}`.

Sometimes we need to express constraints using sub-queries instead of explicit values, as in "this year's lecturers that were also (our) students", doable with `lecturer/course_edition$(@year,lecturer^person/student)`. The operator `^` ("is a") assumes an attribute chain on the left but a query on the right, so `lecturer` is interpreted as an attribute but `student` as a concept.

The dual of `^` is `~` ("is not a"). Both exist also as prefix (rather than infix) operators (meaning respectively "there is a" and "there isn't a") over query expressions. But if we use e.g. `A$(···^B$X···)` we generally want, inside `X`, to relate attributes of `B` to attributes of `A`. For this we use the `*` prefix to move one level up in the context of attribute interpretation. As an example we can express "the students enrolled in only one course this year" with

```
student / enrollment$( @year, ~enrollment$( @year, *student,
                                            course \= *course )
```

where `*student` can be read as "the same student" and is just shorthand for `student = *student`, equating the student of the inner and outer enrollments.

Similar contextual sub-queries can appear in the projection part of a query, e.g. we get "this year's courses and the lecturers that ever taught them" with

```
(course,lecturer/course_edition$(*course))/course_edition$(@year).
```

Queries such as this, yielding for each course a number of lecturers, suggest the usefulness of packing the answer accordingly. This is achieved by using "`;`" instead of "`,`" where the grouping is needed. So, each solution of the alternative query `(course;lecturer···)/··· <? CL` binds `CL` to a term c`:[`l_1`,···,`l_n`]` with a course c and a list of lecturers l_i of c.

We can specify group projections using prefix operators for sum (`+`), average (`+/`) or count (`#`). For example, "the number of students enrolled in each course···" is simply expressed as `(#student,course)/enrollment$···`. The grouping is implicit in the regular projection elements, in this case `course`.

Another facility is the expression, with the usual syntax, of external functions available in the database engine (e.g. arithmetic, string and date functions). An example would be a query about enrollments in the previous year, expressed simply with `enrollment$(@year-1)`.

3.2 A Formal Account of Query Answers

Although queries really produce *sequences* of answers, our semantic account will be given in terms of *sets*, avoiding both the implicit and explicit ordering—an orthogonal issue with a standard meaning—and also the variant multiset reading—a straightforward adaptation from sets.

We can assume, without loss of generality, that our queries are of the form

<query> ::= <projection>/<constrained-concept>

<constrained-concept> ::= <concept>$<constraints>

All other queries are easily converted into this format, using the self attribute `{}` and the null constraint `[]`:

$$\begin{array}{rcl} c & \mapsto & \texttt{\{\} /}\ c \\ p\ \texttt{/}\ c & \mapsto & p\ \texttt{/}\ c\ \texttt{\$ []} \\ p\ \texttt{/ ?}c\ \texttt{\$}\ x & \mapsto & \texttt{(}\ p\texttt{, \{\}) /}\ c\ \texttt{\$}\ x \end{array}$$

Given a query $p/c\,\$\,x$, the semantic intuition is that the constraints x denote a Boolean function acting as a filter on the individuals of c, and the projection p (for constrained c) a function projecting the filtered individuals into values of the projection tuple type, i.e. the answers. Formally,

$$^{Q}[\![\, p/c\,\$\,x \,]\!] = {}^{P}[\![\, p \,]\!]_c(\{\, t \in \Delta_c \mid {}^{F}[\![\, x \,]\!]_c^t \,\})$$

But in general queries can be nested, and there must be a notion of conceptual *context* parametrizing the semantics. Recall the example with `*course` used in a context with two instances of `enrollment`. So the equation above is just a particular case, with ${}^{F}[\![\,.\,]\!]$ parametrized on a single concept c and applying to a single tuple t. In general we must make both ${}^{Q}[\![\,.\,]\!]$ and ${}^{F}[\![\,.\,]\!]$ parametric on a *sequence* (stack) σ of concepts and applicable to a corresponding sequence τ of tuples, with the empty sequence ε as the base:

$$^{Q}[\![\, p/c\,\$\,x \,]\!] = {}^{Q}[\![\, p/c\,\$\,x \,]\!]_{\varepsilon}^{\varepsilon} \tag{1}$$

$$^{Q}[\![\, p/c\,\$\,x \,]\!]_{\sigma}^{\tau} = {}^{P}[\![\, p \,]\!]_c(\{\, t \in \Delta_c \mid {}^{F}[\![\, x \,]\!]_{c\sigma}^{t\tau} \,\}) \tag{2}$$

Constraints. Let us consider the core sub-language of constraint expressions:

<constraints> ::= <constraint>
| <constraints>;<constraints>
| <constraints>,<constraints>
<constraint> ::= <attribute-chain><relation-op><value-exp>
| <existential-op><query>
| []
<attribute-chain> ::= <attribute>
| <attribute-chain>/<attribute>
<relation-op> ::= = | \= | > | < | >= | =< | <existential-op>
<existential-op> ::= ^ | ~

As with queries, we assume that alternative simplified forms in the concrete NADI syntax are mapped into this core language. For example,

{<value>} ↦ {}=<value>

For null, conjunction and disjunction the semantics is straightforward:[2]

$$^{F}[\![\, [] \,]\!]_{\sigma}^{\tau} = \top$$
$$^{F}[\![\, x\,,y \,]\!]_{\sigma}^{\tau} = {}^{F}[\![\, x \,]\!]_{\sigma}^{\tau} \wedge {}^{F}[\![\, y \,]\!]_{\sigma}^{\tau}$$
$$^{F}[\![\, x\,;y \,]\!]_{\sigma}^{\tau} = {}^{F}[\![\, x \,]\!]_{\sigma}^{\tau} \vee {}^{F}[\![\, y \,]\!]_{\sigma}^{\tau}$$

The semantics of existential constraints is defined from the emptiness of the denotation (answer set) of the argument query.

$$^{F}[\![\, \hat{}\,q \,]\!]_{\sigma}^{\tau} = (\, {}^{Q}[\![\, q \,]\!]_{\sigma}^{\tau} \neq \emptyset \,)$$
$$^{F}[\![\, \tilde{}\,q \,]\!]_{\sigma}^{\tau} = (\, {}^{Q}[\![\, q \,]\!]_{\sigma}^{\tau} = \emptyset \,)$$

[2] We use $\top$ for the Boolean "true".

The most common constraint is the one expressing a relation between the value of a *partial generalized attribute*, expressed by an <attribute-chain>, and a *generalized value* expressed by <value-exp>. The generalized (by chaining) attribute is partial because it may not yield a value. The expression `user_id\=X` is a syntactically valid constraint under the concept `person`, but semantically a person may not have a user id, its identity being present in the `person` but not in the `user` database table. The constraint should be understood as "the user id exists and is different from `X`". To capture the partiality of a generalized attribute we formulate its semantics ${}^{A}[\![\,.\,]\!]$ as returning a set, which may be empty or a singleton. Actually larger sets may also be returned, as explained later, giving extra meaning to the "generalized" qualification. The semantics a relational constraint becomes existential, expressed as follows from the partial generalized attribute and generalized value semantics ${}^{A}[\![\,.\,]\!]$ and ${}^{V}[\![\,.\,]\!]$, with ${}^{R}[\![\,r\,]\!]$ the relation denoted by a <relation-op> r in the union of all applicable domains:

$$ {}^{F}[\![\,a\,r\,v\,]\!]^{t\tau}_{c\sigma} = (\,(\,{}^{A}[\![\,a\,]\!]^{t}_{c} \times \{\,{}^{V}[\![\,v\,]\!]^{t\tau}_{c\sigma}\,\}\,) \cap {}^{R}[\![\,r\,]\!] \neq \emptyset\,) \tag{3} $$

Notice that a filter demands a non-empty context, to apply a partial generalized attribute to (just) its topmost (current level) tuple for a concept. Generalized values may require the whole context, being possibly (contextual) sub-queries.

Partial generalized attributes. An atomic <attribute-chain> a must be one of the applicable attributes ${}^{A}\!A_c = {}^{L}\!A_c \uplus {}^{N}\!A_c$ for the contextual concept c. If local ($a \in {}^{L}\!A_c$), its value is obtained by a simple (local) projection $\pi^{a}_{c}(t)$ of the contextual tuple $t \in \Delta_c$. If non-local ($a \in {}^{N}\!A_c$), it must be valuated through the projection $\pi^{a}_{c'}(t')$ of a (non-local) tuple $t' \in \Delta_{c'}$ for a hierarchically related concept $c' = \lambda^{a}_{c} \neq c$ satisfying an identity *join* $(\,\pi^{\{\}}_{c'}(t') = \pi^{\{\}}_{c}(t)\,)$ with the (local) tuple $t \in \Delta_c$; t' always exists for a total attribute ($a \in {}^{T}\!A_c$), but possibly not for a partial one ($a \in {}^{P}\!A_c$). Partial generalized attributes expressed by chains such as `acronym/department/course`, "the acronym of the department of the course", are (recursively) partial generalized attributes of concepts referenced by an applicable attribute, requiring the corresponding join—in this example $\pi^{\{\}}_{\texttt{organization}}(t') = \pi^{\texttt{department}}_{\texttt{course}}(t)$ to allow the final projection $\pi^{\texttt{acronym}}_{\texttt{organization}}(t')$. Partial generalized attributes are indeed partial since joins may fail.

We define partial generalized attributes ${}^{A}[\![\,.\,]\!]$ indirectly, through an auxiliary syntactic mapping γ, the *generalized attribute location*, from attribute chains and their base concepts to auxiliary terms of type <location>.

<location> ::= <attribute> | `@(`<attribute>`,`<concept>`,`<location>`)`

The *indirect* `@`-structured locations give rise to joins in the semantics. In a location `@(`a`,`c'`,`l`)` for a concept c, c' is either a direct attribute reference $r \in R^{a}_{c}$ or a super-concept ($r \sqsubset c'$) or sub-concept ($c' \sqsubset r$) thereof, with l a location for c'.

Here are some examples of γ mappings:

$$
\begin{aligned}
(\texttt{name},\ \texttt{agent}) &\mapsto \texttt{name}\\
(\texttt{name}, \texttt{person}) &\mapsto \texttt{@(\{\},agent,name)}\\
(\texttt{name/student}, \texttt{enrollment}) &\mapsto \texttt{@(student,student,@(person,agent,name))}\\
(\texttt{name}, \texttt{enrollment}) &\not\mapsto
\end{aligned}
$$

The first case is explained by `name` being a dependent, and therefore a local attribute of `agent`. In the second case `name` is not a dependent attribute of `person`, but it is a non-local hierarchical one; under our assumption of a canonical scheme, it has a unique location in a hierarchically related concept, in this case `agent`, joinable through the common identity. The last case shows two effects: sub-attribute inheritance, expressable in our scheme definition language NACS, that allows the attribute `name` to be applied to a `student` meaning the `name` of its `person`; and the chained location of that attribute in the root concept `agent` of the one (`person`) referenced by the attribute `person` in `student`. The γ mapping is naturally partial as e.g. `name` is not an applicable attribute of `enrollment`.

In order to define γ, please remember that condition 3 of the canonicity definition 4 imposes a unique root on an attribute's conceptual references. Since hierarchical attributes are defined from the root (definition 5.1), we can handle attribute references through a simpler alternative to R, namely the *root reference* mapping $\overline{R} : dom(A) \rightharpoonup C$ defined by

$$\overline{R}_c^a = r \quad \text{if} \quad \{\, \overline{x} \mid x \in R_c^a \,\} = \{r\}$$

The definition of γ is split into the base case, when the attribute chain is an atomic attribute, and the recursive case:

$$\gamma_c(a) = \begin{cases} a & \text{if} \quad a \in {}^{L}\!A_c \\ \texttt{@(\{\},}\lambda_c^a\texttt{,}a\texttt{)} & \text{if} \quad a \in {}^{N}\!A_c \end{cases}$$

$$\gamma_c(a_2\texttt{/}a_1) = \begin{cases} \texttt{@(}a_1\texttt{,}\overline{R}_c^{a_1}\texttt{,}\gamma_{\overline{R}_c^{a_1}}(a_2)\texttt{)} & \text{if} \quad \gamma_c(a_1) = a_1 \\ \texttt{@(}a'\texttt{,}c'\texttt{,@(}a_1\texttt{,}\overline{R}_{c'}^{a_1}\texttt{,}\gamma_{\overline{R}_{c'}^{a_1}}(a_2)\texttt{))} & \text{if} \quad \gamma_c(a_1) - \texttt{@(}a'\texttt{,}c'\texttt{,}a_1\texttt{)} \end{cases}$$

In our implementation the base case of γ is precompiled when processing the NACS database scheme, for direct use by the NADI interpreter. We also apply the following equivalence to minimize joins:

$$\texttt{@(}a\texttt{,}\overline{R}_c^a\texttt{,@(\{\},}c'\texttt{,}l\texttt{))} \quad \equiv \quad \texttt{@(}a\texttt{,}c'\texttt{,}l\texttt{)}$$

Our goal of defining partial generalized attributes is realized in terms of a partial location semantics for the γ images, applicable to the contextual tuple of a given concept.

$${}^{A}[\![\, a \,]\!]_c^t \;=\; {}^{L}[\![\, \gamma_c(a) \,]\!]_c^t$$

For the location semantics we project local attributes and recursively switch to the tuple of the non-local concept whose identity joins with the local attribute.

$${}^{L}[\![\, a \,]\!]_c^t = \{\, \pi_c^a(t) \,\} \qquad \text{if} \quad a \in {}^{L}\!A_c$$

$${}^{L}[\![\, \texttt{@(}a\texttt{,}c'\texttt{,}l\texttt{)} \,]\!]_c^t = \bigcup_{t' \in \Delta_{c'}} \{\, {}^{L}[\![\, l \,]\!]_{c'}^{t'} \mid \pi_{c'}^{\{\}}(t') = \pi_c^a(t) \,\}$$

The somewhat dense formalization in the last definition hides the simple fact that at most one t' satisfies the required join, given the uniqueness of identity. The join may fail if c' is not a reference of a in c nor a super-concept thereof, i.e. $x \in R_c^a \Rightarrow x \not\sqsubseteq c'$, thereby yielding partiality (the empty set). An example is $\gamma_{\texttt{student}}^{\texttt{user\_id}} = \texttt{@(person,user,user\_id)}$ with $R_{\texttt{student}}^{\texttt{person}} = \{\texttt{person}\}$.

Generalized values. Our syntax of relational constraints is asymmetric for pragmatic reasons, without sacrificing expressive power. The notion of generalized value, appearing as the right argument, includes (besides plain values) fully contextual attribute chains and (sub-)queries.

<value-exp> ::= <value>
| =<attribute-chain>
| *<contextual-attribute-chain>
| <query>

<contextual-attribute-chain> ::= <attribute-chain>
| *<contextual-attribute-chain>

In a constraint we can then relate two attributes of a concept, using the `=` prefix on the right, e.g. `name \= =common_name`. The prefix is needed to disambiguate the interpretation of an atomic name as either a value or an attribute, on the right-hand side only—thus the asymmetry of the relational constraint.

The semantics for generalized values can now be stated.

$$
\begin{aligned}
^{V}[\![\, v \,]\!]^{\tau}_{\sigma} &= v \qquad \text{if} \quad v : \text{<value>} \\
^{V}[\![\, \texttt{=}a \,]\!]^{t\tau}_{c\sigma} &= {}^{A}[\![\, a \,]\!]^{t}_{c} \\
^{V}[\![\, \ast a \,]\!]^{tt'\tau}_{cc'\sigma} &= \begin{cases} ^{V}[\![\, a \,]\!]^{t'\tau}_{c'\sigma} & \text{if} \quad a = \ast a' \\ ^{A}[\![\, a \,]\!]^{t'}_{c'} & \text{otherwise} \end{cases} \\
^{V}[\![\, q \,]\!]^{t\tau}_{c\sigma} &= {}^{Q}[\![\, q \,]\!]^{t\tau}_{c\sigma} \qquad \text{if} \quad q : \text{<query>}
\end{aligned}
$$

The contextual marker $\ast$ signals the descent of one level in the dual context of concepts and their tuples, to interpret there (and not in the current level) the sub-expression. Queries can only appear under a <existential-op>, whose relational reading is $^{R}[\![\, \hat{~} \,]\!] = (\in)$, $^{R}[\![\, \tilde{~} \,]\!] = (\notin)$.

Projections. Let us start by considering just standard projections without group operators, ordering or external functions. Their core syntax is

<projection> ::= <attribute-chain>
| <query>
| <projection>,<projection>

Sub-queries in projections are supposedly contextual, as in the example about courses and lecturers towards the end of section 3.1. The concrete syntax allows conjunctions inside attribute chains, equivalent to their distribution over the chaining operator:

$$(a,b)/c \quad \mapsto \quad a/c,\ b/c$$

We may recall, from the semantic equation 2 for queries, that answers result from applying the denotation of the projection to the *set* of database tuples for the concept filtered by the constraints. The set argument is needed for the semantics of group operators (sum, max, etc.), but for standard projections the semantics is *flat*—obtained locally (as a set of tuples) from each tuple:

$$^{P}[\![\, p \,]\!]_{c}(T) = \bigcup \{\, ^{\Pi}[\![\, p \,]\!]^{t}_{c} \mid t \in T \,\}$$

We have seen the partial generalized attribute semantics attached to an <attribute-chain> in a constraint. Its projection semantics is basically similar, except that where the other is partial—returning the empty set—this one returns a singleton with a *null* tuple (`[]`, ..., `[]`) of the appropriate size. This alternative encoding of partiality with nulls corresponds, in database parlance, to *outer joins* rather than *inner joins*. The query `(name,user_id)/student/enrollment$...` yields answers with the names of all the students in question along with their user id, if recorded in `user`, otherwise a null. A contextual sub-query in a projection is also linked through an outer join. The upshot is that *every* filtered tuple yields a projected answer tuple—exactly one if the projection consists only of strict[3] attribute chains, or possibly more if sub-queries are present, e.g. in the aforementioned example in section 3.1, where for each course we may get several lecturers. So here is the definition of our tuple projection semantics:

$$
\begin{aligned}
{}^{\Pi}[\![\, p_1 , p_2 \,]\!]^t_c &= {}^{\Pi}[\![\, p_1 \,]\!]^t_c \otimes {}^{\Pi}[\![\, p_2 \,]\!]^t_c && (\, A \otimes B = \{\, \alpha\beta \mid \alpha \in A,\ \beta \in B \,\}\,) \\
{}^{\Pi}[\![\, a \,]\!]^t_c &= {}^{L}[\![\, \gamma^a_c \,]\!]^t_c \cup \{\, \texttt{[]}^a_c \mid {}^{L}[\![\, \gamma^a_c \,]\!]^t_c = \emptyset \,\} && \text{if} \quad a : \text{<attribute-chain>} \\
{}^{\Pi}[\![\, q \,]\!]^t_c &= {}^{Q}[\![\, q \,]\!]^t_c \cup \{\, \texttt{[]}_q \mid {}^{Q}[\![\, q \,]\!]^t_c = \emptyset \,\} && \text{if} \quad q : \text{<query>}
\end{aligned}
$$

The null tuple mappings are $\texttt{[]}_{(a_1,\ldots,a_n)/c\$x} = \texttt{[]}^{a_1}_c \cdots \texttt{[]}^{a_n}_c$ and $\texttt{[]}^a_c = {}^{\texttt{[]}}[\![\, \gamma^a_c \,]\!]$ for a suitable adaptation ${}^{\texttt{[]}}[\![\, . \,]\!]$ of ${}^{L}[\![\, . \,]\!]$ to chase indirect locations even through failed joins and use the lexical arity of the final attribute for the null tuple.

The projection semantics for group functions is more involved. When asking for e.g. `(course,#student)/enrollment$(@year)` (how many students enrolled in each course this year) one must consider the equivalent classes of the `enrollment` tuples filtered under their `course` projection, which are the groups, then the application of the group function (count, in this case) to each group's `student` projection, and finally the concatenation of each projected course with its student count.

3.3 Derived Attributes and Universal Quantification

The attribute names defined in the scheme correspond to (possibly partial) functions, and we've seen the corresponding attribute semantics ${}^{A}[\![\, . \,]\!]$ yielding singletons or the null set. However, in natural language certain nouns are used exactly like attributive ones but with a relational, rather than functional, meaning. An example is "daughter"; yielding possibly more than one value, when applied to a person, it must generally be used along with quantifiers: "one daughter..." or "all daughters...".

Our framework allows for such *derived* (pseudo-)attributes, by naming conceptual expressions with outstanding contextual references to the target concept. If e.g. `person` has (standard) attributes `father` and `mother`, we may define

```
   child  =  person$( father= *{}; mother= *{} )
daughter  =  person$( sex=f, ( father= *{}; mother= *{} ) )
```

[3] Not involving manifold attributes, explained next.

Now ${}^{A}[\![\,\texttt{child}\,]\!]^{t}_{\texttt{person}}$ can be a set with more than one member. Since the default interpretation of constraints is existential, as expressed in equation 3, the constraint `sex/child=f` is interpreted as "with (at least) one daughter". It becomes necessary to introduce extra syntax for signalling universal quantification; we do this by enclosing the (generalized) attribute chain in braces. So, we can ask for persons having no sons with `person$({sex/child}=f)`. Supposing `person` with an attribute `age`, and `son` defined analogously to `daughter`, we may ask `person$({age/daughter}>{age/son})` for those whose daughters are older than any son.

We have to qualify equation 3 with the restriction that a and v are not braced expressions, and define the universal cases, such as e.g.

$$^{F}[\![\,\{a\}\,r\,\{a'\}\,]\!]^{t_i}_{c\sigma} = (\,(\,^{A}[\![\,a\,]\!]^{t}_{c} \times \{\,^{A}[\![\,a'\,]\!]^{t}_{c}\,\}\,) \subseteq {}^{R}[\![\,r\,]\!]\,)$$

The `not` operator is also available for constraints, with the obvious semantics of Boolean negation, so that the last example above can be equivalently stated as `person$(not(age/daughter=< =(age/son)))`.

3.4 Manifold Attributes

Most concepts and attributes in the real world have a temporal validity, i.e. their individual existence and values change with time. If this happens with periodic regularity, as with the course editions in an academic institution, the temporal structure is explicitly ascribed to attributes in the scheme (we've used `year`, `period`). Most of the temporal variability is, however, non-periodic—a user's identifier should be changeable at any time, as well as the name (e.g. through marriage). We may want to register such changes in the database, to be able to look at the evolution of things, but also wish to retain simplicity in most queries, as in saying e.g. "the student's user id" to mean the current (real-time) value.

Another prevalent variability is that of names, acronyms, etc. with language (e.g. English, French). Again, we ideally want a database scheme accommodating this multilingual variability but avoiding explicit mention of language in queries and commands where it can be assumed in context.

Achieving these goals is a highlight of our approach. We provide special notation in NACS, and the corresponding treatment in NADI, for what we call *manifold* attributes, whose value for a given individual may vary along a certain manifold dimension. Temporal and multilingual are the most common examples of such manifolds.

Temporal attributes. Take the example of a user id. Some persons may never get one, while others may have different ones over time, not necessarily all the time. Given this, the temporal dimension is considered a *fluid* manifold. In our example `user_id` is no longer a local attribute of `user`, becoming an attribute of a different sort of concept, the *fluid manifolding* `agent_with_user_id`, whose identity is the relationship between agents and maximal validity time intervals for their user id's. The temporal manifold is a virtual concept with attributes `start` and `end` (with inclusive and exclusive reading, respectively) of type `date` (in our example) or moment. Since start fully identifies each (disjoint) interval, we end up with $A^{\{\}}_{\mathtt{agent\_with\_user\_id}} = (\mathtt{agent}, \mathtt{start})$ and ${}^{D}\!A_{\mathtt{agent\_with\_user\_id}} = \{\mathtt{end}, \mathtt{user\_id}\}$.

Queries abstract away from these implementation details. In fact, asking simply for user_id/student/··· retrieves by default the *current* user id's for the students in question. NADI therefore exhibits upward compatibility [11] when transforming a regular into a temporal attribute. Added expressive power comes with the possible attachment of temporal constraints to temporal attribute occurrences in queries. NACS allows us to predefine shorthand for these, such as e.g. (<T) for (end=<T) or simply T for (start=<T,end>T). An example of usage is user_id~d(2005,12,31)/··· asking for id's valid at the end of 2005. The expression user_id~[] uses the empty constraint to denote *all* the user id's (at all times). This can occur in a projection to list them all, or e.g. in a constraint user_id~[]=X to assert that the user id at some point in time is X; remember the existential semantics of relational constraints expressed in equation 3.

The default constraint (applied when no other is available) is now, standing for the dynamically evaluated current time value (of type moment or date). It can be implicitly overridden by another contextual default, assigned to the global parameter temporal_validity. This is useful for avoiding explicit constraints in multiple queries under the same temporal validity assumption.

What about querying the temporality associated to values? We simply prefix the projected attribute, e.g. ~user_id/··· asks for the time interval associated with the current user id, followed by it, and ~user_id~[]/··· retrieves all the (start, end, user_id) triples. The extreme temporal values are implementation-dependent, and generally understood as "unknown".

Multilingual attributes. The multilingual manifold, contrary to the temporal, is *solid* rather than fluid. This is because a multilingual attribute always returns a value, either the variant for the required language or the base value that always exists (for some language). This behaviour allows the unbroken progressive adaptation of existing services to another language, as translation data gets filled in.

A multilingual attribute, in contrast to a fluid one, remains local in its concept, to hold the base value, along with the extra dependent attribute language. An example might be the name of a course. We get $\{\mathtt{name}, \mathtt{language}\} \in {}^{D}\!A_{\mathtt{course}}$, and course name translations get stored in the auxiliary *solid manifolding* concept course_ml,[4] with $A^{\{\}}_{\mathtt{course\_ml}} = (\mathtt{course}, \mathtt{language})$ and ${}^{D}\!A_{\mathtt{course\_ml}} = \{\mathtt{name}\}$. A database view course_ml_ is also created, as a virtual super-type of course_ml, to achieve the desired effect of defaulting to the base value for name in course when the translation for (course, language) is not in course_ml.

Where the ~ operator was used in fluid attribute expressions, we use ^ for solid ones. The constraints are just values for the language, the generic default being application-dependent, and implicitly overridden by a value assigned to the global parameter language. So, for example, name^en/course might re-

[4] ml stands for multilingual.

fer to the course name in English, also accessed simply by `name/course` in a context where `language=@L` yields `L=en`. Through `^name^[]/course` we get all (`language,name`) pairs, and `name^{}/course` refers to the base name, recorded in the `course` database table.

Manifold combination. Manifolds can be combined. If we define the `name` of an `organization` as being both temporal and multilingual, we may then ask `name~d(2005,12,31)^en/department`··· for a department's name at the end of 2005 in English, or `~^name^{}/department`··· for the validity and base language of the (and) current name of the department.

Manifold formalization. Lacking the space to fully develop the formal account of manifold attributes, we may nevertheless hint at what it takes to do so. The generalized attribute location γ has to cater for new base cases regarding fluid and solid manifold attributes. In the `user_id` example we would have e.g.

$$\gamma_{person}(\texttt{user\_id}) = \texttt{agent\_with\_user\_id\~{}user\_id}$$

This case would be handled by the location semantics with

$${}^{L}[\![\, c'\tilde{}a \,]\!]^{t}_{c} = \{\, \pi^{a}_{c'}(t') \mid t' \in \Delta_{c'},\ \pi^{\bar{\{\}}}_{c'}(t') = \pi^{\{\}}_{c}(t) \,\}$$

where the *base* identity $\bar{\{\}}$ of a manifolding c' refers to the manifolded concept c. In the example, $A^{\bar{\{\}}}_{\texttt{agent\_with\_user\_id}} = \texttt{agent}$, a super-type of `person`. Actually, the given equation reflects just the case with no manifold constraints. In general we have to consider an extra argument in the location semantics, to carry the abstract constraint to be imposed on t' alongside the identity (join) constraint. Notice that we can refer in the same query to different variants, under appropriate constraints, of the same manifold attribute, e.g. the names before and after a given date.

4 Commands

The major commands are for the *creation*, *deletion* and *update* of concept members, expressed respectively with

+ <constrained-concept>

- <constrained-concept>

<constrained-concept> -+ <equalities>

These procedures are much more powerful than their strict SQL counterparts. Wishing to create a person, for example, we naturally need to specify the values of its total attributes (except its automatically incremented `id_code` identity) but not the actual concepts in the hierarchy where they are located, and we can add attributes for implied sub-concepts of person. For instance, the call

```
+ person$( sex=f, name=N, common_name=CN, user_id=I )
```

will split the specified attributes into their locations `agent` (`name`, `common_name`), `person` (`sex`) and `user` (`user_id`),[5] generate (from a database sequence) the common identity `id_code=IC`, and insert a new tuple for each database table, in their hierarchical order. If `user_id` is a temporal attribute, the very same command still works fine, inserting a tuple in `agent_with_user_id` with the provided `user_id` and the default values for `start` and `end`, which happen to be their respective extreme values (thus meaning forever). For a multilingual attribute the static default value for `language` would be used. The defaults can be overridden with the same syntax used in queries to attach explicit manifold constraints.

We can take much advantage of parameters. Imagine the logic programming code for a service on the Web for students to enroll in courses. Upon its invocation the parameters `student`, `year`, etc. have been assigned values, and when the student clicks on a course its code is transmitted and assigned to `course`, with nothing else needed but to call

```
+ enrollment$( @student, @course_edition ).
```

Equally powerful is the update command. We can simply use, for example,

```
@student -+ ( common_name=N )
```

to update the student's common name in the `agent` tuple whose `id_code` is that of the `student`'s `person` attribute. This comes through the implementation of $\lambda^{\texttt{identifier}}_{\texttt{student}}$ that finds the sub-attribute inheritance of `common_name` from `person` and its location at $\texttt{agent} = \overline{\texttt{person}}$.

Manifold attributes require notions of update going beyond simple equalities. For example, the introduction of a new translation for the name of a course is expressed as an update for the course such as `@course-+(+name^fr=FN)`, that actually inserts a new tuple in the `course_ml` translation table.

The true power of updates, however, is revealed when updating an identity attribute. This change in an individual's identity has to be propagated all over the database tables where the individual is present. In order not to violate foreign keys, this has to performed by creation and deletion, instead of immediate update, and in the correct order when chasing dependencies. The compiled scheme has all the information for this reasoning to be performed flawlessly, which in some cases would be a daunting task if done manually. If, for example, there ever was a reason to change the identity code of a course, the deceptively simple call `@course-+(id_code=C)` would do it, and in the end the course identity would have changed in `course`, `course_edition`, `enrollment`, etc. without ever having violated the database keys during the complex operation.

Deletion is similarly powerful, but presents more occasion for ambiguity and inconsistency. Deleting a concept instance implies, much as for identity updates, to chase dependencies in order to eliminate the instance from the database. But while this is sound for sub-concepts and derived concepts (those where it is just part of the identity), what about super-concepts and dependent concepts (those where it is a dependent attribute)? In both cases we may have a strong or weak reading of the deletion, respectively deleting or not the super-instance or derived concept. If the strong reading might make sense for the super-concept (delete the individual, not just the fact that it belongs to a class in the hierarchy), for derived

[5] Assuming that no attribute is manifold.

concepts it is hard to justify (say, delete enrollments with a peculiar grade that is being deleted). So we opt for the weak reading, resulting in (exception) failure if any of the hard cases happens.

Speaking of failure, it should be mentioned that we provide contextual transactions (`db_transaction:Exec`) that can be nested. Actually, any command raises an exception if not called under a transaction.

5 Summary of Achievements and Further Work

We have shown how to interact with relational databases using a vastly more effective language than SQL, following natural language principles of noun phrase composition with attribute chains and contextual definite references. The natural and concise character of our queries and commands is a match for other approaches based on deductive and/or object-oriented paradigms, with higher impact on the readability of code and ease of its change, and the bonus of requiring only standard and mature relational database technology.

In this paper we exhibited precise formal semantics for the core features of our query language, based on a formal model of canonical schemes and corresponding databases, with our attributive syntax translating into implicit inner and outer joins. Useful features include definite references ("the") to contextual entities, local or global. The abstraction power is much enhanced with a generic treatment of manifold phenomena such as temporal and multilingual attributes, incorporated in the scheme definition and database interaction languages, resulting in very powerful effects with little effort. Commands can be very high-level, with concise statements possibly resulting in large transactions.

Complying with the formal semantics, the NADI interaction language has been implemented with high reliance on the distinguishing features of logic programming, namely structural unification and implicit backtracking, to reason over a compiled version of a database scheme. This compilation is itself a deductive task carried out by a logic program, over a scheme description in the NACS language (described elsewhere [2]) that exploits inheritance and name composition to achieve also a high level of conciseness and readability. The architecture is available to developers of Prolog applications through the scheme compiler, the resulting on-line scheme documentation, and a few interface predicates for queries and commands. A team of around ten people has used it for years to build a very large real-world academic management system [1].

There are several directions for improving and building on this work. One is to embed the NADI interaction language in other programming languages through libraries capable of calling Prolog. Performance-wise we can achieve static optimizations of the code by partial evaluation, which should be quite manageable since we are using a purely compositional alternative to Prolog. It is important also to cope with multiple databases and schemes in the same application. A different and much greater challenge, of vast importance, is to tackle the problem of scheme change. This is a fact of life for most real-world applications, and generally a nightmare for the software development teams. One will have to jump from a purely static view of a scheme to a much higher-level plane where to express the *process* of scheme change rather than purely its *result*, and use this to deduce the impacts, and proceed with the necessary changes, on both the current relational database structure and the database interaction code.

At another level of effort it would be interesting to promote these languages as complementary to the current dogmatic choice of languages for the semantic Web, as we believe there is a misguided misconception of what is "content", and an approach favouring a question-answering paradigm of how to acquire useful information, tapping on the immense potential of existing relational databases, is no less adequate than the idea of extracting "knowledge" as structured data to be reasoned upon. One can easily conceive of a site publishing the scheme of (part of) its relational database, in NACS or its compiled form, and allowing clients to submit corresponding NADI queries to Web services providing answers.

References

1. Porto, A.: An integrated information system powered by prolog. In: Dahl, V., Wadler, P. (eds.) PADL 2003. LNCS, vol. 2562, pp. 92–109. Springer, Heidelberg (2002)
2. Porto, A.: High-level interaction with relational databases in logic programming. In: Gill, A., Swift, T. (eds.) PADL 2009. LNCS, vol. 5418, pp. 152–167. Springer, Heidelberg (2008)
3. Ceri, S., Gottlob, G., Tanca, L.: Logic Programming and Databases. Springer, Heidelberg (1990)
4. Liu, M.: Deductive database languages: problems and solutions. ACM Comput. Surv. 31(1), 27–62 (1999)
5. Kifer, M., Lausen, G., Wu, J.: Logical foundations of object-oriented and frame-based languages. Journal of the ACM 42(1), 741–843 (1995)
6. Niemi, T., Järvelin, K.: Prolog-based meta-rules for relational database representation and manipulation. IEEE Transactions on Software Engineering 17(8), 762–788 (1991)
7. Lenzerini, M., Schaerf, A.: Concept languages as query languages. In: Proceedings of the 9th National Conference on Artificial Intelligence, pp. 471–476. AAAI Press/ The MIT Press (1991)
8. Baader, F., Calvanese, D., McGuinness, D., Nardi, D., Patel-Schneider, P. (eds.): The Description Logic Handbook - Theory, Implementation and Applications. Cambridge University Press, Cambridge (2003)
9. Smith, M.K., Welty, C., McGuinness, D.L.: OWL Web Ontology Language Guide (2004), `http://www.w3.org/TR/owl-guide/`
10. Antoniou, G., van Harmelen, F.: A Semantic Web Primer, 2nd edn. The MIT Press, Cambridge (2008)
11. Bair, J., Bölen, M.H., Jensen, C.S., Snodgrass, R.T.: Notions of upward compatibility of temporal query languages. Wirtschaftsinformatik 39(1), 25–34 (1997)

ISTO: A Language for Temporal Organizational Information Systems

Vitor Nogueira and Salvador Abreu

Universidade de Évora and CENTRIA, Portugal
{vbn,spa}@di.uevora.pt

Abstract. In this paper we propose to extend the logical framework ISCO (Information System COnstruction language) with an expressive means of representing and implicitly using temporal information. Moreover, we also provide a compilation scheme that targets a logic language with modularity and temporal reasoning.

1 Introduction and Motivation

Organizational Information Systems (OIS) have a lot to benefit from Logic Programming (LP) characteristics such as a rapid prototyping ability, the relative simplicity of program development and maintenance, the declarative reading which facilitates both development and the understanding of existing code, the built-in solution-space search mechanism, the close semantic link with relational databases, just to name a few. In [1,2] we find examples of LP languages that were used to develop and maintain Organizational Information Systems.

ISCO (Information System COnstruction language) [3] is based on a Constraint Logic Programming framework to define the schema, represent data, access heterogeneous data sources and perform arbitrary computations. In ISCO, processes and data are structured as *classes* which are represented as typed[1] Prolog predicates. An ISCO class may map to an external data source or sink like a table or view in a relational database, or be entirely implemented as a regular Prolog predicate. Operations pertaining to ISCO classes include a *query* which is similar to a Prolog call as well as three forms of *update*.

In this paper we propose to extend ISCO with an expressive means of representing and implicitly using temporal information. This evolution relies upon the formalism called Temporal Contextual Logic Programming [4,5]. Moreover, having simplicity (syntactic, semantic, etc) as a guideline we present a revised and stripped-down version of ISCO, keeping just some of the core features that we consider indispensable in a language for Temporal Organizational Information Systems. Leaving out aspects such as access control [6] does not mean they are deprecated, only not essential for the purpose at hand. The main motivation of this paper is to provide a language suited to construct and maintain Temporal

[1] The type system applies to class members, which are viewed as Prolog predicate arguments.

S. Abreu and D. Seipel (Eds.): INAP 2009, LNAI 6547, pp. 40–51, 2011.

OIS where contexts aren't explicit but implicit (they are obtained throughout the compilation of this language).

The remainder of this article is structured as follows: Sect. 2 briefly overviews Temporal Contextual Logic Programming. Section 3 presents a revised and stripped-down version of the logical framework ISCO and Sect. 3 proposes the temporal extension. Section 4 discusses a compilation scheme for this language and Section 5 compares it with other approaches. Finally, Sect. 6 draws some conclusions.

2 An Overview of Temporal Contextual Logic Programming

In this section we present an overview of Temporal Contextual Logic Programming (TCxLP). For a more detailed description please consider [4,5]. Since TCxLP combines the modular language Contextual Logic Programming with the temporal paradigm Temporal Annotated Constraint Logic Programming, we begin by briefly overviewing these formalisms.

2.1 Contextual Logic Programming

Contextual Logic Programming (CxLP) [7] is a simple yet powerful language that extends logic programming with mechanisms for modularity. In CxLP a finite set of Horn clauses with a given name is designated by *unit*. Using the syntax of GNU Prolog/CX (recent implementation for CxLP [8]) consider a unit named `employee` to represent some basic facts about university employees:

```
:-unit(employee(NAME, POSITION)).

item :- employee(NAME, POSITION).
employee(bill, teaching_assistant).
employee(joe, associate_professor).

name(NAME).
position(POSITION).
```

The main difference between the example above and a plain logic program is the first line that declares the unit name (`employee`) along with the unit arguments (`NAME, POSITION`). Unit arguments help avoid the annoying proliferation of predicate arguments, which occur whenever a global structure needs to be passed around. A unit argument can be interpreted as a "unit global" variable, i.e. one which is shared by all clauses defined in the unit. Therefore, as soon as a unit argument gets instantiated, all the occurrences of that variable in the unit are replaced accordingly.

Suppose another unit to calculate the salary:

```
:-unit(salary(SALARY)).
```

```
item :-
    position(P),
    index(P, I),
    base_salary(B),
    SALARY is I*B.


index(teaching_assistant, 12).
index(associate_professor, 20).

base_salary(100).
```

A set of units is designated as a *contextual logic program*. With the units above we can build the program `P = {employee, salary}`. Moreover, if we consider that `employee` and `salary` designate sets of clauses, then the resulting program is given by the union of these sets.

For a given CxLP program, we can impose an order on its units, leading to the (run time) notion of *context*. Contexts are implemented as lists of unit designators and each computation has a notion of its *current context*. The program denoted by a particular context is the union of the predicates that are defined in each unit. Moreover, we resort to the *override semantics* to deal with multiple occurrences of a given predicate: only the topmost definition is visible.

To construct contexts, we have the *context extension* operation: the goal $U :> G$ extends the *current context* with unit `U` and resolves goal `G` in the new context. As an illustration, consider a goal that computes Joe's salary:

```
?- employee(joe, P) :> (item, salary(S) :> item).
```

A brief explanation of this goal is as follows: we extend the (initially) empty context with unit employee obtaining context `[employee(joe, P)]` and then resolve query `item`. This leads to `P` being instantiated with `associate_professor`. After `salary/1` being added, the context becomes `[salary(S), employee(joe, associate_professor)]`. Afterwards the second `item` is evaluated and the first matching definition is found in unit `salary`. Goal `position(P)` is called and since there is no rule for this goal in the current unit (`salary`), a search in the context is performed. Since `employee` is the topmost unit that has a rule for `position(P)`, this goal is resolved in the (reduced) context `[employee(joe, associate_professor)]`. In an informal way, we queried the context for the position of whom we want to calculate the salary, obtaining `associate_professor`. The remaining is straightforward, leading to the answer `S = 2000` and `P = associate_professor`.

2.2 Temporal Annotated Constraint Logic Programming

This section presents a brief overview of Temporal Annotated Constraint Logic Programming (TACLP). For a more detailed explanation see for instance [9].

We consider the subset of TACLP where time points are totally ordered, sets of time points are convex and non-empty, and only atomic formulae can be annotated. Moreover clauses are free of negation.

Time can be discrete or dense. Time points are totally ordered by the relation $\leq$. We call the set of time points D and suppose that a set of operations (such as the binary operations $+, -$) to manage such points is associated with it. We assume that the time-line is left-bounded by the number 0 and open the future (∞). A *time period* is an interval $[r, s]$ with $0 \leq r \leq s \leq \infty$, $r \in D$, $s \in D$ and represents the convex, non-empty set of time points $\{t \mid r \leq t \leq s\}$. Therefore the interval $[0, \infty]$ denotes the whole time line.

In TACLP there are the following *annotated formulae*:

- **A at t** means that A holds at time point t.
- **A th I** means that A holds *throughout* I, i.e. at *every* time point in the period I.
- **A in I** means that A holds at *some* time point(s) in the time period I, but there is no knowledge when exactly.

The set of annotations is endowed with a partial order relation $\sqsubseteq$ which turns into a lattice. Given two annotations α and β, the intuition is that $\alpha \sqsubseteq \beta$ if α is "less informative" than β in the sense that for all formulae A, $A\beta \Rightarrow A\alpha$. Assuming $r_1 \leq s_1$, $s_1 \leq s_2$ and $s_2 \leq r_2$, we can summarize the axioms for the lattice operation $\sqsubseteq$ by:

$$in[r_1, r_2] \sqsubseteq in[s_1, s_2] \sqsubseteq in[s_1, s_1] = at\ s_1 = th[s_1, s_1] \sqsubseteq th[s_1, s_2] \sqsubseteq th[r_1, r_2]$$

A TACLP *program* is a finite set of TACLP clauses. A TACLP *clause* is a formula of the form $A\alpha \leftarrow C_1, \ldots, C_n, B_1\alpha_1, \ldots, B_m\alpha_m$ $(m, n \geq 0)$ where A is an atom, α and α_i are optional temporal annotations, the C_j's are the constraints and the B_i's are the atomic formulae.

2.3 Temporal Contextual Logic Programming

The basic mechanism of CxLP is called *context search* and can be described as follows: to solve a goal G in a context C, a search is performed until the topmost unit of C that contains clauses for the predicate of G is found. Temporal Contextual Logic Programming (TCxLP) incorporates temporal reasoning into this mechanism. To accomplish that, temporal annotations are added not only the dynamic part of CxLP (*contexts*) but also to the static one (*units*) and it will be the relation between those two types of annotations that will determine if a given unit is eligible to match a goal during a context search. Although TCxLP has an operational semantics that provides a complete formalization of that behavior, for space reasons here we present only an illustrative example. For further reading please consider [4,5].

Revisiting the University employees example, unit `employee` with temporal information can be written as:

```
:- unit(employee(NAME, POSITION)).


item.
employee(bill, teaching_assistant) th [2004, inf].
employee(joe, teaching_assistant) th [2002, 2006].
employee(joe, associate_professor) th [2007, inf].

name(NAME).
position(POSITION).
```

This way it is possible to represent the *history* of the employees positions: Joe was a teaching assistant between 2002 and 2006. The same person is a associate professor since 2007. Moreover, in this case the rule for predicate `item/0` doesn't need to be "`item :- employee(NAME, POSITION).`" because the goal `item` is true only if the unit is (temporally) eligible and, for that to happen, the unit arguments must be instantiated. To better understand this example, consider the goal that queries Joe's position throughout `[2005,2006]`:

```
?- [employee(joe, P)] th [2005,2006] :< item.
```

In the goal above we introduced a new operator (`:<`) called *context switch* where `C :< G` allows the execution of goal `G` in the temporal annotated context `C`. For the example above `item` is true as long as the unit is eligible in the current context, and this happens when `P` is instantiated with `teaching_assistant`, therefore we get the answer `P = teaching_assistant`.

Moreover, if there is no explicit temporal reference in the context, TCxLP assumes the current time. For instance, the following goal queries Joe's current salary:

```
?- employee(joe, P) :> (item, salary(S) :> item).
```

As the reader might see, the goal above is identical to one used to illustrate CxLP. The difference is that units `employee` and `salary` must be eligible in the temporal context defined. Since there is no mention of time we assume the current time (`at 2009`). Therefore in order for those two units to be eligible we obtain `P = associate_professor` and `S = 20000`.

For simplicity reasons we considered that unit `salary` is atemporal and therefore `base_salary` and `index` are the same throughout time. Nevertheless, it should be clear that it would reasonable to define new temporal units `base_salary` and `index`.

3 The ISTO Language

In this section we describe the language *ISTO* (Information System Temporal cOnstruction language) used to construct and maintain Temporal Organizational Information Systems. This language can be a regarded as a temporal extension of another one called ISCO since it provides a revised and stripped-down version of the ISCO methods, inheritance, composition and persistence together with the temporal extension of the notion of class and data manipulation goals.

3.1 Classes

When dealing with large amounts of data, one must be able to organize information in a modular way. The ISTO proposal for this point are *classes*. Although ISTO classes can be regarded as equivalent to Prolog predicates, they provide the homonym OO concept, along with the related data encapsulation capability.

Let us see an ISTO class that handles data about persons, namely its name and social security number:

Example 1. Class Person.

```
class person.
  name: text.
  ssn: int.
```

In this example after defining the class name to be `person`, we state its arguments and types: `name` type `text` and `ssn` (Social Security Number) type `int`(eger).

Temporal Classes. Temporal classes are syntactically introduced by adding the keyword `temporal` before the keyword `class`. Facts of a temporal class have a temporal dimension, i.e. all tuples have an associated *temporal stamp* which represents instants or intervals (their precise definition will be given in Sect. 3.6). As an illustration, class `employee` can be temporal, since it makes sense that the position and home address of a given employee evolves throughout time. On the other hand class `person` should continue atemporal since the facts it stores shouldn't evolve over time.

Example 2. Temporal class `employee`

```
temporal class employee.
  home: text.
  position: text.
```

3.2 Methods

By defining class arguments we are also implicitly setting class methods for accessing those arguments. For instance, in class `person` we have the predicates `ssn/1` and `name/1`. Therefore to query Joe's ssn, besides the (positional) Prolog goal `?- person(joe, S).` we can equivalently use `?- person(name(joe), ssn(N)).`

Besides these implicit methods, there can also be explicit ones defined by means of regular Horn clauses. As an illustration of an Horn clause, consider that argument `name` of class `person` is an atom with the structure syntax 'SURNAME FIRST_NAME'. In order to obtain the person surname we may add the following clause to the class definition:

```
surname(Surname) :-
            name(Name),
            atom_chars(Name, N_Chrs),
            append(Surname_Chrs, [' '|_], N_Chrs),
            atom_chars(Surname, Surname_Chars).
```

3.3 Inheritance

Inheritance is another Object Oriented feature of ISCO that we would like to retain in our language. The reasons for that are quite natural since it allow us to share not only methods, but also data among different classes.

Considering the class `person` of Example 1 and the class `employee` of Example 2, it should be clear that later is a subclass of the former. Using ISTO syntax we can state this by:

Example 3. Temporal subclass `employee`

```
temporal class employee: person.
  home: text.
  position: text.
```

3.4 Composition

In order to have the OO feature of *composition* we retain the ISCO ability to re-use a class definition as a data type. As an illustration suppose that we want to deal with the employees home address and have the possibility of using the address schema in other classes (e.g. for suppliers). For that we define a new class `address` and re–define the `employee` class adding a new argument (`home`) whose type is `address`:

Example 4. Class address.

```
class address.         temporal class employee: person.
  street: text.          home: address.
  number: int.           position: text.
```

The access to compound types its quite natural, for instance suppose that we want to know Joe's street name:

```
?- employee(name(joe), home(address(street(S)))).
```

Actually, as the reader might see, there is no real need for the basic types since we could develop one class for each. Nevertheless, because they are quite intuitive to use, we decided to keep them.

3.5 Persistence

Having persistence in a Logic Programming language is a required feature to construct actual OIS; this could conceivably be provided by Prolog's internal database but is best accounted for by software designed to handle large quantities of factual information efficiently, as is the case in relational database management systems. The semantic proximity between relational database query languages and logic programming languages have made the former privileged candidates to provide Prolog with persistence.

ISCO's approach for interfacing to existing RDBMS[2] involves providing declarations for an external database together with defining equivalences between classes and database relations.

As an illustration, consider that the `person` facts are stored in a homonym table of a PostgreSQL database named `db` running on the `localhost`:

Example 5. Class person with persistence.

```
external(db_link, postgres(db, localhost)).

external(db_link, person) class person.
  name: text.
  ssn: int.
```

Since the database table has the same name as the class, the `person` inside the `external` term above is optional.

3.6 Data Manipulation Goals

Under the data manipulation operations we include not only insertion, removal and update but also query operations. Since queries were already subject of previous examples in this section we present only the remaining operations.

The modification goals (insert, delete and update) are based on simple queries, non backtrackable and all follow the tuple-at-a-time approach. As an example, suppose that we want to insert the person whose name is `Joe` and ssn is `123456`:

```
?- person(name(joe), ssn(123456)) +.
```

As expected there are also operators for removing (`-`) and updating (`#`).

Temporal Data Manipulation. In here we present the temporal equivalent of the data manipulation goals described above, i.e. we provide a temporal query, insertion, removal and update goals.

Keeping the syntax as simple as possible, temporal operations add a suffix composed by the operator "`@`" and a temporal annotation to the *atemporal* counterparts. The interval representation is the standard one `[T1, T2]` and stands for all time points between `T1` and `T2` (where $T2 \geq T1$). Moreover, in order to be able to handle in-annotated information (see Sect. 2.2), we also allow another type of intervals `[T1; T2]` to represent some time points (not necessarily all) between `T1` and `T2`, i.e. `[T1; T2]` is a subset of `[T1, T2]`.

[2] ISCO access to frameworks beyond relational databases, such as LDAP directory services or web services is out of scope for the present work. We shall stick with to RDMBS only.

Although an instant T can be represented by the interval [T, T], to ease the reading we denote it simply by T. As an illustration consider that we want to know Joe's street name in the year 2007:

Example 6. Joe's street name in the year 2007

```
?- employee(name(joe),
            home(address(street(S)))) @ 2007
S = upstreet
```

The goal above is a temporal version of the one presented in Sect. 3.4.

Finally, as it should be expected, whenever there is no temporal mention in a data manipulation goal that involves temporal classes it is assumed the current time, i.e. there is an implicit "@ now" suffixing the goal.

4 Compilation Scheme for ISTO

The compilation of the non-temporal part of ISTO yields CxLP and from the temporal extension we target TCxLP. Since the temporal aspects are the novelty, in this section we describe more throughly the compilation scheme for these aspects.

4.1 (Temporal) Classes

The translation from an ISTO class to CxLP can be roughly described as: every class is mapped to a corresponding unit, with the class arguments transformed into unit arguments and predicates for accessing these arguments. Moreover, one extra unit argument OID standing for *Object Identifier* is added to every unit and is used to discriminate a given element in a class.

Before presenting the compilation of temporal classes and goals one must observe that non-temporal classes must behave as if they were valid throughout the entire time line. Such a behavior can be obtained simply by adding a fact to each non temporal unit. For instance, to the unit person which has been presented, it suffices to add the fact: `person(_OID, _NAME, _SSN) th [0, inf]`.

Let us now see the result of compiling the temporal class `employee` from Example 2:

```
:- unit(employee(OID, HOME_OID, POSITION)).

oid(OID).

home(address(GOAL)) :-
     [address(HOME_OID, STREET, NUMBER)]
                :< (item, GOAL).

position(POSITION).

item :- :^ item.
```

The main difference from the compilation of the non temporal class is that there is no need for predicate `item` to instantiate the unit arguments, since the temporal context search will do that implicitly. Besides the clauses above there must be also some temporal conditions such as `employee(1, 1, associate_professor) th [2007, inf]` (representing for instance part of Joe's information.) Finally, since `employee` is a subclass of `person`, the context for unit `employee` is of the form `[employee(...), person(...), ...]`, therefore to ensure consistency `item/0` must also be invoked in the context `[person(...), ...]` and that is accomplished by `:^ item`.[3]

4.2 Temporal Data Manipulation Goals

The translation of a temporal query will result in a goal in a temporal context. The ISTO query of Joe's street name in 2007 of Sect. 3.6 is translated into:

```
?- [employee(OID, HOME_OID, POSITION),
    person(OID, NAME, SSN)] (at 2007) :<
      (item, name(joe), home(address(street(S)))).
```

Introducing temporal modification goals needs further considerations. First of all, as mentioned, these goals are extra-logical. Moreover, since now the th-annotated facts can change at runtime, to use the (simplified) semantics of TCxLP one must ensure that the backend of a temporal class always stores the least upper bound of th-annotated unit temporal conditions. In order to guarantee that, every insertion of a th-annotated temporal condition must induce a recomputation of the least upper bound. As an illustration consider again Joe's positions through time:[4]

```
employee(1, teaching_assistant) th [2002, 2006].
employee(1, associate_professor) th [2007, inf].
```

Suppose the following ISTO goal to remove this employee information between 2005 and 2006:

```
?- (employee(name(joe)) -) @ [2005, 2006].
```

It changes the temporal conditions in the following way:

```
employee(1, teaching_assistant) th [2002, 2004].
employee(1, associate_professor) th [2007, inf].
```

Finally, if we add the information that Joe's position between 2005 and 2006 was `associate_professor`:

```
?- (employee(name(joe),
      position(associate_professor)) +) @ [2005, 2006].
```

then the least upper bound must be recomputed, leading to:

```
employee(1, teaching_assistant) th [2002, 2004].
employee(1, associate_professor) th [2005, inf].
```

[3] The operator `:^` is called the supercontext operator.

[4] For simplicity reasons in this illustration we ignore the home address argument.

5 Comparison with Other Approaches

The temporal timestamps of ISTO can regarded as the counterpart of the *valid time* proposed in temporal databases [10]. Although ISTO has no concept similar to the *transaction time*, we consider that one could implement it by adding a log in the ISTO backend unit. However this capability is beyond the scope of the ISTO initial concerns. On the other hand, ISTO *contextual time* enables an expressiveness that lacks in most database products with temporal support. Only in Oracle Workspace Manager [11] we find a concept (workspace) that is related to our temporal context.

As far as we know there are logical languages that have modularity/OO, others that provide temporal reasoning or even persistence. ISTO is the only one that encompasses all those features.

6 Conclusions and Future Work

In this paper we presented a revision of a state-of-the-art logical framework for constructing OIS called ISCO. We proceeded to introduce an extension to this language called ISTO, that includes the expressive means of representing and implicitly using temporal information. Together with a syntactical definition of ISTO we also presented a compilation scheme from this language into Temporal Contextual Logic Programming.

Finally, we consider that ISTO can take advantage of the experience gained from several real-world application developed in ISCO in order to act as backbone for constructing and maintaining Temporal OIS. Therefore we are currently applying the language proposed in an University Information System.

References

1. Porto, A.: An integrated information system powered by prolog. In: Dahl, V., Wadler, P. (eds.) PADL 2003. LNCS, vol. 2562, pp. 92–109. Springer, Heidelberg (2002)
2. Abreu, S., Diaz, D., Nogueira, V.: Organizational information systems design and implementation with contextual constraint logic programming. In: IT Innovation in a Changing World – The 10th International Conference of European University Information Systems, Ljubljana, Slovenia (2004)
3. Abreu, S.: Isco: A practical language for heterogeneous information system construction. In: Proceedings of INAP 2001, Tokyo, Japan, Prolog Association of Japan (2001)
4. Nogueira, V., Abreu, S.: Temporal contextual logic programming. Electr. Notes Theor. Comput. Sci. 177, 219–233 (2007)
5. Nogueira, V., Abreu, S.: Temporal Annotations for a Contextual Logic Programming Language. In: Neves, J., Santos, M., Machado, J., eds.: Progress in Artificial Intelligence, 13th Portuguese Conference on Artificial Intellige nce, EPIA 2007, Universidade do Minho (2007)

6. Abreu, S.: Modeling Role-Based Access Control in ISCO. In: Ribeiro, L.M., dos Santos, J.M. (eds.) The 8th International Conference of European University Information Systems, FEUP Edies (2002) ISBN 972-752-051-0
7. Monteiro, L., Porto, A.: A Language for Contextual Logic Programming. In: Apt, K., de Bakker, J., Rutten, J. (eds.) Logic Programming Languages: Constraints, Functions and Objects, pp. 115–147. MIT Press, Cambridge (1993)
8. Abreu, S.P., Díaz, D.: Objective: In minimum context. In: Palamidessi, C. (ed.) ICLP 2003. LNCS, vol. 2916, pp. 128–147. Springer, Heidelberg (2003)
9. Frühwirth, T.W.: Temporal annotated constraint logic programming. J. Symb. Comput. 22(5/6), 555–583 (1996)
10. Tansel, A.U., Clifford, J., Gadia, S., Jajodia, S., Segev, A., Snodgrass, R. (eds.): Temporal databases: theory, design, and implementation. Benjamin-Cummings Publishing Co., Inc., Redwood City (1993)
11. Corportation, O.: Oracle database 10g workspace manager overview. Oracle White Paper (2005)

Programming Patterns for Logtalk Parametric Objects

Paulo Moura

Dep. of Computer Science, University of Beira Interior, Portugal
Center for Research in Advanced Computing Systems,
INESC Porto, Portugal
pmoura@di.ubi.pt

Abstract. This paper presents a survey of programming patterns for Logtalk *parametric objects*. A parametric object is an object whose identifier is a compound term containing logical variables. These variables play the role of object parameters. Object predicates can be coded to depend on the parameter values. Parametric objects are a common feature of some other object-oriented logic programming languages and Prolog object-oriented extensions. Logtalk extends the usefulness of parametric objects by introducing the concept of *object proxies*. An object proxy is a compound term that can be interpreted as a possible instantiation of the identifier of a parametric object. Object proxies, when represented as predicate facts, allow application memory footprint to be minimized while still taking full advantage of Logtalk object-oriented features for representing and reasoning with taxonomic knowledge.

Keywords: logic programming, programming patterns, parametric objects, object proxies.

1 Introduction

Logtalk [1–3] is an object-oriented logic programming language that can use most Prolog implementations as a back-end compiler. Logtalk extends Prolog with versatile code encapsulation and code reuse constructs based on an interpretation of object-oriented concepts in the context of logic programming. Logtalk features *objects* (both *prototypes* and *classes*), *static* and *dynamic binding* (with predicate lookup caching), *single* and *multiple inheritance*, *protocols* (aka interfaces; sets of predicate declarations that can be implemented by any object), *categories* (fine-grained units of code reuse that can be used as object building blocks), *event-driven programming*, and *high-level multi-threading programming* (and-parallelism and competitive or-parallelism). Objects, protocols, and categories can be either static or dynamic. The use of static entities and static binding results in performance similar to plain Prolog.

Logtalk includes support for *parametric objects*, a feature common to some object-oriented logic programming languages and Prolog object-oriented extensions. A parametric object is an object whose identifier is a compound term

S. Abreu and D. Seipel (Eds.): INAP 2009, LNAI 6547, pp. 52–69, 2011.

containing logical variables. A simple example of a parametric object for representing two-dimensional geometric points could be:

```
:- object(point(_X, _Y)).

:- end_object.
```

The variables in the object identifier play the role of object parameters. Object predicates can be coded to depend on the parameter values. For example, assuming that we needed to compute the distance of a point to the origin, we could write:

```
:- object(point(_X, _Y)).

    :- public(distance/1).
    distance(Distance) :-
        parameter(1, X),
        parameter(2, Y),
        Distance is sqrt(X*X + Y*Y).

:- end_object.
```

After compiling this parametric object we could try queries such as:

```
| ?- point(3.0, 4.0)::distance(Distance).

Distance = 5.0
yes
```

Thus, a parametric object can be regarded as a generic object from which specific *instantiations* can be derived by instantiating the object parameters at runtime. Note, however, that instantiating object parameters does not create new objects. For example, the object identifiers `point(2.0, 1.2)` and `point(3.0, 4.0)` refer to the same parametric object. Parameter instantiation usually takes place when a message is sent to the object. By using logical variables, parameter instantiation is undone on backtracking. Object parameters can be any valid term: logical variables, constraint variables, atomic terms, or compound terms.[1]

Despite the simplicity of the concept, parametric objects proved a valuable asset in a diversity of applications. Parametric objects support several useful programming patterns, presented and illustrated in this paper. The remainder of the paper is organized as follows. Section 2 describes Logtalk built-in methods for accessing object parameters. Section 3 illustrates parameter passing within object hierarchies. Section 4 presents useful parametric object programming patterns, illustrated by examples. Section 5 presents and discusses the concept of *object proxies*, introducing additional programming patterns. Section 6 shows how to use both object proxies and regular objects to represent entities of the same *type* that differ on complexity or size. Section 7 discusses related work. Section 8 presents our conclusions.

[1] Logtalk also supports parametric categories, thus extending the advantages of parametric objects when using programming solutions based on category- based composition.

2 Accessing Object Parameters

Logtalk provides a `parameter/2` built-in method for accessing object parameters. The first argument is the parameter position. The second argument is the object parameter. For example:

```
:- object(ellipse(_Rx, _Ry, _Color)).

    area(Area) :-
        parameter(1, Rx),
        parameter(2, Ry),
        Area is Rx*Ry*pi.
    ...
```

Logtalk compiles the calls to the method `parameter/2` in-line by unifying the second argument with the corresponding object identifier argument in the execution context argument in the translated clause head. A second built-in method, `this/1`, allows access to all object parameters at once:

```
    area(Area) :-
        this(ellipse(Rx, Ry, _)),
        Area is Rx*Ry*pi.
```

As with the `parameter/2` method, calls to the `this/1` method are compiled in-line.

An alternative to the `parameter/2` and `this/1` methods for accessing object parameters would be to interpret parameters as logical variables with global scope within the object. This solution was discarded as it forces the programmer to always be aware of parameter names when coding object predicates. It also collides with the local scope of Logtalk and Prolog variables in directives and predicate clauses.

3 Parameter Passing

Logtalk objects may *extend* (defining parent-prototype relations), *instantiate* (defining instance-class relations), or *specialize* (defining class-superclass relations) other objects. When using parametric objects, parameter passing is established through unification in the object opening directive. As an example, consider the following Logtalk version of a SICStus Objects [4] example:

```
:- object(ellipse(_RX, _RY, _Color)).

    :- public([color/1, rx/1, ry/1, area/1]).

    rx(Rx) :-
        parameter(1, Rx).

    ry(Ry) :-
        parameter(2, Ry).
```

```
        color(Color) :-
            parameter(3, Color).

        area(Area) :-
            this(ellipse(Rx, Ry, _)),
            Area is Rx*Ry*pi.

    :- end_object.

    :- object(circle(Radius, Color),                   % circles are ellipses
        extends(ellipse(Radius, Radius, Color))).      % where Rx = Ry

        :- public(r/1).
        r(Radius) :-
            parameter(1, Radius).

    :- end_object.

    :- object(circle1(Color),
        extends(circle(1, Color))).

    :- end_object.

    :- object(red_circle(Radius),
        extends(circle(Radius, red))).

    :- end_object.
```

A query such as:

```
| ?- red_circle(3)::area(Area).

Area = 28.274334
yes
```

will result in the following instantiation chain of the parametric object identifiers:

```
red_circle(3) -> circle(3, red) -> ellipse(3, 3, red)
```

Note that the predicate `area/1` is declared and defined in the object representing ellipses.

4 Programming Patterns

This section presents a survey of useful parametric object programming patterns. These patterns build upon the basic idea that a parametric object encapsulates a set of predicates for working with compound terms that share the same functor and arity. Additional programming patterns will be described later in this paper when presenting the Logtalk concept of parametric object proxies. The full source code of most examples is included in the current Logtalk distribution.

4.1 Using Parameters for Passing Typing Information

Parameters may be used to represent *type* information. This usage provides functionality akin to e.g. C++ templates or Java generics. There are, however, two important differences. First, the Logtalk runtime parameterization does not create a new object. Second, Logtalk provides runtime parameterization instead of compile-time parameterization. The canonical example is sorting a list of elements of a given type:

```
:- object(sort(_Type)).

    :- public(sort/2).
    sort([], []).
    sort([Pivot| Rest], Sorted) :-
        partition(Rest, Pivot, Small, Large),
        sort(Small, SortedSmall),
        sort(Large, SortedLarge),
        list::append(SortedSmall, [Pivot| SortedLarge], Sorted).

    partition([], _, [], []).
    partition([X| Xs], Pivot, Small, Large) :-
        parameter(1, Type),
        (   (Type::(X < Pivot)) ->
            Small = [X| Small1], Large = Large1
        ;   Small = Small1, Large = [X| Large1]
        ),
        partition(Xs, Pivot, Small1, Large1).

:- end_object.
```

Assuming a `rational` object implementing the Logtalk library `comparing` protocol, we can use queries such as:

```
| ?- sort(rational)::sort([1/8, 2/7, 6/5, 2/9, 1/3], Sorted).

Sorted = [1/8, 2/9, 2/7, 1/3, 6/5]
yes
```

Or simply use the pseudo-object *user*, thus using the Prolog built-in comparison predicates:

```
| ?- sort(user)::sort([3, 1, 4, 2, 9], Sorted).

Sorted = [1, 2, 3, 4, 9]
yes
```

4.2 Customizing Object Predicates

Parameters may be used to customize object predicates, improving code reusing by avoiding repeating similar predicate definitions. For example, assume that we want to define implementations of both *max-heaps* and *min-heaps* (also know as *priority queues*). Inserting a new element on a heap requires comparing it with the existing heap elements in order to ensure that the queue front element is always the one with the top priority. For a max-heap, this will be the element with the maximum priority while for a min-heap this will be the element with the minimum priority. We can use a parameter to represent *how* to compare heap elements:

```
:- object(heap(_Order)).

    % generic heap handling predicates containing calls such as:
    % ..., parameter(1, Order), compare(Order, X, Y), ...

:- end_object.
```

We could use this object directly but we can also define two handy shortcuts:

```
:- object(minheap,
    extends(heap(<))).

:- end_object.


:- object(maxheap,
    extends(heap(>))).

:- end_object.
```

This programing pattern illustrates how we can use parameters to customize object predicates by passing the *operations* to be invoked within those predicates. These operations can be either closures (as in the example above) or goals, linking this programming pattern to the concepts of meta-programming and meta-predicates.

4.3 Simplifying Object Interfaces

Parametric objects can simplify object interfaces by moving core object properties from predicate arguments to object parameters, that is, object parameters can be used to represent object *data*. This also makes the core properties visible without requiring the definition of *accessor* predicates to retrieve them. Consider the following parametric object representing rectangles:

```
:- object(rectangle(_Width, _Height)).

    :- public(area/1).
    area(Area) :-
        this(rectangle(Width, Height)),
        Area is Width*Height.

    :- public(perimeter/1).
    perimeter(Perimeter) :-
```

```
        this(rectangle(Width, Height)),
        Perimeter is 2*(Width + Height).

:- end_object.
```

The rectangle properties *width* and *height* are always accessible. The two rectangle predicates, `area/1` and `perimeter/1`, have a single argument returning the respective computed values.

Assume that our application would also need to compute areas and perimeters of circles, triangles, pentagons, and other (regular or non-regular) polygons. The alternative of using non parametric objects to encapsulate the same functionality would require adding extra arguments to both predicates that would depend on the type of shape. We could use instead a single *data* argument that would accept a compound term representing a shape but that would result in a awkward solution for encapsulating the knowledge about each type of shape in its own object. Another alternative would be to use predicates such as `area_circle/1` and `perimeter_triangle/1` but this solution is hard to extend to new shapes, to new predicates over shapes, and would hinder processing of heterogenous collections of shapes. Parametric objects provide us with a simple, clean, logical, and easily extensible knowledge representation solution.

4.4 Data-Centric Programming

Parametric objects can be seen as enabling a more data-centric programming style where data is represented by *instantiations* of parametric object identifiers. Instead of using a term as a predicate argument, predicates can be called by sending the corresponding message to the term itself.

To illustrate this pattern we will use the well-known example of symbolic differentiation and simplification of arithmetic expressions, which can be found in [5]. The L&O [6] system also uses this example to illustrate parametric theories. The idea is to represent arithmetic expressions as parametric objects whose name is the expression operator with greater precedence, and whose parameters are the operator sub-expressions (that are, themselves, objects). In order to simplify this example, the object methods will be restricted to symbolic differentiation of polynomials with a single variable and integer coefficients. In addition, we will omit any error-checking code. The symbolic simplification of arithmetic expressions could easily be programmed in a similar way.

For an arithmetic expression reduced to a single variable, x, we will have the following object:

```
:- object(x,
    implements(diffp)).   % protocol (interface) declaring a diff/1
                          % symbolic differentiation predicate
    diff(1).

:- end_object.
```

Arithmetic addition, $x + y$, can be represented by the parametric object `'+'(X, Y)` or, using operator notation, `X + Y`. Taking into account that the operands can either be numbers or other arithmetic expressions, a possible definition will be:

```
:- object(_ + _,
    implements(diffp)).

    diff(Diff) :-
        this(X + Y),
        diff(X, Y, Diff).

    diff(I, J, 0) :-
        integer(I), integer(J), !.

    diff(X, J, DX) :-
        integer(J), !, X::diff(DX).

    diff(I, Y, DY) :-
        integer(I), !, Y::diff(DY).

    diff(X, Y, DX + DY) :-
        X::diff(DX), Y::diff(DY).

:- end_object.
```

The object definitions for other simple arithmetic expressions, such as `X - Y` or `X * Y`, are similar. The expression x^n can be represented by the parametric object `X ** N` as follows:

```
:- object(_ ** _).

    :- public(diff/1).

    diff(N * X ** N2) :-
        this(X ** N),
        N2 is N - 1.

:- end_object.
```

By defining a suitable parametric object per arithmetic operator, any polynomial expression can be interpreted as an object identifier. For example, the polynomial `2*x**3 + x**2 - 4*x` ($2x^3 + x^2 - 4x$) will be interpreted as `(2*x**3) + (x**2 - 4*x)` ($(2x^3) + (x^2 - 4x)$). Thus, this expression is an *instantiation* of the `X + Y` parametric object identifier, allowing us to write queries such as:

```
| ?- (2*x**3 + x**2 - 4*x)::diff(D).

D = 2* (3*x**2)+2*x**1-4*1
yes
```

The resulting expression could be symbolically simplified using a predicate defined in the same way as the `diff/1` differentiation predicate.

4.5 Restoring Shared Constraint Variables

Object parameters can be used to restore shared variables between sets of constraints that are encapsulated in different objects. We illustrate this pattern using an example that is loosely based in the declarative process modeling research project ESProNa [7]. Each process can be described by a parametric object, implementing a common protocol (reduced here to a single predicate declaration for the sake of this example):

```
:- protocol(process_description).

    :- public(domain/2).
    :- mode(domain(-list(object_identifier), -callable), one).
    :- info(domain/2, [
        comment is 'Returns the process dependencies and constraints.',
        argnames is ['Dependencies', 'Constraints']]).

    % other process description predicates

:- end_ protocol.
```

Part of the process description is a set of finite domain constraints describing how many times the process can or must be executed. An object parameter is used to provide access to the process constraint variable. For example, the following process, `a(_)`, can be executed two, three, or four times:

```
:- object(a(_),
    implements(process_description)).

    domain([], (A #>= 2, A #=< 4)) :-
        parameter(1, A).

:- end_object.
```

Processes may depend on other processes. These dependency relations can be described using a list of parametric object identifiers. For example:

```
:- object(b(_),
    implements(process_description)).

    domain([a(A)], (B #>= A, B #=< 3)) :-
        parameter(1, B).

:- end_object.

:- object(c(_),
    implements(process_description)).

    domain([a(A), b(B)], (C #= B + 1, C #= A + 1)) :-
        parameter(1, C).

:- end_object.
```

Thus, the parametric object identifiers in the dependencies list allows us to relate the different process constraint variables.

The object parameters allows us to restore shared constraint variables at runtime in order to model sets of inter-dependent processes. For example (using Logtalk with GNU Prolog, with its native finite domain solver, as the back-end compiler):

```
| ?- process_model::solve([c(C)], Dependencies).

C = _#59(3..4)
Dependencies = [b(_#21(2..3)),a(_#2(2..3)),c(_#59(3..4))]
yes
```

The predicate `solve/2` (the code of the `process_model` object is omitted due to the lack of page space) computes this answer by retrieving and solving the conjunction of the constraints of processes `a(_)`, `b(_)`, and `c(_)`.

4.6 Logical Updates of Object State

Parametric objects provide an alternative to represent object dynamic state. This alternative supports logical updates, undone by backtracking, by representing object state using one or more object parameters. A similar solution was first used in the OL(P) [8]. Logtalk supports this solution using a pure logical subset implementation of *assignable variables* [9], available in the library `assignvars`.[2] This library defines *setter* and *getter* methods (`<=/2` and `=>/2`, respectively) and an initialization method (`assignable/2`) to work with assignable variables.

Consider the following simple example, where a parametric object is used to describe a geometric rectangle. The object state is comprised by its read-only dimensions, *width* and *height*, and by its dynamically updatable *position*:

```
:- object(rectangle(_Width, _Height, _Position),
    imports(private::assignvars)).

    :- public([init/0, area/1, move/2, position/2]).

    init :-
        parameter(3, Position),
        ::assignable(Position, (0, 0)).

    area(Area) :-
        this(rectangle(Width, Height, _)),
        Area is Width*Height.

    move(X, Y) :-
        parameter(3, Position),
        ::Position <= (X, Y).
```

[2] This library is implemented as a *category* [1], a fine-grained unit of code reuse that can be virtually imported by any object without code duplication.

```
        position(X, Y) :-
            parameter(3, Position),
            ::Position => (X, Y).

    :- end_object.
```

A sample query could be:

```
| ?- rectangle(2, 3, _)::(init, area(Area), position(X0, Y0),
     move(1, 1), position(X1, Y1), move(2, 2), position(X2, Y2)).

Area = 6
X0 = Y0 = 0
X1 = Y1 = 1
X2 = Y2 = 2
yes
```

Using object parameters for representing mutable state provides a solution that supports clean and logical application semantics, backtracking over state changes, and better performance than using assert and retract operations to update an object dynamic database.

5 Parametric Object Proxies

Compound terms with the same functor and arity as a parametric object identifier may act as *proxies* to a parametric object. Proxies may be stored on the database as Prolog facts and be used to represent different *instantiations* of a parametric object identifier. This representation can be ideal to minimize application memory requirements in the presence of a large number of data objects whose state is immutable. As a simple example, assume that our data represents geometric circles with attributes such as an identifier, the circle radius and the circle color:

```
% circle(Id, Radius, Color)
circle('#1', 1.23, blue).
circle('#2', 3.71, yellow).
circle('#3', 0.39, green).
circle('#4', 5.74, black).
```

We can define the following parametric object for representing circles:

```
:- object(circle(_Id, _Radius, _Color)).

    :- public([id/1, radius/1, color/1, area/1, perimeter/1]).

    id(Id) :-
        parameter(1, Id).

    radius(Radius) :-
```

```
        parameter(2, Radius).

    color(Color) :-
        parameter(3, Color).

    area(Area) :-
        parameter(2, Radius),
        Area is 3.1415927*Radius*Radius.

    perimeter(Perimeter) :-
        parameter(2, Radius),
        Perimeter is 2*3.1415927*Radius.

:- end_object.
```

The `circle/3` parametric object provides a simple solution for encapsulating a set of predicates that perform computations over circle properties, as illustrated by the `area/1` and `perimeter/1` predicates.

Logtalk provides a convenient notational shorthand for accessing proxies represented as Prolog facts when sending a message:

```
| ?- {Proxy}::Message.
```

In this case, Logtalk proves `Proxy` as a Prolog goal and sends the message to the resulting term, interpreted as the identifier of a parametric object.[3] This construct can either be used with a proxy argument that is sufficiently instantiated in order to unify with a single Prolog fact or with a proxy argument that unifies with several facts. Backtracking over the proxy goal is supported, allowing all matching object proxies to be processed by e.g. a simple failure-driven loop. For example, in order to construct a list with the areas of all the circles we can write:

```
| ?- findall(Area, {circle(_, _, _)}::area(Area), Areas).

Areas = [4.75291, 43.2412, 0.477836, 103.508]
yes
```

In non-trivial applications, data objects, represented as object proxies, and the corresponding parametric objects, are tied to large hierarchies representing taxonomic knowledge about the application domain. An example is the LgtSTEP application [10] used for validating STEP files, which is a format for sharing data models between CAD/CAM applications. A typical data model can contain hundreds of thousands of geometrical objects, which are described by a set of hierarchies representing geometric concepts, data types, and consistency rules. In its current version, the LgtSTEP application hierarchies define 252 geometric or related entities, 78 global consistency rules, 68 data types, and 69 support functions. STEP files use a simple syntax for geometrical and related objects. Consider the following fragment:

[3] The `{}/1` functor was chosen as it is already used as a control construct to bypass the Logtalk compiler in order to call Prolog predicates.

```
#1=CARTESIAN_POINT('',(0.E0,0.E0,-3.38E0));
#2=DIRECTION('',(0.E0,0.E0,1.E0));
#3=DIRECTION('',(1.E0,0.E0,0.E0));
#4=AXIS2_PLACEMENT_3D('',#1,#2,#3);
```

The first line above defines a cartesian point instance, whose identifier is `#1`, followed by an empty comment and the point coordinates in a 3D space. Similar for the other lines. This syntax is easily translated to Prolog predicate facts that are interpreted by Logtalk as object proxies:

```
cartesian_point('#1', '', (0.0, 0.0, -3.38)).
direction('#2', '', (0.0, 0.0, 1.0)).
direction('#3', '', (1.0, 0.0, 0.0)).
axis2_placement_3d('#4', '', '#1', '#2', '#3').
```

Complemented by the corresponding parametric objects, object proxies provide a source level representation solution whose space requirements are roughly equal to those of the original STEP file. An alternative representation using one Logtalk object per STEP object results in space requirements roughly equal to 2.2 times the size of the original STEP file in our experiments.[4] For example, the cartesian point above could be represented by the object:

```
:- object('#1',
    instantiates(cartesian_point)).

    comment('').
    coordinates(0.0, 0.0, -3.38).

:- end_object.
```

For simple, immutable data objects, Logtalk object representation provides little benefit other than better readability. Object proxies and parametric objects allows us to avoid using a Logtalk object per data object, providing a bridge between the data objects and the hierarchies representing the knowledge used to reason about the data, while optimizing application memory requirements.

6 Using Both Object Proxies and Regular Objects

While object proxies provide a compact representation, complex domain objects are often better represented as regular objects. Moreover, while in object proxies the meaning of an argument is implicitly defined by its position in a compound term, predicates with meaningful names can be used in regular objects. In some applications it is desirable to be able to choose between object proxies and regular objects on a case-by-case basis. An example is the L-FLAT [11] application, a full rewrite in Logtalk of P-FLAT [12], a Prolog toolkit for teaching Formal Languages and Automata Theory. L-FLAT is a work in progress where one of

[4] Logtalk object representation is currently optimized for execution time performance, not memory space requirements.

the goals is to allow users to use both object proxies and regular objects when representing Turing machines, regular expressions, finite automata, context free grammars, and other concepts and mechanisms supported by L-FLAT. This flexibility allows users to represent e.g. a simple finite automaton with a small number of states and transitions as an object proxy:

```
% fa(Id, InitialState, Transitions, FinalStates)
fa(fa1, 1, [1/a/1, 1/a/2, 1/b/2, 2/b/2, 2/b/1], [2]).
```

It also allows users to represent e.g. a complex Turing machine with dozens of transitions as a regular object:

```
:- object(aibiciTM,
    instantiates(tm)).

    initial(q0).

    transitions([
        q0/'B'/'B'/'R'/q1,
        q1/a/'X'/'R'/q2,    q1/'Y'/'Y'/'R'/q5,  q1/'B'/'B'/'R'/q6,
        q2/a/a/'R'/q2,      q2/'Y'/'Y'/'R'/q2,  q2/b/'Y'/'R'/q3,
        q3/b/b/'R'/q3,      q3/'Z'/'Z'/'R'/q3,  q3/c/'Z'/'L'/q4,
        q4/a/a/'L'/q4,      q4/b/b/'L'/q4,      q4/'Y'/'Y'/'L'/q4,
        q4/'Z'/'Z'/'L'/q4,  q4/'X'/'X'/'R'/q1,
        q5/'Y'/'Y'/'R'/q5,  q5/'Z'/'Z'/'R'/q5,  q5/'B'/'B'/'R'/q6
    ]).

    finals([q6]).

:- end_object.
```

The transparent use of both object proxies and regular objects requires that all predicates expecting e.g. a regular expression object accept both an object identifier and an object proxy as argument. While this may sound as an additional hurdle, the solution is simple. Given that an object proxy is also an instantiation of the identifier of a parametric object, it suffices to define the corresponding parametric object. If, for example, we want to represent some finite automata as instances of a class `fa` and other finite automata as object proxies, we simply define a parametric object as an instance of the class `fa`. The object parameters will be the properties that might be unique for a specific finite automaton. The parametric object define the predicates that give access to these properties. These predicates would be the same used in class `fa` to define all predicates that must access to finite automaton properties:

```
:- object(fa(_Id, _Initial, _Transitions, _Finals),
    instantiates(fa)).

    initial(Initial) :-
        parameter(2, Initial).
```

```
        transitions(Transitions) :-
            parameter(3, Transitions).

        finals(Finals) :-
            parameter(4, Finals).

    :- end_object.
```

Thus, using both object proxies and regular objects is simple, fully transparent, and just a matter of defining the necessary parametric objects.

7 Related Work

Logtalk parametric objects are based on L&O [6] parametric theories and SICStus Objects [4] parametric objects, with some input from the OL(P) [8] representation of object instances. The two main differences are the concept of object proxies (introduced in Logtalk and discussed in this paper) and parameter accessing. While Logtalk parameter values are accessed using the `parameter/1` and `this/1` built-in methods, the scope of the parameters in L&O and SICStus Objects is the whole object. The generic concepts of parametric objects and object parameters are also similar to, respectively, the concepts of *units* and *unit arguments* found on some implementations of Contextual Logic Programming [13]. We take a brief look to each one of these systems in this section.

7.1 L&O Parametric Theories

In L&O, parametric objects are known as parametric theories. A theory is identified by a *label*, a term that is either a constant or a compound term with variables. L&O uses as example a parametric theory describing trains:

```
train(S, Cl, Co):{
    colour(Cl).
    speed(S).
    country(Co).
    journey_time(Distance, T) :-
        T = Distance/S.
}
```

The label variables are universally quantified over the theory. A specific train can be described by instantiating the label variables:

```
train(120, green, britain)
```

Messages can be sent to labels, which act as object identifiers. For example, the following message:

```
train(120, green, britain):journey_time(1000, Time)
```

will calculate a journey time using the value of the label first parameter as the speed of the train.

7.2 SICStus Parametric Objects

SICStus parametric objects are similar to L&O parametric theories, with parameters acting as global variables for the parametric object. The SICStus Objects manual contains the following example, describing ellipses and circles:

```
ellipse(RX, RY, Color) :: {
    color(Color) &
    area(A) :-
        :(A is RX*RY*3.14159265)
}.

circle(R, Color) :: {
    super(ellipse(R, R, Color))
}.

red_circle(R) :: {
    super(circle(R, red))
}.
```

SICStus Objects uses the predicate `super/1` to declare the ancestors of an object. This example illustrates parameter-passing between related objects in a hierarchy, a feature also found in L&O and Logtalk.

7.3 OL(P) Object Instances

OL(P) is a Prolog object-oriented extension that represents object instances using a notation similar to parametric objects. An instance `I` of an object named `Object` is represented as `Object(I)`. The term `I` is a list of attributes and attribute-value pairs. Instance state changes can be accomplished by constructing a new list with the updated and unchanged attributes. The OL(P) system documentation offers the following example:

```
| ?- rect(I)::area(A), rect(I)::move(5, 5, J).
```

The method `move/3` will return, in its third argument, the attribute list `J` resulting from the update of the attribute list `I`. In addition, OL(P) provides a nice notation for accessing and updating attributes. This solution for object state changes implies the use of extra arguments for methods that update attributes. Nevertheless, it is an interesting technique, which preserves the declarative semantics found on pure Prolog programs. We can easily apply this solution to Logtalk programs by using parametric objects. Moreover, we are not restricted to using a list of attributes. If the number of attributes is small, an identifier with the format `Object(V1, V2, ..., Vn)` will provide a more efficient solution.

7.4 GNU Prolog/CX Parametric Units

Contextual Logic Programming defines a modularity concept, *unit*, which supports parameterization in some implementations, such as GNU Prolog/CX [14].

Unit arguments play a similar role as object parameters. As in other systems, the scope of the unit arguments is the whole unit. The GNU Prolog/CX authors present the following example of a simple dictionary implementation using a list of key-value pairs:

```
:- unit(dict(ST)).

dict(ST).

lookup(KEY, VALUE) :- ST=[KEY=VALUE|_].
lookup(KEY, VALUE) :- ST=[_|STx], dict(STx) :> lookup(KEY, VALUE).
```

Instead of augmenting all dictionary predicates with an argument for passing the dictionary term, an unit argument is used to hold this term. Thus, this example is an instance of the programming pattern presented in section 4.3.

8 Conclusions

The main contributions of this paper are a survey of useful parametric object programming patterns and the Logtalk concept of object proxies. The use of these programming patterns and the implementation of objects proxies in other object-oriented logic programming languages and Prolog object-oriented extensions is straightforward.

Parametric objects enable useful programming patterns that complement Logtalk encapsulation and reuse features. Object parameters allow passing *data*, *type information*, and *operations* to object predicates. Parametric objects may be used to encapsulate a set of predicates for reasoning about compound terms sharing the same functor and arity, to simplify object interfaces, to restore shared variables between sets of constraints stored in different objects, to enable a more data-centric style of programming, and to provide a logical alternative to the use of an object dynamic database for representing mutable state. It is also possible to use the *instantiations* of a parametric object identifier to represent the history of object state changes.

Logtalk extends the usefulness of parametric objects by introducing the concept of object proxies, which provide a bridge between Logtalk objects and compact plain Prolog representations. Some applications need to represent a large number of immutable objects. These objects typically represent data that must be validated or used for data mining. This kind of data is often exported from databases and must be converted into objects for further processing. The application domain logic is usually represented by a set of hierarchies with the data objects at the bottom. Although data conversion is most of the time easily scriptable, the resulting objects take up more space than a straightforward representation as plain Prolog facts. By using object proxies, application memory footprint can be minimized while still taking full advantage of Logtalk object-oriented features for representing and reasoning with taxonomic knowledge. The concept of object proxies can be easily adopted and used in other languages supporting parametric objects.

Acknowledgements. This work is partially supported by the FCT research project MOGGY – PTDC/EIA/70830/2006. We are grateful to Paul Crocker for helpful suggestions in improving the Logtalk support for object proxies. We thank also José Silva, Sara C. Madeira, and the anonymous reviewers for their comments and help in revising this paper.

References

1. Moura, P.: Logtalk 2.6 Documentation. Technical Report DMI 2000/1, University of Beira Interior, Portugal (July 2000)
2. Moura, P.: Logtalk – Design of an Object-Oriented Logic Programming Language. PhD thesis, Department of Computer Science, University of Beira Interior, Portugal (September 2003)
3. Moura, P.: Logtalk 2.39.0 User and Reference Manuals (February 2010)
4. Swedish Institute for Computer Science: SICStus Prolog 4.0 User Manual (April 2009)
5. Clocksin, W.F., Mellish, C.S.: Programming in Prolog. Springer, New York (1987)
6. McCabe, F.G.: Logic and Objects. Computer Science. Prentice Hall, Englewood Cliffs (1992)
7. Igler, M., Joblonski, S.: ESProNa – Engine for Semantic Process Navigation (2009), `http://www.ai4.uni-bayreuth.de/`
8. Fromherz, M.: OL(P): Object Layer for Prolog (1993), `ftp://parcftp.xerox.com/ftp/pub/ol/`
9. Kino, N.: Logical assignment of Prolog terms (2005), `http://www.kprolog.com/en/logical_assignment/`
10. Moura, P., Marchetti, V.: Logtalk Processing of STEP Part 21 Files. In: Etalle, S., Truszczyński, M. (eds.) ICLP 2006. LNCS, vol. 4079, pp. 453–454. Springer, Heidelberg (2006)
11. Moura, P., Dias, A.M.: L-FLAT: Logtalk Toolkit for Formal Languages and Automata (2009), `http://code.google.com/p/lflat/`
12. Wermelinger, M., Dias, A.M.: A Prolog Toolkit for Formal Languages and Automata. In: ITiCSE 2005: Proceedings of the 10th Annual SIGCSE Conference on Innovation and Technology in Computer Science Education, pp. 330–334. ACM, New York (2005)
13. Monteiro, L., Porto, A.: A language for contextual logic programming. In: Logic Programming Languages: Constraints, Functions, and Objects, pp. 115–147. MIT Press, Cambridge (1993)
14. Abreu, S., Diaz, D.: Objective: In minimum context. In: Palamidessi, C. (ed.) ICLP 2003. LNCS, vol. 2916, pp. 128–147. Springer, Heidelberg (2003)

Stable Model Implementation of Layer Supported Models by Program Transformation

Luís Moniz Pereira and Alexandre Miguel Pinto

Centro de Inteligência Artificial (CENTRIA)
Universidade Nova de Lisboa, 2829-516 Caparica, Portugal
{lmp,amp}@di.fct.unl.pt

Abstract. For practical applications, the use of top-down query-driven proof-procedures is convenient for an efficient use and computation of answers using Logic Programs as knowledge bases. A 2-valued semantics for Normal Logic Programs (NLPs) allowing for top-down query-solving is thus highly desirable, but the Stable Models semantics (SM) does not allow it, for lack of the relevance property. To overcome this limitation we introduced in [11], and summarize here, a new 2-valued semantics for NLPs — the Layer Supported Models semantics — which conservatively extends the SM semantics, enjoys relevance and cumulativity, guarantees model existence, and respects the Well-Founded Model. In this paper we exhibit a space and time linearly complex transformation, TR, from one propositional NLP into another, whose Layer Supported Models are precisely the Stable Models of the transform, which can then be computed by extant Stable Model implementations, providing a tool for the immediate generalized use of the new semantics and its applications. TR can be used to answer queries but is also of theoretical interest, for it may be used to prove properties of programs.Moreover, TR can be employed in combination with the top-down query procedure of XSB-Prolog, and be applied just to the residual program corresponding to a query (in compliance with the relevance property of Layer Supported Models). The XSB-XASP interface then allows the program transform to be sent to Smodels for 2-valued evaluation.

Keywords: Stable Models, Layer Supported Models, Relevance, Layering, Program Transformation.

1 Introduction and Motivation

The semantics of Stable Models (SM) [7] is a cornerstone for the definition of some of the most important results in logic programming of the past two decades, providing an increase in logic programming declarativity and a new paradigm for program evaluation. When we need to know the 2-valued truth value of all the literals in a logic program for the problem we are modeling and solving, the only solution is to produce complete models. Depending on the intended semantics, in such cases, tools like *SModels* [9] or *DLV* [2] may be adequate because they can indeed compute whole models according to the SM semantics. However, the lack of some important properties of language semantics, like relevance, cumulativity and guarantee of model existence (enjoyed by, say, Well-Founded Semantics [6] (WFS)), somewhat reduces its applicability in practice,

S. Abreu and D. Seipel (Eds.): INAP 2009, LNAI 6547, pp. 70–84, 2011.

namely regarding abduction, creating difficulties in required pre- and post-processing. But WFS in turn does not produce 2-valued models, though these are often desired, nor guarantees 2-valued model existence.

SM semantics does not allow for top-down query-solving precisely because it does not enjoy the relevance property — and moreover, does not guarantee the existence of a model. Furthermore, frequently there is no need to compute whole models, like its implementations do, but just the partial models that sustain the answer to a query. Relevance would ensure these could be extended to whole models.

To overcome these limitations we developed in [11] (reviewed here) a new 2-valued semantics for NLPs — the Layer Supported Models (LSM) — which conservatively extends the SMs, enjoys relevance and cumulativity, guarantees model existence, and respects the Well-Founded Model (WFM) [6]. Intuitively, a program is conceptually partitioned into "layers" which are subsets of its rules, possibly involved in mutual loops. An atom is considered *true* in some layer supported model iff there is some rule for it at some layer, where all the literals in its body which are supported by rules of lower layers are also *true*. That is, a rule in a layer must, to be usable, have the support of rules in the layers below.

1.1 Integrity Constraints and Inconsistencies

There is a generalized consensus that Integrity Constraints (ICs) are denials, i.e., rules with $\bot$ as head, e.g,

$$\bot \leftarrow IC\_Body$$

where IC_Body is the body of the IC we wish to prevent from being true. When an NLP is enriched with such an IC, we say an interpretation containing IC_Body violates the IC and is, thus, inconsistent.

The classical notion of support — an atom a is supported in an interpretation I iff there is some rule in the NLP where *all* the literals of the body of the rule are true in I — the one upon which the SM semantics is defined, focuses on one rule at a time. This approach misses the global structure of the whole program. A consequence of such strict notion of support is that, even when an NLP is not enriched with any ICs, some particular patterns of rules might act as ICs. One of such patterns of rules is the Odd Loop Over Negation (OLON)[1]. This is, in fact, one of the reasons why the SM semantics fails to guarantee model existence for every NLP: the stability condition it imposes on models, stemming from the classical notion of support, is impossible to be complied with by OLONs. Actually, under SM semantics, sometimes OLONs are purposefully written as a means to impose ICs. Unfortunately, this confuses the two distinct aspects of rule-writing (wether with OLONs or not) and IC-writing (as denials).

Example 1. **OLON as IC.** Using SMs, one can write an IC, in order to prevent IC_Body from being in any model, with the single rule for some atom 'a':

$$a \leftarrow not\ a, IC\_Body$$

[1] OLON is a loop with an odd number of default negations in its circular call dependency path.

Since the SM semantics cannot provide a semantics to this rule whenever IC_Body holds, this type of OLON is used as IC. When writing such ICs under SMs one must be careful and make sure there are no other rules for a. But the really unintuitive thing about this kind of IC used under SM semantics is the meaning of the atom a. What does a represent?

The LSM semantics instead provides a semantics to all NLPs (OLONs included) thereby separating OLON semantics from IC compliance. In a practical implementation allowing top-down querying, the latter can be enforced by top-down checking that $not\ \bot$ is also part of the answer to the query.

After notation and background definitions, we summarize the formal definition of LSM semantics and its properties. Thereafter, we present a program transformation, TR, from one propositional (or ground) NLP into another, whose Layer Supported Models are precisely the Stable Models of the transform, which can be computed by extant Stable Model implementations, which also require grounding of programs. TR's linear space and time complexities are then examined. The transformation can be used to answer queries but is also of theoretical interest, for it may be used to prove properties of programs, say. In the Implementation section we show how TR can be employed, in combination with the top-down query procedure of XSB-Prolog, it being sufficient to apply it solely to the residual program corresponding to a query (in compliance with the relevance property of Layer Supported Model). The XSB-XASP interface allows the program transform to be sent for Smodels for 2-valued evaluation. Conclusions and future work close the paper.

2 Background Notation and Definitions

Definition 1. ***Logic Rule.*** *A Logic Rule r has the general form*

$$H \leftarrow B_1, \ldots, B_n, not\ C_1, \ldots, not\ C_m$$

where H, the B_i and the C_j are atoms.

We call H the head of the rule — also denoted by $head(r)$. And $body(r)$ denotes the set $\{B_1, \ldots, B_n, not\ C_1, \ldots, not\ C_m\}$ of all the literals in the body of r. Throughout this paper we will use 'not ' to denote default negation. When the body of the rule is empty, we say the head of rule is a fact and we write the rule just as H.

Definition 2. ***Logic Program.*** *A Logic Program (LP for short) P is a (possibly infinite) set of ground Logic Rules of the form in Definition 1.*

In this paper we focus only on NLPs, those whose heads of rules are positive literals, i.e., simple atoms; and there is default negation just in the bodies of the rules. Hence, when we write simply "program" or "logic program" we mean an NLP.

We write $heads(P)$ to denote the set of heads of rules of P, i.e., $heads(P) = \{head(r) : r \in P\}$. Abusing the default negation notation we write $not\ S$, where S is a set of literals, to denote $\{not\ s : s \in S\}$, and confound $not\ not\ s \equiv s$.

The shifting rule [5,8] may be used to reduce disjunctive programs into NLPs, as may other known transformations, say from Extended LPs into NLPs ([3]).

3 Layering of Logic Programs

The well-known notion of stratification of LPs has been studied and used for decades now. But the common notion of stratification does not cover all LPs, i.e., there are some LPs which are non-stratified. The usual syntactic notions of dependency are mainly focused on atoms. They are based on a dependency graph induced by the rules of the program. Useful as these notions might be, for our purposes they are insufficient since they leave out important structural information about the call-graph of P. To encompass that information we define below the notion of a rule's dependency. Indeed, layering puts rules, not atoms, in layers.

Rules that depend on no other rule (except, possibly, itself) are placed in layer 1. Two rules are in the same layer if they depend on each other. The dependency relation between two rules is the transitive closure of the direct dependency relation, where rule r directly depends on rule r' (denoted as $r \leftarrow r'$) iff $head(r') \in body(r)$ or $not\ head(r') \in body(r)$. Moreover, a rule r is in a layer strictly above that of r' if r depends on r' but not vice-versa. We write $r \twoheadleftarrow r'$ to denote r depends (possibly indirectly) on r'.

The *relevant* part of P for some atom A, represented by $Rel_P(A)$, is the subset of rules of P with head A plus the set of rules of P whose heads the atom A depends on, cf. [4]. The relevant part of P for rule r, represented by $Rel_P(r)$, is the set containing the rule r itself plus the set of rules relevant for each atom r depends on.

Definition 3. ***Rule Layering of a Normal Logic Program*** P. *Let P be an NLP. A rule layering function $Lf/1$ is any function defined over the rules of P, assigning each rule $r \in P$ an ordinal, such that the following holds:*

$$\forall_{r_1,r_2 \in P} \begin{cases} Lf(r_1) = 1 & \Leftarrow \neg\,(r_1 \twoheadleftarrow r_2) \wedge \quad r_2 \neq r_1 \\ Lf(r_1) = Lf(r_2) & \Leftarrow \quad (r_1 \twoheadleftarrow r_2) \wedge \quad (r_2 \twoheadleftarrow r_1) \\ Lf(r_1) > Lf(r_2) & \Leftarrow \quad (r_1 \twoheadleftarrow r_2) \wedge \neg\,(r_2 \twoheadleftarrow r_1) \end{cases}$$

The three cases above, which are patently mutually exclusive, leave out independent rules, i.e., rules that have no dependencies amongst themselves. According to this definition there is no restriction on which ordinal to assign to each independent rule in what the other rules' assignations are concerned.

A rule layering of program P is a partition $\ldots, P^i, P^j, \ldots$ of P such that P^i contains all rules r having $Lf(r) = i$. We write $P^{<\alpha}$ as an abbreviation of $\bigcup_{\beta<\alpha} P^\beta$, $P^{\leq\alpha}$ as an abbreviation of $P^{<\alpha} \cup P^\alpha$, and define $P^0 = P^{\leq 0} = \emptyset$. It follows immediately that $P = \bigcup_\alpha P^\alpha = \bigcup_\alpha P^{\leq\alpha}$, and also that the $\leq$ relation between layers is a total-order.

Amongst the several possible layerings of a program P we can always find the least one, i.e., the layering with least number of layers and where the ordinals of the layers are smallest, whilst respecting the rule layering function assignments. This least layering is easily seen to be unique. In the following, when referring to the program's "layering", we mean just such least layering.

Definition 4. ***Part of the body of a rule in loop.*** *Let P be an NLP, and r a rule of P^i. r^l is the subset of literals in the body of r in loop with r, i.e., their corresponding atoms have rules in the same layer as r.*

Formally, $r^l = body(r) \cap (heads(P^i) \cup not\ heads(P^i))$.

Theorem 1. ***The literals in*** r^l ***are in loop with*** r. *All the atoms of the literals in* r^l *have at least one rule in loop with* r.

Proof. Clearly, r depends on rules for all literals in r^l because this is, by definition, a subset of $body(r)$. If it were true for any atom a of some literal $A \in r^l$ that it had no rule in loop with r, then, by definition 3, that all rules for a would be in layers strictly below that of r. In that case a would not be in $heads(P^i)$ (nor $not\ a$ in $not\ heads(P^i)$) since P^i is the layer where r is placed. Thus, a would not be in r^l contradicting the initial assumption "for any atom a of some literal $A \in r^l$". □

Example 2. **Layering example.** Consider the following program P, depicted along with the layer numbers for its least layering:

$c \leftarrow not\ d, not\ y, not\ a$		Layer 3
$d \leftarrow not\ c$		
$y \leftarrow not\ x$	$b \leftarrow not\ x$	Layer 2
$x \leftarrow not\ x$	b	Layer 1

Atom b has a fact rule: its body is empty, and therefore it is placed in Layer 1. The unique rule for x is also placed in Layer 1 in the least layering of P, because this rule only depends on itself. Both $b \leftarrow not\ x$ and $y \leftarrow not\ x$ are placed in Layer 2 because they depend on $not\ x$, and the unique rule for x is in Layer 1. The unique rule for c is placed in Layer 3 because it depends on $not\ y$. The rule for d is also placed in the same Layer 3 because it is in a loop with the rule for c. This program has two LSMs: $\{b, c, x\}$, and $\{b, d, x\}$.

4 Layer Supported Models Semantics

The Layer Supported Models semantics we now present is the result of the two new notions we introduced: the layering, formally introduced in section 3, which is a generalization of stratification; and the layered support, as a generalization of classical support. These two notions are the means to provide the 2-valued Layer Supported Models semantics.

Definition 5. ***Classically Supported interpretation.*** *An interpretation* M *of* P *is classically supported iff every atom* a *of* M *is classically supported in* M*, and this holds iff* a *has a rule* r *where all the literals in* $body(r)$ *are true in* M.

Definition 6. ***Layer Supported interpretation.*** *An interpretation* M *of* P *is layer supported iff every atom* a *of* M *is layer supported in* M*, and this holds iff* a *has a rule* r *where all the literals in* $(body(r) \setminus r^l)$ *are true in* M.

Theorem 2. ***Classical Support implies Layered Support.*** *Given an NLP* P*, an interpretation* M*, and an atom* a *such that* $a \in M$*, if* a *is classically supported in* M *then* a *is also layer supported in* M.

Proof. Trivial from definitions 5 and 6. □

In programs without odd loops layered supported models are classically supported too.

Intuitively, the minimal layer supported models up to and including a given layer, respect the minimal layer supported models up to the layers preceding it. It follows trivially that layer supported models are minimal models, by definition. This ensures the truth assignment to atoms in loops in higher layers is consistent with the truth assignments in loops in lower layers and that these take precedence in their truth labeling. As a consequence of the layered support requirement, layer supported models of each layer comply with the WFM of the layers equal to or below it. Combination of the (merely syntactic) notion of layering and the (semantic) notion of layered support makes the LSM semantics.

Definition 7. ***Layer Supported Model of*** P. *Let* P *be an NLP. A layer supported interpretation* M *is a Layer Supported Model of* P *iff*

$$\forall_\alpha M_{\leq\alpha} \text{ is a minimal layer supported model of } P^{\leq\alpha}$$

where $M_{\leq\alpha}$ *denotes the restriction of* M *to heads of rules in layers less or equal to* α*:*

$$M_{\leq\alpha} \subseteq M \cap \{head(r) : Lf(r) \leq \alpha\}$$

The Layer Supported semantics of a program is just the intersection of all of its Layer Supported Models.

Example 3. **Layer Supported Models semantics.** Consider again the program from example 2. Its LS models are $\{b, c, x\}$, and $\{b, d, x\}$. According to LSM semantics b and x are *true* because they are in the intersection of all models. c and d are *undefined*, and a and y are *false*.

Layered support is a more general notion than that of perfect models [12], with similar structure. Perfect model semantics talks about "least models" rather than "minimal models" because in strata there can be no loops and so there is always a unique least model which is also the minimal one. Layers, as opposed to strata, may contain loops and thus there is not always a least model, so layers resort to minimal models, and these are guaranteed to exist (it is well known every NLP has minimal models).

The arguments in favor of the LSM semantics are presented in [10,11], and are not detailed here. This paper assumes the LSM semantics and focuses on a program transformation.

4.1 Respect for the Well-Founded Model

Definition 8. ***Interpretation*** M ***of*** P ***respects the WFM of*** P. *An interpretation* M *respects the WFM of* P *iff* M *contains the set of all the* true *atoms of WFM, and it is contained by the set of* true *or* undefined *atoms of the WFM. Formally,* $WFM^+(P) \subseteq M \subseteq WFM^{+u}(P)$.

Theorem 3. ***Layer Supported Models respect the WFM.*** *Let* P *be a NLP. Each sub-LSM* $M_{\leq\alpha}$ *of LSM* M *respects the WFM of* $P^{\leq\alpha}$.

Proof. (The reader can skip this proof without loss for the following). By definition, each $M_{\leq\alpha}$ is a full LSM of $P^{\leq\alpha}$.

Consider $P^{\leq 1}$. Every $M_{\leq 1}$ contains the facts of P, and their direct positive consequences, since the rules for all of these are necessarily placed in the first layer in the least layering of P. Necessarily, $M_{\leq 1}$ contains all the *true* atoms of the WFM of $P^{\leq 1}$. Layer 1 also contains whichever loops that do not depend on any other atoms besides those which are the heads of the rules forming the loop. These loops that have no negative literals in the bodies are deterministic and, therefore, the heads of the rules forming the loop will be all *true* or all *false* in the WFM, depending if the bodies are fully supported by facts in the same layer, or not. In any case, a minimal model of this layer will necessarily contains all the *true* atoms of the WFM of $P^{\leq 1}$, i.e., $WFM^{+}(P^{\leq 1})$. For loops involving default negation, the atoms head of rules forming such loops are *undefined* in the WFM; some of them might be in $M_{\leq 1}$ too. Assume now there is some atom a *false* in the WFM of $P^{\leq 1}$ such that $a \in M_{\leq 1}$. a can only be *false* in the WFM of $P^{\leq 1}$ if either it has no rules or if every rule for a has a false body. In the first case, by definition, a cannot be $M_{\leq 1}$ because only heads of rules can be part of LSMs. In the second case, since in a LSM every atom must be layer supported, if all the bodies of all rules for a are false, a will not be layer supported and so it will not be in any LSM, in particular, not in $M_{\leq 1}$. Since $M_{\leq 1}$ contains all *true* atoms of WFM of$P^{\leq 1}$ and it contains no *false* atoms, it must be contained by the *true* or *undefined* atoms of WFM of $P^{\leq 1}$.

Consider now $P^{\leq i+1}$, and $M_{\leq i}$ a LSM of $P^{\leq i}$. Assuming in P^{i+1} all the atoms of $M_{\leq i}$ as *true*, there might be some bodies of rules of P^{i+1} which are true. In such case, a minimal model of P^{i+1} will also consider the heads of such rules to be *true* — these will necessarily comply with the layered support requirement, and will be *true* in the WFM of $P^{i+1} \cup M_{\leq i}$. For the same reasons indicated for layer 1, no *false* atom in the WFM of $P^{i+1} \cup M_{\leq i}$ could ever be considered *true* in $M_{\leq i+1}$. □

5 Program Transformation

The program transformation we now define provides a syntactical means of generating a program P' from an original program P, such that the SMs of P' coincide with the LSMs of P. It engenders an expedite means of computing LSMs using currently available tools like Smodels [9] and DLV [2]. The transformation can be query driven and performed on the fly, or previously preprocessed.

5.1 Top-Down Transformation

Performing the program transformation in top-down fashion assumes applying the transformation to each atom in the program in the call-graph of a query. The transformation involves traversing the call-graph for the atom, induced by its dependency rules, to detect and "solve" the OLONs, via the specific LSM-enforcing method described below. When traversing the call-graph for an atom, one given traverse branch may end by finding (1) a fact literal, or (2) a literal with no rules, or (3) a loop to a literal (or its default negation conjugate) already found earlier along that branch.

To produce P' from P we need a means to detect OLONs. The OLON detection mechanism we employ is a variant of Tarjan's Strongly Connected Component (SCC) detection algorithm [15], because OLONs are just SCCs which happen to have an odd number of default negations along its edges. Moreover, when an OLON is detected, we need another mechanism to change its rules, that is to produce and add new rules to the program, which make sure the atoms a in the OLON now have "stable" rules which do not depend on any OLON. We say such mechanism is an "OLON-solving" one. Trivial OLONs, i.e. with length 1 like that in Example 1 ($a \leftarrow not\ a, IC\_Body$), are "solved" simply by removing the $not\ a$ from the body of the rule. General OLONs, i.e. with length ≥ 3, have more complex (non-deterministic) solutions, described below.

Minimal Models of OLONs. In general, an OLON has the form

$R_1 = \lambda_1 \leftarrow not\ \lambda_2, \Delta_1$
$R_2 = \lambda_2 \leftarrow not\ \lambda_3, \Delta_2$
$\vdots$
$R_n = \lambda_n \leftarrow not\ \lambda_1, \Delta_n$

where all the λ_i are atoms, and the Δ_j are arbitrary conjunction of literals which we refer to as "contexts". Assuming any λ_i *true* alone in some model suffices to satisfy any two rules of the OLON: one by rendering the head *true* and the other by rendering the body *false*.

$\lambda_{i-1} \leftarrow \sim \lambda_i, \Delta_{i-1}$, and
$\lambda_i \leftarrow \sim \lambda_{i+1}, \Delta_i$

A minimal set of such λ_i is what is needed to have a minimal model for the OLON. Since the number of rules n in OLON is odd we know that $\frac{n-1}{2}$ atoms satisfy $n-1$ rules of OLON. So, $\frac{n-1}{2} + 1 = \frac{n+1}{2}$ atoms satisfy all n rules of OLON, and that is the minimal number of λ_i atoms which are necessary to satisfy all the OLON's rules. This means that the remaining $n - \frac{n+1}{2} = \frac{n-1}{2}$ atoms λ_i must be *false* in the model in order for it to be minimal.

Taking a closer look at the OLON rules we see that λ_2 satisfies both the first and second rules; also λ_4 satisfies the third and fourth rules, and so on. So the set $\{\lambda_2, \lambda_4, \lambda_6, \ldots, \lambda_{n-1}\}$ satisfies all rules in OLON except the last one. Adding λ_1 to this set, since λ_1 satisfies the last rule, we get one possible minimal model for OLON: $M_{OLON} = \{\lambda_1, \lambda_2, \lambda_4, \lambda_6, \ldots, \lambda_{n-1}\}$. Every atom in M_{OLON} satisfies 2 rules of OLON alone, except λ_1, the last atom added. λ_1 satisfies alone only the last rule of OLON. The first rule of OLON — $\lambda_1 \leftarrow not\ \lambda_2, \Delta_1$ — despite being satisfied by λ_1, was already satisfied by λ_2. In this case, we call λ_1 the *top literal* of the OLON under M. The other Minimal Models of the OLON can be found in this manner simply by starting with λ_3, or λ_4, or any other λ_i as we did here with λ_2 as an example. Consider the $M_{OLON} = \{\lambda_1, \lambda_2, \lambda_4, \lambda_6, \ldots, \lambda_{n-1}\}$. Since $\sim \lambda_{i+1} \in body(R_i)$ for every $i < n$, and $\sim \lambda_1 \in body(R_n)$; under M_{OLON} all the $R_1, R_3, R_5, \ldots, R_n$ will have their bodies false. Likewise, all the $R_2, R_4, R_6, \ldots, R_{n-1}$ will have their bodies true under M_{OLON}.

This means that all $\lambda_2, \lambda_4, \lambda_6, \ldots, \lambda_{n-1}$ will have classically supported bodies (all body literals true), namely via rules $R_2, R_4, R_6, \ldots, R_{n-1}$, but not λ_1 — which has only layered support (all body literals of strictly lower layers true). "Solving an OLON" corresponds to adding a new rule which provides classical support for λ_1. Since this new rule must preserve the semantics of the rest of P, its body will contain only the conjunction of all the "contexts" Δ_j, plus the negation of the remaining $\lambda_3, \lambda_5, \lambda_7, \ldots, \lambda_n$ which were already considered *false* in the minimal model at hand.

These mechanisms can be seen at work in lines 2.10, 2.15, and 2.16 of the Transform Literal algorithm below.

Definition 9. ***Top-down program transformation.***

```
input : A program P
output: A transformed program P'
context = ∅
stack = empty stack
P' =P
foreach atom a of P do
    Push (a, stack)
    P' =P' ∪Transform Literal (a)
    Pop (a, stack)
end
```

Algorithm 1. TR Program Transformation

The TR transformation consists in performing this literal transformation, for each individual atom of P. The Transform Literal algorithm implements a top-down, rule-directed, call-graph traversal variation of Tarjan's SCC detection mechanism. Moreover, when it encounters an OLON (line 2.9 of the algorithm), it creates (lines 2.13–2.17) and adds (line 2.18) a new rule for each literal involved in the OLON (line 2.11). The newly created and added rule renders its head true *only when the original OLON's* context *is* true*, but also only when that head is not classically supported, though being layered supported under the minimal model of the OLON it is part of.*

Example 4. **Solving OLONs.** Consider this program, coinciding with its residual:

$$a \leftarrow not\ a, b \qquad b \leftarrow c \qquad c \leftarrow not\ b, not\ a$$

Solving a query for a, we use its rule and immediately detect the OLON on a. The leaf $not\ a$ is removed; the rest of the body $\{b\}$ is kept as the Context under which the OLON on a is "active" — if b were to be false there would be no need to solve the OLON on a's rule. After all OLONs have been solved, we use the Contexts to create new rules that preserve the meaning of the original ones, except the new ones do not now depend on OLONs. The current Context for a is now just $\{b\}$ instead of the original $\{not\ a, b\}$.

Solving a query for b, we go on to solve c — $\{c\}$ being b's current Context. Solving c we find leaf $not\ b$. We remove c from b's Context, and add c's body $\{not\ b, not\ a\}$ to it. The OLON on b is detected and the $not\ b$ is removed from b's Context, which finally is just $\{not\ a\}$. As can be seen so far, updating Contexts is similar to performing an unfolding plus OLON detection and resolution by removing the dependency on the OLON. The new rule for b has final Context $\{not\ a\}$ for body. I.e., the new rule for

input : A literal l
output: A partial transformed program Pa'

```
previous context =context
Pa' =P
atom =atom a of literal l; //removing the eventual not
if a has been visited then
    if a or not a is in the stack then
        scc root indx =lowest stack index where a or not a can be found
        nots seq = sequence of neg. lits from (scc root indx +1) to top indx
        loop length = length of nots seq
        if loop length is odd then
            # nots in body = (loop length−1)/2
            foreach 'not x' in nots seq do
                idx = index of not x in nots seq
                newbody = context
                for i=1 to # nots in body do
                    newbody = newbody ∪
                              {nots seq ((idx + 2 * i) mod loop length )}
                end
                newrule = x ←newbody
                Pa' =Pa' ∪{newrule }
            end
        end
    end
else    // a has not been visited yet
    mark a as visited
    foreach rule r = a ← b_1, ..., b_n, not b_{n+1}, ..., not b_m of P do
        foreach (not )b_i do
            Push ((not )b_i, stack)
            context =context ∪{b_1, ..., (not )b_{i−1}, (not )b_{i+1}, ..., not b_m}
            Transform Literal ((not )b_i)
            Pop ((not )b_i, stack)
            context =previous context
        end
    end
end
```

Algorithm 2. Transform Literal

b is $b \leftarrow not\ a$. Next, continuing a's final Context calculation, we remove b from a's Context and add $\{not\ a\}$ to it. This additional OLON is detected and $not\ a$ is removed from a's Context, now empty. Since we already exhausted a's dependency call-graph, the final body for the new rule for a is empty: a will be added as a fact. Moreover, a new rule for b will be added: $b \leftarrow not\ a$. The final transformed program is:

$a \leftarrow not\ a, b \qquad a \qquad b \leftarrow c \qquad b \leftarrow not\ a \qquad c \leftarrow not\ b, not\ a$

it has only one $SM = \{a\}$ the only LSM of the program. Mark layering is respected when solving OLONs: a's final rule depends on the answer to b's final rule.

Example 5. **Solving OLONs (2).** Consider this program, coinciding with its residual:

$$
\begin{aligned}
&a \leftarrow not\ b, x\\
&b \leftarrow not\ c, y\\
&c \leftarrow not\ a, z\\
&x\\
&y\\
&z
\end{aligned}
$$

Solving a query for a we push it onto the stack, and take its rule $a \leftarrow not\ b, x$. We go on for literal $not\ b$ and consider the rest of the body $\{x\}$ as the current Context under which the OLON on a is "active". Push $not\ b$ onto the stack and take the rule for b. We go on to solve $not\ c$, and add the y to the current Context which now becomes $\{x, y\}$. Once more, push $not\ c$ onto the stack, take c's rule $c \leftarrow not\ a, z$, go on to solve $not\ a$ and add z to the current Context which is now $\{x, y, z\}$. When we now push $not\ a$ onto the stack, the OLON is detected and it "solving" begins. Three rules are created and added to the program $a \leftarrow not\ c, x, y, z$, $b \leftarrow not\ a, x, y, z$, and $c \leftarrow not\ b, x, y, z$. Together with the original program's rules they render "stable" the originally "non-stable" LSM $\{a, b, x, y, z\}$, $\{b, c, x, y, z\}$, and $\{a, c, x, y, z\}$. The final transformed program is:

$$
\begin{aligned}
&a \leftarrow not\ b, x\\
&a \leftarrow not\ c, x, y, z\\
&b \leftarrow not\ c, y\\
&b \leftarrow not\ a, x, y, z\\
&c \leftarrow not\ a, z\\
&c \leftarrow not\ b, x, y, z\\
&x\\
&y\\
&z
\end{aligned}
$$

TR Transformation Correctness. The TR transformation steps occur only when OLONs are detected, and in those cases the transformation consists in adding extra rules. So, when there are no OLONs, the TR transformation's effect is $P' = P$, thus preserving the SMs of the original P. The additional Layer Supported Models of P are obtained by "solving" OLONs (by adding new rules in P'), so that the order of OLON solving complies with the layers of P. This is ensured because the top-down search, by its nature, solves OLONs conditional on their Context, and the latter will include same or lower layer literals, but not above layer ones. Finally, note Stable Models evaluation of P' itself respects the Well-Founded Semantics and hence Contexts evaluation respects layering, by Theorem 3.

5.2 Number of Models

Loop detection and the variety of their possible solutions concerns the number of Strongly Connect Components (SCCs) of the residual program.

Theorem 4. ***Maximum number of SCCs and of LSMs of a strongly connected residual component with*** N ***nodes.*** *They are, respectively,* $\frac{N}{3}$ *and* $3^{\frac{N}{3}}$.

Proof. Consider a component containing N nodes. A single odd loop with N nodes, by itself, contains N LSMs: each one obtained by minimally solving the implicit disjunction of the heads of the rules forming the OLON. Given only two OLONs in the component, with $N_1 + N_2 = N$ nodes, they could conceivably always be made independent of each other. Independent in the sense that each and every solution of one OLON combines separately with each and every solution of the other. To achieve this, iteratively duplicate as needed the rules of each OLON such that the combination of values of literals from the other loop are irrelevant. For example, in a program like

$$a \leftarrow not\ b \qquad b \leftarrow not\ c \qquad c \leftarrow not\ a, e$$
$$e \leftarrow not\ d \qquad d \leftarrow not\ f \qquad f \leftarrow not\ e, c$$

add the new rules $c \leftarrow not\ a, not\ e$ and $f \leftarrow not\ e, not\ c$ so that now the loop on a, b, c becomes independent of the truth of e, and the loop on e, d, f becomes independent of the truth of c. So, in the worst (more complex) case of two OLONs the number of LSMs is $N_1 * N_2$, in this case $3 * 3 = 9$.

Each loop over an even number of default negations (ELON), all by itself contains 2 LSMs, independently of the number N of its nodes. An OLON can always be made independent of an ELON by suitably and iteratively duplicating its rules, as per above. So an OLON with N_1 nodes dependent on a single ELON will, in the worst case, provide $2 * N_1$ LSMs.

It is apparent the highest number of LSMs in a component with N nodes can be gotten by combining only OLONs. Moreover, we have seen, the worst case is when these are independent.

Consider a component with N nodes and two OLONs with nodes $N_1 + N_2 = N$. The largest value of $N_1 * N_2$ is obtained when $N_1 = N_2 = \frac{N}{2}$. Indeed, since $N_2 = N - N_1$, take the derivative $\frac{d(N_1*(N-N_1))}{dN_1} = \frac{d(N*N_1)}{dN_1} - \frac{dN_1^2}{dN_1} = N - 2*N_1$. To obtain the highest value make the derivative $N - 2 * N_1 = 0$, and hence $N_1 = \frac{N}{2}$.

Similarly, for $\sum_i N_i = N$, so $N_i = \frac{N}{i}$ gives the maximum value for $\prod_i N_i$. Thus, the maximum number of LSMs for a component of N nodes is obtained when all its (odd) loops have the same size.

And what is the size i that maximizes this value? Let us again use a derivative in i, in this case $\frac{di^{\frac{N}{i}}}{di}$ as the number of LSMs is $i^{\frac{N}{i}}$. Now $\frac{di^{\frac{N}{i}}}{di} = -N * i$. Equating it to zero we have $i = 0$. But i must be greater than zero and less than N. It is easy to see that the

i that affords the value of the derivative closest to zero is $i = 1$. But OLONs of length 1 afford no choices hence the least i that is meaningful is $i = 3$.

Hence the maximum number of LSMs of a component with N nodes is $3^{\frac{N}{3}}$. □

Theorem 5. ***Maximum number of ELONs and of SMs of a SCC component with N nodes.*** *These are, respectively, $\frac{N}{2}$ and $2^{\frac{N}{2}}$.*

Proof. By the same reasoning as above, the maximum number of SMs of a component with N nodes is $2^{\frac{N}{2}}$, since there are no OLONs in SMs and so i can only be 2. □

Corollary 1. ***Comparison between number of possible models of LSMs and SMs.*** *The highest number of models possible for LSMs, #LSMs, is larger than that for SMs, #SMs.*

Proof. By the two previous theorems, we know that for a component with N nodes, $\frac{\#LSMs}{\#SMs} = \frac{3^{\frac{N}{3}}}{2^{\frac{N}{2}}} = 3^{(N*[\frac{1}{3}-\frac{1}{2}*(log_3 2)])}$. □

6 Implementation

The XSB Prolog system[2] is one of the most sophisticated, powerful, efficient and versatile implementations, with a focus on execution efficiency and interaction with external systems, implementing program evaluation following the WFS for NLPs. The XASP interface [1] (standing for XSB Answer Set Programming), is included in XSB Prolog as a practical programming interface to Smodels [9], one of the most successful and efficient implementations of the SMs over generalized LPs. The XASP system allows one not only to compute the models of a given NLP, but also to effectively combine 3-valued with 2-valued reasoning. The latter is achieved by using Smodels to compute the SMs of the so-called residual program, the one that results from a query evaluated in XSB using tabling [13]. A residual program is represented by delay lists, that is, the set of undefined literals for which the program could not find a complete proof, due to mutual dependencies or loops over default negation for that set of literals, detected by the XSB tabling mechanism. This coupling allows one to obtain a two-valued semantics of the residual, by completing the three-valued semantics the XSB system produces. The integration also allows to make use of and benefit from the relevance property of LSM semantics by queries.

In our implementation, detailed below, we use XASP to compute the query relevant residual program on demand. When the TR transformation is applied to it, the resulting program is sent to Smodels for computation of stable models of the relevant sub-program provided by the residue, which are then returned to the XSB-XASP side.

Residual Program. After launching a query in a top-down fashion we must obtain the relevant residual part of the program for the query. This is achieved in XSB Prolog using the `get_residual/2` predicate. According to the XSB Prolog's manual " the predicate `get_residual/2` unifies its first argument with a tabled subgoal and its

[2] XSB-Prolog and Smodels are freely available, at: `http://xsb.sourceforge.net` and `http://www.tcs.hut.fi/Software/smodels`

second argument with the (possibly empty) delay list of that subgoal. The truth of the subgoal is taken to be conditional on the truth of the elements in the delay list". The delay list is the list of literals whose truth value could not be determined to be *true* nor *false*, i.e., their truth value is *undefined* in the WFM of the program.

It is possible to obtain the *residual* clause of a solution for a query literal, and in turn the *residual* clauses for the literals in its body, and so on. This way we can reconstruct the complete relevant residual part of the KB for the literal — we call this a *residual program* or *reduct* for that solution to the query.

More than one such *residual program* can be obtained for the query, on backtracking. Each *reduct* consists only of partially evaluated rules, with respect to the WFM, whose heads are atoms relevant for the initial query literal, and whose bodies are just the *residual* part of the bodies of the original KB's rules. This way, not only do we get just the relevant part of the KB for the literal, we also get precisely the part of those rules bodies still *undefined*, i.e., those that are involved in Loops Over Negation.

Dealing with the Query and Integrity Constraints. ICs are written as just $falsum \leftarrow IC\_Body$. An Smodels IC preventing $falsum$ from being *true* (`:- falsum`) is enforced whenever a transformed program is sent to Smodels. Another two rules are added to the Smodels clause store through XASP: one creates an auxiliary rule for the initially posed query; with the form: `lsmGoal :- Query`, where `Query` is the query conjunct posed by the user. The second rule just prevents Smodels from having any model where the `lsmGoal` does not hold, having the form: `:- not lsmGoal`.

The XSB Prolog source code for the meta-interpreter, based on this program transformation, is available at `http://centria.di.fct.unl.pt/~amp/software.html`

7 Conclusions and Future Work

We have recapped the LSMs semantics for *all* NLPs, complying with desirable requirements: 2-valued semantics, conservatively extending SMs, guarantee of model existence, relevance and cumulativity, plus respecting the WFM.

We have exhibited a space and time linearly complex transformation, TR, from one propositional NLP into another, whose Layer Supported Models are precisely the Stable Models of the transform, which can then be computed by extant Stable Model implementations. TR can be used to answer queries but is also of theoretical interest, for it may be used to prove properties of programs. Moreover, it can be employed in combination with the top-down query procedure of XSB-Prolog, and be applied solely to the residual program corresponding to a query. The XSB-XASP interface subsequently allows the program transform to be sent for Smodels for 2-valued evaluation.

The applications afforded by LSMs are *all* those of SMs, plus those where odd loops over default negation (OLONs) are actually employed for problem domain representation, as we have shown in examples 4 and 5. The guarantee of model existence is essential in applications where knowledge sources are diverse (like in the Semantic Web), and wherever the bringing together of such knowledge (automated or not) can give rise to OLONs that would otherwise prevent the resulting program from having a semantics, thereby brusquely terminating the application. A similar situation can be brought about by self- and mutually-updating programs, including in the learning setting, where unforeseen OLONs would stop short an ongoing process if the SM semantics were in use. Hence, apparently there is only to gain in exploring the adept move from SM semantics to the more general LSM one, given that the latter is readily implementable through the program transformation TR, introduced here for the first time.

Work under way [14] concerns an XSB engine level efficient implementation of the LSM semantics, and the exploration of its wider scope of applications with respect to ASP, and namely in combination with abduction and constructive negation.

Finally, the concepts and techniques introduced in this paper are readily adoptable by other logic programming systems and implementations.

References

1. Castro, L., Swift, T., Warren, D.S.: XASP: Answer Set Programming with XSB and Smodels (1999), `http://xsb.sourceforge.net/packages/xasp.pdf`
2. Citrigno, S., Eiter, T., Faber, W., Gottlob, G., Koch, C., Leone, N., Mateis, C., Pfeifer, G., Scarcello, F.: The dlv system: Model generator and advanced frontends (system description). In: Workshop in Logic Programming (1997)
3. Damásio, C.V., Pereira, L.M.: Default negated conclusions: Why not? In: Herre, H., Dyckhoff, R., Schroeder-Heister, P. (eds.) ELP 1996. LNCS (LNAI), vol. 1050, pp. 103–118. Springer, Heidelberg (1996)
4. Dix, J.: A Classification-Theory of Semantics of Normal Logic Programs: I, II. Fundamenta Informaticae XXII(3), 227–255, 257–288 (1995)
5. Dix, J., Gottlob, G., Marek, V.W., Rauszer, C.: Reducing disjunctive to non-disjunctive semantics by shift-operations. Fundamenta Informaticae 28, 87–100 (1996)
6. Van Gelder, A., Ross, K.A., Schlipf, J.S.: The well-founded semantics for general logic programs. J. of ACM 38(3), 620–650 (1991)
7. Gelfond, M., Lifschitz, V.: The stable model semantics for logic programming. In: ICLP/SLP, pp. 1070–1080. MIT Press, Cambridge (1988)
8. Gelfond, M., Przymusinska, H., Lifschitz, V., Truszczynski, M.: Disjunctive defaults. In: KR 1991, pp. 230–237 (1991)
9. Niemelä, I., Simons, P.: Smodels - an implementation of the stable model and well-founded semantics for normal logic programs. In: Fuhrbach, U., Dix, J., Nerode, A. (eds.) LPNMR 1997. LNCS (LNAI), vol. 1265, pp. 420–429. Springer, Heidelberg (1997)
10. Pereira, L.M., Pinto, A.M.: Layered models top-down querying of normal logic programs. In: Gill, A., Swift, T. (eds.) PADL 2009. LNCS, vol. 5418, pp. 254–268. Springer, Heidelberg (2008)
11. Pereira, L.M., Pinto, A.M.: Layer Supported Models of Logic Programs. In: Erdem, E., Lin, F., Schaub, T. (eds.) LPNMR 2009. LNCS (LNAI), vol. 5753, pp. 450–456. Springer, Heidelberg (2009), `http://centria.di.fct.unl.pt/~lmp/publications/online-papers/LSMs.pdf`
12. Przymusinski, T.C.: Perfect model semantics. In: ICLP/SLP, pp. 1081–1096 (1988)
13. Swift, T.: Tabling for non-monotonic programming. AMAI 25(3-4), 201–240 (1999)
14. Swift, T., Pinto, A.M., Moniz Pereira, L.: Incremental answer completion in xsb-prolog. In: Hill, P.M., Warren, D.S. (eds.) ICLP 2009. LNCS, vol. 5649, pp. 519–524. Springer, Heidelberg (2009)
15. Tarjan, R.: Depth-first search and linear graph algorithms. SIAM J. Computing 1(2), 146–160 (1972)

Towards Computing Revised Models for FO Theories

Johan Wittocx*, Broes De Cat**, and Marc Denecker

Department of Computer Science, K.U. Leuven, Belgium
{johan.wittocx,broes.decat,marc.denecker}@cs.kuleuven.be

Abstract. In many real-life computational search problems, one is not only interested in finding a solution, but also in maintaining a solution under varying circumstances. For example, in the area of network configuration, an initial configuration of a computer network needs to be obtained, but also a new configuration when one of the machines in the network breaks down. Currently, most such revision problems are solved manually, or with highly specialized software.

A recent declarative approach to solve (hard) computational search problems involving a lot of domain knowledge, is by finite model generation. Here, the domain knowledge is specified as a logic theory T, and models of T correspond to solutions of the problem. In this paper, we extend this approach to solve revision problems. In particular, our method allows to use the same theory to describe the search problem and the revision problem, and applies techniques from current model generators to find revised solutions.

1 Introduction

In many real-life search problems, one searches for objects of a complex nature, such as an assignment, a plan or a schedule. Often, these objects can be represented by a finite structure and implicitly described by a logic theory. This observation led to declarative problem solving paradigms based on finite model generation such as Answer Set Programming [8,12], NP-SPEC [2] and the Model Expansion framework [11]. Several efficient solvers for these frameworks have been developed, making them applicable in practice.

Often, one is not (only) interested in a single solution to a search problem, but also in *revising* this solution under varying circumstances. For instance, a network administrator is interested in computing an initial configuration of a computer network as well as in maintaining the configuration when one of the machines in the network breaks down. Typically, the following are requirements for a revised solution:

1. To allow fast reaction to new circumstances, computing a revision should be efficient.

* Research assistant of the Fund for Scientific Research - Flanders (FWO-Vlaanderen).
** Research assistant of the agency for Innovation through Science and Technology (IWT).

S. Abreu and D. Seipel (Eds.): INAP 2009, LNAI 6547, pp. 85–101, 2011.

2. Executing a proposed revision in the problem domain usually has a certain cost. For example, it takes more time to move a storage server from one computer to another than a DHCP-server. A good revision should preferably have a low cost. I.e., the number of changes required to implement the revision is often a good measure.

Most existing approaches to solve revision problems are tailored towards a specific application such as train rescheduling or updating of university rosters, and hence, they are not (entirely) declarative. In this paper, we present a revision method that is much closer to the declarative problem solving frameworks mentioned above. Formally, we describe a *revision problem* by a logic theory T, a finite model M of T and a set of atoms C: T describes the original search problem, M a solution to that problem and C the atoms that should swap truth value compared to their value in M. A solution to the revision problem is a model M' of T such that for every atom in C, its truth value in M' is opposite to its truth value in M. Revision problems where the theory T or the domain of M is changed can be reduced to this case, as we show in Section 3.2.

In this paper, we describe a method to solve revision problems where T is a first-order logic (FO) theory. Like finite model generation for FO, these problems can easily be reduced to SAT. An off-the-shelf SAT solver can then be used to solve the resulting SAT problem. However, directly using this approach does not satisfy the two requirements mentioned above. It does not guarantee that the revised model is close to the original model and it can take too much time and space to create and store the SAT problem. The method we propose avoids these problems by first constructing a set of atoms S', called the *search bound.* The bound contains all the atoms that we allow to swap truth value to obtain a revised model M' from the original one M. Then the method tries to find such a revised model M', by reducing the bounded problem to SAT. If it does not succeed, the bound S' is enlarged and the process is repeated. However, if it succeeds and S' is relatively small, the two requirements are met. Only a small number of operations will be necessary to obtain M' from M, because the only changes are on atoms in S'. Also, reducing to SAT can be efficient if S' is small.

To make the approach work, the consecutive search bounds should be constructed such that there is a *reasonable chance* that a revised model exists within the bound. In Section 5, we present a non-deterministic algorithm to compute such search bounds. Experiments with a prototype implementation are discussed in Section 6. They indicate that the algorithm often finds small search bounds containing a revision. We end with conclusions and topics for future work.

2 Preliminaries

We assume the reader is familiar with classical first-order logic (FO), see, e.g., [5]. We introduce the conventions and notations used in this paper. Without loss of generality, we consider function-free FO in this paper and assume that all negations ($\neg$) occur directly in front of atoms. I.e., we assume that every formula is in negation normal form.

A vocabulary Σ consists of variables and predicate symbols. Variables are denoted by lowercase letters, predicate symbols by uppercase letters. Sets and tuples of variables are denoted by $\overline{x}$, $\overline{y}$,.... For a formula φ, we often write $\varphi[\overline{x}]$ to denote that $\overline{x}$ are its free variables. A *sentence* is a formula without free variables. If $\varphi[x]$ is a formula and d an element from a domain D, we denote by $\varphi[x/d]$ the result of replacing all free occurrences of x in φ by d.[1] This notation is extended to tuples of variables and domain elements of the same length. A formula ψ occurs negatively in another formula φ if ψ occurs in the scope of a negation in φ. In all other cases ψ is said to occur positively in φ.

A literal is an atom (positive literal) or its negation (negative literal). $|L|$ denotes the atom $P(\overline{x})$ if L is the literal $P(\overline{x})$ or $\neg P(\overline{x})$. For an atom (literal) $L[\overline{x}]$ and a tuple of domain elements $\overline{d}$ from a domain D, $L[\overline{x}/\overline{d}]$ is called a *domain atom (literal) over* D.

A Σ-structure I with domain D is an assignment of a relation $P^I \subseteq D^n$ to every n-ary predicate symbol $P \in \Sigma$. A structure is called *finite* if its domain is finite. In this paper, all structures are finite. We say that a domain atom $P(\overline{d})$ is *true*, respectively *false*, in I if $\overline{d} \in P^I$, respectively $\overline{d} \notin P^I$. We often represent a finite two-valued structure by the set of all domain atoms that are true in it. If R is a set of domain atoms, we denote by $\text{swap}(I, R)$ the structure obtained from I by swapping the truth values of the domain atoms in R. I.e., $\overline{d} \in P^{\text{swap}(I,R)}$ if one of the following holds:

- $\overline{d} \in P^I$ and $P(\overline{d}) \notin R$;
- $\overline{d} \notin P^I$ and $P(\overline{d}) \in R$.

The satisfaction relation relation $\models$ is defined as usual [5].

3 The Revision Problem

3.1 Basic Revision Problems

For the rest of this paper, we assume a fixed vocabulary Σ and finite domain D. Unless stated otherwise, every structure has domain D. We now formally define the revision problem for FO.

Definition 1. *Let T be an FO theory, M a finite model of T, and C a set of domain atoms. A* revision *for input $\langle M, T, C\rangle$ is a set R of domain atoms such that $R \cap C = \emptyset$ and* $\text{swap}(M, R \cup C) \models T$*. The structure* $\text{swap}(M, R \cup C)$ *is called a* revised model.

Intuitively, M describes the original solution to a problem, C the changes that occurred and R the changes that should be made to repair the currently wrong solution $\text{swap}(M, C)$.

[1] More precisely, $\varphi[x/d]$ is the result of replacing the free occurrences of x by a new *constant symbol* d and interpreting that constant symbol by the *domain element* d in every structure with domain D.

Example 1. Consider the problem of placing n non-attacking rooks on an $n \times n$ chessboard. A model with domain $\{1, 2, \ldots, n\}$ of the following theory T_1 describes a solution to this problem. Here, atom $R(r, c)$ means "there is a rook on square (r, c)".

$$\forall r \; \exists c \; R(r, c). \tag{1}$$
$$\forall c \; \exists r \; R(r, c). \tag{2}$$
$$\forall r \forall c_1 \forall c_2 \; (R(r, c_1) \wedge R(r, c_2) \supset c_1 = c_2). \tag{3}$$
$$\forall r_1 \forall r_2 \forall c \; (R(r_1, c) \wedge R(r_2, c) \supset r_1 = r_2). \tag{4}$$

For $n = 3$, $M_1 = \{R(1, 1), R(2, 3), R(3, 2)\}$ is a model. Assume we have computed M_1, but for some reason, we do not want a rook on position $(1, 1)$. That means we have to search for a revision for $\langle T_1, M_1, C_1 \rangle$, where $C_1 = \{R(1, 1)\}$. A possible revision is the set $R_1 = \{R(1, 3), R(2, 1), R(2, 3)\}$, which yields the revised model $\{R(1, 3), R(2, 1), R(3, 2)\}$.

In practice, it is often the case that not all atoms are allowed to swap truth value in order to obtain a revised model. For example in a train rescheduling problem, the truth value of atoms that state the positions of the railway stations should never change, because the position of the stations cannot be changed in reality. To formally describe such a problem, let S be a set of domain atoms, disjoint from C. Intuitively, S is the set of atoms that are allowed to swap truth value, i.e. the search space in which to find a revision. A revision R for $\langle T, M, C \rangle$ is *bounded* by S if $R \subseteq S$.

Definition 2. *Let T be an FO theory, M a finite model of T, and C and S disjoint sets of domain atoms. The* bounded revision problem *with input $\langle T, M, C, S \rangle$ is the problem of finding a revision R for $\langle T, M, C \rangle$ such that $R \subseteq S$.*

3.2 Domain and Theory Changes

Besides the revision problem as described above — computing a new model when the truth values of some domain atoms change — one could also consider the problem of computing a new model when either[2]:

1. A new sentence is added to the theory.
2. A domain element is left out of the original model.
3. A new domain element is added to the original model.

All three problems can easily be reduced to the revision problem defined above.

To reduce (1), let φ be the sentence that is added, let P be a new propositional atom and M a model of T such that P is false in M. Then a revision for $\langle T \cup \{P \supset \varphi\}, M, \{P\} \rangle$ is a model for $T \cup \{\varphi\}$. To reduce (2), let *Used* be a new unary predicate and denote by T' the theory obtained by replacing each

[2] Observe that, due to the monotonicity of FO, it is trivial to compute a new model when a sentence of T is left out.

subformula in T of the form $(\forall x\, \varphi)$, respectively $(\exists x\, \varphi)$, by $(\forall x\, (\mathit{Used}(x) \supset \varphi))$, respectively $(\exists x\, (\mathit{Used}(x) \wedge \varphi))$. Let U be the set of all domain atoms of the form $\mathit{Used}(d)$, M a model of T such that each atom in U is true in M, and denote by d' the domain element that is left out. A revision for $\langle T', M, \{\mathit{Used}(d')\}, \mathcal{H} \setminus U\rangle$, restricted to the atoms not mentioning d', is a model for T. Here, $\mathcal{H}$ denotes the set of all domain atoms over Σ and D, i.e., the Herbrand base. In a similar way, (3) can be reduced.

3.3 Weighted Revision Problems

In real-life revision problems, one is often more interested in a revision with a *low cost*, than in a small revision. For example, suppose some problem in a network can be solved by either moving multiple DHCP servers or by moving only one mail server. Although the revision describing the first solution will have a higher cardinality than the second one, the time neeeded to move all mail data will be much higher than the time needed to move the scripts that constitute the DHCP servers. Another example is train-rescheduling, where the passengers will be much more satisfied if the delay is minimized instead of minimizing the number of schedule changes.

To model revision problems where the cost of the revision plays an important role, a pair (c_+, c_-) of values is assigned to each domain atom $P(\overline{d})$. These two numbers indicate the cost of changing the truth value of $P(\overline{d})$ from false to true, respectively from true to false. For instance, if $P(d)$ means that there is a mail server on machine d, c_+ indicates the cost of installing a mail server on d, while c_- indicates the cost of uninstalling it. A good revision only contains atoms that are false, respectively true, in the original model and are assigned a low c_+, respectively low c_-.

4 Solving the Revision Problem

In the rest of this paper, we assume a fixed T, M, C and S and consider the bounded revision problem for input $\langle T, M, C, S\rangle$. The problem $\langle T, M, C, S\rangle$ can be solved by reducing it to the problem of finding a model of a propositional theory T_g, called a *grounding*. The model generation problem can then be solved by an off-the-shelf efficient SAT solver [10]. To find revisions with low cardinality (or low cost in case of a weighted revision problem), one can use a SAT solver with support for optimization, such as a max-SAT solver [7,15].

4.1 Grounding

A formula φ is in *ground normal form (GNF)* if it is a boolean combination of domain atoms. I.e., φ is a sentence containing no quantifiers or variables. A GNF theory is a theory containing only GNF formulas. Observe that a GNF theory is essentially a propositional theory.

Definition 3. *A* grounding for $\langle T, M, C, S\rangle$ *is a GNF theory* T_g *such that for every* $R \subseteq S$, R *is a revision for* $\langle T, M, C, S\rangle$ *iff* $\text{swap}(M, C \cup R) \models T_g$. *A grounding is called* reduced *if all domain atoms that occur in it belong to* S.

A basic grounding algorithm consists of recursively replacing every universal subformula $\forall x\ \varphi[x]$ in T by the conjunction $\bigwedge_{d \in D} \varphi[x/d]$ and every existential subformula $\exists x\ \varphi[x]$ by $\bigvee_{d \in D} \varphi[x/d]$. The resulting grounding is called the *full grounding.* The size of the full grounding is polynomial in the size of D and exponential in the maximum width of a formula in T. A reduced grounding can be obtained by applying the following result.

Lemma 1. *Let* T_g *be a grounding for* $\langle T, M, C, S\rangle$ *and* φ *a subformula of* T_g. *If for every* $R \subseteq S$, φ *is true (false) in* $\text{swap}(M, C \cup R)$, *then the theory obtained by substituting* $\top$ $(\bot)$ *for* φ *in* T_g *is also a grounding for* $\langle T, M, C, S\rangle$.

According to this lemma, all formulas in T_g that do not contain an atom of S can be replaced by $\top$ or $\bot$, according to their truth value in $\text{swap}(M, C)$. The result is a reduced grounding for $\langle T, M, C, S\rangle$. Observe that for a small search space S, the size of a reduced grounding can be considerably smaller than the full grounding size. Smart grounding algorithms avoid creating the full grounding by applying Lemma 1 as soon as possible (see, e.g., [13,14,17]).

4.2 Optimized Grounding

If the search space S is small, a grounder that produces a reduced grounding spends most of its time evaluating formulas in $\text{swap}(M, C)$. Generally, evaluating a formula φ in a structure takes polynomial space in the size of φ. However, by exploiting the fact that M is a model of T, there are certain subformulas of T that can be evaluated in constant time. Below, we describe a set of subformulas of T with this property. Intuitively, the set contains formulas that are obviously true in M, and certainly remain true in $\text{swap}(M, C)$.

First we introduce a set τ of subformulas of T that are obviously true in M. Inductively define the set $\tau(T)$ by

- If φ is a sentence of T, then $\varphi \in \tau(T)$;
- If $\varphi_1 \wedge \varphi_2 \in \tau(T)$, then $\varphi_1 \in \tau(T)$ and $\varphi_2 \in \tau(T)$;
- If $\forall x\ \varphi[x] \in \tau(T)$, then $\varphi[x] \in \tau(T)$.

If $\varphi[\overline{x}]$ is a formula of $\tau(T)$, then clearly $M \models \varphi[\overline{x}/\overline{d}]$ for every tuple $\overline{d}$ of domain elements. Note that the set $\tau(T)$ can be constructed in time linear in the size of T.

Next, we investigate which of the formulas of $\tau(T)$ remain true in every revised model for a search bound S.

Definition 4. *A domain literal* L *is* dangerous *in a formula* φ *with respect to* S *if* $|L| \in C \cup S$, $M \models L$ *and there exists a tuple* $\overline{d}$ *and a literal* $L'[\overline{x}]$ *that occurs positively in* φ *such that* $L = L'[\overline{x}/\overline{d}]$.

Intuitively, a literal is dangerous in φ if it has a "negative influence" on the truth value of φ in swap$(M, C \cup S)$, while it had a "positive influence" in M.

The set of all dangerous literals in φ with respect to S is denoted by $\mathcal{D}_S(\varphi)$.

Lemma 2. *If* $\mathcal{D}_S(\varphi[\overline{x}]) = \emptyset$ *and* $\overline{d}$ *is a tuple of domain elements, then* $M \models \varphi[\overline{x}/\overline{d}]$ *implies* swap$(M, C \cup R) \models \varphi[\overline{x}/\overline{d}]$ *for every* $R \subseteq S$.

Proof. If φ is a literal $L[\overline{x}]$, then it follows from the assumption $\mathcal{D}_S(\varphi) = \emptyset$ that for every tuple of domain elements $\overline{d}$, either $M \not\models L[\overline{x}/\overline{d}]$ or $L[\overline{x}/\overline{d}] \notin (C \cup S)$. If $M \not\models L[\overline{x}/\overline{d}]$, then obviously for every structure M', including structures of the form swap$(M, C \cup R)$, $M \models L[\overline{x}/\overline{d}]$ implies $M' \models L[\overline{x}/\overline{d}]$. If on the other hand $L[\overline{x}/\overline{d}] \notin (C \cup S)$, then swap$(M, C \cup R) \models L[\overline{x}/\overline{d}]$ iff $M \models L[\overline{x}/\overline{d}]$ for every $R \subseteq S$. We conclude that $M \models L[\overline{x}/\overline{d}]$ implies swap$(M, C \cup R) \models L[\overline{x}/\overline{d}]$ for any $R \subseteq S$. The cases where φ is not a literal follow by structural induction.

Corollary 1. *If* $\varphi[\overline{x}] \in \tau(T)$ *and* $\mathcal{D}_S(\varphi[\overline{x}/\overline{d}]) = \emptyset$, *then* swap$(M, C \cup R) \models \varphi[\overline{x}/\overline{d}]$ *for every* $R \subseteq S$.

Observe that the set of formulas that satisfy the conditions of Corollary 1 is an underestimation of the set of formulas that remain true in all revised models. It now follows from Lemma 1 that a grounder can safely substitute formulas that satisfy the conditions of Corollary 1 by $\top$. Checking these conditions for a formula φ takes only linear time in the size of φ.

Example 2. Let T_1 be the theory from Example 1. The subformula $\exists c\ R(r, c)$ of sentence 1 belongs to $\tau(T_1)$. The formula $(\exists c\ R(r, c))[r/d_r]$ contains no dangerous literals if $M \not\models R(d_r, d_c)$ for every domain element d_c such that $R(d_r, d_c) \in C \cup S$. It follows that in this case, $(\exists c\ R(r, c))[r/d_r]$ can safely be replaced by $\top$.

5 Reducing the Search Space

Directly solving a revision problem $\langle T, M, C, S \rangle$ by reducing it to SAT has the drawback that there is no guarantee that the revised model is *close* to M, i.e., that the cardinality of the corresponding revision is low. The revision R can be as large as S. On the other hand, one can often find a revision with a cardinality much lower than the number of domain atoms that are allowed to swap truth value. For example, in a network configuration problem, a problem in a certain subnet can often be repaired by only making changes within that subnet, not touching the rest of the network. In Example 1, the revision contains three atoms, while there are $n \times n$ domain atoms in total.

5.1 Search Bounds

The observation above suggests the following approach to find a revision for $\langle T, M, C, S \rangle$. First, construct a *small* subset S' of S such that there might exist a revision for $\langle T, M, C, S' \rangle$. We will call S' the *search bound.* Then, try to find a revision for $\langle T, M, C, S' \rangle$ by reducing to SAT. If a revision R is found, this is

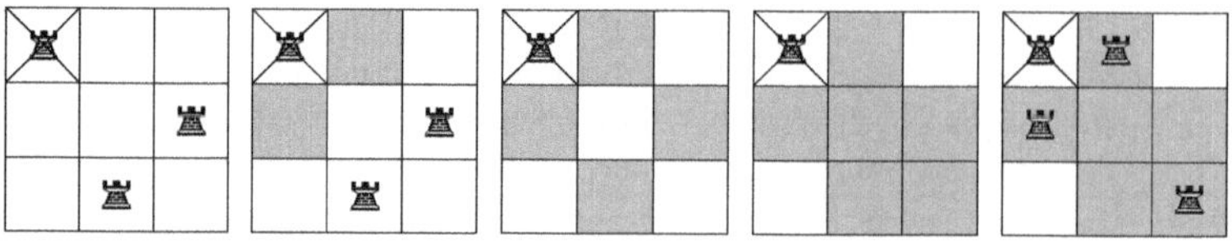

Fig. 1. Enlarging the search bound

also a revision for $\langle T, M, C, S\rangle$, because $R \subseteq S' \subseteq S$. If, on the other hand, there is no revision for $\langle T, M, C, S'\rangle$, the search bound S' is enlarged. This process is repeated until a revision is found or $S' = S$. An example run of this algorithm for Example 1 is shown in Figure 1, where the grey squares represent the domain atoms in the consecutive search bounds. There are several important benefits of using this approach compared to directly reducing to SAT:

- If a small search bound S' can be detected such that there is a revision for $\langle T, M, C, S'\rangle$, such a revision is small. Hence, the corresponding revised model is close to the original model M.
- The size of the reduced grounding for $\langle T, M, C, S'\rangle$ is small when S' is small. Indeed, all atoms that occur in the reduced grounding are atoms of S'. In general, the smaller the grounding, the faster the SAT solver can produce its answer.
- A small S' might speed up the grounding considerably, since the number of formulas that satisfy the conditions of Lemma 2 depends on the size of S'.

5.2 Enlarging the Search Bound

Assume that we have constructed a search bound S' that is not large enough. I.e., there is no revision for $\langle T, M, C, S'\rangle$. Lemma 2 implies that this problem is caused by the dangerous literals in the sentences of T with respect to S'. If we want to enlarge S' to a new search bound S'' such that there is a reasonable chance that there is a revision for $\langle T, M, C, S''\rangle$, we should add atoms to S' that have a "positive influence" on the sentences of T. That is, if they swap truth values compared to M, then some literals that occur positively in T become true. More precisely:

Definition 5. *A domain atom A has* positive, *respectively* negative, influence *on a formula φ if there is a positive occurrence of a literal $L[\overline{x}]$ in φ such that for some tuple $\overline{d}$, $|L[\overline{x}/\overline{d}]| = A$ and $M \not\models L[\overline{x}/\overline{d}]$, respectively $M \models L[\overline{x}/\overline{d}]$. A domain atom has* positive influence on theory *T if it has positive influence on at least one sentence of T.*

Note that if a domain literal L is dangerous in φ with respect to a search bound S', then $|L|$ has negative influence on φ. Observe also that swapping the truth value of an atom with positive influence and no negative influence on a formula that is satisfied in M will never cause that formula to become not satisfied. On the contrary, swapping the truth value of such an atom might cause a formula that was not satisfied in M to become satisfied.

In most cases, it is not beneficial to choose the atoms to add to S' randomly among the atoms with a positive influence on T. Rather, atoms that are added should be able to *neutralize* the negative influence of the dangerous literals. For instance, if a literal $L[\overline{x}/\overline{d}]$ is dangerous in formula $\psi_1 \vee \psi_2$ with respect to S' and $L[\overline{x}]$ occurs in ψ_1, then its negative influence can be neutralized by making ψ_2 true. Hence in this case, one should add atoms to S' that have a positive influence on ψ_2. Observe that a dangerous occurrence of a literal L in a conjunction $\psi_1 \wedge \psi_2$ cannot be neutralized. If ψ_1 is false, then even if ψ_2 is true, the conjunction is false. These intuitions are formalized in the following definitions.

Definition 6. *Let $\varphi[\overline{x}]$ be a subformula of T of the form $\bigvee_i \chi_i$ or $\exists y\ \chi$, L a domain literal and $\overline{d}$ a tuple of domain elements. The sentence $\varphi[\overline{x}/\overline{d}]$ is a* neutralizable sentence *for L if $L \in \mathcal{D}_{S'}(\psi[\overline{x}/\overline{d}])$ and for some $R \subseteq S'$,* swap$(M, C \cup R) \not\models \psi[\overline{x}/\overline{d}]$.

The condition swap$(M, C \cup R) \not\models \psi[\overline{x}/\overline{d}]$ expresses that ψ might become false when some of the atoms in S' swap truth value. That is, $\psi[\overline{x}/\overline{d}]$ can be a reason that there is no revision bounded by S'.

Definition 7. *Let ψ be a neutralizable sentence for a domain literal L. A domain atom A is a* neutralizer for L in ψ *if one of the following holds:*

- *$\psi = \bigvee_{1 \leq i \leq n} \chi_i$, $L \in \mathcal{D}_{S'}(\chi_j)$ and A has positive influence in χ_k for some $k \neq j$.*
- *$\psi = \exists x\ \chi[x]$, $L \in \mathcal{D}_{S'}(\chi[x/d'])$ and A has positive influence in $\chi[x/d'']$ for some domain element $d'' \neq d'$.*

Example 3. Let φ be the propositional formula $((P \vee Q) \wedge R) \vee (U \wedge V)$ and let $M = \{P, R, V\}$, $C = \{P\}$ and $S' = \emptyset$. Then P is dangerous in φ. Its negative influence is clear: $M \models \varphi$, but swap$(M, C \cup S') \not\models \varphi$. There are two neutralizable sentence for P: $P \vee Q$ and φ. Q is a neutralizer for the former, U for the latter. Observe that both swap$(M, C \cup \{Q\})$ and swap$(M, C \cup \{U\})$ satisfy φ. This suggests to add Q and/or U to S' to obtain a new search bound.

Example 4 (Ctd. from Example 1). Let $S' = \{R(2,1)\}$. Then $R(1,1)$ is dangerous in $\forall r\, \exists c\, R(r,c)$. The only neutralizing sentence in this case is $\exists c\, R(1,c)$, yielding $R(1,2)$ and $R(1,3)$ as neutralizers. $\neg R(2,1)$ is dangerous in $\forall r \forall c_1 \forall c_2\, (R(r,c_1) \wedge R(r,c_2) \supset c_1 = c_2)$. The neutralizable sentence is $R(2,1) \wedge R(2,3) \supset 1 = 3$, resulting in $R(2,3)$ as neutralizer.

So to reduce the search space, the first step in the revision algorithm consists of computing a non-empty set V of neutralizers for literals in $\mathcal{D}_{S'}(T)$ such that $V \subseteq S$ and $V \cap S' = \emptyset$. Then, $V \cup S'$ is used as the next search bound.

As a summary, Algorithm 1 presents the complete algorithm for computing revisions. For input $\langle T, M, C, S \rangle$, the search bound S' is initially the empty set (line 1). In lines 3–6, grounding (line 3) and propositional model generation (line 4) are applied to find a revision for $\langle T, M, C, S' \rangle$. If such a revision does not exists, the search bound S' is enlarged (lines 7–12) as follows. First, the set N of all neutralizers that do not yet belong to S' is computed. If this set is empty, it is concluded that no revision for $\langle T, M, C, S\rangle$ exists. Else, a subset V of N is chosen and S' is updated to $S' \cup V$.

Algorithm 1. Computing revisions

Input: A theory T, model M of T and disjoint sets of domain atoms C and S.
Output: A revision for $\langle T, M, C, S\rangle$ if it exists. Otherwise, FAIL is returned.

1 $S' := \emptyset$;
2 **while** *true* **do**
3     $T_g :=$ `ground`$(\langle T, M, C, S'\rangle)$;
4   **if** T_g *is satisfiable* **then**
5         $M' :=$ a model of T_g;
6   **return** $\{A \in S' \mid M(A) \neq M'(A)\}$;
7   **else**
8         $N := \{A \in (S \setminus S') \mid A$ is a neutralizer for a literal $L \in \mathcal{D}_{S'}(T)\}$;
9   **if** $N = \emptyset$ **then return** *FAIL*;
10   **else**
11   Choose a non-empty subset V of N;
12             $S' := S' \cup V$;

Because S' increases each time the while loop is executed, and $S' \subseteq S$, it follows that Algorithm 1 terminates. The correctness of the algorithm follows from the next proposition.

Proposition 1. *Let $S' \subseteq S$ and let N be the set*

$$\{A \in (S \setminus S') \mid A \textit{ is a neutralizer for a literal } L \in \mathcal{D}_{S'}(T)\}.$$

If there is no revision for $\langle T, M, C, S'\rangle$ and $N = \emptyset$, then there is no revision for $\langle T, M, C, S\rangle$.

Proof. Assume there is no revision for $\langle T, M, C, S'\rangle$ and there exists a revision R for $\langle T, M, C, S\rangle$. We have to show that $N \neq \emptyset$. Because there is no revision for $\langle T, M, C, S'\rangle$, there exists a sentence φ of T such that $\mathrm{swap}(M, C \cup (R \cap S')) \not\models \varphi$. We now show by structural induction that either $\mathrm{swap}(M, C \cup R) \not\models \varphi$ or $N \neq \emptyset$. Since R is a revision, it follows that the former case is impossible, and therefore $N \neq \emptyset$, as desired.

For the base case of the induction, assume φ is a literal L. Because $M \models L$ and $\mathrm{swap}(M, C \cup (R \cap S')) \not\models L$, it follows that $|L|$ belongs to $(C \cup R)$. Hence $\mathrm{swap}(M, C \cup R) \not\models \varphi$.

Now assume φ is the conjunction $\psi_1 \wedge \psi_2$. Then $M \models \psi_1$ and $M \models \psi_2$. Also, $\mathrm{swap}(M, C \cup (R \cap S')) \not\models \psi_1$ or $\mathrm{swap}(M, C \cup (R \cap S')) \not\models \psi_2$. Without loss of generality, we assume $\mathrm{swap}(M, C \cup (R \cap S')) \not\models \psi_1$. By the induction hypothesis, it follows that either $\mathrm{swap}(M, C \cup R) \not\models \psi_1$ or $N \neq \emptyset$. The case where φ is of the form $\forall x\ \psi[x]$ is similar.

Finally, assume φ is the disjunction $\psi_1 \vee \psi_2$. Because swap$(M, C \cup (R \cap S')) \not\models \varphi$, it follows that swap$(M, C \cup (R \cap S')) \not\models \psi_1$. If both M and swap$(M, C \cup R)$ satisfy ψ_1, the induction hypothesis guarantees that $N \neq \emptyset$. Similarly if M and swap$(M, C \cup R)$ both satisfy ψ_2. Now assume M satisfies ψ_1 but not ψ_2, and swap$(M, C \cup R)$ satisfies ψ_2 but not ψ_1. Because swap$(M, C \cup (R \cap S')) \not\models \psi_1$, it follows from Lemma 2 that $\mathcal{D}_{S'}(\psi_1) \neq \emptyset$ and hence $\mathcal{D}_{S'}(\varphi) \neq \emptyset$. Let L be a domain literal that belongs to $\mathcal{D}_{S'}(\psi_1)$. Since swap$(M, C \cup (R \cap S')) \not\models \varphi$, φ is a neutralizable sentence for L. To prove that $N \neq \emptyset$, it now suffices to show that there exists a neutralizer for L in φ. Because swap$(M, C \cup R) \models \psi_2$ while swap$(M, C \cup (R \cap S')) \not\models \psi_2$, it follows that there exists a literal $L'[\overline{x}]$ that occurs positively in ψ_2 and a tuple of domain elements $\overline{d}$ such that swap$(M, C \cup (R \cap S')) \not\models L'[\overline{x}/\overline{d}]$ and $|L'[\overline{x}/\overline{d}]| \in (R \setminus S')$. Hence $M \not\models L'[\overline{x}/\overline{d}]$. Therefore $|L'[\overline{x}/\overline{d}]|$ has positive influence on ψ_2. We conclude that $|L'[\overline{x}/\overline{d}]|$ is a neutralizer for L in φ. The case where φ is of the form $\exists x\ \psi[x]$ is similar.

In the above, we did not specify how to choose a set of atoms V from amongst the neutralizers in N to enlarge the search bound (line 11 in Algorithm 1). Several heuristics can be thought of. A thorough theoretical and experimental investigation of heuristics is part of future work. We implemented the following simple heuristics, but none of them produced significantly better results than making random choices:

- In order to neutralize multiple dangerous literals at once, prefer to add atoms to S' that are a neutralizer for more than one literal in $\mathcal{D}_{S'}(T)$.
- Prefer to add atoms to S' that have negative influence on few subformulas of T. This minimizes the increase in the number of dangerous literals in the next iteration of the while loop.
- A weighted sum of the two heuristics above.

A more sophisticated heuristic, based on the trace of the SAT solver applied in line 4 of Algorithm 1, was investigated in [3]. Also this heuristic did not produce significantly better results than randomly choosing a subset V from N. In the experiments of the next section, all results are obtained with random heuristics.

6 Implementation and Experiments

We made a prototype implementation of Algorithm 1 on top of the model generator IDP. The IDP system uses GIDL [17] as grounder and MINISAT(ID) [9] as propositional solver. The latter is an adaption of the SAT solver MiniSAT [4]. As mentioned, we implemented line 11 by choosing a random subset V of the neutralizers for literals in $\mathcal{D}_{S'}(T)$ (the set N in Algorithm 1).

6.1 Implementation of the Grounding Phase

As mentioned in Section 4.1, smart grounders simplify the propositional theories they produce as soon as possible in order to avoid creating the full grounding.

In GIDL, this is done by constructing a vocabulary σ, an σ-structure I_σ and for every subformula $\varphi[\overline{x}]$ of the input theory T a pair $(\varphi_{\text{ct}}[\overline{x}], \varphi_{\text{cf}}[\overline{x}])$ of formulas over σ such that for every $\overline{d}$,

- if $I_\sigma \models \varphi_{\text{ct}}[\overline{x}/\overline{d}]$, then $\text{swap}(M, C \cup R) \models \varphi[\overline{x}/\overline{d}]$ for every $R \subseteq S$;
- if $I_\sigma \models \varphi_{\text{cf}}[\overline{x}/\overline{d}]$, then $\text{swap}(M, C \cup R) \models \neg\varphi[\overline{x}/\overline{d}]$ for every $R \subseteq S$.

The formulas φ_{ct} and φ_{cf} are called a *certainly true bound* (ct-bound), respectively *certainly false bound* (cf-bound) for φ. When grounding, e.g., a sentence of the form $\forall \overline{x}\ \varphi[\overline{x}]$ where $\overline{x}$ are n variables, GIDL produces the conjunction

$$\bigwedge_{\overline{d} \in \{\overline{d} \mid I_\sigma \not\models \varphi_{\text{ct}}[\overline{x}/\overline{d}]\}} \varphi[\overline{x}/\overline{d}]$$

instead of the larger full grounding $\bigwedge_{\overline{d} \in D^n} \varphi[\overline{x}/\overline{d}]$. Moreover, if there exists a tuple $\overline{d}$ such that $I_\sigma \models \varphi_{\text{cf}}[\overline{x}/\overline{d}]$, the grounding of $\forall \overline{x}\ \varphi[\overline{x}]$ is substituted by $\bot$. According to Lemma 1 and the above definition of bounds, this is a correct grounding. Likewise, a formula of the form $\exists \overline{x}\ \varphi[\overline{x}]$ is grounded to $\top$ is there exists a tuple $\overline{d}$ such that $I_\sigma \models \varphi_{\text{ct}}[\overline{x}/\overline{d}]$ and to $\bigvee_{\overline{d} \in \{\overline{d} \mid I_\sigma \not\models \varphi_{\text{cf}}[\overline{x}/\overline{d}]\}} \varphi[\overline{x}/\overline{d}]$ otherwise.

We implemented the optimized grounding techniques described in Section 4.2 as follows with the help of ct-bounds. For an input $\langle T, M, C, S \rangle$ over vocabulary Σ, let σ be the vocabulary consisting of two predicates P_M/n and P_{ps}/n for each predicate $P/n \in \Sigma$. Let I_σ be the σ- structure defined by $\overline{d} \in P_M^{I_\sigma}$ iff $\overline{d} \in P^M$ and $\overline{d} \in P_{\text{ps}}^{I_\sigma}$ iff $P(\overline{d}) \in C \cup S$. That is, P_M denotes the interpretation of P in M and P_{ps} denotes the domain atoms that are certainly or possibly swapped in a revision. Introduce for each positive literal $P(\overline{x})$ the formula $\nu_{P(\overline{x})}$ over σ defined by

$$P_M(\overline{x}) \supset \neg P_{\text{ps}}(\overline{x}).$$

For each negative literal $\neg P(\overline{x})$, let $\nu_{\neg P(\overline{x})}$ be the formula

$$\neg P_M(\overline{d}) \supset \neg P_{\text{ps}}(\overline{x}).$$

Now we compose a ct-bound φ_{ct} for each of the formulas $\varphi \in \tau(T)$.

Lemma 3. *Let $\varphi[\overline{x}] \in \tau(T)$ and let $L_1, \ldots, L_n$ be all literals that occur positively in φ. Denote by $\overline{y}$ the variables that occur free in $L_1, \ldots, L_n$ but do not belong to $\overline{x}$. Then $\forall \overline{y}\ (\nu_{L_1} \wedge \ldots \wedge \nu_{L_n})$ is a ct-bound for φ over σ.*

Proof. Let $\overline{d}_x$ be a tuple such that $I_\sigma \models \forall \overline{y}\ (\nu_{L_1} \wedge \ldots \wedge \nu_{L_n})[\overline{x}/\overline{d}_x]$. We have to prove that for every $R \subseteq S$, $\text{swap}(M, C \cup R) \models \varphi[\overline{x}/\overline{d}_x]$. Observe that $\mathcal{D}_S(\varphi[\overline{x}/\overline{d}_x]) = \emptyset$. Indeed, if a literal L_i occurs positively in φ then $I_\sigma \models \nu_{L_i}[\overline{x}/\overline{d}_x, \overline{y}/\overline{d}_y]$ for every tuple $\overline{d}_y$. Hence for every $\overline{d}_y$, $M \models L_i[\overline{x}/\overline{d}_x, \overline{y}/\overline{d}_y]$ iff $|L_i[\overline{x}/\overline{d}_x, \overline{y}/\overline{d}_y]| \notin C \cup S$. From Corollary 1, we conclude that $\text{swap}(M, C \cup R) \models \varphi[\overline{x}/\overline{d}_x]$ for every $R \subseteq S$.

Example 5 (Example 1 ctd.). Consider the theory T_1 from Example 1. The subformula $\exists c\ R(r, c)$ of sentence (1) belongs to $\tau(T_1)$. The only literal that occurs positively in this formula is the literal $R(r, c)$. It follows that $\forall c\ (R_M(r, c) \supset \neg R_{\text{ps}}(r, c))$ is a ct-bound for $\exists c\ R(r, c)$. Intuitively, this ct-bound states that if each rook on row r cannot be moved, there is still a rook on row r in the revised model. It follows that instead of grounding $\exists c\ R(r, c)$ for each row r, it is sufficient to only ground it for the rows containing a rook that can possibly be moved.

The subformula $R(r, c_1) \wedge R(r, c_2) \supset c_1 = c_2$ of sentence (3) also belongs to $\tau(T_1)$. The three literals that occur positively in this formula are $\neg R(r, c_1)$, $\neg R(r, c_2)$ and $c_1 = c_2$. Hence, the formula

$$(\neg R_M(r, c_1) \supset \neg R_{\text{ps}}(r, c_1)) \wedge (\neg R_M(r, c_2) \supset \neg R_{\text{ps}}(r, c_2))$$

is a ct-bound for $R(r, c_1) \wedge R(r, c_2) \supset c_1 = c_2$. It states that if no extra rooks can be placed on a row r, there is still at most one rook on that row.

6.2 Experiments

We tested our implementation on three different problems:

N-Rooks: The N-Rooks puzzle as described in Example 1. For each of the instances, C contains three atoms. I.e., at least three atoms swap truth value compared to the given model.

N-Queens: The classical N-Queens puzzle. C contains exactly one atom for each of the instances.

$M \times N$-Queens: An adaption of the N-Queens puzzle. Here, M chess-boards of dimension $N \times N$ are placed in a circle. On each board, a valid N-Queens solution is computed. Moreover, if a board contains a queen on square (x, y), then the neighbouring boards may not contain a queen on (x, y). C contains one atom for each of the instances. In this case, it often suffices to revise one of the boards to revise the whole problem.

In the tables below, *MG* stands for *Model generation.* Times and sizes in columns marked *MG* denote times and sizes obtained when solving the problem from scratch with the IDP system. *MR* stands for *Model revision.* Numbers in these columns are obtained with our system. All sizes are expressed in the number of propositional literals. The grounding size for model revision is the grounding size for the final search bound. The *full bound size* is the size of the entire search space, the *final bound size* is the average size of the first search bound containing a revision. *Iter* denotes the average number of iterations, *Changes* denotes the average number of changes with respect to the original model. We used a time-out (###) of 600 seconds. All results are averaged over 10 runs. In each experiment, the cardinality of the randomly chosen subset V from the set of neutralizers N was restricted to a maximum of 10 domain atoms.

On the N-rooks problems, the revision algorithm scores well. Up to dimension 5000 is solved within 30 seconds, while model generation was impossible for dimensions above 500. Around 3 iterations are needed to find a sufficiently large search bound. This is as expected, since this problem is not strongly constrained: it is possible to find revisions of low cardinality. On average, 5 rooks were moved to obtain a revised model.

The results on the N-Queens show the weakness of the random heuristic on strongly constrained problems. Model revision turns out to be far slower than generating a new model from scratch. Also, many queens are moved to obtain the revised model. E.g., for dimension 40 and 50, 15 queens are moved.

The $M \times N$-queens problems show the strength of the revision algorithm. For problems consisting of a large number of small subproblems, the algorithm is able to revise an affected subproblem without looking at the other subproblems. On large problems, this results in far better times compared to model generation.

Table 1. N-Rooks

	Time (sec.)		Grounding size		Bound size			
	MG	MR	MG	MR	Full	Final	Iter.	Changes
10	0	1	$3.8 \cdot 10^3$	585	100	28	2.8	10.0
50	0	1	$5.0 \cdot 10^5$	479	2500	24	2.4	10.4
100	2	1	$3.9 \cdot 10^6$	698	10000	28	2.8	10.4
250	30	1	$6.2 \cdot 10^7$	903	62500	29	2.9	10.6
500	###	1	$5.0 \cdot 10^8$	1116	$2.5 \cdot 10^5$	28	2.8	10.4
1000	###	2	###	1998	$1.0 \cdot 10^6$	28	2.8	11.0
5000	###	29	###	5575	$2.5 \cdot 10^7$	26	2.6	11.0

Table 2. N-Queens

	Time (sec.)		Grounding size		Bound size			
	MG	MR	MG	MR	Full	Final	Iter.	Changes
10	0	1	3140	1943	100	83	8.3	14
20	0	2	25880	6133	400	93	9.3	14
30	0	7	88220	16690	900	121	12.1	26
40	1	12	210160	30083	1600	135	13.5	30
50	2	24	411700	49317	2500	149	14.9	30
60	4	###	712840	###	3600	###	###	###

7 Related and Future Work

Most literature on revision of solutions focuses on particular applications such as train rescheduling. We are not aware of papers describing techniques to handle the general revision problem for FO described in this paper. In work dealing with propositional logic, e.g. [6], the heuristics take large parts of the propositional theory into account, which becomes infeasible for problems with large domains. In the area of Answer Set Programming (ASP), [1] presents a method for updating answer sets of a logic program when a rule is added to it. The method

Table 3. $M \times N$-Queens

	Time (sec.)		Grounding size		Bound size			
	MG	MR	MG	MR	Full	Final	Iter.	Changes
10×10	0	2	33400	4387	1000	95	10.1	14
100×10	1	5	334000	5932	10000	127	13.3	17
1000×10	###	29	3340000	5932	100000	127	14.6	17
10×25	1	58	521000	34872	6250	408	41.4	25
100×25	178	104	5210000	39540	62500	475	48.1	27
1000×25	###	277	52100000	39540	625000	475	44.6	27

is completely different from the one we presented: it does not rely on existing ASP or SAT solvers, it cannot handle the case where a rule is removed from the program and it works on the propositional level.

Instead of using our method with a DPLL based SAT solver as back-end, one could directly use a local search SAT solver [16] on the grounding of $\langle T, M, C, S\rangle$ and provide the original model M as starting point for the search. The main difference with our approach is the way conflicts (dangerous literals) are handled. A local search solver immediately swaps the truth value of neutralizers and hence maintains a two-valued structure, while our approach implicitly assigns the truth value *unknown* to all atoms in the search bound and hence maintains a three-valued structure. In [3] a comparison is made on propositional model revision between DPLL-based and local search-based SAT-solvers.

The following are topics for future work:

- A thorough theoretical and experimental study of heuristics. A promising approach is to analyze the proof of unsatisfiability produced by the SAT-solver on an input $\langle T, M, C, S'\rangle$. This analysis then guides the extension of the search bound S'. Also heuristics applied in local search SAT and constraint solvers could be of use. A different approach consists of developing a more interactive system where the user can guide the search.
- The current implementation spends most of its time in grounding. For two search bounds $S' \subseteq S''$, the grounding for $\langle T, M, C, S'\rangle$ is a subtheory of the grounding for $\langle T, M, C, S''\rangle$. As such the same subtheory is grounded multiple times. It is part of future work on the implementation to avoid this overhead by grounding in an incremental way.
- Many search and revision problems cannot be expressed in a natural manner in FO. This is for example the case for problems involving reachability. Therefore, we plan to extend the revision algorithm to the logic FO(.) [18] used in the IDP system, which is an extension of classical logic with a.o. aggregates, inductive definitions and arithmetic.

8 Conclusions

We defined the model revision problem for FO, the problem of computing a new model of an FO theory when certain changes to an existing model are required. We showed that several interesting variants of the revision problem can be reduced to the basic revision problem. Furthermore, we outlined a conflict-based method to solve revision problems and investigated how this method can be improved by restricting the search space for finding a revised model. If no revised model is found, the search space is gradually increased. Preliminary results obtained with a prototype implementation indicate that our method is often capable of computing revised models that are close to the original model and can be found fast.

References

1. Brain, M., Watson, R., De Vos, M.: An interactive approach to answer set programming. In: Answer Set Programming. CEUR Workshop Proceedings, vol. 142 (2005), `CEUR-WS.org`
2. Cadoli, M., Ianni, G., Palopoli, L., Schaerf, A., Vasile, D.: NP-SPEC: an executable specification language for solving all problems in NP. Computer Languages 26(2-4), 165–195 (2000)
3. De Cat, B.: Ontwikkeling van algoritmes voor modelrevisie, met toepassingen in treinplanning en netwerkconfiguratie. Master's thesis, Katholieke Universiteit Leuven, Leuven, Belgium (June 2009) (in Dutch)
4. Eén, N., Sörensson, N.: An Extensible SAT-solver. In: Giunchiglia, E., Tacchella, A. (eds.) SAT 2003. LNCS, vol. 2919, pp. 502–518. Springer, Heidelberg (2004)
5. Enderton, H.B.: A Mathematical Introduction To Logic. Academic Press, London (1972)
6. Fox, M., Gerevini, A., Long, D., Serina, I.: Plan stability: Replanning versus plan repair. In: Long, D., Smith, S.F., Borrajo, D., McCluskey, L. (eds.) ICAPS, pp. 212–221. AAAI, Menlo Park (2006)
7. Li, C.M., Manyà, F., Planes, J.: New inference rules for max-sat. J. Artif. Intell. Res. (JAIR) 30, 321–359 (2007)
8. Marek, V.W., Truszczyński, M.: Stable models and an alternative logic programming paradigm. In: Apt, K.R., Marek, V.W., Truszczyński, M., Warren, D.S. (eds.) The Logic Programming Paradigm: a 25-Year Perspective, pp. 375–398. Springer, Heidelberg (1999)
9. Mariën, M., Wittocx, J., Denecker, M., Bruynooghe, M.: SAT(ID): Satisfiability of Propositional Logic Extended with Inductive Definitions. In: Kleine Büning, H., Zhao, X. (eds.) SAT 2008. LNCS, vol. 4996, pp. 211–224. Springer, Heidelberg (2008)
10. Mitchell, D.G.: A SAT solver primer. Bulletin of the European Association for Theoretical Computer Science 85, 112–132 (2005)
11. Mitchell, D.G., Ternovska, E., Hach, F., Mohebali, R.: Model expansion as a framework for modelling and solving search problems. Technical Report TR 2006-24, Simon Fraser University, Canada (2006)
12. Niemelä, I.: Logic programs with stable model semantics as a constraint programming paradigm. Annals of Mathematics and Artificial Intelligence 25(3-4), 241–273 (1999)
13. Patterson, M., Liu, Y., Ternovska, E., Gupta, A.: Grounding for model expansion in k-guarded formulas with inductive definitions. In: Veloso, M.M. (ed.) IJCAI, pp. 161–166 (2007)

14. Perri, S., Scarcello, F., Catalano, G., Leone, N.: Enhancing DLV instantiator by backjumping techniques. Annals of Mathematics and Artificial Intelligence 51(2-4), 195–228 (2007)
15. Pipatsrisawat, K., Darwiche, A.: Clone: Solving Weighted Max-SAT in a Reduced Search Space. In: Orgun, M.A., Thornton, J. (eds.) AI 2007. LNCS (LNAI), vol. 4830, pp. 223–233. Springer, Heidelberg (2007)
16. Selman, B., Kautz, H., Cohen, B.: Local search strategies for satisfiability testing. In: DIMACS Series in Discrete Mathematics and Theoretical Computer Science, pp. 521–532 (1995)
17. Wittocx, J., Mariën, M., Denecker, M.: GIDL: A grounder for FO^+. In: Pagnucco, M., Thielscher, M. (eds.) NMR, pp. 189–198. University of New South Wales (2008)
18. Wittocx, J., Mariën, M., Denecker, M.: The IDP system: a model expansion system for an extension of classical logic. In: Denecker, M. (ed.) LaSh, pp. 153–165 (2008)

Adaptive Reasoning for Cooperative Agents

Luís Moniz Pereira and Alexandre Miguel Pinto

Centro de Inteligência Artificial - CENTRIA
Universidade Nova de Lisboa
{lmp,amp}@di.fct.unl.pt

Abstract. Using explicit affirmation and explicit negation, whilst allowing for a third logic value of undefinedness, can be useful in situations where decisions have to be taken on the basis of scarce, ambiguous, or downright contradictory information. In a three-valued setting, we consider an agent that learns a definition for both the target concept and its opposite, considering positive and negative examples as instances of two disjoint classes. Explicit negation is used to represent the opposite concept, while default negation is used to ensure consistency and to handle exceptions to general rules. Exceptions are represented by examples covered by the definition for a concept that belong to the training set for the opposite concept.

One single agent exploring an environment may gather only so much information about it and that may not suffice to find the right explanations. In such case, a cooperative multi-agent strategy, where each agent explores a part of the environment and shares with the others its findings, might provide better results. We describe one such framework based on a distributed genetic algorithm enhanced by a Lamarckian operator for belief revision. The agents communicate their candidate explanations — coded as chromosomes of beliefs — by sharing them in a common pool. Another way of interpreting this communication is in the context of argumentation. In the process of taking all the arguments and trying to find a common ground or consensus we might have to change, or review, some of assumptions of each argument.

The resulting framework we present is a collaborative perspective of argumentation where arguments are put together at work in order to find the possible 2-valued consensus of opposing positions of learnt concepts in an evolutionary pool in order to find the "best" explanation to the observations.

1 Introduction

Expressing theories as Logic Programs has become more natural and common as the field of Computational Logic has grown mature and other fields started to use its tools and results. Theories are usually expressed as a set of 'if-then' rules and facts which allow for the derivation, through the use of logic inference, of non-obvious results. When writing such rules and facts, explicit negation, just like explicit affirmation, can be used to formalize sure knowledge which provides inevitable results.

Theories can be further refined by adding special rules taking the form of Integrity Constraints (ICs). These impose that, whatever the assumptions might be, some conditions must be met. One implicit constraint on every reasonable theory is overall consistency, i.e, it must not be possible to derive one conclusion and its opposition.

S. Abreu and D. Seipel (Eds.): INAP 2009, LNAI 6547, pp. 102–116, 2011.

Since in the real world the most common situation is one where there is incomplete and updatable information, any system making a serious attempt at dealing with real situations must cope with such complexities. To deal with this issue, the field of Computational Logic has also formalized another form of negation, Default Negation, used to express uncertain knowledge and exceptions, and used to derive results in the absence of complete information. When new information updates the theory, old conclusions might no longer be available (because they were relying on assumptions that became false with the new information), and further new conclusions might now be derived (for analogous reasons).

The principle we use is thus the *Unknown World Assumption* (UWA) where everything is unknown or undefined until we have some solid evidence of its truthfulness or falseness. This principle differs from the more usual *Closed World Assumption* (CWA) where everything is assumed false until there is solid evidence of its truthfulness. We believe the UWA stance is more skeptical, cautious, and even more realistic than the CWA. We do not choose a fuzzy logic approach due to its necessity of specific threshold values. For such an approach we would need to compute those values *a priori*, possibly recurring to a probabilistic frequency-based calculation. Accordingly, we use a 3-valued logic (with the *undefined* truth value besides the *true* and *false* ones) instead of a more classical 2-valued logic.

We start by presenting the method for theory building from observations we use — a 3-valued logic rule learning method, — and in the following section we focus on a method to analyze observations and to provide explanations for them given the learned theory. We show how the possible alternative explanations can be viewed as arguments for and against some hypotheses, and how we can use these arguments in a collaborative way to find better consensual explanations. Conclusions and outlined future work close this paper.

2 Theory Building and Refinement

Complete information about the world is impossible to achieve and it is necessary to reason and act on the basis of the available partial information coming from distinct agents. In situations of incomplete knowledge, it is important to distinguish between what is true, what is false, and what is unknown or undefined.

Such a situation occurs, for example, when each agent incrementally gathers information from the surrounding world and has to select its own actions on the basis of acquired knowledge. If the agent learns in a two-valued setting, it can encounter the problems that have been highlighted in [10]. When learning in a specific to general way, it will learn a cautious definition for the target concept and it will not be able to distinguish what is false from what is not yet known. Supposing the target predicate represents the allowed actions, then the agent will not distinguish forbidden actions from actions with a still unknown outcome and this can restrict the agent's acting power. If the agent learns in a general to specific way (i.e., the agent starts with a most general concept and progressively restricts it by adding exceptions as he learns), instead, it will not know the difference between what is true and what is unknown and, therefore, it can try actions with an unknown outcome. Rather, by learning in a three-valued setting, it will be able to distinguish between allowed actions, forbidden actions, and actions with an unknown outcome. In this way, the agent will know which part of the domain needs to be further explored and will not try actions with an unknown outcome unless it is trying to expand its knowledge.

In [25] the authors showed that various approaches and strategies can be adopted in Inductive Logic Programming (ILP, henceforth) for learning with Extended Logic Programs (ELP) — including explicit negation — under an extension of well-founded semantics. As in [18,19], where answer-sets semantics is used, the learning process starts from a set of positive and negative examples plus some background knowledge in the form of an extended logic program. Positive and negative information in the training set are treated equally, by learning a definition for both a positive concept p and its (explicitly) negated concept $\neg p$.

Default negation is used in the learning process to handle *exceptions* to general rules. Exceptions are examples covered by the definition for the positive concept that belong to the training set for the negative concept or examples covered by the definition for the negative concept that belong to the training set for the positive concept.

In this work, we consider standard ILP techniques to learn a concept and its opposite. Indeed, separately learned positive and negative concepts may conflict and, in order to handle possible *contradiction*, contradictory learned rules are made defeatable by making the learned definition for a positive concept p depend on the default negation of the negative concept $\neg p$, and vice-versa, i.e., each definition, possibly arising from distinct agents, is introduced as an exception to the other.

The learned theory will contain rules of the form:

$$p(\boldsymbol{X}) \leftarrow Body^{+}(\boldsymbol{X}) \qquad\qquad \neg p(\boldsymbol{X}) \leftarrow Body^{-}(\boldsymbol{X})$$

for every target predicate p, where $\boldsymbol{X}$ stands for a tuple of arguments. In order to satisfy the completeness requirement, the rules for p will entail all positive examples while the rules for $\neg p$ will entail all (explicitly negated) negative examples. The consistency requirement is satisfied by ensuring that both sets of rules do not entail instances of the opposite element in either of the training sets.

The ILP techniques to be used depend on the level of generality that we want to have for the two definitions: we can look for the Least General Solution (LGS) or the Most General Solution (MGS) of the problem of learning each concept and its complement. In practice, LGS and MGS are not unique and real systems usually learn theories that are not the least nor most general, but closely approximate one of the two. In the following, these concepts will be used to signify approximations to the theoretical concepts.

2.1 Strategies for Combining Different Generalizations

The generality of concepts to be learned is an important issue when learning in a three-valued setting. In a two-valued setting, once the generality of the definition is chosen, the extension (i.e., the generality) of the set of false atoms is automatically decided, because it is the complement of the true atoms set. In a three-valued setting, rather, the extension of the set of false atoms depends on the generality of the definition learned for the negative concept. Therefore, the corresponding level of generality may be chosen independently for the two definitions, thus affording four epistemological cases. The adoption of ELP allows case combination to be expressed in a declarative and smooth way.

When classifying an as yet unseen object as belonging to a concept, we may later discover that the object belongs to the opposite concept. The more we generalize a concept, the higher is the number of unseen atoms covered by the definition and the higher is the risk of an erroneous classification. Depending on the damage that may derive from such a mistake, we may decide to take a more cautious or a more confident approach. If the possible damage from an over extensive concept is high, then one should learn the LGS for that concept, if the possible damage is low then one can generalize the most and learn the MGS. The overall risk will depend also on the use of the learned concepts within other rules: we need to take into account the damage that may derive from mistakes made on concepts depending on the target one.

The problem of selecting a solution of an inductive problem according to the cost of misclassifying examples has been studied in a number of works. PREDICTOR [15] is able to select the cautiousness of its learning operators by means of meta-heuristics. These meta-heuristics make the selection based on a user-input penalty for prediction error. In [33] Provost provides a method to select classifiers given the cost of misclassifications and the prior distribution of positive and negative instances. The method is based on the Receiver Operating Characteristic (ROC) [16] graph from signal theory that depicts classifiers as points in a graph with the number of false positives on the X axis and the number of true positive on the Y axis. In [28] it is discussed how the different costs of misclassifying examples can be taken into account into a number of algorithms: decision tree learners, Bayesian classifiers and decision list learners.

As regards the confidence in the training set, we can prefer to learn the MGS for a concept if we are confident that examples for the opposite concept are correct and representative of the concept. In fact, in top-down methods, negative examples are used in order to delimit the generality of the solution. Otherwise, if we think that examples for the opposite concept are not reliable, then we should learn the LGS.

2.2 Strategies for Eliminating Learned Contradictions

The learned definitions of the positive and negative concepts may overlap. In this case, we have a contradictory classification for the objective literals[1] in the intersection. In order to resolve the conflict, we must distinguish two types of literals in the intersection: those that belong to the training set and those that do not, also dubbed *unseen* atoms.

In the following we discuss how to resolve the conflict in the case of unseen literals and of literals in the training set. We first consider the case in which the training sets are disjoint, and we later extend the scope to the case where there is a non-empty intersection of the training sets, when they are less than perfect. From now onwards, $\boldsymbol{X}$ stands for a tuple of arguments.

For unseen literals, the conflict is resolved by classifying them as undefined, since the arguments supporting the two classifications are equally strong. Instead, for literals in the training set, the conflict is resolved by giving priority to the classification stipulated

[1] An 'objective literal' in a Logic Program is just an atom, possibly explicitly negated.

by the training set. In other words, literals in a training set that are covered by the opposite definition are considered as *exceptions* to that definition.

Contradiction on Unseen Literals. For unseen literals in the intersection, the undefined classification is obtained by making opposite rules mutually defeasible, or "non-deterministic" (see [3,6]). The target theory is consequently expressed in the following way:

$$p(\boldsymbol{X}) \leftarrow p^{+}(\boldsymbol{X}), not\ \neg p(\boldsymbol{X}) \qquad\qquad \neg p(\boldsymbol{X}) \leftarrow p^{-}(\boldsymbol{X}), not\ p(\boldsymbol{X})$$

where $p^{+}(\boldsymbol{X})$ and $p^{-}(\boldsymbol{X})$ are, respectively, the definitions learned for the positive and the negative concept, obtained by renaming the positive predicate by p^{+} and its explicit negation by p^{-}. From now onwards, we will indicate with these superscripts the definitions learned separately for the positive and negative concepts.

We want both $p(\boldsymbol{X})$ and $\neg p(\boldsymbol{X})$ to act as an exception to the other. In case of contradiction, this will introduce mutual circularity, and hence undefinedness according to *WFSX*. For each literal in the intersection of p^{+} and p^{-}, there are two stable models, one containing the literal, the other containing the opposite literal.

Contradiction on Examples. Theories are tested for consistency on all the literals of the training set, so we should not have a conflict on them. However, in some cases, it is useful to relax the consistency requirement and learn clauses that cover a small amount of counterexamples. This is advantageous when it would be otherwise impossible to learn a definition for the concept, because no clause is contained in the language bias that is consistent, or when an overspecific definition would be learned, composed of many specific clauses instead of a few general ones. In such cases, the definitions of the positive and negative concepts may cover examples of the opposite training set. These must then be considered exceptions, which are then due to abnormalities in the opposite concept.

Let us start with the case where some literals covered by a definition belong to the opposite training set. We want of course to classify these according to the classification given by the training set, by making such literals *exceptions*. To handle exceptions to classification rules, we add a negative default literal of the form $not\ abnorm_p(\boldsymbol{X})$ (resp. $not\ abnorm_{\neg p}(\boldsymbol{X})$) to the rule for $p(\boldsymbol{X})$ (resp. $\neg p(\boldsymbol{X})$), to express possible abnormalities arising from exceptions. Then, for every exception $p(\boldsymbol{t})$, an individual fact of the form $abnorm_p(\boldsymbol{t})$ (resp. $abnorm_{\neg p}(\boldsymbol{t})$) is asserted so that the rule for $p(\boldsymbol{X})$ (resp. $\neg p(\boldsymbol{X})$) does not cover the exception, while the opposite definition still covers it. In this way, exceptions will figure in the model of the theory with the correct truth value. The learned theory thus takes the form:

$$p(\boldsymbol{X}) \leftarrow p^{+}(\boldsymbol{X}), not\ abnorm_p(\boldsymbol{X}), not\ \neg p(\boldsymbol{X}) \tag{1}$$

$$\neg p(\boldsymbol{X}) \leftarrow p^{-}(\boldsymbol{X}), not\ abnorm_{\neg p}(\boldsymbol{X}), not\ p(\boldsymbol{X}) \tag{2}$$

3 Explaining Observations and Meta-learning

After a theory is built it can now be used to analyze observations and to provide explanations for them. Such explanations are sets of abductive hypotheses which, when assumed true under the theory at hand, yield the observations as conclusions. There can be, of course, many different possible explanations. In the end, most of the times, we want to find the single "best" explanation for the observations, and hence we must have some mechanism to identify the "best" solution among the several alternative ones.

3.1 Abduction

Deduction and abduction differ in the direction in which a rule like "a entails b" is used for inference. Deduction allows deriving b as a consequence of a ; i.e., deduction is the process of deriving the consequences of what is known. Abduction allows deriving a as a hypothetical explanation of b.

3.2 Finding Alternative Explanations for Observations

Trying to find explanations for observations can be implemented by simply finding the alternative abductive models that satisfy both the theory's rules and the observations. The latter can be coded as Integrity Constraints (ICs) which are added to the theory thereby imposing the truthfulness of the observations they describe.

Example 1. Running example

We will use this running example throughout the rest of the chapter.

Consider the following Logic Program consisting of four rules. According to this program a 'professional' is someone who is a regular employee or someone who is a boss in some company. Also, a non-employee is assumed to be a student as well as all those who are junior (all children should go to school!).

$$professional(X) \leftarrow employee(X) \qquad student(X) \leftarrow not\ employee(X)$$
$$professional(X) \leftarrow boss(X) \qquad student(X) \leftarrow junior(X)$$

For now keep this example in mind as we will use it to illustrate the concepts and methods we are about to describe. Assume that '$employee/1$', '$boss/1$', and '$junior/1$' are abducible hypotheses.

Adding one single IC to the theory might yield several alternative 2-valued models (sets of abductive hypotheses) satisfying it, let alone adding several ICs.

In the example above, adding just the Integrity Constraint '$\bot \leftarrow not\ professional(john)$' — coding the fact that John is a professional — would yield two alternative abductive solutions: $\{employee(john)\}$ and $\{boss(john)\}$.

When the information from several observations comes in at one single time, several ICs must be added to the theory in order to be possible to obtain the right explanations for the corresponding observations.

Our concern is with finding explanations to observations. In a nutshell, we split the set of observations into several smaller subsets; then we create several agents and give each agent the same base theory and a subset of the observations coded as ICs. We then allow each agent to come up with several alternative explanations to its ICs; the explanations need not be minimal sets of hypotheses.

Going back again to our running example, if we also know that John is a student, besides adding the '$\bot \leftarrow not\ professional(john)$' IC we must also add the '$\bot \leftarrow not\ student(john)$' IC.

Finding possible alternative explanations is one problem; finding which one(s) is(are) the "best" is another issue. In the next section we assume "best" means minimal set of hypotheses and we describe the method we use to find such best.

3.3 Choosing the Best Explanation

One well known method for solving complex problems widely used by creative teams is that of 'brainstorming'. In a nutshell, every agent participating in the 'brainstorm' contributes by adding one of his/her ideas to the common idea-pool shared by all the agents. All the ideas, sometimes clashing and oppositional among each other, are then mixed, crossed and mutated. The solution to the problem arises from the pool after a few iterations of this evolutionary process.

The evolution of alternative ideas and arguments in order to find a collaborative solution to a group problem is the underlying inspiration of this work.

Evolutionary Inspiration. Darwin's theory is based on the concept of natural selection: only those individuals that are most fit for their environment survive, and are thus able to generate new individuals by means of reproduction. Moreover, during their lifetime, individuals may be subject to random mutations of their genes that they can transmit to offspring. Lamarck's [21] theory, instead, states that evolution is due to the process of adaptation to the environment that an individual performs in his/her life. The results of this process are then automatically transmitted to his/her offspring, via its genes. In other words, the abilities learned during the life of an individual can modify his/her genes.

Experimental evidence in the biological kingdom has shown Darwin's theory to be correct and Lamarck's to be wrong. However, this does not mean that the process of adaptation (or learning) does not influence evolution. Baldwin [4] showed how learning could influence evolution: if the learned adaptations improve the organism's chance of survival then the chances for reproduction are also improved. Therefore there is selective advantage for genetically determined traits that predisposes the learning of specific behaviors. Baldwin moreover suggests that selective pressure could result in new individuals to be born with the learned behavior already encoded in their genes. This is known as the Baldwin effect. Even if there is still debate about it, it is accepted by most evolutionary biologists.

Lamarckian evolution [22] has recently received a renewed attention because it can model cultural evolution. In this context, the concept of "meme" has been developed. A meme is the cognitive equivalent of a gene and it stores abilities learned by an individual during his lifetime, so that they can be transmitted to his offspring.

In the field of genetic programming [20], Lamarckian evolution has proven to be a powerful concept and various authors have investigated the combination of Darwinian and Lamarckian evolution.

In [24] the authors propose a genetic algorithm for belief revision that includes, besides Darwin's operators of selection, mutation and crossover, a logic based Lamarckian operator as well. This operator differs from Darwinian ones precisely because it modifies a chromosome coding beliefs so that its fitness is improved by experience rather than in a random way. There, the authors showed that the combination of Darwinian and Lamarckian operators are useful not only for standard belief revision problems, but especially for problems where different chromosomes may be exposed to different constraints, as in the case of a multi-agent system. In these cases, the Lamarckian and Darwinian operators play different roles: the Lamarckian one is employed to bring a given chromosome closer to a solution (or even find an exact one) to the current belief revision problem, whereas the Darwinian ones exert the role of randomly producing alternative belief chromosomes so as to deal with unencountered situations, by means of exchanging genes amongst them.

Evolving Beliefs. Belief revision is an important functionality that agents must exhibit: agents should be able to modify their beliefs in order to model the outside world. What's more, as the world may be changing, a pool of separately and jointly evolved chromosomes may code for a variety of distinct belief evolution potentials that can respond to world changes as they occur. This dimension has been explored in [24] with specific experiments to that effect. Mark that it is not our purpose to propose here a competitor to extant classical belief revision methods, in particular as they apply to diagnosis. More ambitiously, we do propose a new and complementary methodology, which can empower belief revision — any assumption based belief revision — to deal with time/space distributed, and possibly intermittent or noisy laws about an albeit varying artifact or environment, possibly by a multiplicity of agents which exchange diversified genetically encoded experience. We consider a definition of the belief revision problem that consists in removing a contradiction from an extended logic program by modifying the truth value of a selected set of literals corresponding to the abducible hypotheses. The program contains as well clauses with *falsum* ($\bot$) in the head, representing ICs. Any model of the program must ensure the body of ICs false for the program to be non-contradictory. Contradiction may also arise in an extended logic program when both a literal L and its opposite $\neg L$ are obtainable in the model of the program. Such a problem has been widely studied in the literature, and various solutions have been proposed that are based on abductive logic proof procedures. The problem can be modeled by means of a genetic algorithm, by assigning to each abducible of a logic program a gene in a chromosome. In the simplest case of a two valued revision, the gene will have the value 1 if the corresponding abducible is *true* and the value 0 if the abducible is *false*. The fitness functions that can be used in this case are based on the percentage of ICs that are satisfied by a chromosome. This is, however, an over-simplistic approach since it assumes every abducible is a predicate with arity 0, otherwise a chromosome would have as many genes as the number of all possible combinations of ground values for variables in all abducibles.

Specific Belief Evolution Method. In multi-agent joint belief revision problems, agents usually take advantage of each other's knowledge and experience by explicitly communicating messages to that effect. In our approach, however, we introduce a new and complementary method (and some variations of it), in which we allow knowledge and experience to be coded as genes in an agent. These genes are exchanged with those of other agents, not by explicit message passing but through the crossover genetic operator. Crucial to this endeavor, a logic-based technique for modifying cultural genes, i.e. memes, on the basis of individual agent experience is used.

The technique amounts to a form of belief revision, where a meme codes for an agent's belief or assumptions about a piece of knowledge, and which is then diversely modified on the basis of how the present beliefs may be contradicted by laws (expressed as ICs). These mutations have the effect of attempting to reduce the number of unsatisfied constraints. Each agent possesses a pool of chromosomes containing such diversely modified memes, or alternative assumptions, which cross-fertilize Darwinianly amongst themselves. Such an experience in genetic evolution mechanism is aptly called Lamarckian.

Since we will subject the sets of beliefs to an evolutionary process (both Darwinian and Lamarckian) we will henceforth refer to this method as "Belief Evolution" (BE) instead of the classical "Belief Revision" (BR).

General Description of the Belief Evolution Method. Each agent keeps a population of chromosomes and finds a solution to the BE problem by means of a genetic algorithm. We consider a formulation of the distributed BE problem where each agent has the same set of abducibles and the same program expressed theory, but is exposed to possibly different constraints. Constraints may vary over time, and can differ because agents may explore different regions of the world. The genetic algorithm we employ allows each agent to cross over its chromosomes with chromosomes from other agents. In this way, each agent can be prepared in advance for situations that it will encounter when moving from one place to another.

The algorithm proposed for BE extends the standard genetic algorithm in two ways:

- crossover is performed among chromosomes belonging to different agents,
- a Lamarckian operator called Learn is added in order to bring a chromosome closer to a correct revision by changing the value of abducibles

The Structure of a Chromosome. In BR and BE, each individual hypothesis is described by the truth value of all the abducibles. In our present setting, however, each gene encodes a ground literal, i.e., all its variables are bound to fixed values.

So, we represent a chromosome as a list of genes and memes, and different chromosomes may contain information about different genes. This implies a major difference to traditional genetic algorithms where every chromosome refers exactly to the same genes and the crossover and mutation operations are somewhat straightforward.

The memes in a chromosome will be just like genes — representing abducibles — but they will have extra information. Each meme has associated with it a counter keeping record of how many times the meme has been confirmed or refuted. Each time a meme is confirmed this value is increased, and each time it is refuted the value decreases. This value provides thus a measure of confidence in the corresponding meme.

Example 2. Running example (cont.)

Continuing with our running example, let us assume that both $professional(john)$ and $student(john)$ have been observed. We can create two agents, each with the same rule-set theory, and split the observations among them. We would have thus

Agent 1: $\leftarrow not\ professional(john)$

Agent 2: $\leftarrow not\ student(john)$

Agent 1 and Agent 2:

$$
\begin{array}{lll}
professional(X) & \leftarrow & employee(X) \\
professional(X) & \leftarrow & boss(X) \\
student(X) & \leftarrow & not\ employee(X) \\
student(X) & \leftarrow & junior(X)
\end{array}
$$

In the simplest case where a gene encodes an abductive ground literal Agent 1 would come up with two alternative abductive solutions for its IC '$\perp \leftarrow not\ professional(john)$': $\{employee(john)\}$ and $\{boss(john)\}$. Moreover, Agent 2 would come up with two other alternative abductive solutions for its IC '$\perp \leftarrow not\ student(john)$': $\{not\ employee(john)\}$ and $\{junior(john)\}$.

Crossover. Since each agent knows only some ICs the abductive answer the algorithm seeks should be a combination of the partial answers each agent comes up with. In principle, the overlap on abducibles among two chromosomes coming from different agents should be less than total — after all, each agent is taking care of its own ICs which, in principle, do not refer to the exact same abducibles. Therefore, crossing over such chromosomes can simply turn out to be the merging of the chromosomes, i.e., the concatenation of the lists of abducibles.

If several ICs refer to the exact same abducibles the chromosomes from different agents will contain either the same gene — in which case we can see this as an 'agreement' between the agents as far as the corresponding abducible is concerned — or genes stating contradictory information about the same abducible. In this last case if the resulting concatenated chromosome turns out to be inconsistent in itself the fitness function will filter it out by assigning it a very low value.

Example 3. Running example (cont.)

Continuing with our running example, recall that Agent 1 would come up with two alternative abductive solutions for its IC '$\perp \leftarrow not\ professional(john)$': $\{employee(john)\}$ and $\{boss(john)\}$. Moreover, Agent 2 would come up with two other alternative abductive solutions for its IC '$\perp \leftarrow not\ student(john)$': $\{not\ employee(john)\}$ and $\{junior(john)\}$.

The crossing over of these chromosomes will yield the four combinations $\{employee(john), not\ employee(john)\}$, $\{employee(john), junior(john)\}$, $\{boss(john), not\ employee(john)\}$, and $\{boss(john), junior(john)\}$.

The first resulting chromosome is contradictory so it will be filtered out by the fitness function. The second chromosome correspond to the situation where John is a junior employee who is still studying — a quite common situation, actually. The third chromosome corresponds to the situation where John is a senior member of a company — a 'boss' — who is taking some course (probably a post-graduation study). The last chromosome could correspond to the situation of a young entrepreneur who, besides owning his/hers company, is also a student — this is probably an uncommon situation and, if necessary, the fitness function can reflect that "unprobability".

Mutation. When considering a list of abducible literals the mutation operation resembles the standard mutation of genetic algorithms by changing one gene to its opposite; in this case negating the truth value of the abducted literal.

Example 4. Running example (cont.)

In the example we have been using this could correspond to mutating the chromosome $\{not\ employee(john)\}$ to $\{employee(john)\}$, or to mutating the chromosome $\{junior(john)\}$ to $\{not\ junior(john)\}$.

The Lamarckian Learn operator. The Lamarckian operator Learn can change the values of variables of an abducible in a chromosome c_i so that a bigger number of constraints is satisfied, thus bringing c_i closer to a solution. Learn differs from a normal belief revision operator because it does not assume that all abducibles are false by CWA before the revision but it starts from the truth values that are given by the chromosome c_i. Therefore, it has to revise the values of variables of some abducibles and, in the particular case of an abducible without variables, from *true* to *false* or from *false* to *true*. This Lamarckian $Learn$ operator will introduce an extra degree of flexibility allowing for changes to a chromosome to induce the whole belief evolution algorithm to search a solution considering new values for variables.

In the running example this could correspond, for example, to changing the chromosome $\{junior(john)\}$ to $\{junior(mary)\}$, where 'mary' is another value in the domain range of the variable for abducible $junior/1$.

The Fitness Functions. Various fitness functions can be used in belief revision. The simplest fitness function is the following $Fitness(c_i) = (n_i/n)/(1 + NC)$, where n_i is the number of integrity constraints satisfied by chromosome c_i, n is the total number of integrity constraints, and NC is the number of contradictions in chromosome c_i. We will call it an accuracy fitness function.

4 Argumentation

In [12], the author shows that preferred maximal scenarios (with maximum default negated literals — the hypotheses) are always guaranteed to exist for NLPs; and that when these yield 2-valued complete (total), consistent, admissible scenarios, they coincide with the Stable Models of the program. However, preferred maximal scenarios are, in general, 3-valued. The problem we address now is how to define 2-valued complete models based on preferred maximal scenarios. In [31] the authors took a step further from what was achieved in [12], extending its results. They did so by completing a preferred set of hypotheses rendering it approvable, ensuring whole model consistency and 2-valued completeness.

The resulting semantics thus defined, dubbed Approved Models [31], is a conservative extension to the widely known Stable Models semantics [14] in the sense that every Stable Model is also an Approved Model. The Approved Models are guaranteed to exist for every Normal Logic Program, whereas Stable Models are not. Concrete examples in [31] show how NLPs with no Stable Models can usefully model knowledge, as well as produce additional models. Moreover, this guarantee is crucial in program composition (say, from knowledge originating in divers sources) so that the result has a semantics. It is important too to warrant the existence of semantics after external updating, or in Stable Models based self-updating [1].

For the formal presentation and details of the Approved Models semantics see [31].

4.1 Intuition

Most of the ideas and notions of argumentation we are using here come from the Argumentation field — mainly from the foundational work of Phan Minh Dung in [12]. In [31] the *Reductio ad Absurdum* reasoning principle is also considered. This has been studied before in [29], [30], and [32]. In this paper we consider an *argument* (or set of hypotheses) as a set S of abducible literals of a NLP P.

We have seen before examples of Extended Logic Programs — with explicit negation. In [8] the authors show that a simple syntactical program transformation applied to an ELP produces a Normal Logic Program with Integrity Constraints which has the exact same semantics as the original ELP.

Example 5. Transforming an ELP into a NLP with ICs

Taking the program

$$\begin{aligned} dangerous\_neighborhood &\leftarrow not\ \neg dangerous\_neighborhood \\ \neg dangerous\_neighborhood &\leftarrow not\ dangerous\_neighborhood \end{aligned}$$

we just transform the explicitly negated literal $\neg dangerous\_neighborhood$ into the positive literal $dangerous\_neighborhood^-$, and the original $dangerous\_neighborhood$ literal is converted into $dangerous\_neighborhood^+$

Now, in order to ensure consistency, we just need to add the IC $\bot \leftarrow dangerous\_neighborhood^+, dangerous\_neighborhood^-$. The resulting transformed program is

$$\begin{aligned} dangerous\_neighborhood^+ &\leftarrow not\ dangerous\_neighborhood^- \\ dangerous\_neighborhood^- &\leftarrow not\ dangerous\_neighborhood^+ \\ \bot \leftarrow\ & dangerous\_neighborhood^+, dangerous\_neighborhood^- \end{aligned}$$

Now know that we can just consider NLPs with ICs without loss of generality and so, henceforth, we will assume just that case. NLPs are in fact the kind of programs most Inductive Logic Programming learning systems produce.

4.2 Assumptions and Argumentation

Previously, we have seen that assumptions can be coded as abducible literals in Logic Programs and that those abducibles can be packed together in chromosomes. The evolutionary operators of genetic and memetic crossover, mutation and fitness function applied to the chromosomes provide a means to search for a consensus of the initial assumptions since it will be a consistent mixture of these.

Moreover, the 2-valued contradiction removal method presented in subsection 2.2 is a very superficial one. That method removes the contradiction between $p(\boldsymbol{X})$ and $\neg p(\boldsymbol{X})$ by forcing a 2-valued semantics for the ELP to choose either $p(\boldsymbol{X})$ or $\neg p(\boldsymbol{X})$

since they now are exceptions to one another. It is a superficial removal of the contradiction because the method does not look into the reasons why both $p(\boldsymbol{X})$ and $\neg p(\boldsymbol{X})$ hold simultaneously. The method does not go back to find the underlying assumptions supporting both $p(\boldsymbol{X})$ and $\neg p(\boldsymbol{X})$ to find out which assumptions should be revised in order to restore overall consistency. Any one such method must fall back into the principles of argumentation: to find the arguments supporting one conclusion in order to prevent it if it leads to contradiction.

4.3 Collaborative Opposition

In [12] the author shows that the Stable Models of a NLP coincide with the 2-valued complete Preferred Extensions which are self-corroborating arguments.

The more challenging environment of a Semantic Web is one possible 'place' where the future intelligent systems will live in. Learning in 2-values or in 3-values are open possibilities, but what is most important is that knowledge and reasoning will be shared and distributed. Different opposing concepts and arguments will come from different agents. It is necessary to know how to conciliate those opposing arguments, and how to find 2-valued consensus as much as possible instead of just keeping to the least-commitment 3-valued consensus. In [31] the authors describe another method for finding such 2-valued consensus in an incremental way. In a nutshell, we start by merging together all the opposing arguments into a single one. The conclusions from the theory plus the unique merged argument are drawn and, if there are contradictions against the argument or contradictions inside the argument we non-deterministically choose one contradicted assumption of the argument and revise its truth value. The iterative repetition of this step eventually ends up in a non-contradictory argument (and all possibilities are explored because there is a non-deterministic choice).

In a way, the evolutionary method we presented in subsection 3.3 implements a similar mechanism to find the consensus non-contradictory arguments.

5 Conclusions

The two-valued setting that has been adopted in most work on ILP and Inductive Concept Learning in general is not sufficient in many cases where we need to represent real world data.

Standard ILP techniques can be adopted for separate agents to learn the definitions for the concept and its opposite. Depending on the adopted technique, one can learn the most general or the least general definition and combine them in different ways.

We have also presented an evolution-inspired algorithm for performing belief revision in a multi-agent environment. The standard genetic algorithm is extended in two ways: first the algorithm combines two different evolution strategies, one based on Darwin's and the other on Lamarck's evolutionary theory and, second, chromosomes from different agents can be crossed over with each other. The Lamarckian evolution strategy is obtained be means of an operator that changes the genes (or, better, the memes) of agents in order to improve their joint fitness.

We have presented too a new and productive way to deal with oppositional concepts in a cooperative perspective, in different degrees. We use the contradictions arising from opposing agents' arguments as hints for the possible collaborations. In so doing, we extend the classical conflictual argumentation giving a new treatment and new semantics to deal with the contradictions.

References

1. Alferes, J.J., Brogi, A., Leite, J.A., Pereira, L.M.: Evolving logic programs. In: Flesca, S., et al. (eds.) JELIA 2002. LNCS (LNAI), vol. 2424, pp. 50–61. Springer, Heidelberg (2002)
2. Alferes, J.J., Damásio, C.V., Pereira, L.M.: SLX - A top-down derivation procedure for programs with explicit negation. In: Bruynooghe, M. (ed.) Proc. Int. Symp. on Logic Programming. The MIT Press, Cambridge (1994)
3. Alferes, J.J., Pereira, L.M.: Reasoning with Logic Programming. LNCS (LNAI), vol. 1111. Springer, Heidelberg (1996)
4. `http://www.psych.utoronto.ca/museum/baldwin.htm`
5. Baral, C., Gelfond, M., Rushton, J.N.: Probabilistic Reasoning With Answer Sets. In: Lifschitz, V., Niemelä, I. (eds.) LPNMR 2004. LNCS (LNAI), vol. 2923, pp. 21–33. Springer, Heidelberg (2003)
6. Baral, C., Gelfond, M.: Logic programming and knowledge representation. Journal of Logic Programming 19/20, 73–148 (1994)
7. Damásio, C.V., Nejdl, W., Pereira, L.M.: REVISE: An extended logic programming system for revising knowledge bases. In: Doyle, J., Sandewall, E., Torasso, P. (eds.) Knowledge Representation and Reasoning, pp. 607–618. Morgan Kaufmann, San Francisco (1994)
8. Damásio, C.V., Pereira, L.M.: Default Negated Conclusions: Why Not? In: Herre, H., Dyckhoff, R., Schroeder-Heister, P. (eds.) ELP 1996. LNCS, vol. 1050, pp. 103–117. Springer, Heidelberg (1996)
9. De Raedt, L., Bruynooghe, M.: Towards friendly concept-learners. In: Procs. of the 11th Intl. Joint Conf. on Artificial Intelligence, pp. 849–856. Morgan Kaufmann, San Francisco (1989)
10. De Raedt, L., Bruynooghe, M.: On negation and three-valued logic in interactive concept learning. In: Procs. of the 9th European Conf. on Artificial Intelligence (1990)
11. De Raedt, L., Bruynooghe, M.: Interactive concept learning and constructive induction by analogy. Machine Learning 8(2), 107–150 (1992)
12. Dung, P.M.: On the acceptability of arguments and its fundamental role in nonmonotonic reasoning, logic programming and n-person games. Artif. Intell. 77(2), 321–358 (1995)
13. Esposito, F., Ferilli, S., Lamma, E., Mello, P., Milano, M., Riguzzi, F., Semeraro, G.: Cooperation of abduction and induction in logic programming. In: Flach, P.A., Kakas, A.C. (eds.) Abductive and Inductive Reasoning, Pure and Applied Logic. Kluwer, Dordrecht (1998)
14. Gelfond, M., Lifschitz, V.: The stable model semantics for logic programming. In: Kowalski, R., Bowen, K.A. (eds.) Procs. of the 5th Int. Conf. on Logic Programming, pp. 1070–1080. MIT Press, Cambridge (1988)
15. Gordon, D., Perlis, D.: Explicitly biased generalization. Computational Intelligence 5(2), 67–81 (1989)
16. Green, D.M., Swets, J.M.: Signal detection theory and psychophysics. John Wiley and Sons Inc., New York (1966) ISBN 0-471-32420-5
17. Greiner, R., Grove, A.J., Roth, D.: Learning active classifiers. In: Procs. of the Thirteenth Intl. Conf. on Machine Learning, ICML 1996 (1996)
18. Inoue, K.: Learning abductive and nonmonotonic logic programs. In: Flach, P.A., Kakas, A.C. (eds.) Abductive and Inductive Reasoning, Pure and Applied Logic. Kluwer, Dordrecht (1998)

19. Inoue, K., Kudoh, Y.: Learning extended logic programs. In: Procs. of the 15th Intl. Joint Conf. on Artificial Intelligence, pp. 176–181. Morgan Kaufmann, San Francisco (1997)
20. Koza, J.R.: Genetic Programming: On the Programming of Computers by Means of Natural Selection. MIT Press, Cambridge (1992)
21. Lamarck, J.B.: `http://www.ucmp.berkeley.edu/history/lamarck.html`
22. Grefenstette, J.J.: Lamarckian learning in multi-agent environments (1991)
23. Lamma, E., Riguzzi, F., Pereira, L.M.: Learning in a three-valued setting. In: Procs. of the Fourth Intl. Workshop on Multistrategy Learning (1988)
24. Lamma, E., Pereira, L.M., Riguzzi, F.: Belief revision via lamarckian evolution. New Generation Computing 21(3), 247–275 (2003)
25. Lamma, E., Riguzzi, F., Pereira, L.M.: Strategies in combined learning via logic programs. Machine Learning 38(1-2), 63–87 (2000)
26. Lapointe, S., Matwin, S.: Sub-unification: A tool for efficient induction of recursive programs. In: Sleeman, D., Edwards, P. (eds.) Procs. of the 9th Intl. Workshop on Machine Learning, pp. 273–281. Morgan Kaufmann, San Francisco (1992)
27. Lavrač, N., Džeroski, S.: Inductive Logic Programming: Techniques and Applications. Ellis Horwood (1994)
28. Pazzani, M.J., Merz, C., Murphy, P., Ali, K., Hume, T., Brunk, C.: Reducing misclassification costs. In: Procs. of the Eleventh Intl. Conf. on Machine Learning (ML 1994), pp. 217–225 (1994)
29. Pereira, L.M., Pinto, A.M.: Revised stable models – A semantics for logic programs. In: Dias, G., et al. (eds.) EPIA 2005. LNCS (LNAI), vol. 3808, pp. 29–42. Springer, Heidelberg (2005)
30. Pereira, L.M., Pinto, A.M.: Reductio ad absurdum argumentation in normal logic programs. In: Argumentation and Non-monotonic Reasoning (ArgNMR 2007) Workshop at LPNMR 2007, pp. 96–113 (2007)
31. Pereira, L.M., Pinto, A.M.: Approved Models for Normal Logic Programs. In: Dershowitz, N., Voronkov, A. (eds.) LPAR 2007. LNCS (LNAI), vol. 4790, pp. 454–468. Springer, Heidelberg (2007)
32. Pinto, A.M.: Explorations in revised stable models — a new semantics for logic programs. Master's thesis, Universidade Nova de Lisboa (February 2005)
33. Provost, F.J., Fawcett, T.: Analysis and visualization of classifier performance: Comparison under imprecise class and cost distribution. In: Procs. of the Third Intl. Conf. on Knowledge Discovery and Data Mining (KDD 1997). AAAI Press, Menlo Park (1997)
34. Quinlan, J.: Learning logical definitions from relations. Machine Learning 5, 239–266 (1990)
35. Vere, S.A.: Induction of concepts in the predicate calculus. In: Procs. of the Fourth Intl. Joint Conf. on Artificial Intelligence (IJCAI 1975), pp. 281–287 (1975)
36. Whitley, D., Rana, S., Heckendorn, R.B.: The Island Model Genetic Algorithm: On Separability, Population Size and Convergence (1998)

Extending XQuery for Semantic Web Reasoning

Jesús Manuel Almendros-Jiménez

Dpto. de Lenguajes y Computación,
Universidad de Almería, Spain
jalmen@ual.es

Abstract. In this paper we investigate an extension of the XQuery language for querying and reasoning with OWL-style ontologies. The proposed extension incorporates new primitives (i.e. boolean operators) in XQuery for the querying and reasoning with OWL-style triples in such a way that XQuery can be used as query language for the Semantic Web. In addition, we propose a Prolog-based implementation of the extension.

1 Introduction

XQuery [31,11] is a typed functional language devoted to express queries against XML documents. It contains *XPath 2.0* [30] as a sublanguage. *XPath 2.0* supports navigation, selection and extraction of fragments from XML documents. XQuery also includes expressions to construct new XML documents and to join multiple documents. The *Web Ontology Language (OWL)* [32] is a proposal of the *W3C consortium*[1] for ontology modeling. OWL is an ontology language based on the so-called *Description Logic (DL)* [6]. OWL is syntactically layered on the *Resource Description Framework (RDF)* [29], whose underlying model is based on triples. The *RDF Schema (RDFS)* [28] is also an ontology language, enriching RDF with meta-data, however, OWL offers more complex relationships than RDF(S). OWL includes, among others, means to infer that items with various properties are members of a particular class, means to define complex vocabularies: equivalence and inclusion between entities, symmetric, inverse and transitive properties, cardinality restrictions on properties, etc.

In this paper we present an extension of XQuery for querying and reasoning with OWL-style ontologies. Such extension incorporates to XQuery mechanisms for the traversal and reasoning with OWL statements. The main features of our proposal can be summarized as follows:

- XQuery has been developed for querying XML documents, however, Web data can be also represented by means of RDF(S) and OWL. Therefore, XQuery should support the simultaneous querying of XML data by both its structure and by its associated meta-data given in form of OWL-style ontologies. This is an important problem for supporting data discovery tasks

[1] http://www.w3.org

S. Abreu and D. Seipel (Eds.): INAP 2009, LNAI 6547, pp. 117–134, 2011.

against collections of XML data. The problem of simultaneous querying of both data and meta-data has been intensely studied for other data models, but the topic is in its infancy for XML data. Our approach could be used in large-scale document repositories allowing document meta-data to be used in the generation of reports and aggregate documents. The proposed extension allows to query XML/RDF(S)/OWL documents and to obtain as output the same kind of documents.

- In his current form, XQuery can be used for querying RDF(S) and OWL assuming a XML representation of RDF(S) and OWL. However, the representation of RDF(S) and OWL in XML is not standarized. While query languages for XML + RDF do exist, their application in practice is restricted by the assumption of a particular encoding of the ontology hierarchy in XML. In addition, expressing queries in XQuery against RDF and OWL in XML format can be too sophisticated. The proposed extension is independent of the XML encoding of ontologies, working directly on the conceptual RDF(S) (and OWL) data model: triples.
- RDF(S) and OWL querying should be combined with reasoning. RDF(S) and OWL allow to express and infer complex relationships between entities which should be exploited by means of a query language. The proposed extension is able to use semantic information inferred from RDF(S) and OWL resources.
- Finally, we will propose an implementation of the extension in Prolog.

Now, we will review the existing proposals of query languages for the Semantic Web and we will present the advantages of our proposal.

A great effort has been made for defining query languages for RDF(S)/OWL documents (see [7,17] for surveys about this topic). The proposals mainly fall on extensions of *SQL*-style syntax for handling the *triple-based RDF structure*. In this line the most representative languages are SquishQL [22], SPARQL [14] and RQL [19]. However, they are designed for RDF(S) and OWL querying in the following sense. The syntax of the previous languages resemble SQL extensions for expressing queries in which the database contains RDF triples. The answers to such queries resemble to SQL answers (i.e. tables). In our proposal, the extension of XQuery can express answers as XML documents, and, in particular, as RDF documents, and therefore XML/RDF(S)/OWL documents work as input and as output of the XQuery extension. It does not mean that the existing proposals of RDF(S)/OWL query languages cannot produce XML documents as output but they require the use of *ad-hoc* languages for formatting the output. This is the case, for instance, of SPARQL which incorporates to the queries the so-called *SPARQL Results Document* which defines the XML format of the answers. In our case, we take advantage of the XQuery mechanisms for obtaining XML documents as output.

There exist in the literature some proposals of extensions of *XPath*, *XSLT* and *XQuery* languages for the handling of RDF(S) and OWL. XPath, XSLT were also designed for XML, and therefore the proposals are *XML-based* approaches. In this line the most representative languages are XQuery for RDF (*'the Syntactic Web Approach"*) [23], RDF Twig [33], RDFPath [26], RDFT [12] and

XsRQL [20]. Such languages assume the serialization (i.e. encoding, representation) of RDF(S) and OWL in XML. However, such serialization is not standard. Our proposal aims to amalgamate the SPARQL (SquishQL and RQL) design with the XML-based approaches in the following sense. In our proposed extension of XQuery we do not assume a fixed serialization of RDF(S) and OWL in XML, rather than, we extend the XQuery syntax in order to admit the traversal of RDF triples similarly to SPARQL-style query languages. However, we retain the XQuery capability to generate XML documents as output. In addition, our proposal extends the syntax of XQuery but XQuery can be still used for expressing queries against XML documents. Therefore, with our extension XQuery can be used for expressing queries which combine input resources which can have XML/RDF(S)/OWL format, any of them. As far as we know, our proposal is the first one in which heterogeneous resources can be combined in a query.

Finally, there are some proposals of logic-based query languages for the Semantic Web. This is the case of TRIPLE [25], N3QL [8] and XCerpt [24,15]. They have their own syntax similar to *deductive logic languages*, and handle RDF(S)/OWL (in the case of TRIPLE and N3QL) and XML/RDF (in the case of XCerpt). Our proposal aims to define an extension of an standarized query language like XQuery rather than defining a new query language (i.e. syntax and semantics). However, our work is close to logic-based query languages in the following sense. We will propose a logic-based implementation of XQuery using Prolog as host language.

The question now is, why Prolog? The existing XQuery implementations either use functional programming (with *Objective Caml* as host language) or Relational DataBase Management Systems (RDBMS). In the first case, the *Galax* implementation [21] encodes XQuery into *Objective Caml*, in particular, encodes XPath. Since XQuery is a functional language (with some extensions) the main encoding is related with the type system for allowing XML documents and XPath expressions to occur in a functional expression. With this aim an specific type system for handling XML tags, the hierarchical structure of XML, and sequences of XML items is required. In addition, XPath expressions can implemented from this representation. In the second case, XQuery has been implemented by using a RDBMS. It evolves in most of cases the encoding of XML documents by means of relational tables and the encoding of XPath and XQuery. The most relevant contribution in this research line is *MonetDB/XQuery* [9]. It consists of the *Pathfinder* XQuery compiler [10] on top of the *MonetDB* RDBMS, although *Pathfinder* can be deployed on top of any RDBMS. MonetDB/XQuery encodes the XML tree structure in a relational table following a pre/post order traversal of the tree (with some variant). XPath can be implemented from such table-based representation. XQuery can be implemented by encoding *flwor* expressions into the *relational algebra*, extended with the so-called *loop-lifted staircase join*.

The motivation for using a logic-based language for implementing XQuery is that our extension of XQuery has to handle OWL-style ontologies. However, RDF(S) and OWL should be handled not only as a database of triples, but reasoning with RDF(S) and OWL should be incorporated. The underlying model of RDF(S) and OWL is suitable for reasoning about data and metadata. For instance, class and property (i.e. concepts and roles) hierarchies can define complex models in which a given individual can belong to more than one complex class. Inferencing and reasoning is then required. Logic programming (and in particular, Prolog) is a suitable framework for inferencing and reasoning. It has been already noted by some authors. In this area of research, some authors [16,27] have studied the intersection of Description Logic and Logic Programming, in other words, which fragment of Description Logic can be expressed in Logic Programming. In [16], they have defined the so-called *Description Logic Programming (DLP)*, which corresponds with a fragment of $\mathcal{SHIQ}$. With this aim, firstly, the fragment of DL is encoded into a fragment of FOL; and after the fragment of FOL is encoded into logic programming. Other fragments of OWL/DL can be also encoded into logic programming, in particular, Volz [27] has encoded fragments of $\mathcal{SHOIN}$ into *Datalog*, *Datalog(=)*, *Datalog(=,IC)* and *Prolog(=,IC)*; where "=" means "with equality", and "IC" means "with Integrity constraints". Some other proposals have encoded the fragment $\mathcal{SHIQ}$ into *disjunctive Datalog* [18], and into *Datalog(IC,≠,not)* [13], where "not" means "with negation".

Implementing XQuery by means of Prolog we will have a logic based implementation in which we can accommodate the Semantic Web extension. In previous works [4,5] we have proposed a Prolog based implementation of the XQuery (and XPath) languages. In such proposal, XML documents are translated into a Prolog program by means of facts and rules. Then, a query of XQuery is encoded by means of Prolog rules, and an specific goal is used for obtaining the answer. The rules of the encoding of the query specializes the Prolog program representing the input XML document. From the Prolog computed answers we are able to rebuild the output XML document. The contribution of this paper is that both XQuery constructs and RDF(S)/OWL reasoning can be expressed by means of rules and therefore a Prolog based implementation of the extension of XQuery can be easily defined.

In our proposal, we have focused on one of the Volz's fragments [27] which can be encoded into *Datalog*. It is a fragment of $\mathcal{SHOIN}$, which includes the OWL vocabulary: $rdf : type$, $rdfs : subClassOf$, $rdfs : subPropertyOf$, $owl : equivalent Property$, $owl : equivalentClass$, $rdfs : domain$, $rdfs : range$, $owl : someValues From$, $owl : has\ Value$ and $owl : allValuesFrom$, and handles $owl : union$ and $owl : inter\ section$ operators, and $owl : TransitiveProperty$, $owl : SymmetricPro perty$ and $owl : inverseOf$ properties. All of them are used with some restrictions. Since the main aim of our approach is to exhibit the combination of querying of XML, RDF and OWL, the restriction to a simple kind of ontology makes our work easier. However, it does not affect substantially to the relevance of the approach since interesting examples can be handled in our query language. We believe that more complex ontologies which can be encoded into extensions of Datalog could be also integrated in our approach following the same ideas presented here. Such extensions are considered as future work.

We would like to remark that our work also continues a previous work about XQuery. In [1], we have studied how to define an extension of XQuery for

$C \sqsubseteq D$	(`rdfs:subClassOf`)	$E \equiv F$	(`owl:equivalentClass`)
$P \sqsubseteq Q$	(`rdfs:subPropertyOf`)	$P \equiv Q$	(`owl:equivalentProperty`)
$P \equiv Q^-$	(`owl:inverseOf`)	$P \equiv P^-$	(`owl:SymmetricProperty`)
$P^+ \sqsubseteq P$	(`owl:TransitiveProperty`)	$\top \sqsubseteq \forall P^-.D$	(`rdfs:domain`)
$\top \sqsubseteq \forall P.D$	(`rdfs:range`)	$P(a,b)$	(property fillers)
$A(a)$	(individual assertions)		

Fig. 1. TBox and ABox Formulas (see [27])

querying RDF documents. Similarly to the current proposal, such extension allows to query XML and RDF resources with XQuery, and queries can take as input XML and RDF documents, obtaining also as output both kind of documents. The proposed RDF extension of XQuery uses the **for** construction of XQuery for traversing RDF triples. In addition, our RDF extension of XQuery is equipped with built-in boolean operators for RDF/RDFS properties like *rdf:type*, *rdfs:domain*, *rdfs:range*, *rdfs:subClassOf*, *rdfs:subPropertyOf*, and so on. Such built-in boolean operators can be used for reasoning about RDF, that is, for using the RDFS entailment relationship in the queries. In addition, we have studied a Prolog based implementation of this extension.

Finally, we have tested the proposal of this paper by means of a prototype implemented in SWI-Prolog. The prototype consists of a XQuery implementation and a RDF(S)/OWL reasoning module. The *XQuery* implementation can be downloaded from `http://indalog.ual.es/XQuery` and the RDF(S)/OWL module from `http://indalog.ual.es/OProlog`.

The structure of the paper is as follows. Section 2 will present the kind of ontologies we consider in our framework. Section 3 will describe the extension of XQuery for RDF(S)/OWL. Section 4 will show the implementation in Prolog and, finally, Section 5 will conclude and present future work.

2 Ontology Representation

In this section we will show which kind of ontologies will be handled in our framework. We will restrict ourselves to the case of a subset of DL expressible in Datalog [27], and therefore in Prolog. Such kind of DL ontologies contains a **TBox** and a **ABox** of axioms whose syntax is shown in Figure 1. In Figure 1, E and F are class descriptions of type $\mathcal{E}$ (see Figure 2), C is a class description of left-hand side type (type $\mathcal{L}$, see Figure 2), and D is a class description of right-hand side type (type $\mathcal{R}$, see Figure 2), P and Q are property names, a, b are individual names, and A is an atomic class.

Basically, the proposed subset of DL restricts the form of class descriptions in right and left hand sides of subclass and class equivalence axioms. Such restriction is required to be encoded by means of Datalog rules. Roughly speaking, the universal quantification is only allowed in the right hand side of DL formulas, which corresponds in the encoding to the occurrences of the same quantifier in the left hand side (i.e. head) of rules. The same kind of reasoning can be used

type $\mathcal{E}$	
A	atomic class
$E_1 \sqcap E_2$	`owl:intersectionOf`
$\exists P.\{o\}$	`owl:hasValue`

type $\mathcal{L}$	
A	atomic class
$C_1 \sqcap C_2$	`owl:intersectionOf`
$\exists P.\{o\}$	`owl:hasValue`
$C_1 \sqcup C_2$	`owl:unionOf`
$\exists P.C$	`owl:someValuesFrom`

type $\mathcal{R}$	
A	atomic class
$D_1 \sqcap D_2$	`owl:intersectionOf`
$\exists P.\{o\}$	`owl:hasValue`
$\forall P.D$	`owl:allValuesFrom`

Fig. 2. Allowed Types (see [27])

TBox	
(1) $Man \sqsubseteq Person$	(2) $Woman \sqsubseteq Person$
(3) $Person \sqcap \exists author\_of.Manuscript \sqsubseteq Writer$	(4) $Paper \sqcup Book \sqsubseteq Manuscript$
(5) $Book \sqcap \exists topic.\{\text{“XML”}\} \sqsubseteq XMLbook$	(6) $Manuscript \sqcap \exists reviewed\_by.Person \sqsubseteq Reviewed$
(7) $Manuscript \sqsubseteq \forall rating.Score$	(8) $Manuscript \sqsubseteq \forall topic.Topic$
(9) $author\_of \equiv writes$	(10) $average\_rating \sqsubseteq rating$
(11) $authored\_by \equiv author\_of^-$	(12) $\top \sqsubseteq \forall\ author\_of.Manuscript$
(13) $\top \sqsubseteq \forall\ author\_of^-.Person$	(14) $\top \sqsubseteq \forall\ reviewed\_by.Person$
(15) $\top \sqsubseteq \forall\ reviewed\_by^-.Manuscript$	
ABox	
(1) *Man(“Abiteboul”)*	
(2) *Man(“Buneman”)*	(3) *Man(“Suciu”)*
(4) *Book(“Data on the Web”)*	(5) *Book(“XML in Scottland”)*
(6) *Paper(“Growing XQuery”)*	(7) *Person(“Anonymous”)*
(8) *author_of(“Abiteboul”, “Data on the Web”)*	(9) *authored_by(“Data on the Web”, “Buneman”)*
(10) *author_of(“Suciu”, “Data on the Web”)*	(11) *author_of(“Buneman”, “XML in Scottland”)*
(12) *writes(“Simeon”, “Growing XQuery”)*	(13) *reviewed_by(“Data on the Web”, “Anonymous”)*
(14) *reviewed_by(“Growing”, “Almendros”)*	(15) *average_rating(“Data on the Web”, “good”)*
(16) *rating(“XML in Scottland”, “excellent”)*	(17) *average_rating(“Growing XQuery”, “good”)*
(18) *topic(“Data on the Web”, “XML”)*	(19) *topic(“Data on the Web”, “Web”)*
(20) *topic(“XML in Scottland”, “XML”)*	

Fig. 3. An Example of Ontology

for explaining why existential quantifiers can only occur in left hand sides of DL formulas. Union formulas are required to appear in left hand sides which corresponds with the definition of two or more rules in the encoding. The details about the encoding can be found in Section 4.1. Let us see now an example of a such DL ontology (see Figure 3).

The ontology of Figure 3 describes, in the **TBox**, meta-data in which the elements of *Man* and the elements of *Woman* are elements of *Person* (cases (1) and (2)); and the elements of *Paper* and *Book* are elements of *Manuscript* (case (4)). In addition, a *Writer* is a *Person* who is the *author_of* a *Manuscript* (case (3)), and the class *Reviewed* contains the elements of *Manuscript reviewed_by* a *Person* (case (6)). Moreover, the *XMLBook* class contains the elements of *Manuscript* which have as *topic* the value “XML” (case (5)). The classes *Score* and *Topic* contain, respectively, the values of the properties *rating* and *topic* associated to *Manuscript* (cases (7) and (8)). The property *average_rating* is a subproperty of *rating* (case (10)). The property *writes* is equivalent to *author_of* (case (9)), and *authored_by* is the inverse property of *author_of* (case (11)). Finally, the property *author_of*, and conversely, *reviewed_by*, has as domain a *Person* and as range a *Manuscript* (cases (12)-(15)).

```
xquery:= namespace name : resource in xquery | flwr | value
    | xmldoc | < tag att ='{' vexpr '}' ,...,att ='{' vexpr '}'> xquery,...,xquery < /tag > .
xmldoc:= document(doc) '/' expr.          rdfdoc := rdfdocument(doc).
owldoc := owldocument(doc).               tripledoc:= rdfdoc | owldoc.
flwr:= for $var in vexpr [where constraint] return xqvar
        | for ($var,$var,$var) in tripledoc [where constraint] return xqvar
        | let $var :=  vexpr [where constraint] return xqvar.
xqvar:= '{'vexpr'}' | < tag att ='{'vexpr'}',...,att ='{'vexpr'}'> xqvar,...,xqvar < /tag >
        | flwr | value.
vexpr:= $var | $var '/' expr | xmldoc | value.      expr:= text() | @att | tag | tag[expr] | '/' expr.
constraint := Op(vexpr,...,vexpr) | constraint 'or' constraint | constraint 'and' constraint.
```

Fig. 4. Extension of the Core of XQuery

The **ABox** describes data about two elements of *Book*: "Data on the Web" and "XML in Scotland" and a *Paper*: "Growing XQuery". It describes the *author_of* and *authored_by* relationships for the elements of *Book* and the *writes* relation for the elements of *Paper*. In addition, the elements of *Book* and *Paper* have been reviewed and rated, and they are described by means of a topic.

3 Extended XQuery

Now, we would like to show how to query an OWL-style ontology by means of XQuery. The grammar of the extended XQuery for querying XML, RDF(S) and OWL is described in Figure 4, where "name : resource" assigns name spaces to URL resources; "value" can be strings, numbers or XML trees; "tag" elements are XML labels; "att" elements are attribute names; "doc" elements are URLs; and finally, *Op* elements can be selected from the usual binary operators: <=, >=, <, >, =, =/=, and from *OWL/RDF(S) built-in boolean operators*. Basically, the XQuery language has been extended as follows:

- The **namespace** statement has been added allowing the declaration of URIs.
- A new kind of **for** expression has been added for traversing triples from a RDF document whose location is specified by means of the **rdfdocument** primitive; analogously, a new kind of **for** expression has been added for traversing triples from an OWL document whose location is specified by means of the **owldocument** primitive.
- In addition, the **where** construction includes boolean conditions of the form *Op* (*vexpr*, ..., *vexpr*) which can be used for checking RDF(S)/OWL properties. The boolean operator *Op* can be one of *rdf:type*, *rdfs:subClassOf*, *owl:equivalentClass*, etc.

The above XQuery is a typed language in which there are two kinds of variables: those variables used in XPath expressions, and those used in RDF(S)/OWL triples. However they can be compared by means of boolean expressions, and they can be used together for the construction of the answer. We have considered a subset of the XQuery language in which some other built-in constructions for XPath can be added, and also it can be enriched with other XQuery constructions, following the W3C recommendations [31]. However, with this small extension of the core of XQuery we are able to express interesting queries against XML, RDF and OWL documents.

Now, we would like to show an example of query in order to give us an idea about how the proposed extension of XQuery is suitable for OWL querying and reasoning. The query we like to show is *"Retrieve the authors of manuscripts"*. It can be expressed in our proposed extension of XQuery as follows:

```
namespace mns : "http://www.ontologies.org/manuscripts/#" in
< list > {
for  ($Author,$Property,$Manuscript) in owldocument(''ex.owl'') return
for  ($Manuscript,$Property2,$Type) in owldocument(''ex.owl'')
where rdfs:subPropertyOf($Property,mns:author_of)
and $Property2=rdf:typeOf and rdfs:subClassOf($Type,mns:manuscript) return
<author>{ $Author } </author >
} </ list >
```

In the example we can see the following elements:

- OWL triples are traversed by means of the new **for** expression of XQuery. Each triple is described by means of three variables (prefixed with '$' as usual in XQuery). Given that we have to query two properties, that is, *rdf:typeOf* and *author_of*, we have to combine two **for** expressions.
- The **where** expression has to check whether the first property, that is, *$Property*, is a subproperty of *author_of*, and the second property is *rdf:typeOf*. Let us remark that we could write *$Property=mns:author_of* instead of *rdfs:subPropertyOf($Property,mns:author_of)* but in such a case only triples "*author_of*" would be considered, and not subproperties of "*author_of*".
- The type of the manuscripts should be "*Manuscript*", as it is checked by means of *rdfs:subClassOf($Type,mns:manuscript)*.
- Finally, the output of the query is shown by means of XML in which each element (i.e. the author) is labeled by means of "*author*".

In this case the answer would be:

<list>
<author>Abiteboul</author>
<author>Suciu</author>
<author>Buneman</author>
<author>Buneman</author>
<author>Simeon</author>
</list>

Let us remark that our proposed query language is able to reason with OWL, that is, it uses that *Book* and *Paper* are subclasses of *Manuscript* and the relationship *author_of* is equivalent to *writes.*

4 Prolog Implementation

In this section, we will propose the implementation of the extension of XQuery in Prolog. Firstly, we will describe the encoding of the subset of OWL into Prolog. Secondy, we will show the encoding of XQuery in Prolog. The encoding of the extension of XQuery will use the encoding of XPath studied in [5], and the encoding of XQuery studied in [4].

```
triple(man,rdfs:subClassOf,person).
triple(woman,rdfs:subClassOf,person).
triple(inter([person,exists(author_of,manuscript)]),rdfs:subClassOf,writer).
triple(union([paper,book]),rdfs:subClassOf,manuscript).
triple(inter([book,hasvalue(topic,''XML'')]),rdfs:subClassOf,xmlbook).
triple(inter([manuscript,exists(reviewed_by,person)]),rdfs:subClassOf,reviewed).
triple(manuscript,rdfs:subClassOf,forall(rating,score)).
triple(manuscript,rdfs:subClassOf,forall(topic,topic)).
triple(author_of,owl:equivalentProperty,writes).
triple(authored_by,owl:equivalentProperty,inv(author_of)).
triple(average_rating,rdfs:subPropertyOf,rating).
triple(owl:thing,rdfs:subClassOf, forall(author_of, manuscript)).
triple(owl:thing,rdfs:subClassOf, forall(inv(author_of), person)).
triple(owl:thing, rdfs:subClassOf, forall(reviewed_by,person)).
triple(owl:thing, rdfs:subClassOf, forall(inv(reviewed_by),manuscript)).
triple(''Abiteboul'',rdf:type,man).
triple(''Buneman'',rdf:type,man).
triple(''Suciu'',rdf:type,man).
triple(''Data on the Web'',rdf:type,book).
triple(''XML in Scottland'',rdf:type,book).
triple(''Growing XQuery'',rdf:type,paper).
triple(''Anonymous'',rdf:type,person).
triple(''Abiteboul'',author_of,''Data on the Web'').
triple(''Data on the Web'',authored_by,''Buneman'').
triple(''Suciu'',author_of,''Data on the Web'').
triple(''Buneman'',author_of,''XML in Scottland'').
triple(''Simeon'',writes,''Growing XQuery'').
triple(''Data on the Web'',reviewed_by,''Anonymous'').
triple(''Growing XQuery'',reviewed_by,''Almendros'').
triple(''Data on the Web'',average_rating,''good'').
triple(''XML in Scottland'',rating,''excellent'').
triple(''Growing XQuery'',rating,''good'').
triple(''Data on the Web'',topic,''XML'').
triple(''Data on the Web'',topic,''Web'').
triple(''XML in Scottland'',topic,''XML'').
```

Fig. 5. Representation of Ontology instances

4.1 Ontology Encoding

The encoding of the ontologies defined in Section 2 consists of Prolog facts and rules. Facts are used for representing a given ontology instance. Rules are used for representing the ontology reasoning.

1. Ontology Instance Encoding: The encoding introduces Prolog facts about a predicate called *triple*. There is one fact for each element of the ontology instance. The encoding of DL formulas is as follows. Class and property names are represented by means of Prolog atoms. Quantified formulas are represented by means of Prolog terms, that is, $\forall P.C$, $\exists P.C$ and $\exists P.\{o\}$ are represented by means of Prolog term *forall*(p, c), *exists*(p, c) and *hasvalue*(p, o), respectively. Unions (i.e. $C_1 \sqcup .... \sqcup C_n$) and intersections (i.e. $C_1 \sqcap ... \sqcap C_n$) are also represented as *union*$([C_1, \ldots, C_n])$ and *inter*$([C_1, \ldots, C_n])$, respectively. Inverse and transitivity properties (i.e. P^- and P^+) are represented as Prolog terms: *inv*(P) and *trans*(P). Finally OWL relationships: *rdfs:subClassOf*, *rdf:type*, etc are represented as atoms in Prolog. In the running example, we will have the facts of Figure 5.

2. OWL Reasoning Encoding: Now, the second element of the encoding consists of Prolog rules defining how to reason about OWL properties. Such rules express the semantic information deduced from a given ontology instance. Such

$fol^t(C \sqsubseteq D) = \forall x.fol^t_x(C) \rightarrow fol^t_x(D)$	
$fol^t(E \equiv F) = \forall x.fol^t_x(E) \leftrightarrow fol^t_x(F)$	$fol^t_x(A) = triple(x, rdf : type, A)$
$fol^t(P \sqsubseteq Q) = \forall x, y.triple(x, p, y) \rightarrow triple(x, q, y)$	$fol^t_x(C \sqcap D) = fol^t_x(C) \wedge fol^t_x(D)$
$fol^t(P \equiv Q) = \forall x, y.triple(x, p, y) \leftrightarrow triple(x, q, y)$	$fol^t_x(C \sqcup D) = fol^t_x(C) \vee fol^t_x(D)$
$fol^t(P = Q^-) = \forall x, y.triple(x, p, y) \leftrightarrow triple(y, q, x)$	$fol^t_x(\exists P.C) = \exists y.triple(x, p, y) \wedge fol^t_y(C)$
$fol^t(P \equiv P^-) = \forall x, y.triple(x, p, y) \leftrightarrow triple(y, p, x)$	$fol^t_x(\forall P.C) = \forall y.triple(x, p, y) \rightarrow fol^t_y(C)$
$fol^t(P^+ \sqsubseteq P) = \forall x, y, z.triple(x, p, y) \wedge triple(y, p, z) \rightarrow triple(x, p, z)$	$fol^t_x(\forall P^-.C) = \forall y.triple(y, p, x) \rightarrow fol^t_y(C)$
$fol^t(\top \sqsubseteq \forall P.C) = \forall x.fol^t_x(\forall P.C)$	$fol^t_x(\exists P.\{o\}) = \exists y.triple(x, p, y) \wedge y = o$
$fol^t(\top \sqsubseteq \forall P^-.C) = \forall x.fol^t_x(\forall P^-.C)$	

Fig. 6. Triple-based encoding of DL in FOL

rules infer new relationships between the data in the form of triples. Therefore new Prolog terms make true the predicate *triple*. For instance, new triples for *rdf:type* are defined from the *rdfs:subClassOf* and previously inferred *rdf:type* relationships. In order to define the encoding, we have to follow the encoding of DL into FOL, which is described in Figure 6. Such encoding is based on a representation by means of triples of the DL formulas. In such encoding, class and property names are considered as constants in FOL. The encoding of OWL reasoning by means of rules is shown in Table 1.

The rules from **(Eq1)** to **(Eq4)** handle inference about equivalence. **(Eq1)** infers equivalence by reflexivity, **(Eq2)** infers equivalence by transitivity, and **(Eq3)** infers equivalence by symmetry. **(Eq4)** infers equivalence from the subclass relationship. The rules from **(Sub1)** to **(Sub13)** handle inference about subclasses. Cases from **(Sub3)** to **(Sub7)** define new subclass relationships from union and intersection operators. Cases from **(Sub8)** to **(Sub13)** define new subclass relationships for complex formulas. The rules **(Type1)** to **(Type7)** infer type relationships from subclass and equivalence relationships. The most relevant ones are the cases from **(Type2)** to **(Type5)** defining the meaning of complex formulas with regard to individuals. Finally, the rules **(Prop1)** to **(Prop11)** infer relationships about roles. The most relevant ones are the case **(Prop8)** and **(Prop9)** about the inverse of a property and the case **(Prop10)** about the transitivity relationship.

Our rules are able to infer new information from a given ontology. For instance, `triple(''Data on the Web'',rdf:type,reviewed)`, using the following **TBox** and **ABox** information:

```
triple(''Data on the Web'',rdf:type,book).
triple(book,rdfs:subClassOf,manuscript).
triple(''Anonymous'',rdf:type,person).
triple(''Data on the Web'',reviewed_by,'Anonymous'').
triple(inter([manuscript,exists(reviewed_by,person)]),rdfs:subClassOf, reviewed).
```

In order to avoid the looping of the rules, a bottom-up interpreter in Prolog has been implemented (for instance, the rule (**Sub2**) of Figure 1 loops in Prolog). Fortunately, the rules of Figure 1 satisfy a nice property. Applying the rules in a bottom-up fashion they compute a finite set of OWL relationships, that is, a finite set of triples. Therefore, the reasoning in the selected fragment of OWL is finite. It does not hold in general in description logic. Therefore, the implemented RDF(S)/OWL reasoner actually can be used for the pre-processing

Table 1. OWL reasoning rules

Rule Name	Prolog Rule
(Eq1)	triple(E, owl : equivalentClass, E) : −class(E).
(Eq2)	triple(E, owl : equivalentClass, G) : −triple(E, owl : equivalentClass, F), triple(F, owl : equivalentClass, G).
(Eq3)	triple(E, owl : equivalentClass, F) : −triple(F, owl : equivalentClass, E).
(Eq4)	triple(E, owl : equivalentClass, F) : −triple(E, rdfs : subClassOf, F), triple(F, rdfs : subClassOf, E).
(Sub1)	triple(E, rdfs : subClassOf, F) : −triple(E, owl : equivalentClass, F).
(Sub2)	triple(C, rdfs : subClassOf, E) : −triple(C, rdfs : subClassOf, D), triple(D, rdfs : subClassOf, E).
(Sub3)	triple(D, rdfs : subClassOf, E) : −triple(union(U), rdfs : subClassOf, E), member(D, U).
(Sub4)	triple(E, rdfs : subClassOf, C) : −triple(E, rdfs : subClassOf, inter(I)), member(C, I).
(Sub5)	triple(inter(I2), rdfs : subClassOf, D) : −triple(inter(I1), rdfs : subClassOf, D), member(C, I1), triple(E, rdfs : subClassOf, C), replace(I1, C, E, I2).
(Sub6)	triple(union(U2), rdfs : subClassOf, D) : −triple(union(U1), rdfs : subClassOf, D), member(C, U1), triple(E, rdfs : subClassOf, C), replace(U1, C, E, U2).
(Sub7)	triple(C, rdfs : subClassOf, inter(I2)) : −triple(C, rdfs : subClassOf, inter(I1)), member(D, I1), triple(D, rdfs : subClassOf, E), replace(I1, D, E, I2).
(Sub8)	triple(hasvalue(Q, O), rdfs : subClassOf, D) : −triple(Q, owl : subPropertyOf, P), triple(hasvalue(P, O), rdfs : subClassOf, D).
(Sub9)	triple(exists(Q, C), rdfs : subClassOf, D) : −triple(Q, owl : subPropertyOf, P), triple(exists(P, C), rdfs : subClassOf, D).
(Sub10)	triple(exists(P, E), rdfs : subClassOf, D) : −triple(E, rdfs : subClassOf, C), triple(exists(P, C), rdfs : subClassOf, D).
(Sub11)	triple(C, rdfs : subClassOf, hasvalue(Q, O)) : −triple(P, owl : subPropertyOf, Q), triple(C, rdfs : subClassOf, hasvalue(P, O)).
(Sub12)	triple(C, rdfs : subClassOf, forall(Q, D)) : −triple(Q, owl : subPropertyOf, P), triple(C, rdfs : subClassOf, forall(P, D)).
(Sub13)	triple(C, rdfs : subClassOf, forall(P, E)) : −triple(D, rdfs : subClassOf, E), triple(C, rdfs : subClassOf, forall(P, D)).
(Type1)	triple(A, rdf : type, D) : −triple(C, rdfs : subClassOf, D), triple(A, rdf : type, C).
(Type2)	triple(A, rdf : type, D) : −triple(inter(E), rdf : type, D), triple_cond(A, E).
(Type3)	triple(A, rdf : type, D) : −triple(exists(P, C), rdfs : subClassOf, D), triple(B, rdf : type, C), triple(A, P, B).
(Type4)	triple(A, rdf : type, D) : −triple(hasvalue(P, O), rdfs : subClassOf, D), triple(A, P, O), individual(O).
(Type5)	triple(B, rdf : type, D) : −triple(forall(P, C), rdfs : subClassOf, D), triple(A, P, B), triple(A, rdf : type, C).
(Type6)	triple(A, rdf : type, D) : −triple(forall(inv(P), C), rdfs : subClassOf, D), triple(A, P, B), triple(A, rdf : type, C).
(Type7)	triple(A, rdf : type, owl : thing) : −individual(A).
(Prop1)	triple(P, owl : equivalentProperty, P) : −property(P).
(Prop2)	triple(P, owl : equivalentProperty, R) : −triple(P, owl : equivalentProperty, Q), triple(Q, owl : equivalentProperty, R).
(Prop3)	triple(P, owl : equivalentProperty, Q) : −triple(Q, owl : equivalentProperty, P).
(Prop4)	triple(P, owl : equivalentProperty, Q) : −triple(P, rdfs : subPropertyOf, Q), triple(Q, rdfs : subPropertyOf, P).
(Prop5)	triple(P, rdfs : subPropertyOf, Q) : −triple(P, owl : equivalentProperty, Q).
(Prop6)	triple(P, rdfs : subPropertyOf, R) : −triple(P, rdfs : subPropertyOf, Q), triple(Q, rdfs : subPropertyOf, R).
(Prop7)	triple(A, Q, B) : −triple(P, rdfs : subPropertyOf, Q), triple(A, P, B).
(Prop8)	triple(B, Q, A) : −triple(P, rdfs : subPropertyOf, inv(Q)),triple(A, P, B).
(Prop9)	triple(B, P, A) : −triple(inv(Q), rdfs : subPropertyOf, P),triple(A, Q, B).
(Prop10)	triple(A, P, C) : −triple(trans(P), rdfs : subPropertyOf, P), triple(A, P, B), triple(B, P, C).
(Prop11)	triple(A, P, O) : −triple(C, rdfs : subClassOf, hasvalue(P, O)), triple(A, rdf : type, C).

```
xquery:= namespace name : resource in xquery | flwr | value
        | < tag att ='{ 'vexpr '} ', . . . , att ='{ 'vexpr '} '> xquery, . . . , xquery < /tag >.
owldoc := owldocument(doc).          vexpr:= $var | value.
flwr:= for ($var,$var,$var) in owldoc [where constraint] return xqvar.
xqvar:= '{' vexpr '}' | < tag att ='{ 'vexpr '} ', . . . , att ='{ 'vexpr '} '> xqvar, . . . , xqvar < /tag >
        | flwr | value.
constraint := Op(vexpr, . . . , vexpr) | constraint 'or' constraint | constraint 'and' constraint.
```

Fig. 7. A Subset of the Core XQuery

OWL documents in order to be used in the solving of queries. It improves the efficience of the proposed language.

Now, we would like to show how the extended XQuery language can be encoded in Prolog, in such a way that the queries formulated in our proposed query language can be executed under Prolog. In order to make the paper self-contained we will restrict to a fragment of the extended XQuery for querying and reasoning with OWL triples and for generating XML documents as output. Now, the fragment to be encoded will consist in the grammar of the Figure 7, where *Op* can be one of the OWL built-in boolean operators. The reader can check that such fragment has been used in the example of the previous section. Now, a crucial point is the encoding of XML documents in Prolog. Such encoding will allow the encoding of the output of the query.

4.2 Encoding of XML Documents

In this section we will show an example of encoding of XML documents. A formal and complete definition can be found in [5]. Let us consider the following document called "b.xml":

```
<books>
<book year="2003">
    <author>Abiteboul</author>
    <author>Buneman</author>
    <author>Suciu</author>
    <title>Data on the Web</title>
<review>A <em>fine</em> book.</review>
</book>
<book year="2002">
    <author>Buneman</author>
    <title>XML in Scottland</title>
    <review><em>The <em>best</em> ever!</em></review>
</book>
</books>
```

Now, it can be represented by means of a Prolog program as in Figure 8. In our XML encoding we can distinguish the so-called *schema rules* which define the structure of the XML document, and *facts* which store the leaves of the XML tree (and therefore the values of the XML document). Each tag is translated into a predicate name: *books*, *book*, etc. Each predicate has four arguments. The first one, used for representing the XML document structure, is encapsulated into a function symbol with the same name as the tag adding the suffix *type*. Therefore, we have *bookstype*, *booktype*, etc. The second argument is used for numbering each node (a list of natural numbers identifying each node); the third argument of the predicates is used for numbering each type (a natural number identifying

Rules (Schema):	Facts (Document):
`books(bookstype(Book, []), NBooks,1,Doc) :- book(Book, [NBook|NBooks],2,Doc).`	`year('2003', [1, 1], 3,''b.xml").`
`book(booktype(Author, Title, Review, [year=Year]),NBook ,2,Doc) :-`	`author('Abiteboul', [1, 1, 1], 3,''b.xml").`
`author(Author, [NAu|NBook],3,Doc),`	`author('Buneman', [2,1, 1], 3,''b.xml").`
`title(Title, [NTitle|NBook],3,Doc),`	`author('Suciu', [3,1,1], 3,''b.xml").`
`review(Review, [NRe|NBook],3,Doc),`	`title('Data on the Web', [4, 1, 1], 3,''b.xml").`
`year(Year, NBook,3,Doc).`	`unlabeled('A', [1, 5, 1, 1], 4,''b.xml").`
`review(reviewtype(Un,Em,[]),NReview,3,Doc):-`	`em('fine', [2, 5, 1, 1], 4,''b.xml").`
`unlabeled(Un,[NUn|NReview],4,Doc),`	`unlabeled('book.', [3, 5, 1, 1], 4,''b.xml").`
`em(Em,[NEm|NReview],4,Doc).`	`year('2002', [2, 1], 3,''b.xml").`
`review(reviewtype(Em,[]),NReview,3,Doc):-`	`author('Buneman', [1, 2, 1], 3,''b.xml").`
`em(Em,[NEm|NReview],5,Doc).`	`title('XML in Scottland', [2, 2, 1], 3,''b.xml").`
`em(emtype(Unlabeled,Em,[]),NEms,5,Doc) :-`	`unlabeled('The', [1, 1, 3, 2, 1], 6,''b.xml").`
`unlabeled(Unlabeled,[NUn|NEms],6,Doc),`	`em('best', [2, 1, 3, 2, 1], 6,''b.xml").`
`em(Em, [NEm|NEms],6,Doc).`	`unlabeled('ever!', [3, 1, 3, 2, 1], 6,''b.xml").`

Fig. 8. Encoding of XML documents

each type); and the last argument represents the document name. The key element of our encoding is to be able to recover the original XML document from the set of rules and facts. The encoding has the following peculiarities. In order to specify the order of an XML document in a fact based representation, each fact is numbered (from left to right and by levels in the XML tree). In addition, the hierarchical structure of the XML records is described by means of the identifier of each fact: the number of the children is a suffix of the number of the parent. The type number makes possible to map schema rules with facts.

4.3 Encoding of XQuery

Now, we will show how to encode the proposed extension of XQuery. We can summarize the encoding as follows. The encoding combines the schema rules of the output document with rules which call the *triple* predicate. A new predicate is defined called *join*. The join predicate calls to *triple* predicate in order to carry out the join of the triples. Now, let us see examples of queries in our proposal and the corresponding encoding.

Query 1: Let us suppose the query *"Retrieve the authors of manuscripts"* which is defined in XQuery as follows:

```
< list > {
for ($Author,$Property,$Manuscript) in owldocument(''ex.owl'') return
for ($Manuscript,$Property2,$Type) in owldocument(''ex.owl'')
where rdfs:subPropertyOf($Property,author_of)
and $Property2=rdf:typeOf and rdfs:subClassOf($Type,manuscript) return
<author>{ $Author } </author >
} </ list >
```

Now, the encoding is as follows:

```
(1) list(listtype(Author,[]),NList,1,Doc):-author(Author,[NAuthor|NList],2,Doc).
(2) author(authortype(Author,[]),NAuthor,2,''result.xml''):-join(Author,NAuthor).
(3) join(Author,[NAuthor,[1]]):-
        triple(Author,Property,Manuscript,NAuthor,''ex.owl''),
        triple(Manuscript,Property2,Type,_,''ex.owl''),
        triple(Property,rdfs:subPropertyOf,author_of,_,''ex.owl''),
        Property2=rdf:typeOf,
        triple(Type,rdfs:subClassOf,manuscript,_,''ex.owl'').
```

The encoding takes into account the following elements.

- The **return** expression generates an XML document, and therefore the encoding includes the schema rules of the output document. In the previous example, this is the case of rule **(1)**, describing that the *list* tag includes elements labeled as *author*.
- The rules **(2)** and **(3)** are the main rules of the encoding, in which the elements of the output document are computed by means of the so-called *join* predicate.
- The *join* predicate is the responsible of the encoding of the **for** and **where** constructs. Each **for** associated to an OWL triple is encoded by means of a call to the *triple* predicate with variables.
- Now, the **where** expression is encoded as follows. In the case of binary operators like "=", ">", ">=", etc, they are encoded by means of calls to the corresponding Prolog operator. In the case of built-in boolean operators of the kind *rdf:typeOf*, *rdfs:subClassOf*, etc, a call to the *triple* predicate is achieved.
- Finally, we have to incorporate to the *triple* predicate two new arguments in facts and rules. The first new argument is a list of natural numbers identifying the triple. Each element of the **TBox** and the **ABox** is identified by means of [1], [2], etc. The triples inferred from the **TBox** and the **ABox** can be identified by appending the identifiers of the triples used for the inference. Therefore, in general, each triple can be identified as a list of natural numbers (for instance, $[1, 4, 5]$). Triple identifiers are required for representing the order of the elements of the output XML document, according to our encoding. The second new argument is the name of the document which stores the triple.

Now, the Prolog goal `?-author(Author,Node,Type,Doc)` has the following answers:

```
Author=authortype("Abiteboul",[]),Node=[...],Type=2,Doc=''result.xml''
Author=authortype("Suciu",[]),Node=[...],Type=2,Doc=''result.xml''
Author=authortype("Buneman",[]),Node=[...],Type=2,Doc=''result.xml''
Author=authortype("Buneman",[]),Node=[...],Type=2,Doc=''result.xml''
Author=authortype("Simeon",[]),Node=[...],Type=2,Doc=''result.xml''
```

From the schema rule (rule **(1)**), and these computed answers, we can rebuild the output XML document:

```
<list>
<author>Abiteboul</author>
<author>Suciu</author>
<author>Buneman</author>
<author>Buneman</author>
<author>Simeon</author>
</list>
```

Query 2: The second query we would like to show is *"Retrieve the reviewed manuscripts and their writers"*. In this case, the query can be expressed in XQuery as follows:

```
< list > {
for ($Writer,$Property,$Manuscript) in owldocument(''ex.owl'') return
for ($Manuscript,$Property2,$Type) in owldocument(''ex.owl'')
where rdfs:subPropertyOf($Property,writes)
and $Property2=rdf:typeOf and rdfs:subClassOf($Type,reviewed) return
<item>
<manuscript> { $Manuscript } </ manuscript >
<writer>{ $Writer } </writer >
</item>
} </ list >
```

In this case, the properties to be checked are *"writes"* and *"rdf:typeOf"*. The boolean operator *rdfs : subPropertyOf ($Property, writes)* is also true for triples in which the *$Property* is *"author_of"* given that both are equivalent properties in the given ontology. A more concise way to express the previous query is:

```
< list > {
for ($Writer,$Property,$Manuscript) in owldocument(''ex.owl'')
where rdfs:subPropertyOf($Property,writes) and rdf:type(Manuscript,reviewed) return
<item>
<manuscript> { $Manuscript } </ manuscript >
<writer>{ $Writer } </writer >
</item>
} </ list >
```

It uses the built-in boolean operator *rdf:type* whose semantics takes into account the inclusion and equivalence relationships of the input ontology. In this case the answer would be:

```
<list>
<item><manuscript>Data on the Web</manuscript>
<writer>Abiteboul</writer></item>
<item><manuscript>Data on the Web</manuscript>
<writer>Suciu</writer></item>
<item><manuscript>Data on the Web</manuscript>
<writer>Buneman</writer></item>
<item><manuscript>XML in Scottland</manuscript>
<writer>Buneman</writer></item>
<item><manuscript>Growing XQuery</manuscript>
<writer>Simeon</writer></item>
</list>
```

Now, the goal is ? − `item(Item, Node, Type, Doc)` and the encoding is as follows:

```
list(listtype(Item,[]),NL,1,Doc):- item(Item,[NItem|NL],2,Doc).
item(itemtype(manuscripttype(Manuscript,[]),writertype(Writer,[]),[]),NItem,2,''result.xml''):-
                              join(Manuscript,Writer,NItem).
join(Manuscript,Writer,[NM,[1]]):-
                              triple(Writer,Property,Manuscript,NM,''ex.owl''),
                              triple(Manuscript,Property2,Type,_,''ex.owl''),
                              triple(Property,rdfs:subPropertyOf,writes,_,''ex.owl''),
                              Property2=rdf:typeOf,
                              triple(Type,rdfs:subClassOf,reviewed,_,''ex.owl'').
```

Query 3: Finally, we would like to show the query *"Retrieve the equivalent properties of the ontology"*, in which we can extract from the input ontology some properties and we can represent the output of the query as an ontology:

```
< owl:Ontology > {
for ($Object1,$Property,$Object2) in owldocument(''ex.owl'')
where $Property=owl:equivalentProperty return
<owl:ObjectProperty rdf:about=''{$Object1}''/>
<owl:equivalentProperty rdf:resource=''{$Object2}''/>
</owl:ObjectProperty>
} </ owl:Ontology >
```

Now, the goal is ? − owlObjectProperty(OwlObjectProperty, Node, Type, Doc), and the query is encoded as follows:

```
owlOntology(owlOntologytype(OwlObjectProp,[]),Nowl,1,Doc):-
     owlObjectProperty(OwlObjectProp,[Nowlo|Nowl],2,Doc).
owlObjectProperty(owlObjectPropertytype(owlequivalentPropertytype('''',[rdf:resource=Object2]),
       [rdf:about=Object1]),Nowlp,2,''result.xml''):-join(Object1,Object2,Nowlp).
join(Object1,Object2,[NTriple,[1]]):-
       triple(Object1,Property,Object2,NTriple,''ex.owl''),
       Property=owl:equivalentProperty.
```

5 Conclusions and Future Work

In this paper we have studied an extension of XQuery for the querying and reasoning with OWL style ontologies. Such extension combines RDF(S)/OWL and XML documents as input/output documents. By means of built-in boolean operators XQuery can be equipped with inference mechanism for OWL properties. We have also studied how to implement/encode such language in Prolog. We have developed an implementation of the XQuery language and a RDF(S) / OWL reasoner which can be downloaded from our Web site: http://indalog.ual.es/XQuery and http://indalog.ual.es/OProlog. More details about the implementation of the RDF(S)/OWL reasoner and the XQuery implementation can be found in [2,3]. As future work, we would like to extend our work with the handling of more complex ontologies in the line of [18,27]. In addition, we are now developing an implementation of the proposed extension as a XQuery library, using the available extension mechanisms of XQuery. We believe that it can be significant for the widespread acceptance of the approach.

Acknowledgements

The author would like to thank the anonymous referees for their insightful comments and suggestions. This work has been partially supported by the Spanish MICINN under grant TIN2008-06622-C03-03.

References

1. Almendros-Jiménez, J.M.: An RDF Query Language based on Logic Programming. Electronic Notes in Theoretical Computer Science 200(3), 67–85 (2008)
2. Almendros-Jiménez, J.M.: An encoding of xQuery in prolog. In: Bellahsène, Z., Hunt, E., Rys, M., Unland, R. (eds.) XSym 2009. LNCS, vol. 5679, pp. 145–155. Springer, Heidelberg (2009)

3. Almendros-Jiménez, J.M.: A Query Language for OWL based on Logic Programming. In: 5th Int'l Workshop on Automated Specification and Verification of Web Systems, WWv 2009, pp. 69–84 (2009)
4. Almendros-Jiménez, J.M., Becerra-Terón, A., Enciso-Baños, F.J.: Integrating XQuery and Logic Programming. In: Seipel, D., Hanus, M., Wolf, A. (eds.) INAP 2007. LNCS (LNAI), vol. 5437, pp. 117–135. Springer, Heidelberg (2009)
5. Almendros-Jiménez, J.M., Becerra-Terón, A., Enciso-Baños, F.J.: Querying XML documents in logic programming. TPLP 8(3), 323–361 (2008)
6. Baader, F., Horrocks, I., Sattler, U.: Description logics, pp. 3–28. Springer, Heidelberg (2004)
7. Bailey, J., Bry, F., Furche, T., Schaffert, S.: Web and Semantic Web Query Languages: A Survey. In: Eisinger, N., Małuszyński, J. (eds.) Reasoning Web. LNCS, vol. 3564, pp. 35–133. Springer, Heidelberg (2005)
8. Berners-Lee, T.: N3QL-RDF Data Query Language. Technical report, Online only (2004)
9. Boncz, P., Grust, T., van Keulen, M., Manegold, S., Rittinger, J., Teubner, J.: MonetDB/XQuery: a fast XQuery processor powered by a relational engine. In: Proceedings of the 2006 ACM SIGMOD International Conference on Management of Data, pp. 479–490. ACM, New York (2006)
10. Boncz, P.A., Grust, T., van Keulen, M., Manegold, S., Rittinger, J., Teubner, J.: Pathfinder: XQuery - The Relational Way. In: Proc. of the International Conference on Very Large Databases, pp. 1322–1325. ACM Press, New York (2005)
11. Chamberlin, D., Draper, D., Fernández, M., Kay, M., Robie, J., Rys, M., Simeon, J., Tivy, J., Wadler, P.: XQuery from the Experts. Addison Wesley, Boston (2004)
12. Davis, I.: RDF Template Language 1.0. Technical report, Online only (September 2003)
13. de Bruijn, J., Lara, R., Polleres, A., Fensel, D.: OWL DL vs. OWL Flight: conceptual modeling and reasoning for the semantic Web. In: WWW 2005: Proceedings of the 14th International Conference on World Wide Web, pp. 623–632. ACM Press, New York (2005)
14. de Laborda, C.P., Conrad, S.: Bringing Relational Data into the Semantic Web using SPARQL and Relational OWL. In: Procs. of ICDEW 2006. IEEE Computer Society, Los Alamitos (2006)
15. Furche, T., Bry, F., Bolzer, O.: Marriages of Convenience: Triples and Graphs, RDF and XML in Web Querying. In: Fages, F., Soliman, S. (eds.) PPSWR 2005. LNCS, vol. 3703, pp. 72–84. Springer, Heidelberg (2005)
16. Grosof, B.N., Horrocks, I., Volz, R., Decker, S.: Description Logic Programs: Combining Logic Programs with Description Logic. In: Proc. of the International Conference on World Wide Web, USA, pp. 48–57. ACM Press, New York (2003)
17. Haase, P., Broekstra, J., Eberhart, A., Volz, R.: A Comparison of RDF query languages. In: McIlraith, S.A., Plexousakis, D., van Harmelen, F. (eds.) ISWC 2004. LNCS, vol. 3298, pp. 502–517. Springer, Heidelberg (2004)
18. Hustadt, U., Motik, B., Sattler, U.: Reasoning in Description Logics by a Reduction to Disjunctive Datalog. J. Autom. Reasoning 39(3), 351–384 (2007)
19. Karvounarakis, G., Alexaki, S., Christophides, V., Plexousakis, D., Scholl, M.: RQL: a declarative query language for RDF. In: WWW 2002: Proceedings of the 11th International Conference on World Wide Web, pp. 592–603. ACM Press, New York (2002)
20. Katz, H.: XsRQL: an XQuery-style Query Language for RDF. Technical report, Online only (2004)

21. Marian, A., Simeon, J.: Projecting XML Documents. In: Proc. of International Conference on Very Large Databases, Burlington, USA, pp. 213–224. Morgan Kaufmann, San Francisco (2003)
22. Miller, L., Seaborne, A., Reggiori, A.: Three Implementations of SquishQL, a Simple RDF Query Language. In: Horrocks, I., Hendler, J. (eds.) ISWC 2002. LNCS, vol. 2342, pp. 423–435. Springer, Heidelberg (2002)
23. Robie, J., Garshol, L.M., Newcomb, S., Biezunski, M., Fuchs, M., Miller, L., Brickley, D., Christophides, V., Karvounarakis, G.: The Syntactic Web: Syntax and Semantics on the Web. Markup Languages: Theory & Practice 4(3), 411–440 (2002)
24. Schaffert, S., Bry, F.: A Gentle Introduction to Xcerpt, a Rule-based Query and Transformation Language for XML. In: Proc. of International Workshop on Rule Markup Languages for Business Rules on the Semantic Web, Aachen, Germany. CEUR Workshop Proceedings, vol. 60, pages 22 (2002)
25. Sintek, M., Decker, S.: *TRIPLE*–A Query, Inference, and Transformation Language for the Semantic Web. In: Horrocks, I., Hendler, J. (eds.) ISWC 2002. LNCS, vol. 2342, pp. 364–378. Springer, Heidelberg (2002)
26. Souzis, A.: RxPath: a mapping of RDF to the XPath Data Model. In: Extreme Markup Languages (2006)
27. Volz, R.: Web Ontology Reasoning with Logic Databases. PhD thesis, Universität Fridericiana zu Karlsruhe (2004)
28. W3C. RDF Vocabulary Description Language 1.0: RDF Schema. Technical report (2004), `www.w3.org`
29. W3C. Resource Description Framework (RDF). Technical report (2004), `www.w3.org`
30. W3C. XML Path Language (XPath) 2.0. Technical report (2007), `www.w3.org`
31. W3C. XML Query Working Group and XSL Working Group, XQuery 1.0: An XML Query Language. Technical report (2007), `www.w3.org`
32. W3C. OWL 2 Web Ontology Language. Technical report (2008), `www.w3.org`
33. Walsh, N.: RDF Twig: Accessing RDF Graphs in XSLT. In: Proceedings of Extreme Markup Languages (2003)

Reference Model and Perspective Schemata Inference for Enterprise Data Integration

Valéria Magalhães Pequeno and João Carlos Moura Pires

CENTRIA, Departamento de Informática,
Faculdade de Ciências e Tecnologia, FCT, Universidade Nova de Lisboa
2829-516, Caparica, Portugal
vmp@fct.unl.pt, jmp@di.fct.unl.pt

Abstract. Sharing and integrating information among multiple heterogeneous and autonomous databases has emerged as a strategic requirement in modern enterprises. We deal with this problem by proposing a declarative approach based on the creation of a reference model and perspective schemata. The former provides a common semantic, while the latter connects schemata. This paper focuses on deduction of new perspective schemata using a proposed inference mechanism. A proof-of-concept prototype, based on Logic Programming, is presented in brief.

1 Introduction

One of leading issues in database research is to develop flexible mechanisms for providing integrated access to multiple, distributed, heterogeneous databases and other information sources. A wide range of techniques has been developed to address this problem, including approaches based on the creation of Data Warehouses (DWs), and Federated Database Systems (FDBSs). DWs are highly specialised database systems which contain the unified history of an enterprise at a suitable level of detail for decision support. All data is integrated into, normally, a single repository, with a generalised and global schema. A FDBS enables a unified virtual view of one or more autonomous sources of information to hide data heterogeneity from applications and users. Closely coupled FDBSs, those that occur in DWs, provide a global schema expressed in a common, "canonical" data model. Unlike a DW, a FDBS leaves data at the source.

In both approaches, the designer usually deals with incompatible data models, characterised by subtle differences in structure and semantics and should define mappings between the global and source information schemata. He/she uses tools in order to do these maps and build the DW (or the FDBS). These tools, although in most part are graphical user-friendly interfaces, generate diverse codes, which hide knowledge of procedures and policies used to create the maps. Because the mapping between schemata is not explicit, it cannot be reused. However, we cannot deduce new maps based on previous ones (i.e., if we have two maps: one from a class A to another class B, and other from class B to class C and want a map from A to C directly, we have to create this map manually).

S. Abreu and D. Seipel (Eds.): INAP 2009, LNAI 6547, pp. 135–152, 2011.

In order to deal with these problems, we propose to take a declarative approach based on the creation of a reference model and perspective schemata. A reference model (conceptual model, business data model, or enterprise data model) is an abstract framework that represents the information used in an enterprise from a business viewpoint. It provides a common semantic that can be used to guide the development of other models and help with data consistency [1]. Also, it serves as basis for multiple products such as application systems, DWs, and FDBSs [1, 2], being a more stable basis for identifying information requirements to the DW systems than user query requirements, which are unpredictable and subject to frequent change [3]. The use of a reference model is not a novelty of our approach. It is very advocated in DW systems [1–5], although some users do not agree with its creation. Nevertheless, it is important to note that, when a reference model is used, it is essentially methodological and is not computable, serving only as reference and guide propose. The novelty of our proposal is that the reference model is formal and plays a more active role.

A perspective schema describes a data model, part or whole (*the target*), in terms of other data models (*the base*). It represents the mapping from one or more schemata (e.g., the information sources) to another (e.g., the reference model). In the proposed approach, the relationship between the base and the target is made explicitly and declaratively through Correspondence Assertions (CAs). By using the perspective schemata the designer has a formal representation, with well defined semantic, which allows: a) definition of diverse points of views of the (same or different) source information; b) dealing with semantic heterogeneity in a declarative way; and c) reusing (a same perspective schema can used simultaneously in several (application, DW, FDBS) systems.

We propose that the relevant parts (those of the interest to the DW) of all schemata are only aligned to the reference model through perspective schemata, and that any other map (e.g., the direct mapping between the sources and the DW) is automatically (or semi-automatically) created using an inference mechanism. An advantage of the proposed approach is that by using the reference model the designer(s) does (do) not need to map each model. This work is theoretically reduced since schemata (source or global) must only align with the reference model, rather than with each participating schema. Thus, the designer of the DW system (or FDBS) – the DW designer – only needs to describe the mapping between the DW and the reference model, and he/she does not need to be involved with the mapping between the different sources. Traditionally, the DW designer must have the knowledge of all necessary information to build a DW. This includes creation of a DW schema (the global schema) based on user requirements and a deep knowledge of each source information that will be used to populate the DW. Even the followers of Inmon approach [4, 5], which also deal with a reference model, need to report to the the source information when they build Extract, Transform and Load (ETL) processes. We suggest that every time that an operational system is built, its designer is responsible for mapping it (in part or whole) to the reference model. This makes possible a division of responsibility appropriate to the understanding of each designer, as the DW designer only has to deal with the reference model. Therefore, the DW designer can describe the global system without concerns about where the sources are or how they are stored. Furthermore, the mapping between the global schema and its sources are automatically generated by the inference mechanism. We argue that the direct mapping between the sources and the global schema validates the reference model, and promotes its consistency and its coverage. This paper focuses on the deduction of new perspective schemata using a proposed inference mechanism.

The remainder of this paper is laid out as follows. Section 2 concisely mentions representative works in the data integration area. Section 3 presents an overview of the reference model-based framework proposed in [6]. Section 4 briefly describes the language to define the perspective schemata. Section 5 details the process to infer new perspective schemata. The paper ends with Section 6, which points out new features of the approach presented here and for ongoing or planned future works on this topic.

2 Related Work

The database community has been engaged for many years in the problem of data integration. Research in this area has developed in several important directions: schema matching and data quality, to cite a couple (see [7] for a survey), which covers different architectures (e.g., FDBSs and DWs), representation of data and involved data models (e.g., relational and non-structured). Recent research in FDBSs has included: behaviour integration [8], integration of non-traditional data (e.g., biomedical [9, 10], intelligence data [11], and web source [12]), interactive integration of data [13, 14], and federated data warehouse systems [15]. All these approaches use a global schema, but do not deal with a reference model. Similar to the research of this paper, [12] uses correspondence assertions (in this case, for specifying the semantics of XML-based mediators). However, their CAs only deal with part of the semantic correspondence managed here. Furthermore, they assume that there is a universal key to determine when two distinct objects are the same entity in the real-world, which is often an unreal supposition.

Research in DWs has focused on technical aspects such as multidimensional data models (e.g., [16–21]) as well as the materialised view definition and maintenance (e.g., [22]). In particular, the most conceptual multidimensional models are extensions to the Entity-Relationship model (e.g., [23–26]) or extensions to Unified Modeling Language (UML) (e.g., [27–29]).

The work in [30] focuses on an ontology-based approach to determine the mapping between attributes from the source and the DW schemata, as well as identifying the transformations required for correctly moving data from source information to the DW. Their ontology, based on a common vocabulary as well as a set of data annotations (both provided by the designer), allows formal and explicit description of the semantic of the sources and the DW schemata. However, their strategy requires a deep knowledge of all schemata involved in the DW system, which is not the usual case. In our research, it is dispensable, since each schema (source or DW) needs to be related only to the reference model. Additionally, we deal with the matching of instances (i.e., the problem to identify the same instances of the real-world that are differently represented in the diverse schemata), and the work in [30] does not.

The closest approach to our research is described in [31]. Similar to our study, their proposal included a reference model (cited as "enterprise model") designed using an Enriched Entity-Relationship (EER) model. However, unlike our research, all their schemata, including the DW, are formed by relational structures, which are defined as views over the reference model. Their proposal provides the user with various levels of abstraction: conceptual, logical, and physical. In their conceptual level, they introduce the notion of intermodel assertions that precisely capture the structure of an EER schema or allow for the specifying of the relationship between diverse schemata. However, any transformation (e.g., restructuring of schema and values) or mapping of instances is deferred for the logical level, unlike the current work. In addition, they did not deal with complex data, integrity constraints, and path expressions, as our research does.

3 The Framework

The proposal presented in [6] offers a way to express the existing data models (source, reference model, and global/integrated schema) and the relationship between them. The approach is based on *Schema language* (L_S) and *Perspective schema language* (L_{PS}).

The language L_S is used to describe the actual data models (source, reference model, and global/integrated schema). The formal framework focuses on an object-relational paradigm, which includes definitions adopted by the main concepts of object and relational models as they are widely accepted([32, 33]).

The language L_{PS} is used to describe *perspective schemata*. A perspective schema is a special kind of model that describes a data model (part or whole) (*the target*) in terms of other data models (*the base*). In Fig. 1, for instance, $\mathsf{P}_{s'1|RM}$, $\mathsf{P}_{s'2|RM}$, $\mathsf{P}_{s4|RM}$, ..., $\mathbf{P}_{sn|RM}$ are perspective schemata that map the reference model (**RM**) in terms of the sources ($\mathbf{S}'_1$, $\mathbf{S}'_2$, $\mathbf{S}_4$, ..., $\mathbf{S}_n$). L_{PS} mainly extends L_S with two components: CAs and Matching Function (MF) signatures. CAs formally specify the relationship between schema components. MF signatures indicate when two data entities represent the same instance of the real world. L_{PS} includes data transformations, such as names conversion and data types conversion.

Figure 1 illustrates the basic components of the proposed architecture and their relationships. The schemata **RM**, $\mathbf{S}_1$,...,$\mathbf{S}_n$ and **G** are defined using the language L_S and represent, respectively, the reference model, the sources $\mathbf{S}_1$,...,$\mathbf{S}_n$, and a global schema. The schemata $\mathbf{S'}_1$ and $\mathbf{S'}_2$ are defined using the language L_{PS}, and represent, respectively, a viewpoint of $\mathbf{S}_1$ and an integrated viewpoint of $\mathbf{S}_2$ and $\mathbf{S}_3$. $\mathbf{S'}_1$ and $\mathbf{S'}_2$ are special kinds of perspective schemata (called *view schema*), since the target is described in the scope of a perspective schema, instead of just referring to an existing model. The relationships between the target and the base are shown through the perspective schemata $\mathbf{P}_{s'1|RM}$, $\mathbf{P}_{s'2|RM}$,

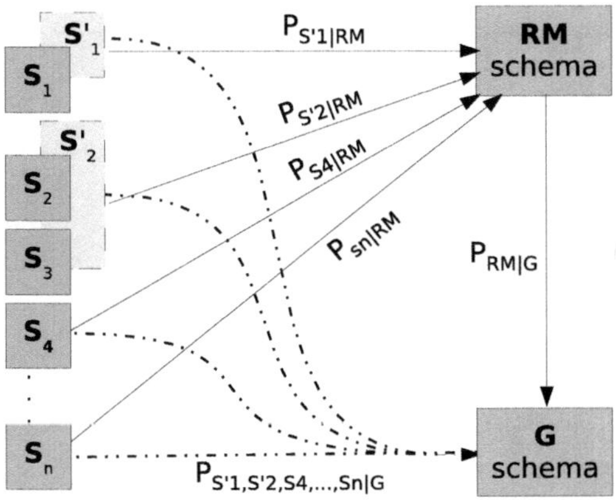

Fig. 1. Proposed architecture

$\mathbf{P}_{s4|RM}$, ..., $\mathbf{P}_{sn|RM}$, $\mathbf{P}_{RM|G}$, and $\mathbf{P}_{s'1,s'2,s4,...,sn|G}$ (denoted by arrows). In the current research, $\mathbf{P}_{s'1,s'2,s4,...,sn|G}$ can be automatically deduced by the proposed inference mechanism. The next Sect. illustrates, through the examples, the language L_{PS}, and the Sect. 5 presents the proposed inference mechanism. For a more detailed and formal description of L_S and L_{PS} languages, the reader is referred to [6, 34, 35].

4 Perspective Schema Language

The remainder of the paper, considers a simple sales scenario comprising two data sources $\mathbf{S}_1$ and $\mathbf{S}_2$, a reference model **RM**, and a global schema **G**. For simplicity, only part of these schemata are shown in Fig. 2. All properties that are key to a relation (or class) are shown in Fig. 2 using "#" before their names.

The language L_{PS}, as we mentioned before, is used to define perspective schemata. A perspective schema is formed by the following components:

1. *Name* is a schema name with the notation: $\mathbf{P}_{\mathbf{B}|\mathbf{T}}$, being **B** the name of one or more schemata (the base) and **T** the name of another schema (the target). In Fig. 1, for instance, $\mathbf{P}_{s'1|RM}$ is a name of a perspective schema whose base is $\mathbf{S}'_1$ and the target is **RM**;
2. *"Require" declarations* express the subset of the components of the target (classes, relations, keys, and foreign keys) that will be used in the perspective schema;
3. *Matching Function signatures* indicate which matching functions must be implemented to determine when two objects/tuples are distinct representations of the same object in the real-world;
4. *Correspondence Assertions* establish the semantic correspondence between schemata's components.

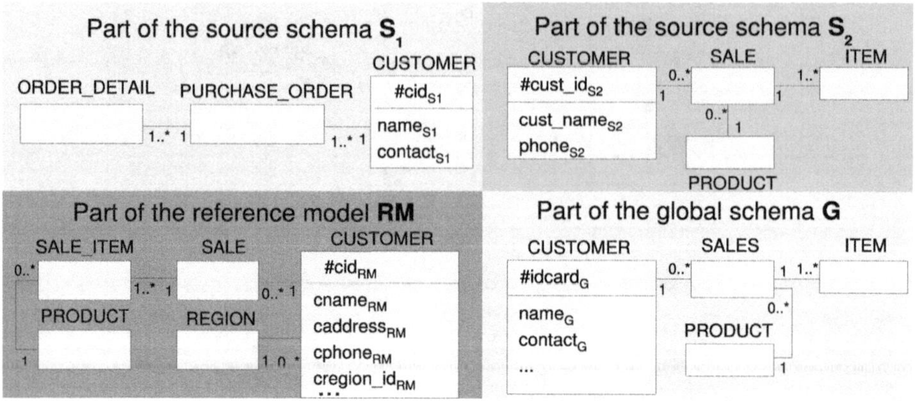

Fig. 2. Motivating example

When a perspective schema is a view schema, the "require" declarations are not defined, rather the components of the view schema are declared in the scope of the perspective schema using the L_S language. Let us see in more detail the components of a perspective schema.

4.1 "Require" Declarations

"Require" declarations explicitly indicate which elements of the target are in the scope of the perspective schema. It is useful, since the target may have much more information than is required to represent in a perspective schema, namely when the target is the reference model. For instance, consider the perspective schema $\mathbf{P}_{\mathbf{S}_2|\mathbf{RM}}$ between the schemata **RM** and $\mathbf{S}_2$, both as presented in Fig. 2. For this perspective schema, four relations from **RM** are needed (PRODUCT, CUSTOMER, SALE, and SALE_ITEM). The "require" declaration to relation CUSTOMER, for example, would be as follows:

$$\text{require}(\text{CUSTOMER}, \{\mathbf{cid}_{\text{RM}}, \mathbf{cname}_{\text{RM}}, \mathbf{cphone}_{\text{RM}}\})$$

Note that, for instance, the properties $\mathbf{cregion\_id}_{\text{RM}}$ and $\mathbf{caddress}_{\text{RM}}$ from **RM**.CUSTOMER are not declared as being required.

"Require" declarations also have an important role in the verification of mapping between schemata. Once all classes, relations, keys and foreign keys are known, it is easy to confirm if all map between the target and the base were done.

4.2 Matching Functions

From a conceptual viewpoint, it is essential to provide a way to identify instances of different models that represent the same entity in the real-world in order to combine them appropriately. This identification (we call it *the instance matching problem*) usually is expensive to compute, due to the complex structure and the character of the data. It is not part of the current research to deal with the full instance matching problem. We assume, usually like the DW designers do, that data quality tools were used and that, for instance, duplicates were removed. Even then, in a data integration context, the instance matching problem still persists. The proposal presented in [6] is using MF signatures, which points to situations that should be considered in a data integration context. These signatures define a 1:1 correspondence between the objects/tuples in families of corresponding classes/relations. In particular, the work shown in [6] is based on the following matching function signature:

$$\mathbf{match} : ((\mathsf{S}_1 \left[\mathrm{R}_1\right], \tau_1) \times (\mathsf{S}_2 \left[\mathrm{R}_2\right], \{\tau_2\})) \rightarrow \mathrm{Boolean} \ , \tag{1}$$

being S_i schema names, R_i class/relation names, and τ_i the data type of the instances of R_i, for i $\in$ {1,2}. When both arguments are instanced, **match** verifies whether two instances are semantically equivalent or not. If only the first argument is instanced (i.e., $\mathsf{S}_1.\mathrm{R}_1$) then it obtains the semantically equivalent $\mathsf{S}_2.\mathrm{R}_2$ instance of the given $\mathsf{S}_1.\mathrm{R}_1$ instance, returning true when it is possible, and false when nothing is found or when there is more than one instance to match. An example of a matching function signature involving schemata of Fig. 2 is as follows:

$$\mathbf{match} : ((\mathsf{RM} \left[\mathrm{CUSTOMER}\right], \tau_1) \times (\mathsf{G} \left[\mathrm{CUSTOMER}\right], \{\tau_2\})) \rightarrow \mathrm{Boolean} \tag{2}$$

In some scenarios one-to-many correspondence between instances are common (e.g., when historical data is stored in the DW). In this case, a variant of **match** should be used, which has the following form:

$$\mathbf{match} : ((\mathsf{S}_1 \left[\mathrm{R}_1\right], \tau_1) \times (\mathsf{S}_2 \left[\mathrm{R}_2 \left(\textsf{\textbf{predicate}}\right)\right], \{\tau_2\})) \rightarrow \mathrm{Boolean} \ . \tag{3}$$

In (3), **predicate** is a boolean condition that determines the context in which the instance matching must be applied in $\mathsf{S}_2.\mathrm{R}_2$, and that ensure the one-to-one correspondence between the instances of both relations or classes ($\mathsf{S}_1.\mathrm{R}_1$ and $\mathsf{S}_2.\mathrm{R}_2$). (3) works similarly than (1), except that only a subset of $\mathsf{S}_2.\mathrm{R}_2$ is evaluated (the set of instances selected by the predicate).

It is not our intention to deal with the full instance matching problem. The MF signatures in a perspective schema only indicate, to a more effective and complete mapping, the situations in which there are instance matching problems and for which must be present implementations. The implementation of the matching functions shall be externally provided, since their implementation is very close to the application domain and to the application itself.

4.3 Correspondence Assertions

The semantic correspondence between schemata's components is declared in the proposal presented in [6] through the CAs, which are used to formally assert the correspondence between schema components in a declarative way. CAs are classified in four groups: Property Correspondence Assertion (PCA), Extension

Table 1. Examples of correspondence assertions

Property Correspondence Assertions (PCAs)
ψ_1: $\mathbf{P}_{\mathbf{RM}\mid\mathbf{G}}$ [CUSTOMER] • **idcard**$_G$ → numberTOtext (**RM** [CUSTOMER] • **cid**$_{RM}$)
ψ_2: $\mathbf{P}_{\mathbf{RM}\mid\mathbf{G}}$ [CUSTOMER] • **contact**$_G$ → **RM** [CUSTOMER] • **cphone**$_{RM}$
Extension Correspondence Assertions (ECAs)
ψ_3: $\mathbf{P}_{\mathbf{RM}\mid\mathbf{G}}$ [CUSTOMER] → **RM** [CUSTOMER]
ψ_4: $\mathbf{S}_v$ [CUSTOMER] → $\mathbf{S}_1$ [CUSTOMER] ⟗ $\mathbf{S}_2$ [CUSTOMER]
Summation Correspondence Assertion (SCA)
ψ_5: $\mathbf{P}_{\mathbf{S}_3\mid\mathbf{RM}}$ [PRODUCT] (**pid**$_{RM}$) → normalise ($\mathbf{S}_3$ [PRODUCT_SALES] (**product_numbers**$_{S3}$))

Correspondence Assertion (ECA), Summation Correspondence Assertion (SCA), and Aggregation Correspondence Assertion (ACA). Examples of CAs are shown in Table 1 and explained in the following text.

PCAs relate properties of the target to the properties of the base. They allow dealing with several kinds of semantic heterogeneity such as: *naming conflict* (for instance synonyms and homonyms properties), *data representation conflict* (that occur when similar contents are represented by different data types), and *encoding conflict* (that occur when similar contents are represented by different formats of data or unit of measures). For example, the PCAs ψ_1 and ψ_2 (see Table 1) deal with, respectively, *data representation conflict* and *naming conflict*. ψ_1 links the property **idcard**$_G$ to the property **cid**$_{RM}$ using the function **numberTOtext** to convert the data type from *number* to *text*. ψ_2 assigns **contact**$_G$ to **cphone**$_{RM}$.

ECAs are used to describe which objects/tuples of the base should have a corresponding semantically equivalent object/tuple in the target. For instance, the relation **G**.CUSTOMER is linked to relation **RM**.CUSTOMER through the ECA ψ_3 presented in Table 1. ψ_3 determines that **G**.CUSTOMER and **RM**.CUSTOMER are equivalent (i.e., for each tuple of CUSTOMER of the schema **RM** there is one semantically equivalent tuple in CUSTOMER of the schema **G**, and vice-versa).

There are five different kinds of ECAs: equivalence, selection, difference, union, and intersection, being the ECA of union similar to the *natural outer-join* of the usual relational models. For instance, consider the view schema $\mathbf{S}_v$ (not presented in any diagram) with the relation CUSTOMER, which is related to the relations CUSTOMER of the schemata $\mathbf{S}_1$ and $\mathbf{S}_2$ through the ECA ψ_4 shown in Table 1. ψ_4 determines that CUSTOMER in $\mathbf{S}_v$ is the union/join of CUSTOMER in $\mathbf{S}_1$ and CUSTOMER in $\mathbf{S}_2$ (i.e., for each tuple in CUSTOMER of $\mathbf{S}_1$ there is one semantically equivalent tuple in CUSTOMER of $\mathbf{S}_v$, or for each tuple in CUSTOMER of $\mathbf{S}_2$ there is one semantically equivalent tuple in CUSTOMER of $\mathbf{S}_v$, and vice-versa). In an ECA, any relation/class can appear with a selection condition, which determines the subset of instances of the class/relation being considered. This kind of ECA is especially important to the DW, because through it the current instances of the DW can be selected and related to the instances of their sources (which usually do not have historical data).

SCAs are used to describe the summary of a class/relation whose instances are related to the instances of another class/relation by breaking them into logical groups that belong together. They are used to indicate that the relationship between classes/relations involve some type of aggregate functions (called SCA of groupby) or a normalisation process (called SCA of normalisation)[1]. For example, consider the source schema $\mathbf{S}_3$ (not presented in any figure), which contains a denormalised relation PRODUCT_SALES(**product_number**$_{S3}$, **product**$_{S3}$, **quantity**$_{S3}$, **price**$_{S3}$, **purchase_order**$_{S3}$) and the schema **RM** presented in Fig. 2. PRODUCT_SALES holds information about sold items in a purchase order as well as information logically related to products themselves, which could be in another relation, as occurring in **RM**. The SCA ψ_5, displayed in Table 1, determines the relationship between PRODUCT_SALES and **RM**.PRODUCT when a normalisation process is involved (i.e., it determines that **RM**.PRODUCT is a normalisation of $\mathbf{S}_3$.PRODUCT_SALES based on distinct values of property **product_number**$_{S3}$).

ACAs link properties of the target to the properties of the base when a SCA is used. ACAs associated to SCAs of groupby contains aggregation functions supported by most of the queries languages, like SQL-99 [36] (i.e., *summation, maximum, minimum, average* and *count*). The ACAs, similar to the PCAs, allow the description of several kinds of situations; therefore, the aggregate expressions can be more detailed than simple property references. Calculations performed can include, for example, ordinary functions (such as sum or concatenate two or more properties' values before applying the aggregate function), and Boolean conditions (e.g., count all male students whose grades are greater to 10).

5 Inference Mechanism

In our proposal, a new perspective schema can be inferred from schemata and perspective schemata. The inference mechanism parameters are:

1. a schema (named *destination* (see Fig. 3(a));
2. another schema (named *intermediary* (see Fig. 3(b));
3. a set of schemata (named *origin*) and perspective schemata (see Fig. 3(c)).

A subset of schemata in the *origin* will be the base of the new perspective schema, while the *destination* will be the target. The *intermediary* here works like a bridge between the *origin* and the *destination*. The perspective schemata are associated to the *destination*, the *intermediary* or to the *origin* in the following way: they take some of the schemata of the *origin* as *base* and the *intermediary* as *target*; or take the *intermediary* as *base* and the *destination* as *target*.

In context of the Fig. 1, the perspective schema $\mathbf{P}_{s'1,s'2,s4,\ldots,sn|G}$ can be inferred taking as destination $\mathbf{G}$, as *intermediary* **RM**, as *origin* the schemata $\mathbf{S}'_1$, $\mathbf{S}'_2$, $\mathbf{S}_4$, ..., $\mathbf{S}_n$, and the perspective schemata $\mathbf{P}_{s'1|RM}$, $\mathbf{P}_{s'2|RM}$, $\mathbf{P}_{s4|RM}$, ..., $\mathbf{P}_{sn|RM}$, $\mathbf{P}_{RM|G}$.

[1] This research also deals with denormalisations, which is defined using *path expressions* (component of the language L_S).

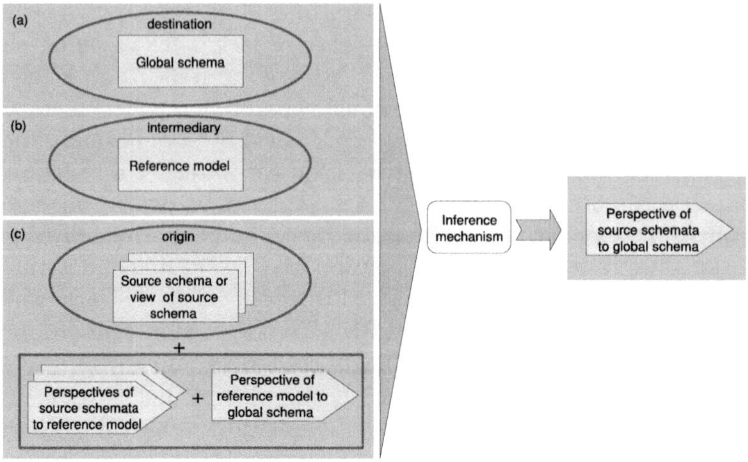

Fig. 3. Sketch of the inference mechanism

The classes, relations, keys and foreign keys of the inferred perspective schema are the same appearing in the *"require" declarations* of the perspective schema associated to the *destination*. The *MF signatures* and *CAs* of the inferred perspective schema will be automatically generated using a rule-based rewriting system, which is described as follows:

5.1 Rewriting Rules

The rule-based rewriting system is formed by a set of rules having the general form:

$$\textbf{Rule}: \frac{X \Rightarrow Y}{Z} \quad \text{(read } X \text{ is rewritten as } Y \text{ if } Z \text{ is valid)} \quad , \tag{4}$$

In (4), **Rule** is the name of the rule. X and Y can be formed by any of the following expressions: a CA pattern expression, a MF pattern signature, or a component pattern expression. CA pattern expressions and MF pattern signatures are expressions conforming to the L_{PS} syntax to declare, respectively, CAs and MF signatures, being that some of their elements are variables to be used in a unification process. Component pattern expressions are expressions conforming to the L_S or the L_{PS} syntax to represent components that can appear in CAs or in MF signatures (e.g., properties, path expressions, functions with n-ary arguments, values, or conditions of selection (predicates)), being that some of their elements are variables to be used in a unification process. Z is a condition formed by a set of CA pattern expressions, a foreign key declaration, or expressions of the form: a) $A \Rightarrow B$ such that A and B are component pattern expressions; b) $\boldsymbol{p}{:}\natural \mathrm{C} \in \boldsymbol{type}(\mathrm{C}')$, such that $\boldsymbol{p}$ is a property name declared in a class/relation C′ that refers to a class C. ***type***() is a function defined in language L_S that returns the type of a relation or class. A condition Z is valid when all of its expressions are valid. More details about it will be shown later.

When X and Y are CA pattern expressions, the rules are rewritten-rules that rewrite CAs in other CAs (RR-CAs). When X and Y are MF pattern signatures, the rules are rewritten-rules that rewrite MF signatures in other MF signatures (RR-MFs). When X and Y are component pattern expressions, the rules are substitution-rules that rewrite components in other components (SR-Cs). The latter are used as an *intermediary* process by the RR-CAs and RR-MFs.

An example of a RR-CA is as follows:

$$\mathbf{RR\text{-}CA1}: \frac{\mathrm{P}_{\mathrm{I|D}}\left[\underline{\mathrm{C}^{\mathrm{D}}}\right] \rightarrow \mathrm{I}\left[\underline{\mathrm{C}^{\mathrm{I}}}\right] \Rightarrow \mathrm{P}_{\underline{S}|\mathrm{D}}\left[\underline{\mathrm{C}^{\mathrm{D}}}\right] \rightarrow \underline{\mathbf{K}^{\mathrm{S}}}}{\mathrm{P}_{\underline{S}|\mathrm{I}}\left[\underline{\mathrm{C}^{\mathrm{I}}}\right] \rightarrow \underline{\mathbf{K}^{\mathrm{S}}}} . \tag{5}$$

In (5), all variables are indicated by an underline. **D** is the *destination*, **I** is the *intermediary*, and **S** is a variable that will be instantiated with some *origin* schemata. C^D is a variable that will be instantiated with a class/relation of **D**; mutatis mutandis to C^I. **K** is a variable that will be instantiated with the right side of a CA pattern expression of extension. The letter "S" in $\mathbf{K}^S$ means that all elements in that expression belong to schema in **S**. The value of **S** and **K** will depend on which CA (declared in the perspective schema associated to some *origin* schemata) will unify with the condition of the rule. The notation in (5) will be used through the paper to explain examples of rules.

The rule **RR-CA1** rewrites an ECA of equivalence in another ECA (maybe other than equivalence) by replacing a class/relation of the *intermediary* (C^I) by one class/relation (or an expression containing classes/relations) of the *origin* schemata ($\mathbf{K}^S$); when is provided an ECA that connects the class/relation C^I to $\mathbf{K}^S$.

An example of a RR-MF is as follows:

$$\mathbf{RR\text{-}MF1}: \frac{\begin{array}{c}\mathbf{match}: \left(\left(\mathrm{I}\left[\underline{\mathrm{C}^{\mathrm{I}}}\right], \underline{\tau^{\mathrm{I}}}\right) \times \left(\mathrm{D}\left[\underline{\mathrm{C}^{\mathrm{D}}}\right], \underline{\tau^{\mathrm{D}}}\right)\right) \rightarrow \mathrm{Boolean} \Rightarrow \\ \mathbf{match}: \left(\left(\underline{\mathbf{S}}\left[\underline{\mathrm{C}^{\mathrm{S}}}\right], \underline{\tau^{\mathrm{S}}}\right) \times \left(\mathrm{D}\left[\underline{\mathrm{C}^{\mathrm{D}}}\right], \underline{\tau^{\mathrm{D}}}\right)\right) \rightarrow \mathrm{Boolean}\end{array}}{\mathrm{P}_{\underline{S}|\mathrm{I}}\left[\underline{\mathrm{C}^{\mathrm{I}}}\right] \rightarrow \underline{\mathbf{S}}\left[\underline{\mathrm{C}^{\mathrm{S}}}\right]} . \tag{6}$$

In (6), τ is a data type. The rule **RR-MF1** rewrites a MF signature that matches a class/relation C^I to a class/relation C^D, into a MF signature that matches a class/relation C^S to C^D, when is provided an ECA of equivalence that connects C^I to C^S.

An example of a SR-C is as follows:

$$\mathbf{SR\text{-}C1}: \frac{\mathrm{I}\left[\underline{\mathrm{C}^{I}}\right] \bullet \underline{\boldsymbol{p}^{\mathrm{I}}} \Rightarrow \underline{\mathbf{A}^{\mathrm{S}}}}{\mathrm{P}_{\underline{S}|\mathrm{I}}\left[\underline{\mathrm{C}^{\mathrm{I}}}\right] \bullet \underline{\boldsymbol{p}^{\mathrm{I}}} \rightarrow \underline{\mathbf{A}^{\mathrm{S}}}} . \tag{7}$$

In (7), $\boldsymbol{p}^I$ is a variable that will be instantiated with a property of a class/relation of the *intermediary* (here the symbol "•" means that $\boldsymbol{p}^I$ is defined in C^I). **A** is a variable that will be instantiated with a component pattern expression. Similar to $\mathbf{K}^{\mathrm{S}}$ in (5), the letter "S" in $\mathbf{A}^{\mathrm{S}}$ means that all elements into that expression belong to schema S. The value of S and $\mathbf{A}$ will depend on which CA declared in the perspective schema associated to some *origin* schemata will unify with the condition of the rule.

The rule **SR-C1** rewrites a property $\boldsymbol{p}^{\mathrm{I}}$ of the *intermediary* into a property, a path expression, or a function of some *origin* schema (here represented by variable $\mathbf{A}^{\mathrm{S}}$); when is provided an PCA that connects $\boldsymbol{p}^{\mathrm{I}}$ to that property, path expression, or function.

We define about 39 rules in our proposal, being 21 RR-CAs, 6 RR-MFs, and 12 SR-Cs. The whole set of proposed rules can be found in [37].

5.2 Inference

A simplified pseudo-code with the iteration of the process to generate a new perspective schema by using the proposed inference mechanism is shown in Algorithm 1.

Algorithm 1. generateNewPerspective(D,I,$\{\mathsf{S}_1, ..., \mathsf{S}_m, P_{\mathrm{D}}, P_1, ..., P_m\}, P_N$)

1: `for each` $CA\ A^{\mathrm{D}} \to A^{\mathrm{I}}$ `in` $P_{\mathrm{D}}.caList$ `do`
2: `infer_CAs(`$A^{\mathrm{D}} \to A^{\mathrm{I}}, \{A^{\mathrm{D}} \to A^{\mathsf{Si}}\}$`);`
3: `add` $CAs\ A^{\mathrm{D}} \to A^{\mathsf{Si}}$ `to` $P_N.caList$;
4: `end for`
5: `for each` $MF\ m$ `in` $P_{\mathrm{D}}.mfList$ `do`
6: `infer_MFs(`$m, \{m'_i\}$`);`
7: `add` $MFs\ m'_i$ `to` $P_N.mfList$
8: `end for`
9: `for each` E `in` $classList/relationList/keyList$ `do`
10: `create a ''require'' declaration to` P_N;
11: `add it, appropriately, to` $P_N.classList/$
12: $P_N.relationList/P_N.keyList$
13: `end for`

In Algorithm 1, D is the *destination*, I is the *intermediary*, S_j, $1 \leq \mathrm{j} \leq \mathrm{m}$, are the *origin* schemata, P_{D} is the perspective schema from the *intermediary* to the *destination*; P_j, $1 \leq \mathrm{j} \leq \mathrm{m}$, are perspective schemata from the *origin* to the *intermediary*; and P_N is the inferred perspective schema from the (subset of) *origin* to the *destination*. All elements of the perspective schemata are grouped in lists: $classList$, $relationList$, $keyList$, $caList$, and $mfList$. The three first lists hold "require" declarations of, respectively, classes, relations, and keys (including foreign keys). $caList$ contains CA declarations, and $mfList$ has MF signatures. Firstly, in the Algorithm 1, new CAs are inferred from CAs defined in P_{D} (lines 1 to 4). The CAs in $P_{\mathrm{D}}.caList$ are firstly organised in accordance to class/relation which them belong, then by their types: ECAs, PCAs, ACAs, and SCAs (in this order). Then, one by one the CAs in $P_{\mathrm{D}}.caList$ are used by the procedure to rewrite CAs (**infer_CAs**) as a start point to create new CAs to P_N. After, new MF signatures to P_N can be created from MF signatures defined in P_{D} (lines 5 to 8), using the procedure to rewrite MF signatures (**infer_MFs**). Finally, new "require" declarations are generated from the "require" declarations of P_{D} (lines 9 to 13), by adding all "require" declarations of P_{D} to P_N. A simplified pseudo-code description of the process to generate new CAs is shown in Algorithm 2.

Algorithm 2. infer_CAs($A^{\mathrm{D}} \rightarrow A^{\mathrm{I}}$,$CAs$)

```
repeat
    find A^D → A^S applying the inference rule R:
    R: (A^D → A^I ⇒ A^D → A^S) / condition
    add A^D → A^S to CAs
until all rules for rewriting CAs have been tested
```

In Algorithm 2, D is the *destination*, I the *intermediary*, and **S**, any of the *origin* schemata. The algorithm tries to find, for each CA of the general form $A^{\mathrm{D}} \rightarrow A^{\mathrm{I}}$ (assigning the *destination* to the *intermediary*), one or more CAs $A^{\mathrm{D}} \rightarrow A^{\mathrm{S}}$ (assigning the *destination* to an *origin* schema) as a result of applying to $A^{\mathrm{D}} \rightarrow A^{\mathrm{I}}$ a rule for rewriting CAs, since the condition of the rule is valid.

The condition of a rule is valid when all of its expressions are valid:

1. a CA pattern expression is valid if there is a CA $A^{\mathrm{S}} \rightarrow A^{\mathrm{I}}$ (and in some cases also $A^{\mathrm{I}} \rightarrow A^{\mathrm{D}}$), which unifies with it;
2. a foreign key is valid if it is required (or defined, in case of the view schemata) in one of the perspective schemata associated with the *origin*;
3. an expression of the form $A \Rightarrow B$, such that A and B are component pattern expressions, is valid if there is a rule which unifies with it and which is recursively applied;
4. an expression $\boldsymbol{p}{:}\natural\mathrm{C} \in \boldsymbol{type}(\mathrm{C}')$ is valid if $\boldsymbol{p}$ is required (or defined, in case of the view schemata) in one of the perspective schemata associated with the *origin*, such that $\boldsymbol{p}$ is defined in C' and $\boldsymbol{p}$ points to C.

The rules are defined in an ordered way in order to reduce the search space. The choice of which rule to use is made by the Prolog unification mechanism. All rules, whose CA $A^{\mathrm{D}} \rightarrow A^{\mathrm{I}}$ unifies with the CA pattern expression above left of the rule, are used, being that each one can create a new CA. Notice that, within the condition of the rule, can exist expressions of the form $A \Rightarrow B$. In this case, the recursivity will be present. Only the Prolog backtracking mechanism is used. An example follows below:

Consider the schemata of Fig. 2 and its associated perspective schemata, being **G** the *destination*, **RM** the *intermediary*, and S_1 and S_2 the *origin* schemata. Consider also the CAs shown in Table 2.

Table 2. More examples of correspondence assertions

Extension Correspondence Assertion (ECA)
ψ_6: $\mathsf{P}_{\mathsf{S1}\vert\mathsf{RM}}$ [CUSTOMER] $\rightarrow$ **S1** [CUSTOMER]
ψ_7: $\mathsf{P}_{\mathsf{S2}\vert\mathsf{RM}}$ [CUSTOMER] $\rightarrow$ **S2** [CUSTOMER]

A new ECA: $\mathsf{P}_{\mathsf{S1}|\mathsf{G}}$ [CUSTOMER] $\rightarrow$ **S1** [CUSTOMER] can be created based on ψ_3 (see Table 1) by using the rule **RR-CA1**. Observe that ψ_3 unifies with the CA pattern expression above left of the **RR-CA1** and ψ_6 unifies with its condition.

The process to create new MF signatures has similarities to the creation of new CAs. However, in the latter can exist compositions of CAs, while in the former there is no composition of MF signatures, just all references to a class/relation of the *intermediary* are changed to a class/relation of an *origin* schemata. A pseudo-code detailing as new MF signatures are deduced is shown in Algorithm 3.

Algorithm 3. infer_MFs(**match**:(**K**×**L**)→Boolean ,MFs)

```
repeat
    find match:(K'×L')→Boolean applying the inference rule R:
    R: match:(K×L)→Boolean⇒match:(K'×L')→Boolean / condition ;
    add match:(K'×L') → Boolean to MFs;
until all rules for rewriting MFs have been tested
```

In Algorithm 3, **K** and **L** are pairs (classes/relations, data type) of the *intermediary* or of the *destination*, while **K**′ and **L**′ are pairs (classes/relations, data type) of some *origin* schema or of the *destination*. For each MF signature **M** that is declared in the perspective schema associated to the *destination*, the algorithm tries to find one or more MF signatures as a result of applying to **M** some rule for rewriting MF signatures. For instance, two new MF signatures:

match:((**S1**[CUSTOMER],τ_1)×(**G**[CUSTOMER],{τ_2}))→Boolean
match:((**S2**[CUSTOMER],τ_1)×(**G**[CUSTOMER],{τ_2}))→Boolean

can be created based on MF signature presented in (2) by using the rule **RR-MF1** twice. Note that, the MF signature 2 unifies with the MF pattern signature above left of the **RR-MF1**, and there are two CAs in Table 2 (ψ_6 and ψ_7) that unifies with the condition of this rule.

5.3 Implementation Details

This mechanism has been developed as part of a proof-of-concept prototype using a Prolog language. Beside the inference mechanism module, the prototype consists of another five cooperating modules: the *schema manager*, the *ISCO translator*, the *ISCO-generated applications*, the *schema repository*, and the *ISCO repository*. The architecture of the prototype is depicted in Fig. 4.

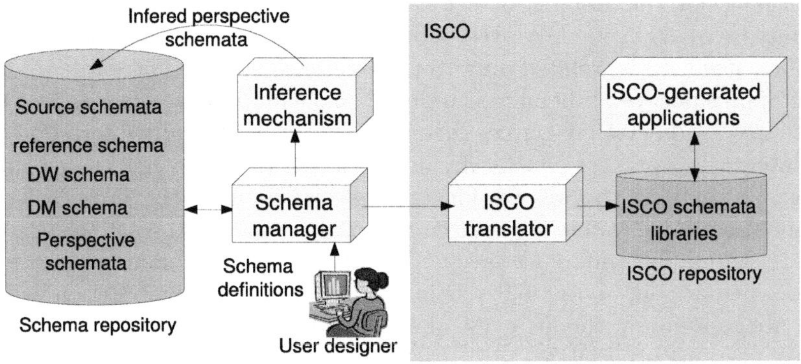

Fig. 4. Prototype architecture

The *schema manager* module is employed by the designer to manage the schemata (in language L_S) as well as the perspective schemata (in language L_{PS}). The designer, using the *schema manager*, should define all source schemata, the data warehouse schema, the reference model schema, and perspective schemata that he/she needs. The *ISCO translator* performs the mapping between schemata written in L_S or L_{PS} languages to schemata defined in a language programming called Information Systems Construction (ISCO) language [38]. ISCO is based on a contextual constraint logic programming that allows the construction of information systems. It can define (object) relational schemata, represent data, and transparently access data from various heterogeneous sources in a uniform way, like a mediator system [39]. The *ISCO-generated applications* includes all files that are necessary to access data from information sources. So, data in any perspective schema mapped to ISCO, specifically any inferred perspective schema between the DW and its sources, can be queried in a transparent way, just as in a mediator approach. The *schema repository* stores both the schemata (in language L_S) and perspective schemata (in language L_{PS}), including any inferred perspective schema created by the inference mechanism. The *ISCO repository* is used to store ISCO schemata and ISCO files (libraries, units, etc.). Details about the prototype can be found in [40].

6 Conclusions and Future Works

We have presented a proposal to automatically connect a global schema to its sources by using an inference mechanism taking into account the explicit mappings between the sources and a reference model. The proposed approach makes clear the mappings that there are in a DW system, and uncouples them in order to make their maintenance easier. Besides, the relationship between the global schema and the source schemata is made explicitly and declaratively through correspondence assertions.

Our approach is particularly useful in data integration systems that define a common or canonical schema, such as in DW systems and in FDBSs. By using the reference model, the designer does not need to have an in depth knowledge of all schemata involved in the DW system or in the FDBSs, since each schema (source or global) needs to be related only to the reference model. The effort to describe the mappings between schemata is reduced, since mappings between the DW and each source (and between sources themselves) is automatically inferred. Thus the data integration process can be divided in small parts, rather than being seen as a whole, making the integration task easier. Besides, the DW designer can describe the global system without concerns about where the sources are or how they are stored. The inference mechanism also allows that changes in the actual source schemata, in the global schema, or in the mapping between schemata, which are common in the life cycle of any system, are completely transparent to the DW systems (or FDBSs).

A prototype, Prolog-based, has been developed to allow the description of schemata and perspective schemata in the proposed language as well as to infer new perspective schemata based on other ones. The matching functions can be implemented using Prolog itself or external functions. In addition, the prototype includes translators from the proposed language to the ISCO one. ISCO [38] allows access to heterogeneous data sources and to perform arbitrary computations. Thus, user-queries can be done, in a transparent way, to access the information sources, as occurs in mediator systems [39].

For future work, investigations will be made into how the perspective schemata can be used to automate the materialisation of the data in the DWs or in another repository of a data integration environment. Another important direction for future work is the development of a graphical user-friendly interface to declare the schemata in the proposed language, and thus, to hide some syntax details.

References

1. Imhoff, C., Galemmo, N., Geiger, J.G.: Mastering Data Warehouse Design - Relational and Dimensional Techniques. Wiley Publishing, Chichester (2003)
2. Geiger, J.G.: Why build a data model? Information Management Magazine (2009)
3. Moody, D.L.: From enterprise models to dimensional models: A methodology for data warehouse and data mart design. In: Proc. of the Intl. Workshop on Design and Management of Data Warehouses (2000)
4. Inmon, W.H., Imhoff, C., Sousa, R.: Corporate Information Factory, 2nd edn. John Wiley & Sons, Chichester (2001)
5. Inmon, W., Strauss, D., Neushloss, G.: DW 2.0: the architecture for the next generalization of data warehousing. Morgan Kaufmann, San Francisco (2008)
6. Pequeno, V.M., Pires, J.C.G.M.: Using perspective schemata to model the ETL process. In: Intl. Conf. on Management Information Systems, France (June 2009)
7. Halevy, A.Y., Rajaraman, A., Ordille, J.J.: Data integration: The teenage years. In: VLDB, pp. 9–16 (2006)
8. Stumptner, M., Schrefl, M., Grossmann, G.: On the road to behavior-based integration. In: First Asia-Pacific Conf. on Conceptual Modelling, pp. 15–22 (2004)
9. Louie, B., Mork, P., Martin-Sanchez, F., Halevy, A., Tarczy-Hornoch, P.: Data integration and genomic medicine. Journal of Biomedical Informatics 40, 5–13 (2007)

10. Naidu, P.G., Palakal, M.J., Hartanto, S.: On-the-fly data integration models for biological databases. In: Proc. of the 2007 ACM Symp. on Applied Computing, pp. 118–122. ACM, USA (2007)
11. Yoakum-Stover, S., Malyuta, T.: Unified architecture for integrating intelligence data. In: DAMA: Europe Conf., UK (2008)
12. Vidal, V.M.P., Lóscio, B.F., Salgado, A.C.: Using correspondence assertions for specifying the semantics of XML-based mediators. In: Workshop on Information Integration on the Web, pp. 3–11 (2001)
13. Ives, Z.G., Knoblock, C.A., Minton, S., Jacob, M., Talukdar, P.P., Tuchinda, R., Ambite, J.L., Muslea, M., Gazen, C.: Interactive data integration through smart copy & paste. In: 4th Biennial Conf. on Innovative Data Systems Research (2009)
14. Mccann, R., Doan, A., Varadarajan, V., Kramnik, E.: Building data integration systems via mass collaboration. In: Intl. Workshop on the Web and Databases, USA (2003)
15. Berger, S., Schrefl, M.: From federated databases to a federated data warehouse system. In: 41st Annual Hawaii Intl. Conf. on System Sciences. IEEE Computer Society, USA (2008)
16. Dori, D., Feldman, R., Sturm, A.: From conceptual models to schemata: An object-process-based data warehouse construction method. Inf. Syst. 33(6), 567–593 (2008)
17. Malinowski, E., Zimányi, E.: A conceptual model for temporal data warehouses and its transformation to the ER and the object-relational models. Data Knowl. Eng. 64(1), 101–133 (2008)
18. Pérez, J.M., Berlanga, R., Aramburu, M.J., Pedersen, T.B.: A relevance-extended multi-dimensional model for a data warehouse contextualized with documents. In: Proc. of the 8th ACM Intl. Workshop on Data Warehousing and OLAP, pp. 19–28. ACM, USA (2005)
19. Golfarelli, M., Maniezzo, V., Rizzi, S.: Materialization of fragmented views in multidimensional databases. Data Knowl. Eng. 49(3), 325–351 (2004)
20. Husemann, B., Lechtenborger, J., Vossen, G.: Conceptual data warehouse modeling. In: Design and Management of Data Warehouses (2000)
21. Rizzi, S.: Conceptual modeling solutions for the data warehouse. In: Data Warehousing and Mining: Concepts, Methodologies, Tools, and Applications (2008); 208–227, copyright, by Information Science Reference, formerly known as Idea Group Reference (an imprint of IGI Global)
22. Wrembel, R.: On a formal model of an object-oriented database with views supporting data materialisation. In: Proc. of the Conf. on Advances in Databases and Information Systems, pp. 109–116 (1999)
23. Franconi, E., Kamble, A.: A data warehouse conceptual data model. In: Proc. of the 16th Intl. Conf. on Scientific and Statistical Database Management, pp. 435–436. IEEE Computer Society, USA (2004)
24. Kamble, A.S.: A conceptual model for multidimensional data. In: Proc. of the 15th on Asia-Pacific Conf. on Conceptual Modelling, pp. 29–38. Australian Computer Society, Inc., Australia (2008)
25. Sapia, C., Blaschka, M., Höfling, G., Dinter, B.: Extending the E/R model for the multidimensional paradigm. In: Proc. of the Workshops on Data Warehousing and Data Mining, pp. 105–116 (1999)
26. Tryfona, N., Busborg, F., Christiansen, J.G.B.: starER: a conceptual model for data warehouse design. In: Proc. of the 2nd ACM Intl. Workshop on Data Warehousing and OLAP, pp. 3–8. ACM, USA (1999)

27. Luján-Mora, S., Trujillo, J., Song, I.Y.: A UML profile for multidimensional modelling in data warehouses. Data Knowl. Eng. 59(3), 725–769 (2005)
28. Nguyen, T.B., Tjoa, A.M., Wagner, R.R.: An object oriented multidimensional data model for OLAP. In: Lu, H., Zhou, A. (eds.) WAIM 2000. LNCS, vol. 1846, pp. 69–82. Springer, Heidelberg (2000)
29. Trujillo, J., Palomar, M., Gómez, J.: Applying object-oriented conceptual modeling techniques to the design of multidimensional databases and OLAP applications. In: Lu, H., Zhou, A. (eds.) WAIM 2000. LNCS, vol. 1846, pp. 83–94. Springer, Heidelberg (2000)
30. Skoutas, D., Simitsis, A.: Designing ETL processes using semantic web technologies. In: DOLAP 2006: Proceedings of the 9th ACM International Workshop on Data Warehousing and OLAP, pp. 67–74. ACM, USA (2006)
31. Calvanese, D., Dragone, L., Nardi, D., Rosati, R., Trisolini, S.M.: Enterprise modeling and data warehousing in TELECOM ITALIA. Inf. Syst. 31(1), 1–32 (2006)
32. Codd, E.F.: A relational model of data for large shared data banks. Communications of the ACM, 377–387 (1970)
33. Cattell, R.G., Barry, D. (eds.): The Object Database Standard ODMG 3.0. Morgan Kaufmann Publishers, San Francisco (2000)
34. Pequeno, V.M., Pires, J.C.G.M.: A formal object-relational data warehouse model. Technical report, Universidade Nova de Lisboa (November 2007)
35. Pequeno, V.M., Pires, J.C.G.M.: Using perspective schemata to model the ETL process. Technical report, Universidade Nova de Lisboa (2009)
36. Elmasri, R., Navathe, S.B.: Fundamentals of database systems, 5th edn. Addison Wesley, Reading (2006)
37. Pequeno, V.M., Pires, J.C.G.M.: Reference model and perspective schemata inference for enterprise data integration. Technical report, Universidade Nova de Lisboa (2009)
38. Abreu, S., Nogueira, V.: Using a logic programming language with persistence and contexts. In: Umeda, M., Wolf, A., Bartenstein, O., Geske, U., Seipel, D., Takata, O. (eds.) INAP 2005. LNCS (LNAI), vol. 4369, pp. 38–47. Springer, Heidelberg (2006)
39. Wiederhold, G.: Mediators in the architecture of future information systems. Computer 25(3), 38–49 (1992)
40. Pequeno, V.M., Abreu, S., Pires, J.C.G.M.: Using contextual logic programming language to acess data in warehousing systems. In: 14th Portuguese Conference on Artificial Intelligence, Portugal (October 2009)

JSquash: Source Code Analysis of Embedded Database Applications for Determining SQL Statements

Dietmar Seipel, Andreas M. Boehm, and Markus Fröhlich

University of Würzburg, Department of Computer Science
Am Hubland, D–97074 Würzburg, Germany
seipel@informatik.uni-wuerzburg.de,
ab@andiboehm.de,
markus.froehlich1@gmx.de

Abstract. In this paper, we analyse Java source code of embedded database applications by means of static code analysis. If the underlying database schema of such an application is subject to refactoring or database tuning, then the SQL statements in the embedding Java program need to be adapted correspondingly. This should be done mostly automatically, since changing software manually is error–prone and time consuming.

For determining the SQL statements that access the database, we can either look at the database logfile, an audit file, or at the Java source code itself. Here, we show how to derive the strings of dynamic SQL statements directly from the Java source code. We do this without using a debugger or a virtual machine technique; instead, we trace the values of variables that contribute to a query string backwards to predict the values of contributing program variables as precisely as possible.

We use PROLOG's declarative features and its backtracking mechanism for code analysis, refactoring, and tuning.

1 Introduction

During the software life–cycle, enterprise–class databases undergo a lot of changes in order to keep up with the ever–changing requirements. The growing space requirements and complexity of productive databases make the task of maintaining a good performance of the database query execution more and more complicated. The performance is highly dependent on the database schema design [16], and additionally, a complex database schema is more prone to design errors.

Increasing the performance and the manageability of a database usually requires analysing and restructuring the database schema and therefore affects the application code indirectly. The application code highly depends on the database schema, because the database queries are embedded in the source code. Usually, they are contained in string variables or, more dynamically, statements are generated step by step by using control structures and string concatenations. Nearly any type of database schema modification implies the adaption of the queries embedded in the application code. Sometimes, the logic of the construction of the query strings has to be changed, too. Some efforts have been made to prescind the applications code from the data persistence in the database [13]. The employed methods require a configuration that tells the database

S. Abreu and D. Seipel (Eds.): INAP 2009, LNAI 6547, pp. 153–169, 2011.

service the mapping between database tables and application objects. Moreover, the relationships between the tables must also be included in that configuration. Therefore, such approaches are also affected by database changes and need to be adjusted accordingly.

We have developed a standardized XML representation of SQL statements and database schemas named SQUASHML, that was introduced within the PROLOG based toolset Squash for *refactoring* and *tuning* relational database applications [2]. Squash is the first tool that supports the analysis and the refactoring of database applications with coordinated simultaneous modification of the SQL code and the database schema definition. Squash also detects inconsistencies and common flaws in SQL statements. It can determine an optimized configuration of indexes as well as of tables, and propose modifications of the database schema that result in an efficiency gain. The changes are applied automatically to both the schema and the SQL statements.

In this paper, we develop an extension of Squash named JSquash that analyses a given Java source code and presents all expressions in the code that influence the construction of the embedded SQL statements. Our approach estimates or even determines the values of variables in the source code of the databases application by static code analyis; this is used to predict the dynamic and static database queries that can be generated by the application.

Related research on *source code analysis* has mainly focussed on static analyis providing information about security issues (secure code) [4,10], model extraction [12], code smells [9], obvious errors [15,17], code metrics [7], flow analysis [6], design patterns [19], call graph analysis [8], and clone recognition [22]. An interactive, scalable, declarative program analysis has been proposed in [1]. Other approaches are supporting the complex task of understanding the run–time behaviour of legacy and non–legacy software systems [7,21]. An extensive amount of research has been dedicated to system analysis by extracting information generated during the run–time of a software system [7]. These approaches require the code being instrumented prior to execution by various techniques, such as wrapping, logging, or extended virtual machines. The output of such an analysis is an execution trace containing information about the run–time behaviour of the system, such as call hierarchies of methods and object creation. Such traces of productive software systems are often very voluminous, and usually the values of interesting variables are missing.

In contrast, our approach focusses on the detection of the parts of the source code that contribute to the construction of embedded SQL statements based on a sophisticated code analysis.

The rest of the paper is organized as follows: Section 2 summarizes the basic concepts of managing source code with PROLOG in the JSquash repository. Section 3 describes some basic methods of static code analysis supported by JSquash, such as the calculation of metrics and the detection of code smells. Section 4 presents the strategies of JSquash used for recursively evaluating the control flow of the source code in order to determine values of variables contributing to embedded SQL statements at run–time. Section 5 shows how JSquash can visualise the creation of embedded SQL statements using HTML 4, CSS, and JavaScript technology, and how Squash can visualise join conditions of complex SELECT statements. Finally, Section 6 summarizes our work.

2 Management of Java Source Code with PROLOG

The first step of the process consists of parsing the Java code followed by a transformation into the XML representation JAML [11], that provides all syntactic information about the source code. Subsequently, a source code *repository* is derived that suitably represents the constructs of the analysed programming language. It is essential to choose an adequate format for the repository, such that the analysis can handle the data as efficiently as possible. The analysis is implemented using the declarative logic programming system SWI–PROLOG [5,23].

2.1 Representation of Java Source Code in XML

The XML representation JAML completely resembles the Java source code; it even conserves the layout of the source code. JAML enables standardised access to the source code. Generally, XML is a markup language for representing hierarchically structured data, which is often used for the exchange of data between different applications; as a particular XML language, JAML is a very good candidate for an intermediate representation during the creation of the repository out of the Java source code. It comes with a plugin that can be installed as an online update in the integrated development environment Eclipse, that performs the transformation from Java to XML on–the–fly while programming. For each type of expressions, i.e., variables, statements, and control structures, there is a special XML element in JAML, which holds the hierarchical design of the program as well as detailed information about the represented Java component.

According to the W3C XML 1.1 recommendation, the terseness in XML markup is of minimal importance, and JAML increases the volume by a factor of about 50. To meet our requirements, the contained information has to be condensed; e.g., the single indenting white spaces are of no interest for JSquash.

For example, the Java variable declaration `int a = 5`, that additionally includes an initialisation, is presented in JAML, as shown in the listing below; for clarity, the representation has been strongly simplified. The Java declaration is represented by a `variable-declaration-statement` element in JAML. The included `type` element sets the data type of the variable `a` to integer. The assignment is represented by the `variable-declaration` subelement: the identifier of the variable is given by the `identifier` element, and the literal expression is given by an `expression` element.

```
<variable-declaration-statement>
  <type kind="primitive-type">
    <primitive-type>
      <int>int</int>
    </primitive-type>
  </type> <whitespace/>
  <variable-declaration-list>
    <variable-declaration>
      <identifier>a</identifier> <whitespace/>
```

```
      <initializer>
        <equal>=</equal> <whitespace/>
        <expression>
          <literal-expression type-ref-"int">
            <literal>
              <number-literal>5</number-literal>
            </literal>
          </literal-expression>
        </expression>
      </initializer>
    </variable-declaration>
  </variable-declaration-list>
</variable-declaration-statement>
```

For deriving the JSquash repository, the JAML data are represented in field notation and processed using the XML query, transformation, and update language FNQuery [18,20]. The query part of the language resembles an extension of the well–known XML query language XQuery [3]; but FNQuery is implemented in and fully interleaved with PROLOG. The usual axes of XPath are provided for selection and modification of XML documents. Moreover, FNQuery embodies transformation features, which go beyond XSLT, and also update features.

2.2 The JSquash Repository

The JSquash repository stores the relevant elements of the Java code, which are extracted from the JAML representation, in the form of PROLOG facts. These facts represent information that at least consists of the type and a description of the location within the source code including the locations of the surrounding code blocks. Additionally, necessary parameters can be added, depending on the type.

The construct of a *path* reflects the hierarchy of the code nesting. A path starts with the file number of the source code; the further elements of the path are derived from the position attributes (`pos`) of the JAML representation.

The JSquash repository supports access to variables, objects, classes as well as method calls. E.g., a variable declaration is represented in the repository using a fact

```
jsquash_repository(
   Path:'variable-declaration', Type, Id, P:T).
```

where `Path` is the path of the statement, `Type` is the type and `Id` is the name of the variable, and `P:T` is an optional reference to the in–place initialisation.

As an example, the representation of the following fragment of a Java source code, which starts at position `101` in the Java source file, in the JSquash repository will be explained in more detail.

```
1: int a = 5;
2: int b = 10;
3: int c = a + b;
4: int d = c;
```

Due to surrounding blocks and preceeding statements, all paths have the common prefix "`0, 49, 3, 49, 94`", which we abbreviate by "`...`". Since "a" starts at position `105` and "5" starts at position `109`, the declaration "`int a = 5`" in line 1 is represented by the two facts:

```
jsquash_repository(
   [..., 105]:'variable-declaration', int, a,
   [..., 105, 109]:'literal-expression').
jsquash_repository(
   [..., 105, 109]:'literal-expression', int, 5).
```

The type `variable-declaration` requires two parameters: the type of the variable and its name. In this example, the in–place initialisation with the value "5" is represented in the repository by the path of that expression as a reference, here `[..., 105, 109]`, together with the fact of the referenced expression. Such expressions are represented in JSquash by the type `literal-expression`.

The source code of line 2 is represented by two similar facts, where "5" is replaced by "`10`", "`105`" is replaced by "`119`", and "`109`" is replaced by "`123`".

Line 3 is more complex, because it contains the sum of `a` and `b` in the initialisation, a binary expression that comes in the repository as the type `binary-expression`.

```
jsquash_repository(
   [..., 134]:'variable-declaration', int, c,
   [..., 134, 138]:'binary-expression').
jsquash_repository(
   [..., 134, 138]:'binary-expression',
   [..., 134, 138, 138]:'variable-access-expression', +,
   [..., 134, 138, 142]:'variable-access-expression').
jsquash_repository(
   [..., 134, 138, 138]:'variable-access-expression', a).
jsquash_repository(
   [..., 134, 138, 142]:'variable-access-expression', b).
```

The reference of the declaration fact points to the description of the binary expression, which holds two references, one for the left and one for the right expression; in our case, both are accesses to variables.

Line 4 contains an access to a variable instead of a literal expression. This is represented in the repository by the type `variable-access-expression`, which works like `literal-expression`, but it has no qualifier for local variables – as in our example.

```
jsquash_repository(
   [..., 152]:'variable-declaration', int, d,
   [..., 152, 156]:'variable-access-expression').
jsquash_repository(
   [..., 152, 156]:'variable-access-expression', c).
```

In this paper, the notation described above is used for convenience to improve the readability of rules refering to the repository. For *efficiency* reasons, however, we store other facts with the predicate symbols `jsquash_repository_/3,4,5` in the repository; then we can make use of the index on the first argument to search for facts of a given type. The predicates from above are derived using the following simple rules:

```
jsquash_repository(P1:T1, P2:T2, Op, P3:T3) :-
   !,
   jsquash_repository_(T1, P2:T2, Op, P3:T3, P1).
jsquash_repository(P1:T1, Type, Id, P2:T2) :-
   jsquash_repository_(T1, Type, Id, P2:T2, P1).
jsquash_repository(P:T, Id) :-
   jsquash_repository_(T, Id, P).
```

E.g., we frequently search for the type, which is given by the first argument of the facts for `jsquash_repository_/3,4,5` in the repository.

Using the design of a repository described here, JSquash is able to work efficiently with application code of any complexity.

3 Static Code Analysis

Source code analysis comprises the manual, tooled or automated verification of source code regarding errors, coding conventions, programming style, test coverage, etc.

The tool JSquash supports some standard methods of static code analysis, such as the calculation of metrics and the detection of code smells. In the following, we will show some examples.

3.1 Local and Global Variables

The following rule determines the classes and identifiers of all local (if `Type` is given by `'variable-declaration'`) or global (if `Type` is `'field-declaration'`) variables within the source code, respectively:

```
variables_in_system(Type, Class, Id) :-
   jsquash_repository([N]:'java-class', _, Class),
   jsquash_repository([N|_]:Type, _, Id, _).
```

Note, that the repository facts for Java classes have a path consisting of only one number. Each variable in a Java class has this number as the first element of its path.

3.2 Detection of Flaws and Code Smells

JSquash supports the detection of some types of code flaws, i.e., code sections that could be sources of potential errors.

The following rule determines the method signatures of all methods having more than one `return` statement:

```
methods_with_several_returns(
      Class, Method, Signature) :-
   jsquash_repository([N]:'java-class', _, Class),
   jsquash_repository([N|Ns]:'method-declaration',
      Method, Signature, _),
   findall( Path,
      ( jsquash_repository(
           Path:'return-expression', _, _),
        append([N|Ns], _, Path) ),
      Paths ),
   length(Paths, Length),
   Length > 1.
```

The method declarations within a Java class have the position of the class as the first element in their path. Accordingly, the return expressions of a method have the path of the method as a prefix of their path.

The following rule detects all `if` conditions that always evaluate to `false`. It determines the sections of all such `if` statements within the analysed code. If all possible evaluations of an `if` condition are `false`, then the `if` statement is unnecessary.

```
unnecessary_if_statements(If_Path) :-
   jsquash_repository(
      If_Path:'if-statement', P:T, _, _),
   init_run_time(R),
   set_run_time(R, R2, [
      searched_expression@path=P,
      searched_expression@type=T]),
   forall( eval(R2:P:T, Value),
      Value = [boolean, false|_] ).
```

After initialising the run–time – which will be explained in the following section – with `init_run_time/1`, the path and the type of the searched expression are stored in the run–time using `set_run_time/3`.

All of these features make use of the basic code analysis that is supported and integrated in JSquash. This comprises the detection of the following facts: which code sections influence the values of variables, which methods are calling other methods (call dependencies), and which objects are created at which time by which other objects. The predicate `eval/2` for backward tracing the flow of control leading to the values of variables will be explained in the following section.

4 Backward Tracing of the Control Flow

While determining the current values of variables, JSquash recursively calls the predicate `eval/2` until the evaluation reaches assignments having literal expressions on their right hand side. As literal expressions need not to be evaluated, their values can

```
public | |class| |Sender| {

    public void sendMessage() {

        String tCondColumns = { "a","b","c" };
        String tCondValues = { "1","2","3" };
        String tOrderByColumns = { "c","d" };

        String tSQL = "SELECT * FROM training";
        tSQL += " WHERE ";
        tSQL += tCondColumns[0] + " = " + tCondValues[0] + " AND ";
        tSQL += tCondColumns[1] + " = " + tCondValues[1] + " AND ";
        tSQL += tCondColumns[2] + " = " + tCondValues[2];

        tSQL += " ORDER BY ";
        tSQL += tOrderByColumns[0] + ", ";
        tSQL += tOrderByColumns[1];
        tSQL += " ASCENDING";

        Connection con = DBTools.getConnection();

        try {
            PreparedStatement st = con.prepareStatement(tSQL);
            st.execute();
        }catch {Exception e)
            e.printStackTrace();
        }
    }
}
```

Fig. 1. A code example that uses arrays of strings to construct an SQL statement

immediately be used as arguments in complex expressions. After the recursion is rolled out completely, the calculated values of the partial expressions are returned until the value of the examined expression is determined.

For example, during the search for the current value of `d` in line 4 of the code fragment of Section 2.2, first the variable `c` in the right side of the assignment has to be evaluated. Therefore, JSquash detects the assignment in line 3, where `c` can be evaluated by determining the current values of `a` in line 1 and `b` in line 2 and by returning their sum. Another example using arrays of strings to construct an SQL statement is shown in Figure 1.

The current state of the analysed program plays an important role for `eval/2` , because it determines the control flow of the applications's calculations. The program state is the set of all variables and their current values that are needed for evaluation of the control structures involved in the calculation of the value of the examined variable.

4.1 Overview of the Evaluation Strategy

Evaluating a specific variable means accessing it at a specific point of run–time. As variables always receive their values strictly via assignment expressions, the analysis component recursively has to find the last assignment before the currently examined access to the variable. Therefore, a *simulation* of the control flow has been implemented in JSquash, that can also handle statements such as loops and `if-then-else` constructs. This machine recognizes, if a program block directly or indirectly influences the value of the examined variable.

The search for the current value of a variable has been implemented in the predicate `eval/2`. Given the reference to a variable, it returns the corresponding value, depending on the current state. On backtracking, it determines all further value assignments for the given variable. E.g., `if` statements may lead to alternative value assignments, if the condition cannot be evaluated and the `then` or `else` part assigns a value to the examined variable. But, often there is only one possible value assignment.

`eval/2` is always called with the first argument of the form `R:P:T`. The *run–time* object `R` holds fundamental information for determining the values of variables including the current state of the automata. It is represented as an XML object in field notation, which holds the following information:

- the current position of the analysis in the source code,
- the analysed control structure,
- the state of the variables defining the current state and control flow,
- the currently examined variable, and
- the currently examined assignment.

The run–time is needed as a supporting data structure for analysing the lifetime behavior of loops and other constructs that have nested blocks, including recursive method calls. In these cases, it is used for holding the distinct states of the blocks passed during the analysis. The value history of the run–time is used extensively to reflect the construction and dependencies of each single variable value.

`P:T` *references* the currently searched expression. Based on the type of the referenced expressions, JSquash can decide which rule of `eval/2` has to be used for determining the actual value of the given expression. In the case of variable accesses, the `eval/2` rule – shown in the listing below – determines the current value of the referenced variable at the time of the access.

For each type `T` of *control structure*, a rule has been developed that simulates its behaviour and functionality. These rules implement evaluation strategies that yield the current value for all type primitives. The handling of local and global variables (class fields) is implemented separately, since the evaluation strategies differ.

Using the techniques described below, JSquash is able to derive the values of variables based on dependencies that can be resolved solely within the source code. Working with values that rely on other resources is a challange and does yield the exact value of the specific variable.

In the following, we will show some examples; more complicated cases, such as the handling of Java loops, cannot be shown due to the inherent complexity of their evaluation.

4.2 Variable Access Expressions

While processing the Java code fragment of Section 2.2, JSquash has at first to resolve the identifier `d`. The JSquash repository fact

```
jsquash_repository(
   [..., 152, 156]:'variable-access-expression', c).
```

shows that the variable access expression at `[..., 152, 156]` refers to the variable `c`. Based on the repository fact

```
jsquash_repository(
    [..., 134]:'variable-declaration', int, c,
    [..., 134, 138]:'binary-expression').
```

the predicate `next/2` finds out that the most recent assignment defining `c` was the binary expression at `[..., 134, 138]`, cf. line 3 of the Java code fragment:

```
eval(R:P:T, Value) :-
    T = 'variable-access-expression',
    jsquash_repository(P:T, Id),
    set_run_time(R, R2, [
        @searched_id=Id,
        @search_mode=variable,
        @scope=T ]),
    next(R2:P:T, R3:P3:T3),
    eval(R3:P3:T3, V),
    handle_postfix(P3:T3, V, Value).
```

Similarly, the repository fact

```
jsquash_repository(
    [..., 105]:'variable-declaration', int, a,
    [..., 105, 109]:'literal-expression').
```

is used later during the computation to find out that the variable `a` is declared using a literal expression.

For finding the most recent assignment to the examined variables, the predicate `next/2` has to traverse the JSquash repository facts in inverse code order. This can be supported by further PROLOG facts in the repository, which link a statement to its preceding statement in the code order.

4.3 Binary Expressions

The repository fact

```
jsquash_repository([..., 134, 138]:'binary-expression',
    [..., 134, 138, 138]:'variable-access-expression', +,
    [..., 134, 138, 142]:'variable-access-expression').
```

shows that the binary expression for `c` refers to two variable access expressions. After evaluating them, the resulting values are combined using the binary operator (in our case +) indicated by the fact from the repository:

```
eval(R:P:T, Value) :-
    T = 'binary-expression',
    jsquash_repository(P:T, P1:T1, Op, P2:T2),
    eval(R:P1:T1, V1),
    eval(R:P2:T2, V2),
    apply(Op, [V1, V2, Value]).
```

If we evaluate the following code fragment, then both expressions within the binary expression in line 2 are evaluated w.r.t. the same run–time `R`, but with different references `P1:T1` and `P2:T2`, respectively:

```
1: int a = 5;
2: int c = a++ + a;
```

The first call `eval(R:P1:T1,V1)` evaluates the left expression "`a++`" to "`5`"; only afterwards, the value of "a" is incremented to the new value "`6`". The second call `eval(R:P2:T2,V2)` for the right expression "a" re–evaluates the left expression, since the new value of "a" is relevant. Thus, the right expression "a" correctly evaluates to "`6`", and finally, "c" evaluates to "`11`", i.e. "`5 + 6`".

4.4 Literal Expressions

The repository fact

```
jsquash_repository(
   [..., 105, 109]:'literal-expression', int, 5).
```

shows that the value of the literal expression at `[..., 105, 109]` is "5". This type of expression is evaluated using the following rule:

```
eval(R:P:T, Value) :-
   T = 'literal-expression',
   jsquash_repository(P:T, _, Value).
```

4.5 Management of Loops

From the field of compiler construction, it is known that there is an equivalence between `while`–, `do-while`–, and `for`–loops; all of them can be translated into a `while`–loop. The `for`–loop can be replaced by a `while`–loop with the next–part of the loop as its last statement and a preceding initialization of the loop's variables. The `do-while`–loop can be translated into a `while`–loop by simply appending one copy of its complete body in front. For example, the following two loops are equivalent:
`for`–loop:

```
int j = 0;
for (int i = 1; i < 10; i++) {
   j += i;
}
```

`while`–loop:

```
int i = 1, j = 0;
while (i < 10) {
   j += i; i++;
}
```

Thus, only the two rules of translation had to be implemented in JSquash together with a single mechanism for evaluating the `while`–loop itself.

4.6 Input Operations

If some parts of an SQL statement are obtained by input operations at run–time, then they cannot be determined by static code analysis. If our backward tracing strategy detects such a situation, then it returns a don't know marker to be included in the finally produced SQL statement. Fortunately, this rarely happens in practical database applications.

5 Embedded SQL Statements

The tool JSquash can detect and analyse SQL statements embedded in the Java source code of database applications.

5.1 Visualization of SQL Statements in the Source Code

For presenting the results of the analysis to the user, JSquash includes a generator component, that produces an HTML document containing the complete information about the detected SQL statements, including the full SQL code and the source code that contributes to each SQL statement. This HTML document comprises a fully functional graphical user interface (GUI) that can be opened and used with any Web browser. The GUI is implemented in HTML 4 using cascading style sheets (CSS) and JavaScript; the JavaScript helps building a dynamic GUI.

The expressions that contribute to the following generated SQL statement have been detected by JSquash and are automatically highlighted, see Figure 1. JSquash was also able to build the full SQL statement by only analyzing the source code:

```
SELECT * FROM training
WHERE a = 1 AND b = 2 AND c = 3
ORDER BY c, d ASCENDING
```

The second SQL statement of Figure 2 is visualised in the GUI depicted in Figure 3. The left side in of the GUI shown in Figure 3 displays all the class files of the source code that contribute to the detected SQL statements. Clicking on the buttons at the left side of the class name opens (+) or closes (−) the source code, respectively. At the upper right side, all detected SQL statements are shown. Below is the block of settings, that allow for changing the highlighting colors.

When an SQL statement of the list is selected, then the corresponding code sections and expressions are automatically highlighted in the listings at the left side, cf. Figure 3. Thus, the user can easily analyse all code sections that contribute to the selected SQL statement. This feature is implemented in JavaScript and CSS, making extensive use of the path information from the repository.

To know the places in the source code of the application that contribute to a given SQL statement is a big aid for software engineers. This becomes extremely beneficial in a situation, where a table is changed in the database and the programmer must ensure that the application still works well with that changed database schema.

In such a case, the engineer wants to know, starting with a given table name, where in the source code of the application SQL statements are generated that use this table. JSquash can assist in such a situation and helps performing the required manual refactoring.

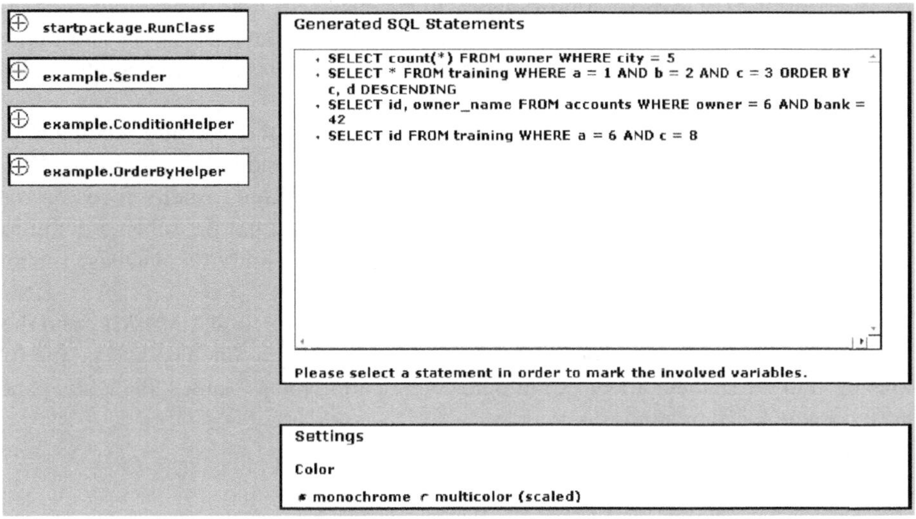

Fig. 2. The GUI of JSquash. No SQL statement is selected

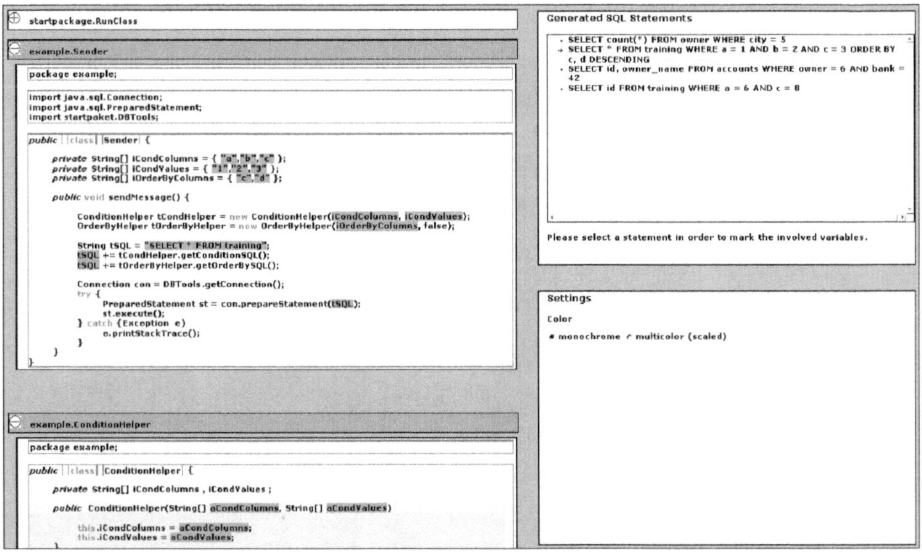

Fig. 3. All contributing values and variables of the selected second SQL statement are marked

5.2 XML Representation of SQL Statements

Recently, we have developed the tool Squash for analysing, tuning and refactoring relational database applications [2]. It uses an extensible and flexible XML representation for SQL database schema definitions and queries called SQUASHML, that is designed for representing schema objects, as well as database queries and data modification statements.

The core of SQUASHML follows the SQL standard, but it also allows for system–specific constructs of different SQL dialects; for example, some definitions and storage parameters from the Oracle database management system have been integrated as optional XML elements.

This format allows for easily processing and evaluating the database schema information. Currently, supported schema objects include table and index definitions. Other existing XML representations of databases, such as SQL/XML, usually focus on representing the database contents, i.e., the table contents, and not the schema definition itself [14]. SQUASHML was developed specifically to map only the database schema and queries, without the current contents of the database.

The SQL statements detected by JSquash are transformed to SQUASHML, and then the tool Squash can be used for the visualisation of the single statements. E.g., the following SELECT statement from a biological application joins 9 tables; the table names have been replaced by aliases A, ..., I:

```
SELECT * FROM A, B, C, D, E, F, G, H
WHERE A.ID_DICT_PEPTIDE IN (
   SELECT ID_PEPTIDE FROM I
   WHERE I.ID_SEARCH = 2025
   GROUP BY ID_PEPTIDE
   HAVING COUNT(ID_SEARCH_PEPTIDE) >=1 )
AND A.ID_SEARCH = 2025 AND c1 AND c2
AND A.FLAG_DELETED = 0
AND c3 AND c6 (+) AND c7 (+) AND c4 AND c5
AND E.LEN >= 6 AND A.NORMALIZED_SCORE >= 1.5
ORDER BY ...
```

The following 7 join conditions are used:

```
c1: A.ID_SEARCH_PEPTIDE = B.ID_SEARCH_PEPTIDE
c2: A.ID_SPECTRUM = G.ID_SPECTRUM
c3: A.ID_SEARCH_PEPTIDE = C.ID_PEPTIDE
c4: C.ID_SEQUENCE = D.ID_SEQUENCE
c5: A.ID_SEARCH = H.ID_SEARCH
c6: B.ID_PEPTIDE = E.ID_DICT_PEPTIDE
c7: B.ID_PEPTIDE_MOD = F.ID_DICT_PEPTIDE
```

This query is parsed into the following SQUASHML element; we leave out some opening and closing tags, respectively:

```
<select>
  <subquery id="subquery_1">
    <select_list> <expr> <simple_expr>
      <object table_view="A"
        column="ID_SEARCH"/> ...
    <from> <table_reference> ...
      <simple_query_table_expression
```

```
          object="A" schema="USER"/> ...
      <where> ...
      <order_by> ...
  </select>
```

The conditions in the WHERE part (e.g., the join condition c1) look like follows:

```
  <condition>
    <simple_comparison_condition operator="=">
      <left_expr> <expr> <simple_expr>
        <object table_view="A"
          column="ID_SEARCH_PEPTIDE"/> ...
      <right_expr> ...
        <object table_view="B"
          column="ID_SEARCH_PEPTIDE"/> ...
  </condition>
```

5.3 Visualization of Database Schemas and SQL Statements

Squash provides a number of different visualization methods for the database schema and the queries [2]. Complex select statements tend to include many tables in join operations. Therefore, Squash uses a graph representation for query visualization, cf. Figure 4. If a SELECT statement contains nested subqueries (like the statement shown above), then these queries can be included in the graphical output if desired.

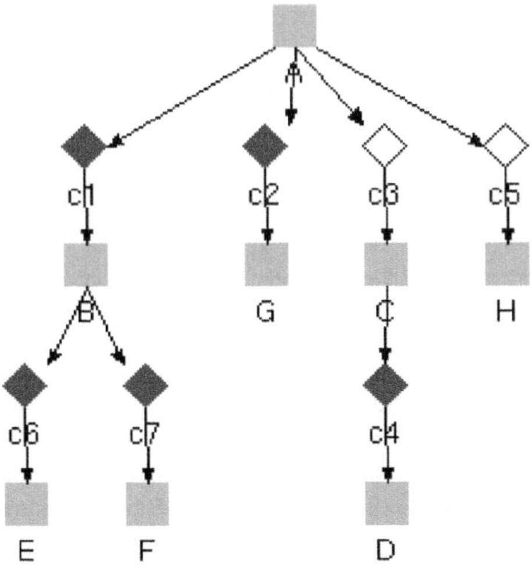

Fig. 4. Join Conditions in a Query

6 Conclusions

We have shown, how to derive the content of application variables using means of static code analysis implemented in PROLOG. Now, we are able to analyse embedded

SQL statements of a given database application, either by analysing audit files of the database connection using the basic tool Squash [2], or by static source code analysis with the extended tool JSquash.

The statements derived from the source code of the database application can be imported into Squash, which can then generate database modifications for improving the performance of the application.

Future work will be on developing methods that preserve the linkage between the detected single SQL statement fragments and their positions as well as each of their effects in the completed statement. This extension to SQUASHML will then overcome a current limitation of our system: it will allow for automatically injecting the changes proposed by Squash into the original source code of the application and help conducting the appropriate changes there – which so far have to be done by hand. These techniques can then be integrated into integrated development environments such as Eclipse and will help developers of database applications.

Moreover, we will try to apply similar techniques of static code analysis to PROLOG programs with embedded SQL statements as well.

References

1. Benton, W.C., Fischer, C.N.: Interactive, Scalable, Declarative Program Analysis: From Prototype to Implementation. In: Proc. Intl. Conference on Principles and Practice of Declarative Programming, PPDP 2007, pp. 13–24 (2007)
2. Boehm, A.M., Seipel, D., Sickmann, A., Wetzka, M.: Squash: A Tool for Analyzing, Tuning and Refactoring Relational Database Applications. In: Seipel, D., Hanus, M., Wolf, A. (eds.) INAP 2007. LNCS, vol. 5437, pp. 82–98. Springer, Heidelberg (2009)
3. Chamberlin, D.: XQuery: a Query Language for XML. In: Proc. ACM International Conference on Management of Data, SIGMOD 2003, p. 682. ACM Press, New York (2003)
4. Chess, B., McGraw, G.: Static Analysis for Security. IEEE Security & Privacy 2(6), 76–79 (2004)
5. Clocksin, W.F., Mellish, C.S.: Programming in PROLOG, 5th edn. Springer, Heidelberg (2003)
6. Corbett, J.C., Dwyer, M.B., Hatcliff, J., Laubach, S., Pasareanu, C.S., Zheng, R.H.: Bandera: Extracting Finite State Models From Java Source Code. In: Proc. Intl. Conference on Software Engineering, ICSE 2000, pp. 439–448 (2000)
7. Ducasse, S., Lanza, M., Bertuli, R.: High–Level Polymetric Views of Condensed Run–Time Information. In: Proc. 8th European Conference on Software Maintenance and Reengineering, CSMR 2004, pp. 309–318 (2004)
8. Hopfner, M., Seipel, D., Wolff von Gudenberg, J., Fischer, G.: Reasoning About Source Code in XML-Representation. In: Workshop on Software-Reengineering, WSR 2003 (2003)
9. van Emden, E., Moonen, L.: Java Quality Assurance by Detecting Code Smells. In: Proc. 9th Working Conference on Reverse Engineering, WCRE 2002, pp. 97–108. IEEE Computer Society, Los Alamitos (2002)
10. Evans, D., Larochelle, D.: Improving Security Using Extensible Lightweight Static Analysis. IEEE Software 19(1), 42–51 (2002)
11. Fischer, D., Lusiardi, J.: JAML: XML Representation of Java Source Code. Technical Report, University of Würzburg, Department of Computer Science (2008)

12. Holzmann, G.J., Smith, M.H.: Extracting Verification Models by Extracting Verification Models. In: Proc. Joint International Conference on Formal Description Techniques, FORTE 1999, and Protocol Specification, Testing, and Verification, PSTV 1999, pp. 481–497. Kluwer, Dordrecht (1999)
13. JBoss: Red Hat: Hybernate, `https://www.hibernate.org/`
14. INTL. ORGANIZATION FOR STANDARDIZATION: ISO/IEC 9075–14:2003 Information Technology – Database Languages – SQL – Part 14: XML Related Specifications, SQL/XML (2003)
15. Marinescu, R.: Detection Strategies: Metrics–Based Rules for Detecting Design Flaws. In: Proc. 20th IEEE Intl. Conference on Software Maintenance, ICSM 2004, pp. 350–359 (2004)
16. Ramakrishnan, R., Gehrke, J.: Database Management Systems, 3rd edn. McGraw-Hill, New York (2003)
17. Ren, X., Shah, F., Tip, F., Ryder, B.G., Chesley, O.: Chianti: A Tool for Change Impact Analysis of Java Programs. ACM SIGPLAN Notices 39(10), 432–448 (2004)
18. Seipel, D.: Processing XML Documents in PROLOG. In: Proc. 17th Workshop on Logic Programmierung, WLP 2002 (2002)
19. Seipel, D., Hopfner, M., Heumesser, B.: Analyzing and Visualizing PROLOG Programs based on XML Representations. In: Proc. Intl. Workshop on Logic Programming Environments, WLPE 2003 (2003)
20. Seipel, D., Baumeister, J., Hopfner, M.: Declarative Querying and Visualizing Knowledge Bases in XML. In: Seipel, D., Hanus, M., Geske, U., Bartenstein, O. (eds.) INAP/WLP 2004. LNCS (LNAI), vol. 3392, pp. 16–31. Springer, Heidelberg (2005)
21. Systä, T., Yu, P., Müller, H.: Analyzing Java Software by Combining Metrics and Program Visualization. In: Proc. 4th European Conference on Software Maintenance and Reengineering, CSMR 2000, pp. 199–208. IEEE Computer Society, Los Alamitos (2000)
22. Wahler, V., Seipel, D., Wolff von Gudenberg, J., Fischer, G.: Clone Detection in Source Code by Frequent Itemset Techniques. In: Proc. 4th IEEE Intl. Workshop on Source Code Analysis and Manipulation, SCAM 2004, pp. 128–135. IEEE Computer Society, Los Alamitos (2004)
23. Wielemaker, J.: An Overview of the SWI–PROLOG Programming Environment. In: Proc. 13th International Workshop on Logic Programming Environments, WLPE 2003, pp. 1–16 (2003)
24. Wielemaker, J.: SWI–PROLOG. Version (2007), `http://www.swi-prolog.org/`

Elder Care via Intention Recognition and Evolution Prospection

Luís Moniz Pereira and The Anh Han

Centro de Inteligência Artificial (CENTRIA)
Universidade Nova de Lisboa, 2829-516 Caparica, Portugal
lmp@di.fct.unl.pt, h.anh@fct.unl.pt

Abstract. We explore and exemplify the application in the Elder Care context of the ability to perform Intention Recognition and of wielding Evolution Prospection methods. This is achieved by means of an articulate use of Causal Bayes Nets (for heuristically gauging probable general intentions), combined with specific generation of plans involving preferences (for checking which of such intentions are plausibly being carried out in the specific situation at hand). The overall approach is formulated within a coherent and general logic programming framework and implemented system. The paper recaps required background and illustrates the approach via an extended application example.

Keywords: Intention Recognition, Elder Care, Causal Bayes Nets, P-Log, Evolution Prospection, Preferences.

1 Introduction

In the last twenty years there has been a significant increase of the average age of the population in most western countries and the number of elderly people has been and will be constantly growing. For this reason there has been a strong development of supportive technology for elderly people living independently in their own homes, for example, RoboCare Project [8] – an ongoing project developing robots for assisted elderly people's living, SINDI – a logic-based home monitoring system [9].

For the Elder Care application domain, in order to provide contextually appropriate help for elders, it is required that the assisting system has the ability to observe the actions of the elders, recognize their intentions, and then provide suggestions on how to achieve the recognized intentions on the basis of the conceived plans. In this paper we focus on the latter two steps in order to design and implement an elder care logic programming based assisting system. The first step of perceiving elders' actions is taken for granted. For elders' intention recognition based on their observable actions, we employ our work on Intention Recognition system using Causal Bayes Networks and plan generation techniques, described in [1]. The intention recognition component is indispensable for living-alone elders, in order to provide them with timely suggestions. The next step, that of providing action suggestions for realizing the recognized

S. Abreu and D. Seipel (Eds.): INAP 2009, LNAI 6547, pp. 170–187, 2011.

intention gleaned from the previous stage, is implemented using our Evolution Prospection Agent (EPA) system [2,3]. The latter can prospectively look ahead into the future to choose the best course of evolution whose actions achieve the recognized intention, while being aware of the external environment and of an elder's preferences and already scheduled future events. Expectation rules and a priori preferences take into account the physical state (health reports) information of the elder to guarantee that only contextually safe healthy choices are generated; then, information such as the elder's pleasure, interests, etc. are taken into account by a posteriori preferences and the like. In this manner, the system guarantees, in the first place, the safety for the elder's health, before considering his pleasure choices, which may sometimes not be suitable to his current health conditions. In addition, the advance and easiness of expressing preferences in EPA [3] enable to closely take into account the elders' preferences—which we believe—would increase the degree of acceptance of the elders w.r.t. the technological help—an important issue of the domain [10].

Recently, there have been many works addressing the problem of intention recognition as well as its applications in a variety of fields. As in Heinze's doctoral thesis [11], intention recognition is defined, in general terms, as the process of becoming aware of the intention of another agent and, more technically, as the problem of inferring an agent's intention through its actions and their effects on the environment. According to this definition, one approach to tackling intention recognition is by reducing it to plan recognition, i.e. the problem of generating plans achieving the intentions and choosing the ones that match the observed actions and their effects in the environment of the intending agent. This has been the main stream so far [11,14].

One of the main issues of that approach is that of finding an initial set of possible intentions (of the intending agent) that the plan generator is going to tackle, and which must be imagined by the recognizing agent. Undoubtedly, this set should depend on the situation at hand, since generating plans for all intentions one agent could have, for whatever situation he might be in, is unrealistic if not impossible.

In this paper, we use an approach to solve this problem employing so-called *situation-sensitive Causal Bayes Networks* (CBN) - That is, CBNs [18] that change according to the situation under consideration, itself subject to ongoing change as a result of actions. Therefore, in some given situation, a CBN can be configured dynamically, to compute the likelihood of intentions and filter out the much less likely intentions. The plan generator (or plan library) thus only needs, at the start, to deal with the remaining more relevant because more probable or credible intentions, rather than all conceivable intentions. One of the important advantages of our approach is that, on the basis of the information provided by the CBN the recognizing agent can see which intentions are more likely and worth addressing; so, in case of having to make a quick decision, it can focus on the most relevant ones first. CBNs, in our work, are represented in P-log [4,6,5], a declarative language that combines logical and probabilistic reasoning, and uses Answer Set Programming (ASP) as its logical and CBNs as its probabilistic foundations. Given a CBN, its situation-sensitive version is constructed by attaching to it a logical component to dynamically compute situation specific probabilistic information—which is forthwith inserted into the P-log program representing that CBN. The computation is dynamic in the sense that there is a process of inter-feedback between the logical component and the CBN; i.e. the result from the updated CBN is also given back to the logical component, and that might give rise to further updating, etc.

In addition, one more advantage of our approach, in comparison with those using solely BNs [12,13] is that these just use the available information for constructing CBNs. For complicated tasks, e.g. in recognizing hidden intentions, not all information is observable. The approach of combining with plan generation provides a way to guide the recognition process: which actions (or their effects) should be checked for whether they were or will be (hiddenly) executed by the intending agent. In practice, one can make use of any plan generators or plan libraries available. For integration's sake, we can use the ASP based conditional planner called ASCP [16] from XSB Prolog using the XASP package [7,24] for interfacing with Smodels [22]—an answer set solver—or, alternatively, rely on plan libraries so obtained.

In the sequel we briefly describe the intention recognition and evolution prospection systems, but not the planner. Then we show in detail how to combine them to provide contextual help for elderly people, illustrating with an extended example.

2 Intention Recognition

2.1 Causal Bayes Networks

We briefly recall Causal Bayes Networks (CBN) here for convenience in order to help understand their use for intention recognition and their realization in P-log. Firstly, let us recall some preliminary definitions.

Definition 1 (Directed Acyclic Graph). *A directed acyclic graph, also called a dag, is a directed graph with no directed cycles; that is, for any node v, there is no nonempty directed path that starts and ends on v.*

Definition 2. *Let G be a dag that represents causal relations between its nodes. For two nodes A and B of G, if there is an edge from A to B (i.e. A is a direct cause of B), A is called a parent of B, and B is a child of A. The set of parent nodes of a node A is denoted by* ***parents(A)****. Ancestor nodes of A are parents of A or parents of some ancestor nodes of A. If node A has no parents ($parents(A) = \emptyset$), it is called a* ***top node****. If A has no child, it is called a* ***bottom node****. The nodes which are neither top nor bottom are said* ***intermediate****. If the value of a node is observed, the node is said to be an* ***evidence node****.*

Definition 3 (Causally Sufficient Set [17]). *Let V be a set of variables with causal relations represented by a dag. V is said to be causally sufficient if and only if for any $Y, Z \in V$ with $Y \neq Z$ and X is a common cause of Y and Z, then*

$X \in V$. That is to say, V is causally sufficient if for any two distinct variables in V, all their common causes also belong to V.

Definition 4 (Causal Markov Assumption - CMA [17]). *Let X be any variable in a causally sufficient set S of variables or features whose causal relations are represented by a dag G, and let P be the set of all variables in S that are direct causes of X (i.e. parents of X in G). Let Y be any subset of S such that no variable in Y is a direct or indirect effect of X (i.e., there is no directed path in G from X to any member of Y). Then X is independent (in probability) of Y conditional on P.*

The CMA implies that the joint probability of any set of values of a causally sufficient set can be factored into a product of conditional probabilities of the value of each variable on its parents. More details and a number of examples can be found in [17].

Definition 5 (Bayes Networks). *A Bayes Network is a pair consisting of a dag whose nodes represent variables and missing edges encode conditional independencies between the variables, and an associated probability distribution satisfying the Causal Markov Assumption.*

If the dag of a BN is intended to represent causal relations and its associated probability distribution is intended to represent those that result from the represented mechanism, then the BN is said to be causal. To do so, besides CMA, the associated probability distribution needs to satisfy an additional condition, as more formally shown in the following definition

Definition 6 (Causal Bayes Network). *A Bayes Network is causal if its associated probability distribution satisfies the condition specifying that if a node X of its dag is actively caused to be in a given state x (an operation written as $do(x)$, e.g. in P-log syntax), then the probability density function changes to the one of the network obtained by cutting the links from X's parents to X, and setting X to the caused value x [18].*

With this condition being satisfied, one can predict the impact of external interventions from data obtained prior to intervention.

In a BN, associated with each intermediate node of its dag is a specification of the distribution of its variable, say A, conditioned on its parents in the graph, i.e. $P(A|parents(A))$ is specified. For a top node, the unconditional distribution of the variable is specified. These distributions are called Conditional Probability Distribution (CPD) of the BN.

Suppose nodes of the dag form a causally sufficient set, i.e. no common causes of any two nodes are omitted, then implied by CMA [17], the joint distribution of all node values of a causally sufficient can be determined as the product of conditional probabilities of the value of each node on its parents

$$P(X_1, ..., X_N) = \prod_{i=1}^{N} P(X_i|parents(X_i))$$

where $V = \{X_i | 1 \leq i \leq N\}$ is the set of nodes of the dag.

Suppose there is a set of evidence nodes in the dag, say $O = \{O_1, ..., O_m\} \subset V$. We can determine the conditional probability of a variable X given the observed value of evidence nodes by using the conditional probability formula

$$P(X|O) = \frac{P(X,O)}{P(O)} = \frac{P(X, O_1, ..., O_m)}{P(O_1, ..., O_m)} \tag{1}$$

where the numerator and denominator are computed by summing the joint probabilities over all absent variables w.r.t. V as follows

$$P(X = x, O = o) = \sum_{av \in ASG(AV_1)} P(X = x, O = o, AV_1 = av)$$

$$P(O = o) = \sum_{av \in ASG(AV_2)} P(O = o, AV_2 = av)$$

where $o = \{o_1, ..., o_m\}$ with $o_1, ..., o_m$ being the observed values of $O_1, ..., O_m$, respectively; $ASG(Vt)$ denotes the set of all assignments of vector Vt (with components are variables in V); AV_1, AV_2 are vectors components of which are corresponding absent variables, i.e. variables in $V \setminus \{O \cup \{X\}\}$ and $V \setminus O$, respectively.

In short, to define a BN, one needs to specify the structure of the network, its CPD and the prior probability distribution of the top nodes.

2.2 Intention Recognition with Causal Bayesian Networks

The first phase of the intention recognition system is to find out how likely each possible intention is, based on current observations such as observed actions of the intending agent or the effects its actions (either actually observed, or missed direct observations) have in the environment. It is carried out by using a CBN with nodes standing for binary random variables that represent causes, intentions, actions and effects.

Intentions are represented by intermediate nodes whose ancestor nodes stand for causes that give rise to intentions. Intuitively, we extend Heinze's tri-level model [11] with a so-called pre-intentional level that describes the causes of intentions, used to estimate prior probabilities of the intentions. This additional level guarantees the causal sufficiency condition of the set of nodes of the dag. However, if these prior probabilities can be specified without considering the causes, intentions are represented by top nodes. These reflect the problem context or the intending agent's mental state.

Observed actions are represented as children of the intentions that causally affect them. Observable effects are represented as bottom nodes. They can be children of observed action nodes, of intention nodes, or of some unobserved actions that might cause the observable effects that are added as children of the intention nodes.

The causal relations among nodes of the BNs (e.g. which causes give rise to an intention, which intentions trigger an action, which actions have an effect), as well as their CPD and the distribution of the top nodes, are specified by domain experts. However, they might be learnt mechanically. By using formula 1 the conditional probabilities of each intention on current observations can be determined, X being an intention and O being the set of current observations.

Example 1 (Elder Care). An elder stays alone in his apartment. The intention recognition system observes that he is looking for something in the living room. In order to assist him, the system needs to figure out what he intends to find. The possible things are: something to read (*book*); something to drink (*drink*); the TV remote control (*Rem*); and the light switch (*Switch*). The CBN, with CPD and top nodes distribution, representing this scenario is that of Figure 1.

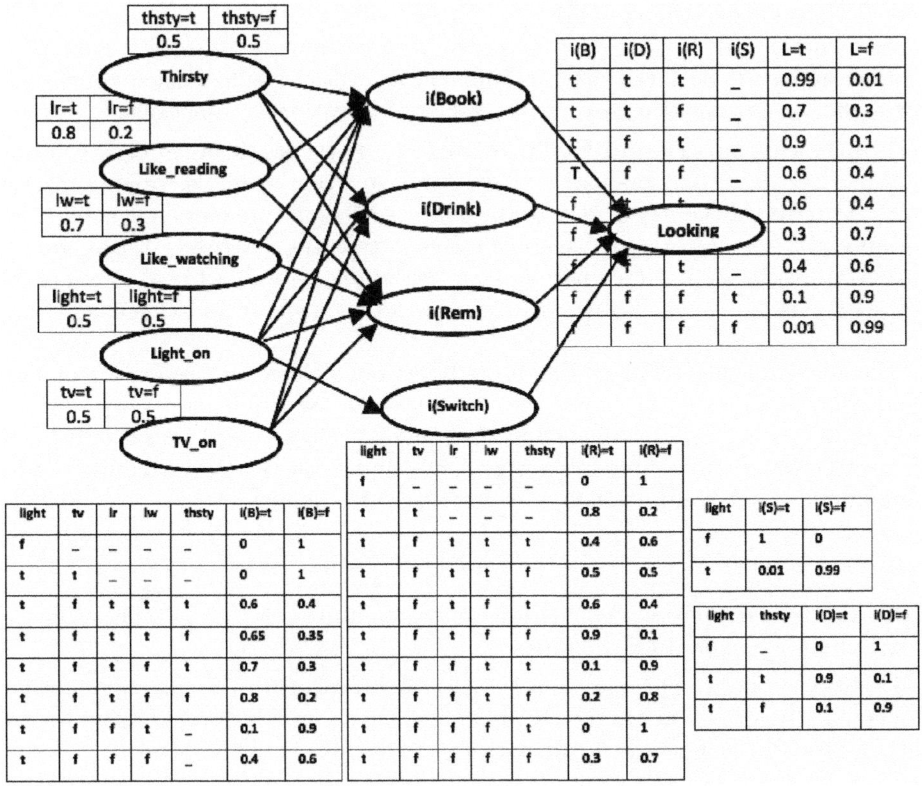

thsty=t	thsty=f
0.5	0.5

lr=t	lr=f
0.8	0.2

lw=t	lw=f
0.7	0.3

light=t	light=f
0.5	0.5

tv=t	tv=f
0.5	0.5

i(B)	i(D)	i(R)	i(S)	L=t	L=f
t	t	t	_	0.99	0.01
t	t	f	_	0.7	0.3
t	f	t	_	0.9	0.1
T	f	f	_	0.6	0.4
f	t	t		0.6	0.4
f	[illegible]	[illegible]	[illegible]	0.3	0.7
f	f	t	_	0.4	0.6
f	f	f	t	0.1	0.9
f	f	f	f	0.01	0.99

light	tv	lr	lw	thsty	i(B)=t	i(B)=f
f	_	_	_	_	0	1
t	t	_	_	_	0	1
t	f	t	t	t	0.6	0.4
t	f	t	t	f	0.65	0.35
t	f	t	f	t	0.7	0.3
t	f	t	f	f	0.8	0.2
t	f	f	t	_	0.1	0.9
t	f	f	f	_	0.4	0.6

light	tv	lr	lw	thsty	i(R)=t	i(R)=f
f	_	_	_	_	0	1
t	t	_	_	_	0.8	0.2
t	f	t	t	t	0.4	0.6
t	f	t	t	f	0.5	0.5
t	f	t	f	t	0.6	0.4
t	f	t	f	f	0.9	0.1
t	f	f	t	t	0.1	0.9
t	f	f	t	f	0.2	0.8
t	f	f	f	t	0	1
t	f	f	f	f	0.3	0.7

light	i(S)=t	i(S)=f
f	1	0
t	0.01	0.99

light	thsty	i(D)=t	i(D)=f
f	_	0	1
t	t	0.9	0.1
t	f	0.1	0.9

Fig. 1. Elder's intentions CBN

2.3 P-Log

The computation in CBNs is automated using P-log, a declarative language that combines logical and probabilistic reasoning, and ASP as its logical and CBNs as its probabilistic foundations. We recap it here for self-containment, to the extent we use it.

The original P-log [4,6] uses ASP as a tool for computing all stable models of the logical part of P-log. Although ASP has been proved to be a useful paradigm for solving a variety of combinatorial problems, its non-relevance property [7] makes the P-log system sometimes computationally redundant. Newer developments of P-log [5] use the XASP package of XSB Prolog [24] for interfacing with Smodels [22] – an answer set solver. The power of ASP allows the representation of both classical and default negation in P-log easily. Moreover, the new P-log uses XSB as the underlying processing platform, allowing arbitrary Prolog code for recursive definitions. Consequently, it allows more expressive queries not supported in the original version, such as meta queries (probabilistic built-in predicates can be used as usual XSB predicates, thus allowing full power of probabilistic reasoning in XSB) and queries in the form of any XSB predicate expression [5]. Moreover, the tabling mechanism of XSB [23] significantly improves the performance of the system.

In general, a P-log program Π consists of 5 components detailed below: a sorted signature, declarations, a regular part, a set of random selection rules, a probabilistic information part, and a set of observations and actions.

(i) Sorted signature and Declaration. The sorted signature Σ of Π contains a set of constant symbols and term-building function symbols, which are used to form terms in the usual way. Additionally, the signature contains a collection of special reserved function symbols called attributes. Attribute terms are expressions of the form $a(\bar{t})$, where a is an attribute and $\bar{t}$ a vector of terms of the sorts required by a. A literal is an atomic statement, p, or its explicit negation, neg_p.

The declaration part of a P-log program can be defined as a collection of sorts and sort declarations of attributes. A sort c can be defined by listing all the elements $c = \{x_1, ..., x_n\}$, specifying the range of values $c = \{L..U\}$ where L and U are the integer lower bound and upper bound of the sort c. Attribute a with domain $c_1 \times ... \times c_n$ and range c_0 is represented as follows:

$$a : c_1 \times ... \times c_n \texttt{ --> } c_0$$

If attribute a has no domain parameter, we simply write $a : c_0$. The range of attribute a is denoted by $range(a)$.

(ii) Regular part. This part of a P-log program consists of a collection of rules, facts, and integrity constraints (ICs) in the form of denials, formed using literals of Σ. An IC is encoded as a rule with the `false` literal in the head.

(iii) Random Selection Rule. This is a rule for attribute a having the form:

$$random(RandomName, a(\bar{t}), DynamicRange) \texttt{ :- } Body$$

This means that the attribute instance $a(\bar{t})$ is random if the conditions in *Body* are satisfied. The *DynamicRange*, not used in the particular examples in the sequel, allows to restrict the default range for random attributes. The *RandomName* is a syntactic mechanism used to link random attributes to the corresponding probabilities. If there is no precondition, we simply put *true* in the body. A constant *full* can be used in *DynamicRange* to signal that the dynamic domain is equal to $range(a)$.

(iv) Probabilistic Information. Information about probabilities of random attribute instances $a(\bar{t})$ taking a particular value y is given by probability atoms (or simply pa-atoms) which have the following form:

$$pa(RandomName, a(\bar{t}, y), d\_(A, B)) \text{:-}\ Body.$$

meaning that if the *Body* were true, and the value of $a(\bar{t})$ were selected by a rule named *RandomName*, then *Body* would cause $a(\bar{t}) = y$ with probability $\frac{A}{B}$.

(v) Observations and Actions. These are, respectively, statements of the forms $obs(l)$ and $do(l)$, where l is a literal. Observations are used to record the outcomes of random events, i.e. of random attributes and attributes dependent on them. The statement $do(a(t, y))$ indicates that $a(t) - y$ is enforced true as the result of a deliberate action, not an observation.

2.4 Elder Intention Recognition

To begin with, we need to declare two sorts:

```
bool = {t,f}.    elder_intentions = {book,drink,rem,switch}.
```

where the second one is the sort of possible intentions of the elder. There are five top nodes, named *thirsty*(*thsty*), *like_reading*(*lr*), *like_watching*(*lw*), *tv_on*(*tv*), *light_on*(*light*), belonging to the pre-intentional level to describe the causes that might give rise to the considered intentions. The values of the last two nodes are observed (evidence nodes). The corresponding random attributes are declared as

```
thsty:bool. lr:bool. lw:bool. tv:bool. light:bool.
random(rth,thsty,full). random(rlr,lr,full).
random(rlw,lw,full).    random(rtv,tv,full).    random(rl, light, full).
```

and their independent probability distributions are encoded with pa-rules as

```
pa(rth,thsty(t),d_(1,2)). pa(rlr,lr(t),d_(8,10)).
pa(rlw,lw(t),d_(7,10)). pa(rtv,tv(t),d_(1,2)). pa(rl,light(t),d_(1,2)).
```

The possible intentions reading is afforded by four nodes, representing the four possible intentions of the elder, as mentioned above. The corresponding random attributes are coded specifying an attribute with domain *elder_intentions* and receive boolean values

```
i:elder_intentions --> bool.  random(ri, i(I), full).
```

The probability distribution of each intention node conditional on the causes are coded in P-log below. Firstly, for *i*(*book*):

```
pa(ri(book),i(book,t),d_(0,1))       :-light(f).
pa(ri(book),i(book,t),d_(0,1))       :-light(t),tv(t).
pa(ri(book),i(book,t),d_(6,10))      :-light(t),tv(f),lr(t),lw(t),thsty(t).
pa(ri(book),i(book,t),d_(65,100))    :-light(t),tv(f),lr(t),lw(t),thsty(f).
pa(ri(book),i(book,t),d_(7,10))      :-light(t),tv(f),lr(t),lw(f),thsty(t).
pa(ri(book),i(book,t),d_(8,10))      :-light(t),tv(f),lr(t),lw(f),thsty(f).
pa(ri(book),i(book,t),d_(1,10))      :-light(t),tv(f),lr(f),lw(t).
pa(ri(book),i(book,t),d_(4,10))      :-light(t),tv(f),lr(f),lw(f).
```

For $i(drink)$:

```
pa(ri(drink),i(drink,t),d_(0,1))   :- light(f).
pa(ri(drink),i(drink,t),d_(9,10))  :- light(t), thsty(t).
pa(ri(drink),i(drink,t),d_(1,10))  :- light(t), thsty(f).
```

For $i(rem)$:

```
pa(ri(rem),i(rem,t),d_(0,1))   :-light(f).
pa(ri(rem),i(rem,t),d_(8,10))  :-light(t),tv(t).
pa(ri(rem),i(rem,t),d_(4,10))  :-light(t),tv(f),lw(t),lr(t),thsty(t).
pa(ri(rem),i(rem,t),d_(5,10))  :-light(t),tv(f),lw(t),lr(t),thsty(f).
pa(ri(rem),i(rem,t),d_(6,10))  :-light(t),tv(f),lw(t),lr(f),thsty(t).
pa(ri(rem),i(rem,t),d_(9,10))  :-light(t),tv(f),lw(t),lr(f),thsty(f).
pa(ri(rem),i(rem,t),d_(1,10))  :-light(t),tv(f),lw(f),lr(t),thsty(t).
pa(ri(rem),i(rem,t),d_(2,10))  :-light(t),tv(f),lw(f),lr(t),thsty(f).
pa(ri(rem),i(rem,t),d_(0,1))   :-light(t),tv(f),lw(f),lr(f),thsty(t).
pa(ri(rem),i(rem,t),d_(3,10))  :-light(t),tv(f),lw(f),lr(f),thsty(f).
```

For $i(switch)$:

```
pa(ri(switch),i(switch,t),d_(1,1))    :- light(f).
pa(ri(switch),i(switch,t),d_(1,100)) :- light(t).
```

There is only one observation, namely, that is the elder is looking for something (*look*). The declaration of the corresponding random attribute and its probability distribution conditional on the possible intentions are given as follows:

```
look : bool.  random(rla, look, full).
pa(rla,look(t),d_(99,100)) :-i(book,t),i(drink,t),i(rem,t).
pa(rla,look(t),d_(7,10))   :-i(book,t) i(drink,t),i(rem,f).
pa(rla,look(t),d_(9,10))   :-i(book,t),i(drink,f),i(rem,t).
pa(rla,look(t),d_(6,10))   :-i(book,t),i(drink,f),i(rem,f).
pa(rla,look(t),d_(6,10))   :-i(book,f),i(drink,t),i(rem,t).
pa(rla,look(t),d_(3,10))   :-i(book,f),i(drink,t), i(rem,f).
pa(rla,look(t),d_(4,10))   :-i(book,f),i(drink,f),i(rem,t).
pa(rla,look(t),d_(1,10))   :-i(book,f),i(drink,f),i(rem,f),i(switch,t).
pa(rla,look(t),d_(1,100))  :-i(book,f),i(drink,f),i(rem,f),i(switch,f).
```

Recall that the two nodes *tv_on* and *light_on* are observed. The probabilities that the elder has the intention of looking for *book, drink, remote control* and *light switch* given the observations that he is looking around and of the states of the light (on or off) and TV (on or off) can be found in P-log with the following queries, respectively:

$$? -\ \mathrm{pr}(\mathrm{i}(\mathrm{book},\mathrm{t}) \mid (\mathrm{obs}(\mathrm{tv}(\mathrm{S}_1))\ \&\ \mathrm{obs}(\mathrm{light}(\mathrm{S}_2))\ \&\ \mathrm{obs}(\mathrm{look}(\mathrm{t}))), \mathrm{V}_1).$$
$$? -\ \mathrm{pr}(\mathrm{i}(\mathrm{drink},\mathrm{t}) \mid (\mathrm{obs}(\mathrm{tv}(\mathrm{S}_1))\ \&\ \mathrm{obs}(\mathrm{light}(\mathrm{S}_2))\ \&\ \mathrm{obs}(\mathrm{look}(\mathrm{t}))), \mathrm{V}_2).$$
$$? -\ \mathrm{pr}(\mathrm{i}(\mathrm{rem},\mathrm{t}) \mid (\mathrm{obs}(\mathrm{tv}(\mathrm{S}_1))\ \&\ \mathrm{obs}(\mathrm{light}(\mathrm{S}_2))\ \&\ \mathrm{obs}(\mathrm{look}(\mathrm{t}))), \mathrm{V}_3).$$
$$? -\ \mathrm{pr}(\mathrm{i}(\mathrm{switch},\mathrm{t}) \mid (\mathrm{obs}(\mathrm{tv}(\mathrm{S}_1))\ \&\ \mathrm{obs}(\mathrm{light}(\mathrm{S}_2))\ \&\ \mathrm{obs}(\mathrm{look}(\mathrm{t}))), \mathrm{V}_4).$$

where S_1, S_2 are boolean values (t or f) instantiated during execution, depending on the states of the light and TV. Let us consider the possible cases

- If the light is off ($S_2 = f$), then $V_1 = V_2 = V_3 = 0$, $V_4 = 1.0$, regardless of the state of the TV.
- If the light is on and TV is off ($S_1 = t, S_2 = f$), then $V_1 = 0.7521, V_2 = 0.5465, V_3 = 0.5036, V_4 = 0.0101$.
- If both light and TV are on ($S_1 = t, S_2 = t$), then $V_1 = 0, V_2 = 0.6263, V_3 = 0.9279, V_4 = 0.0102$.

Thus, if one observes that the light is off, definitely the elder is looking for the light switch, given that he is looking around. Otherwise, if one observes the light is on, in both cases where the TV is either on or off, the first three intentions *book, drink, remote control* still need to be put under consideration in the next phase, generating possible plans for each of them. The intention of looking for the light switch is very unlikely to be the case comparing with other three, thus being ruled out. When there is light one goes directly to the light switch if the intention is to turn it off, without having to look for it.

Situation-sensitive CBNs. Undoubtedly, CBNs should be situation-sensitive since using a general CBN for all specific situations (instances) of a problem domain is unrealistic and most likely imprecise. However, consulting the domain expert to manually change the CBN w.r.t. each situation is also very costly. We here provide a way to construct situation-sensitive CBNs, i.e. ones that change according to the given situation. It uses Logic Programming (LP) techniques to compute situation specific probabilistic information, which is then introduced into a CBN which is general for the problem domain.

The LP techniques can be deduction with top-down procedure (Prolog) (to deduce situation-specific probabilistic information) or abduction (to abduce probabilistic information needed to explain observations representing the given situation). However, we do not exclude various other types of reasoning, e.g. integrity constraint satisfaction, contradiction removal, preferences, or inductive learning, whose results can be compiled (in part) into an evolving CBN.

The general issue of how to update a CBN with new probabilistic information can take advantage of the advances in LP semantics for evolving programs by means of rule updates [19,20,21]. In this paper, however, we do not need such general updates, and make do with a simpler way, shown in the sequel.

Example 2 (Elder Care, cont'd). In this scenario, the CBN may vary depending on some observed factors, for example, the time of day, the current temperature, etc. We design a logical component for the CBN to deal with those factors:

```
pa_rule(pa(rlk,lr(t),d_(0,1)),[])       :-time(T), T>0, T<5, !.
pa_rule(pa(rlk,lr(t),d_(1,10)),[])      :-time(T), T>=5, T<8, !.
pa_rule(pa(rlw,lw(t),d_(9,10)),[])      :-time(T),schedule(T,football),!.
pa_rule(pa(rlw,lw(t),d_(1,10)),[])      :-time(T), (T>23; T<5), !.
pa_rule(pa(rth,thsty(t),d_(7,10)),[])   :-temp(T), T>30, !.
pa_rule(pa(rlk,lr(t),d_(1,10)),[])      :-temp(TM), TM >30, !.
pa_rule(pa(rlw,lw(t),d_(3,10)),[])      :-temp(TM), TM>30, !.
```

Given P-log probabilistic information by $pa/3$ rules, then the corresponding so-called situation-sensitive $pa\_rule/2$ predicates take the head and body of some *pa*/3 rule as its first and second arguments, respectively, and includes conditions for its activation in its own body. Now, a situation is given by asserted facts representing it and, in order to find the probabilistic information specific to the given situation, we simply use the XSB Prolog built-in *findall/3* predicate to find all true *pa*/3 literals expressed by the *pa_rule*/2 rules with true bodies in the situation. For example, when the time and temperature are defined (the assisting system should be aware of such information), they are asserted using predicates *time*/1 and *temp*/1. Note that in this modelling, to guarantee the consistency of the P-log program (there must not be two pa-rules for the same attribute instance with non-exclusive bodies) we consider time with a higher priority than temperature, enacted by using XSB Prolog *cut* operator, as can be seen in the *rlk* and *rlw* cases.

2.5 Plan Generation

The second phase of the intention recognition system is to generate conceivable plans that can achieve the most likely intentions surviving after the first phase. The plan generation phase can be carried out by ASCP – an ASP logic programming based conditional planner [16], as in our work [1], which details the method and the language for expressing actions. For lack of space, we will simply assume here that the system has been furnished a plan library that provides recipes for achieving the recognized intentions in the situation. This alternative method has also been employed in several works of plan recognition, e.g. [11,14].

3 Elder Assisting with Evolution Prospection

3.1 Preliminary

We next describe constructs of the evolution prospection system that are necessary for representation of the example. A full presentation can be found in [2]. The separate formalism for expressing actions can be found in [1] or [16].

Language. Let $\mathcal{L}$ be a first order language. A domain literal in $\mathcal{L}$ is a domain atom A or its default negation *not* A. The latter is used to express that the atom is false by default (Closed World Assumption). A domain rule in $\mathcal{L}$ is a rule of the form:

$$A \leftarrow L_1, \ldots, L_t \qquad (t \geq 0)$$

where A is a domain atom and $L_1, \ldots, L_t$ are domain literals. An integrity constraint in $\mathcal{L}$ is a rule with an empty head. A (logic) program P over $\mathcal{L}$ is a set of domain rules and integrity constraints, standing for all their ground instances.

Active Goals. In each cycle of its evolution the agent has a set of active goals or desires. We introduce the *on_observe*/1 predicate, which we consider as representing active goals or desires that, once triggered by the observations figuring in its rule bodies, cause the agent to attempt their satisfaction by launching all the queries standing for them, or using preferences to select them. The rule for an active goal AG is of the form:

$$on\_observe(AG) \leftarrow L_1, ..., L_t \ (t \geq 0)$$

where L_1,...,L_t are domain literals. During evolution, an active goal may be triggered by some events, previous commitments or some history-related information. When starting a cycle, the agent collects its active goals by finding all the $on\_observe(AG)$ that hold under the initial theory without performing any abduction, then finds abductive solutions for their conjunction.

Preferring abducibles. Every program P is associated with a set of abducibles $\mathcal{A} \subseteq \mathcal{L}$. These, and their default negations, can be seen as hypotheses that provide hypothetical solutions or possible explanations to given queries. Abducibles can figure only in the body of program rules. An abducible A can be assumed only if it is a considered one, i.e. if it is expected in the given situation, and, moreover, there is no expectation to the contrary

$$consider(A) \leftarrow expect(A), not\ expect\_not(A), A$$

The rules about expectations are domain-specific knowledge contained in the theory of the program, and effectively constrain the hypotheses available in a situation. To express preference criteria among abducibles, we envisage an extended language $\mathcal{L}^\star$. A preference atom in $\mathcal{L}^\star$ is of the form $a \lhd b$, where a and b are abducibles. It means that if b can be assumed (i.e. considered), then $a \lhd b$ forces a to be assumed too if it can. A preference rule in $\mathcal{L}^\star$ is of the form:

$$a \lhd b \leftarrow L_1, ..., L_t \ (t \geq 0)$$

where $L_1, ..., L_t$ are domain literals over $\mathcal{L}^\star$. This preference rule can be coded as follows:

$$expect\_not(b) \leftarrow \ L_1, ..., L_n, not\ expect\_not(a), expect(a), not\ a$$

In fact, if b is considered, the consider–rule for abducible b requires $expect\_not(b)$ to be false, i.e. every rule with the head $expect\_not(b)$ cannot have a true body. Thus, $a \lhd b$, that is if its body in the preference rule holds, and if a is expected, and not counter-expected, then a must be abduced so that this particular rule for $expect\_not(b)$ also fails, and the abduction of b may go through if all the other rules for $expect\_not(b)$ fail as well.

A priori preferences are used to produce the most interesting or relevant conjectures about possible future states. They are taken into account when generating possible scenarios (abductive solutions), which will subsequently be preferred amongst each other a posteriori.

A posteriori Preferences. Having computed possible scenarios, represented by abductive solutions, more favorable scenarios can be preferred a posteriori.

Typically, *a posteriori* preferences are performed by evaluating consequences of abducibles in abductive solutions. An *a posteriori* preference has the form:

$$A_i \ll A_j \leftarrow holds\_given(L_i, A_i),\ holds\_given(L_j, A_j)$$

where A_i, A_j are abductive solutions and L_i, L_j are domain literals. This means that A_i is preferred to A_j a posteriori if L_i and L_j are true as the side-effects of abductive solutions A_i and A_j, respectively, without any further abduction when testing for the side-effects. Optionally, in the body of the preference rule there can be any Prolog predicate used to quantitatively compare the consequences of the two abductive solutions.

Evolution result a posteriori preference. While looking ahead a number of steps into the future, the agent is confronted with the problem of having several different possible courses of evolution. It needs to be able to prefer amongst them to determine the best courses from its present state (and any state in general). The *a posteriori* preferences are no longer appropriate, since they can be used to evaluate only one-step-far consequences of a commitment. The agent should be able to also declaratively specify preference amongst evolutions through quantitatively or qualitatively evaluating the consequences or side-effects of each evolution choice.

A posteriori preference is generalized to prefer between two evolutions. An *evolution result a posteriori* preference is performed by evaluating consequences of following some evolutions. The agent must use the imagination (look-ahead capability) and present knowledge to evaluate the consequences of evolving according to a particular course of evolution. An *evolution result a posteriori preference* rule has the form:

$$E_i \lll E_j \leftarrow holds\_in\_evol(L_i, E_i), holds\_in\_evol(L_j, E_j)$$

where E_i, E_j are possible evolutions and L_i, L_j are domain literals. This preference implies that E_i is preferred to E_j if L_i and L_j are true as evolution history side-effects when evolving according to E_i or E_j, respectively, without making further abductions when just checking for the side-effects. Optionally, in the body of the preference rule there can be recourse to any Prolog predicate, used to quantitatively compare the consequences of the two evolutions for decision making.

3.2 Evolution Prospection as an Intention Consumer

Having recognized the intention of another agent, EPA system can be used to provide the best courses of evolution for that agent to achieve its own intention. These courses of evolution might be provided to the other agent as suggestions.

In Elder Care domain, assisting systems should be able to provide contextually appropriate suggestions for the elders based on their recognized intentions. The assisting system is supposed to be better aware of the environment, the elders' physical states, mental states as well as their scheduled events, so that it can provide good and safe suggestions, or simply warnings. We continue with the Elder Care example from a previous section for illustration.

Example 3 (Elder Care, cont'd). Suppose in Example 1, the final confirmed intention is that of looking for a drink. The possibilities are natural pure *water, tea, coffee* and *juice.* EPA now is used to help the elder in choosing an appropriate one. The scenario is coded with the program in Figure 2.

The elder's physical states are employed in a priori preferences and expectation rules to guarantee that only choices that are contextually safe for the elder are generated. Note that a priori preferences and expectation rules are transformed into appropriate forms during preprocessing and directly participate in generating prior abductive solutions (see [3] for details). Only after that other aspects, for example the elder's pleasure w.r.t. to each kind of drink, are taken into account, in a posteriori preferences. In this manner, the system guarantees, in the first place, the safety for the elder's health, before considering his pleasure choices, which may sometimes not be suitable to his current health conditions (that he is not aware of).

The information regarding the environment (e.g. current time, current temperature) and the physical states of the elder is coded in the Prolog part of the program (lines 9-11). The assisting system is supposed to be aware of this information in order to provide good suggestions.

Line 1 is the declaration of program abducibles: *water, coffee, tea*, and *juice.* All of them are always expected (line 2). Line 3 picks up a recognized intention verified by the planner. The counter-expectation rules in line 4 state that *coffee* is not expected if the elder has high blood pressure, experiences difficulty to sleep or it is late; and juice is not expected if it is late. Note that the reserved predicate *prolog/1* is used to allow embedding Prolog code in an EPA program. More details can be found in [2,3]. The integrity constraints in line 5 say that is is not allowed to have at the same time the following pairs of drink: tea and coffee, tea and juice, coffee and juice, and tea and water. However, it is the case that the elder can have coffee or juice together with water at the same time.

The a priori preferences in line 6 say in the morning coffee is preferred to tea, water and juice. And if it is hot, juice is preferred to all other kinds of drink and water is preferred to tea and coffee (line 7). In addition, the a priori preferences in line 8 state if the weather is cold, tea is the most favorable, i.e. preferred to all other kinds of drink.

Now let us look at the suggestions provided by the Elder Care assisting system modelled by this EPA program, considering some cases:

1. time(24) (*late*); temperature(16) (*not hot, not cold*); no high blood pressure; no sleep difficulty: there are two a priori abductive solutions: [*tea*], [*water*]. Final solutions: [*tea*] (since it has greater level of pleasure than water, which is ruled out by the a posteriori preference in line 12).
2. time(8) (*morning time*); temperature(16) (*not hot, not cold*); no high blood pressure; no sleep difficulty: there are two abductive solutions: [*coffee*], [*coffee, water*]. Final: [*coffee*], [*coffee, water*].

```
1. abds([water/0, coffee/0, tea/0, juice/0]).
2. expect(coffee). expect(tea). expect(water). expect(juice).
3. on_observe(drink) <- has_intention(elder,drink).
   drink <- tea. drink <- coffee. drink <- water. drink <- juice.
4. expect_not(coffee) <-  prolog(blood_high_pressure).
   expect_not(coffee) <- prolog(sleep_difficulty).
   expect_not(coffee) <- prolog(late).
   expect_not(juice) <- prolog(late).
5. <- tea, coffee.    <- coffee, juice.
   <- tea, juice.     <- tea, water.
6. coffee '<|' tea <- prolog(morning_time).
   coffee '<|' water <- prolog(morning_time).
   coffee '<|' juice  <- prolog(morning_time).
7. juice '<|' coffee <- prolog(hot). juice '<|' tea <- prolog(hot).
   juice '<|' water <- prolog(hot).  water '<|' coffee <- prolog(hot).
   water '<|' tea <- prolog(hot).
8. tea '<|' coffee <- prolog(cold).  tea '<|' juice <- prolog(cold).
   tea '<|' water <- prolog(cold).
9. pleasure_level(3) <- coffee. pleasure_level(2) <- tea.
   pleasure_level(1) <- juice.  pleasure_level(0) <- water.
10.sugar_level(1) <- coffee. sugar_level(1) <- tea.
   sugar_level(5) <- juice.  sugar_level(0) <- water.
11.caffein_level(5) <- coffee.  caffein_level(0) <- tea.
   caffein_level(0) <- juice.  caffein_level(0) <- water.
12.Ai << Aj <- holds_given(pleasure_level(V1), Ai),
               holds_given(pleasure_level(V2), Aj), V1 > V2.

13.on_observe(health_check) <- time_for_health_check.
   health_check <- precise_result.
   health_check <- imprecise_result.
14.expect(precise_result) <- no_hight_sugar, no_high_caffein.
   expect(imprecise_result).
   no_high_sugar <- sugar_level(L), prolog(L < 2).
   no_high_caffein <- caffein_level(L), prolog(L < 2).
15.Ei <<< Ej <- holds_in_evol(precise_result, Ei),
          holds_in_evol(imprecise_result, Ej).

 beginProlog.
   :- assert(scheduled_events(1, [has_intention(elder,drink)])),
   assert(scheduled_events(2, [time_for_health_check])).
   late :- time(T), (T > 23; T < 5).
   morning_time :- time(T), T > 7, T < 10.
   hot :- temperature(TM), TM > 32.
   cold :- temperature(TM), TM < 10.
   blood_high_pressure :- physical_state(blood_high_pressure).
   sleep_difficulty :- physical_state(sleep_difficulty).
 endProlog.
```

Fig. 2. Elder Care: Suggestion for a Drink

3. time(18) (*not late, not morning time*); temperature(16) (*not cold, not hot*); no high blood pressure; no sleep difficulty: there are six abductive solutions: *[coffee]*, *[coffee,water]*, *[juice]*, *[juice,water]*, *[tea]*, and *[water]*. Final: *[coffee]*, *[coffee,water]*.
4. time(18) *(not late, not morning time*); temperature(16) (*not cold, not hot*); high blood pressure; no sleep difficulty: there are four abductive solutions: *[juice]*, *[juice,water]*, *[tea]*, and *[water]*. Final: [*tea*].
5. time(18) (*not late, not morning time*); temperature(16) (*not cold, not hot*); no high blood pressure; sleep difficulty: there are four abductive solutions: *[juice]*, *[juice,water]*, *[tea]*, and *[water]*. Final: [*tea*].
6. time(18) (*not late, not morning time*); temperature(8) (*cold*); no high blood pressure; no sleep difficulty: there is only one abductive solution: *[tea]*.
7. time(18) (*not late, not morning time*); temperature(35) (*hot*); no high blood pressure; no sleep difficulty: there are two abductive solutions: *[juice]*, *[juice, water]*. Final: *[juice]*, *[juice,water]*.

If the *evolution result a posteriori preference* in line 15 is taken into account and the elder is scheduled to go to the hospital for health check in the second day: the first and the second cases do not change. In the third case: the suggestions are [*tea*] and [*water*] since the ones that have *coffee* or juice would cause high caffein and sugar levels, respectively, which can make the checking result (health) imprecise (lines 13-15). Similarly for other cases ...

Note future events can be asserted as Prolog code using the reserved predicate *schedule_events*/2. For more details of its use see [2,3].

As one can gather, the suggestions provided by this assisting system are quite contextually appropriate. We might elaborate current factors (time, temperature, physical states) and even consider more factors to provide more appropriate suggestions if the situation gets more complicated.

4 Conclusions and Future Work

We have shown a coherent LP-based system for assisting elderly people based on an intention recognizer and Evolution Prospection system. The recognizer is to figure out intentions of the elders based on their observed actions or the effects their actions have in the environment, via a combination of situation-sensitive Causal Bayes Nets and a planner. The implemented Evolution Prospection system, being aware of the external environment, elders' preferences and their note future events, is then employed to provide contextually appropriate suggestions that achieve the recognized intention. The system built-in expectation rules and a priori preferences take into account the physical state (health reports) information of the elder to guarantee that only contextually safe healthy choices are generated; then, information such as the elder's pleasure, interests, scheduled events, etc. are taken into account by a posteriori and evolution result a posteriori preferences.

We believe to have shown the usefulness and advantage of our approach of combining several needed features to tackle the application domain, by virtue of an integrated logic programming approach.

One future direction is to implement meta-explanation about evolution prospection. It would be quite useful in the considered setting, as the elder care assisting system should be able to explain to elders the whys and wherefores of suggestions made. In addition, it should be able to produce the abductive solutions found for possible evolutions, keeping them labeled by the preferences used (in a partial order) instead of exhibiting only the most favorable ones. This would allow for final preference change on the part of the elder.

We plan to deploy our system to tackle actual situations of the Elder Care domain, combining with an activity recognition system to supply inputs for the intention recognition system. Based on that, we hope to obtain more insights in order to improve and provide its more comprehensive evaluation.

Acknowledgment

Han The Anh is supported by FCT grant SFRH/BD/62373/2009. We also thank the anonymous referees for their useful comments, which enabled the improvement of the submitted version.

References

1. Pereira, L.M., Han, T.A.: Intention Recognition via Causal Bayes Networks Plus Plan Generation. In: Lopes, L.S., Lau, N., Mariano, P., Rocha, L.M. (eds.) EPIA 2009. LNCS (LNAI), vol. 5816, pp. 138–149. Springer, Heidelberg (2009)
2. Pereira, L.M., Han, T.A.: Evolution Prospection. In: Nakamatsu, K. (ed.) Procs. Intl. Symposium on Intelligent Decision Technologies (KES-IDT 2009). Springer Studies in Computational Intelligence, vol. 199, pp. 51–63 (2009)
3. Pereira, L.M., Han, T.A.: Evolution Prospection in Decision Making. Intelligent Decision Technologies (IDT) 3(3), 157–171 (2009)
4. Baral, C., Gelfond, M., Rushton, N.: Probabilistic reasoning with answer sets. In: Lifschitz, V., Niemelä, I. (eds.) LPNMR 2004. LNCS (LNAI), vol. 2923, pp. 21–33. Springer, Heidelberg (2003)
5. Han, T.A., Kencana Ramli, C.D.P., Damásio, C.V.: An implementation of extended P-log using XASP. In: Garcia de la Banda, M., Pontelli, E. (eds.) ICLP 2008. LNCS, vol. 5366, pp. 739–743. Springer, Heidelberg (2008)
6. Baral, C., Gelfond, M., Rushton, N.: Probabilistic reasoning with answer sets. Theory and Practice of Logic Programming 9(1), 57–144 (2009)
7. Castro, L., Swift, T., Warren, D.S.: XASP: Answer set programming with xsb and smodels, `http://xsb.sourceforge.net/packages/xasp.pdf`
8. Cesta, A., Pecora, F.: The Robocare Project: Intelligent Systems for Elder Care. In: AAAI Fall Symposium on Caring Machines: AI in Elder Care, USA (2005)
9. Mileo, A., Merico, D., Bisiani, R.: A Logic Programming Approach to Home Monitoring for Risk Prevention in Assisted Living. In: Garcia de la Banda, M., Pontelli, E. (eds.) ICLP 2008. LNCS, vol. 5366, pp. 145–159. Springer, Heidelberg (2008)
10. Giuliani, M.V., Scopelliti, M., Fornara, F.: Elderly people at home: technological help in everyday activities. In: IEEE International Workshop on In Robot and Human Interactive Communication, pp. 365–370 (2005)

11. Heinze, C.: Modeling Intention Recognition for Intelligent Agent Systems, Doctoral Thesis, the University of Melbourne, Australia (2003), `http://www.dsto.defence.gov.au/publications/scientific_record.php?record=3367`
12. Tahboub, K.A.: Intelligent Human-Machine Interaction Based on Dynamic Bayesian Networks Probabilistic Intention Recognition. J. Intelligent Robotics Systems 45(1), 31–52 (2006)
13. Schrempf, O.C., Albrecht, D., Hanebeck, U.D.: Tractable Probabilistic Models for Intention Recognition Based on Expert Knowledge. In: Procs. 2007 IEEE/RSJ Intl. Conf. on Intelligent Robots and Systems (IROS 2007), pp. 1429–1434 (2007)
14. Kautz, H.A., Allen, J.F.: Generalized plan recognition. In: Procs. 1986 Conf. of the American Association for Artificial Intelligence, pp. 32–37. AAAI, Menlo Park (1986)
15. Eiter, T., Faber, W., Leone, N., Pfeifer, G., Polleres, A.: A Logic Programming Approach to Knowledge State Planning, II: The $DLV^{\mathcal{K}}$ System. Artificial Intelligence 144(1-2), 157–211 (2003)
16. Tu, P.H., Son, T.C., Baral, C.: Reasoning and Planning with Sensing Actions, Incomplete Information, and Static Causal Laws using Answer Set Programming. Theory and Practice of Logic Programming 7(4), 377–450 (2007)
17. Glymour, C.: The Mind's Arrows: Bayes Nets and Graphical Causal Models in Psychology. MIT Press, Cambridge (2001)
18. Pearl, J.: Causality: Models, Reasoning, and Inference. Cambridge U.P, Cambridge (2000)
19. Alferes, J.J., Brogi, A., Leite, J.A., Pereira, L.M.: Evolving logic programs. In: Flesca, S., Greco, S., Leone, N., Ianni, G. (eds.) JELIA 2002. LNCS (LNAI), vol. 2424, pp. 50–61. Springer, Heidelberg (2002)
20. Alferes, J.J., Banti, F., Brogi, A., Leite, J.A.: The Refined Extension Principle for Semantics of Dynamic Logic Programming. Studia Logica 79(1), 7–32 (2005)
21. Alferes, J.J., Leite, J.A., Pereira, L.M., Przymusinska, H., Przymusinski, T.C.: Dynamic updates of non-monotonic knowledge bases. J. Logic Programming 45(1-3), 43–70 (2000)
22. Niemelä, I., Simons, P.: Smodels: An implementation of the stable model and well-founded semantics for normal logic programs. In: Fuhrbach, U., Dix, J., Nerode, A. (eds.) LPNMR 1997. LNCS (LNAI), vol. 1265, pp. 420–429. Springer, Heidelberg (1997)
23. Swift, T.: Tabling for non-monotonic programming. Annals of Mathematics and Artificial Intelligence 25(3-4), 201–240 (1999)
24. The XSB System Version 3.0 Vol. 2: Libraries, Interfaces and Packages (July 2006)

Knowledge Management Strategy and Tactics for Forging Die Design Support

Masanobu Umeda[1] and Yuji Mure[2]

[1] Kyushu Institute of Technology, 680-4 Kawazu, Iizuka 820-8502, Japan
umerin@ci.kyutech.ac.jp
[2] Kagoshima Prefectural Institute of Industrial Technology, 1445-1 Hayato-Oda, Kirishima 899-5105, Japan
mure@kagoshima-it.go.jp

Abstract. The design tasks of cold forged products are very important because they have a great influence on the quality of the final products and the life of the forging dies. However, the design expertise required for the design tends to get scattered and lost, and therefore there is a need for a framework that will enable the accumulation, utilization and evolution of this expertise. The authors have been developing a knowledge-based system to support process planning and the design of dies and die-sets for cold forged products. The knowledge base contains design knowledge on cold forging, which is systematized based on the formal definition of die design problems and on methods with high generality for resolving these problems. These features facilitate the improvement of product quality using an exhaustive search of process plans and die structures, and the improvement of design performance by automating the design work. They also make it easier to pass on and evolve expertise by allowing design experts to self audit and maintain their own knowledge base. The proposed system has been applied to several cold forged products. Experiments show that it can generate multiple forging process plans, dies, and die-sets based on the design knowledge, and that feasible solutions can be obtained within a practical time span.

1 Introduction

Parts formed by cold forging are popularly used in many products such as automobiles, aircrafts and home electrical appliances. This is because they have the advantages of productivity in mass production, dimensional accuracy and precision, and improvements in mechanical properties. The design tasks of cold forged products are very important because they have great influence on the quality of the final products and the life of the forging dies. In these design tasks, many kinds of expertise in forging process planning and the design of dies and die-sets are required for high-quality and low-cost production. Such expertise, however, tends to get scattered and lost for a range of reasons such as the loss or retirement of experienced experts. This expertise has been poorly

S. Abreu and D. Seipel (Eds.): INAP 2009, LNAI 6547, pp. 188–204, 2011.

documented and typically has been transferred as individual skills through informal communication. To systematically pass on this expertise, it is essential to realize a framework that enables the design knowledge of experienced experts to be accumulated as important knowledge-based software assets, so that they can be continuously utilized and evolved within an organization or industrial community.

A number of knowledge-based systems have been developed to ensure the productivity of forging process planning and die design. They can be roughly classified into two categories. Case- or pattern-based systems [1, 2] formulate past successful design results as design cases or patterns, and derive solutions from similar cases. Although these systems generally achieve adequate results, the variety of applicable products strongly depends on the cases or patterns that have been accumulated. Conventional rule-based systems [3–7] represent design guidelines or expertise as production rules, and have the advantage of adaptability to new products. However, production rules are difficult to maintain and extend, because interference between rules, and combinatorial explosion and execution control of rules become serious problems if a knowledge base becomes too large [8, 9].

The authors have been developing a knowledge-based system to support process planning and the design of dies and die-sets for cold forged products. The knowledge base contains design knowledge on cold forging, which is systematized based on the formal definition of die design problems and on methods with high generality for resolving these problems. The knowledge representation language of the knowledge base is suitable for representing design procedures involving trial and error without any side-effects, and can be used to comprehensively enumerate all possible solutions of forging processes and die structures. These features facilitate the improvement of product quality using an exhaustive search of process plans and die structures and the improvement of design performance by automating the design work. They also make it easier to inherit the available expertise and evolve it by allowing design experts to self audit and maintain their own knowledge base.

This paper first describes an overview of the integrated die design support system for cold forging, design object models of cold forged products and associated dies, and the formalization and systematization methodology for forging die design knowledge. The implementation of the system is then briefly introduced. Finally, experimental results applied to several cold forged products are shown.

2 System Overview

Generally, the design process of a cold forged product is as follows. First, based on a final product design and considering post machining processes, the shape of a forged product is designed. Then, the forging process planning is undertaken to decide parameters such as the number of stages of the forming process, the shape of an intermediate forged product, and the forming methods. In the

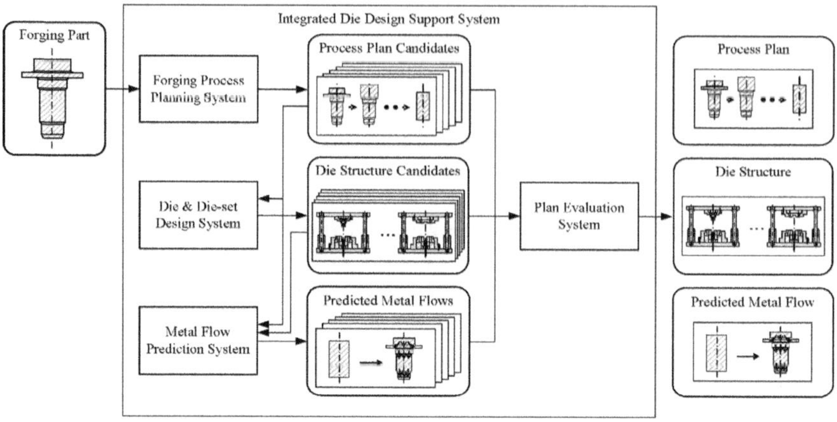

Fig. 1. Overview of the integrated die design support system

planning, various design constraints, such as the load capacity of press machines and the forming limits and metal flow of materials are taken into account. Finally, dies and die-sets are designed for each stage of the forming processes by considering the product quality, the die life and the production cost. If necessary, the metal flow is evaluated using experimental analysis or FEM analysis. Although the degree of geometric deformation freedom is generally high in forging process planning, design constraints, such as the forming limits and metal flow of materials, dominate. Therefore, it is difficult, even for experienced experts, to find an appropriate solution from countless process plans and their die structures.

The integrated die design support system is intended to consistently support this design process. It consists of the following four subsystems shown in Fig. 1: forging process planning, die and die-set design, metal flow prediction, and plan evaluation.

The forging process planning system is to support the planning of a cold forging process for a given axisymmetrical forged product. It can propose multiple deformable process plans using the Adjustment of Stepped Cylinder (ASC) method [10]. Because the ASC method is based on a combination of simple geometric deformations and fundamental design constraints, it can generate appropriate plans even if no similar best practices can be found in a case-based knowledge base.

The die and die-set design system generates multiple die structures and the detailed shapes of their components, such as die inserts, stress rings, and knock-out pins, for the generated process plans. Because dies are subjected to high stress, they are prone to breakage, such as stress cracks. Therefore, the die life has to be taken into account by considering empirical actions, such as partitioning a die insert into pieces and stacking pressure pads that receive the pressure on the dies.

The forming limits of materials, such as reduction in area, are taken into account by these two subsystems. It is still necessary to evaluate the metal flow using experimental analysis or FEM analysis in the case of an unknown or unfamiliar shape, because it is not sufficient to evaluate the surface and internal defects. It is, however, time consuming or impractical to evaluate the metal flow of all the generated solutions using the usual analytic methods. The metal flow prediction system [11] is designed to help make a rough and quick quantitative evaluation of metal flow using the knowledge of experienced experts and deformation characteristics.

Candidates for forging process plans and die structures are often obtained from these two subsystems. Therefore, it is not easy to choose an optimal candidate manually, because many aspects of the candidates must be considered. The plan evaluation system is designed to help choose an optimal candidate by evaluating the candidates overall in terms of product quality, production cost, and production lead time.

3 Modeling of Forged Product and Die

3.1 Shape Representation

Because the shape of a cold forged product is axisymmetric, the principal shapes of companion forging dies are also axisymmetric. Therefore, both a forged product shape and a die shape can be represented as a series of axisymmetrical representation units called **basic elements** (BEs). Figure 2 shows a list of the basic elements. Each basic element has geometric attributes, such as element type, diameter, and height. Figure 3 shows examples of the shape representations of a forged product and a die. In these examples, the shape of a forged product can be represented by an outer shape `[C1,TU1,C1,TU1,C1]`. The shape of a hollow die can be represented by the combination of an outer shape `[TL1]` and an inner shape `[C1,TU1,C1,TU1,C1]`. This uniform representation simplifies the shape representation of a forged product and a die, and the knowledge description needed for forging process planning and die design can then easily be integrated.

3.2 Object Model Representation

A forged product, a die, and a die-set are constructively represented as a design object model called an **assembly structure**, which is simplified for use with an axisymmetrical object based on the model proposed for mechanism parts [12]. Figure 4 illustrates the assembly structure of a forged product and that of a die and a die-set, where the arrows indicate the dependency between elements. The assembly structure of the forged product in Fig. 4 (a) represents a billet (or a blank), an intermediate forged product, or a final forged product. The object model of a forged product has outer and inner shapes represented by a series of basic elements, and other attributes, such as material, forming method, and forming load. On the other hand, the assembly structure of the die and die-set

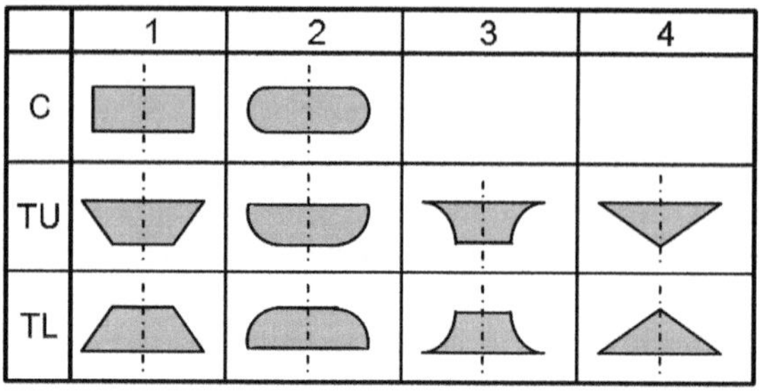

Fig. 2. Basic elements for shape representation

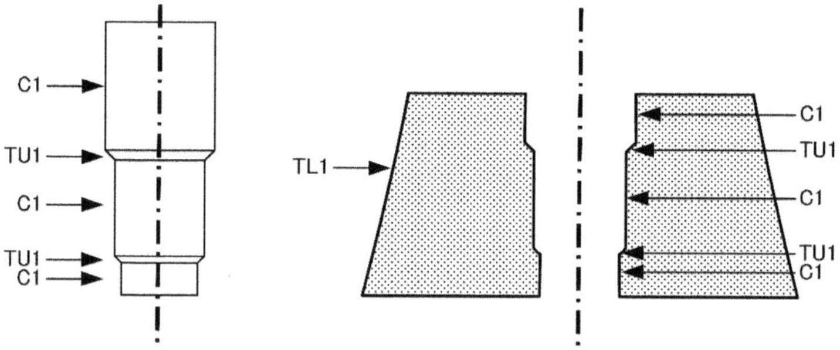

Fig. 3. Shape representation of a product and a die using basic elements

in Fig. 4 (b) represents the whole structure of an upper die, a lower die, and a die-set. The object model of a part, which constructs an upper die, a lower die, or a die-set, has outer and inner shapes and other similar attributes to that of a forged product.

The model based on the assembly structure is easy to extend for the purpose of dealing with dimensional and geometric tolerances. This feature is important because accuracy and precision management of a forged product and a die is essential in cold forging.

4 Formalization of Die and Die-Set Design Problems

Generally speaking, most design tasks can be seen as activities to decide on the structural attributes from the required functional attributes by solving an inverse problem[1]. Because these kinds of problems often involve nonlinear features, it is difficult to solve them analytically, and in the past they were solved typically by trial and error based on experience or intuition. Deriving approximate

[1] On the other hand, a direct problem is solved by deriving functional attributes from structural attributes. This is often called analysis.

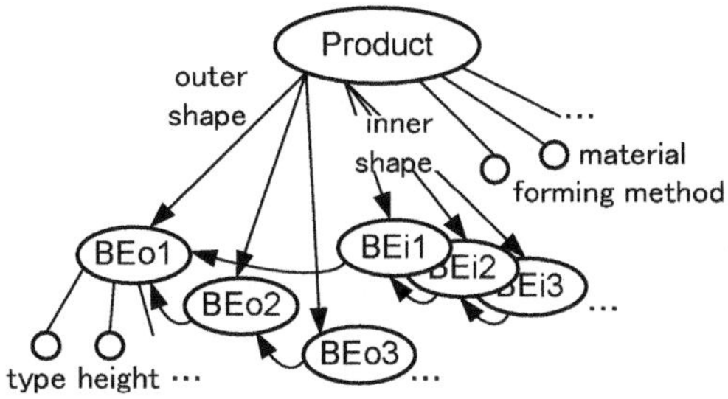

(a) Forged product representation

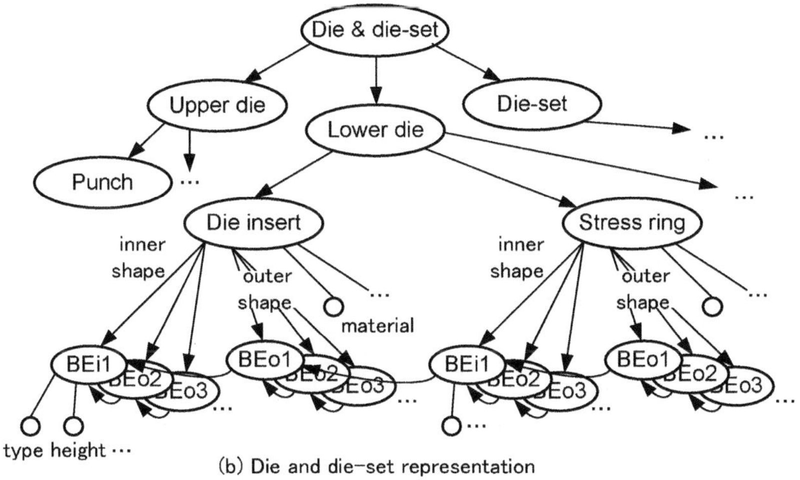

(b) Die and die–set representation

Fig. 4. Assembly structure of a forged product and a die and die-set

solutions from past design results or design constraints using back calculation is an example of how these problems have been solved. These heuristic methods are, however, usually unique to each designer or organization. The design result, productivity, and product quality of a designer usually differ from those of other designers, even for the same problem. For this reason, even if pieces of heuristic knowledge are collected from experienced experts through interviews, and described as production rules, the generality of this knowledge is quite low and its applicability is limited to a narrow range of problems. A knowledge base developed in this way is difficult to maintain and extend and is thus likely to become out of date. In addition, it would seem more effective and efficient for experienced experts to develop and maintain a knowledge base by themselves.

For this reason, it is essential to provide a formalization methodology to allow design experts to reorganize, describe, audit, and maintain their own design knowledge, while enabling them to represent individual heuristic knowledge in as general a form as possible.

4.1 Formal Definition of Design Problem

The authors have applied the **design space** proposed in [13] to the formal definition of die and die-set design problems. The design space Ds is a set of design solutions intentionally defined by the necessary and sufficient design attributes and the design constraints between them. It is represented as a quadruple $<P, D, R, C>$, where P is a set of design attributes, D is a set of the domains of the attributes, R is a set of the equations or functional relationships between the attributes, and C is a set of the logical constraints on the attributes.

Figure 5 illustrates the pressure pads and design space of the design of the pressure pads. The pads belong to a die-set, and are used for absorbing the forming pressure and preventing the deformation of a press machine. This design problem is to decide the number N, thickness T, and radius R of the pads from other attributes, such as the receiving radius $R0$, receiving pressure $P0$, and pressure propagation angle θ, where P is the propagated pressure and r is the radius where the pads actually receive the pressure. The solutions must satisfy the condition that P is smaller than the load limit **LoadLimit** of a press machine.

If a design problem is large and complicated, designers often solve it by dividing it into several sub-problems and solving them step by step. Such a complicated design problem can be represented as a concatenation of design spaces representing the sub-problems. The concatenation indicates the order in which the sub-problems need to be solved, and a set of its solutions can be expressed as a result of several join operations over the design spaces. The join operation, such as a natural join and a direct product, is determined by how a preceding design space and a following design space are combined and the dependency between them. An example of the concatenation of design spaces is shown in Sect. 5.

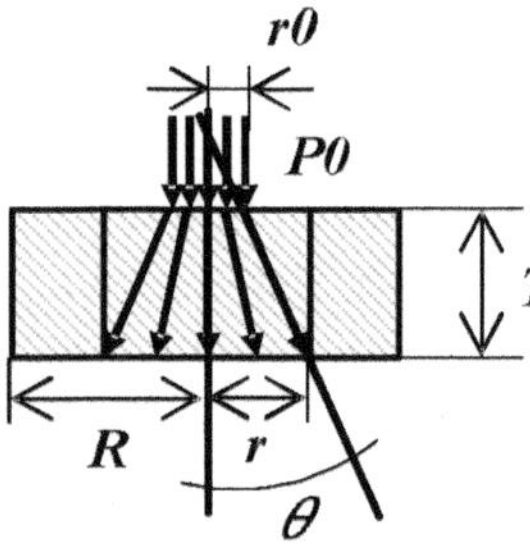

(a) Pressure pads

$$Ds = \langle P, D, R, C \rangle$$
$$P = \{r0,\ \theta,\ P0,\ r,\ T,\ P,\ R,\ N\}$$
$$D = \{r0,\ \theta,\ P0,\ r,\ T,\ P,\ R \in real,\ N \in int\}$$
$$R = \{r = r0*(3/(3-2*tan(\theta)))\hat{}(N-1),\ T = (r - r0)/tan(\theta),\ R = 1.5*r,\ P = (r0/r)\hat{}2*P0\ \}$$
$$C = \{P < \text{LoadLimit}\}$$

(b) Design space of pressure pads design

Fig. 5. Design space of pressure pads design

4.2 Resolving Method of the Design Space

If a design problem is difficult to solve analytically, a trial and error process is usually necessary. In many cases traditional AI techniques for combinatorial optimization problems are ideally applicable to such design problems, but most of these techniques are not adequate for describing design knowledge in a manageable and extendable way. This is because some are limited in applicable scope and may become obstacles to the future extension of a knowledge base, while other techniques are difficult for design experts to use for describing, auditing, and maintaining their own knowledge base.

The generate and test method is a very simple but general method for resolving such a problem in a manageable and extendable way. A design problem defined by a design space can easily be formulated using the generate and test method. That is, for a given design space $<P, D, R, C>$, the solutions can be obtained by assuming the values of base attributes within D, where the base attributes are members of a necessary and sufficient subset of P for specifying a unique design solution, calculating values of other dependent attributes from the base attributes using R, and verifying that C is satisfied. Figure 6 illustrates a data-flow diagram of the resolving method based on the generate and test method for the design space of pressure pads design in Fig. 5.

Once a design problem formulated as a design space is represented using data-flow diagrams, it can easily be translated into executable knowledge descriptions. A knowledge representation language for describing resolving methods based on the generate and test method is described in Sect. 6.

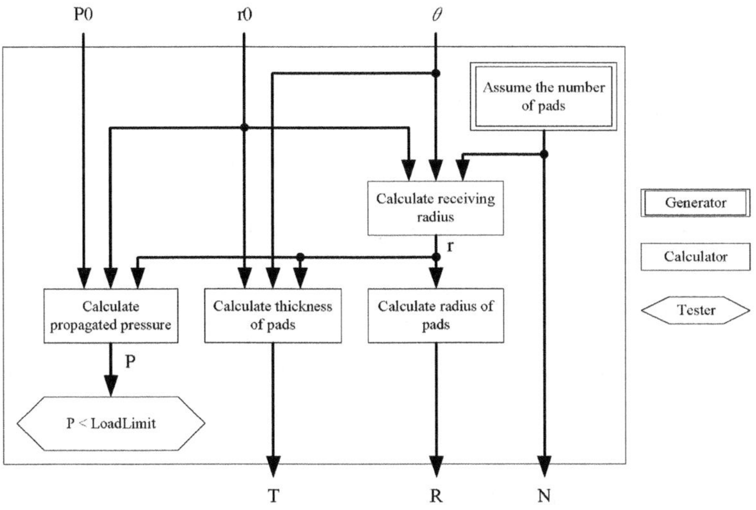

Fig. 6. Data-flow diagram for pressure pads design

5 Systematization of Die and Die-Set Design Knowledge

Parts composing a die and a die-set can be roughly classified into a forming portion, a pressure receiver, and a mounting portion according to their roles. Based on this classification the design procedure for a die and a die-set is standardized. The forming portion, which is prone to breakage, is designed according to the results of the forging process planning, and the pressure receiver is then designed to withstand the forming pressure. Finally, the mounting portion, by which the forming portion and pressure receiver are mounted on a press machine, is designed. Figure 7 illustrates the overall structure of these portions. In this section, the methodology to systematize the design knowledge for dies and die-sets is introduced using examples of the forming portion.

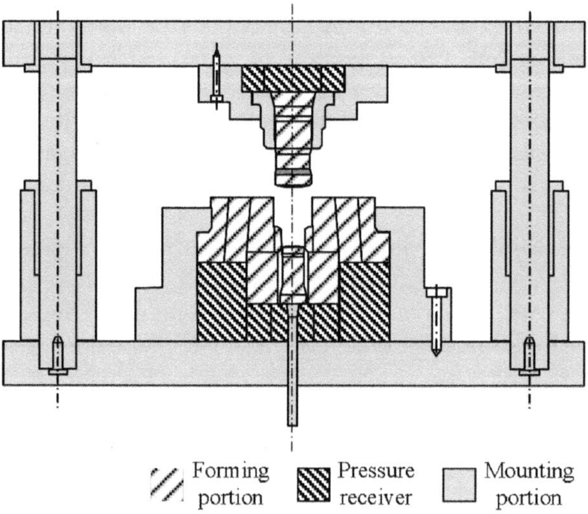

Fig. 7. Overall structure of a die and a die-set

5.1 Design Space of Forming Portion Design

The forming portion, which consists of a punch, a die insert, stress rings, backup rings, and knock-out pins, is directly related to the forming of forged products. Because it is subjected to high stress, the shapes of its parts have to be designed with forming methods and loads in mind in order not to be broken. The design procedure of the forming portion is divided into an outline design and a detailed design. First, the outline shapes of the forming portion are decided according to a process plan by taking into account design constraints, such as the strength and press fit ratio of a die. A number of solutions with different die structures may be available for the same forged or intermediate product if multiple forming methods are applicable. The detailed shapes are then determined by taking into account design constraints, such as the deformation characteristics of materials and the reduction in area.

The design space of the forming portion design can be represented as a concatenation of ten design spaces. Figure 8 illustrates these design spaces. The five design spaces at the beginning correspond to the outline design, and the rest to the detailed design. In the following, the design space of the detailed design of the die insert is briefly explained as an example.

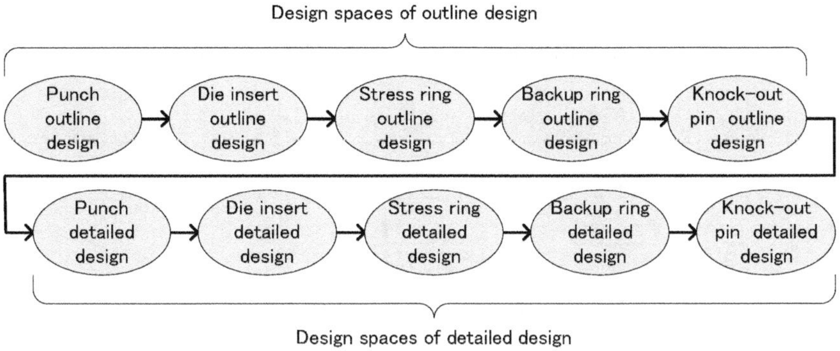

Fig. 8. Concatenated design spaces of the forming portion design

5.2 Design Space of the Detailed Design of the Die Insert

In the detailed design of a die insert, the partition of a die insert, creation of lands, and position alignment of the upper and lower dies have to be solved. For the sake of simplicity, this paper focuses on the partition of a die insert.

Because the forming portion is subjected to high stress as described previously, a die insert and a punch are often damaged by metal fatigue. In such a case, it is usually possible to avoid breakage by changing their geometries to reduce the concentration of the stress. In the case of a die insert, it is effective to partition the die insert into two parts around a stress concentration zone. Repairing the partition of a die insert is low cost, because it is possible to replace only the part of the partitioned die insert that is broken. On the other hand, the partition has disadvantages, because it is costly to produce due to the increased number of components and complicated geometry.

There are roughly two parting methods of a die insert, as illustrated in Fig. 9. The vertical partition (a) is suitable for upsetting because a die insert is subjected to very high stress. The horizontal partition (b) is, instead, suitable for forward extrusion where the reduction in area is not very large, but is applicable to other forming methods. Figure 10 is a data-flow diagram for die insert partition design in the case of forward extrusion. In this diagram, either of the parting methods is assumed only when the constraints on forming load and the reduction in area are satisfied, and the shapes of partitioned die inserts are decided according to the assumed parting method.

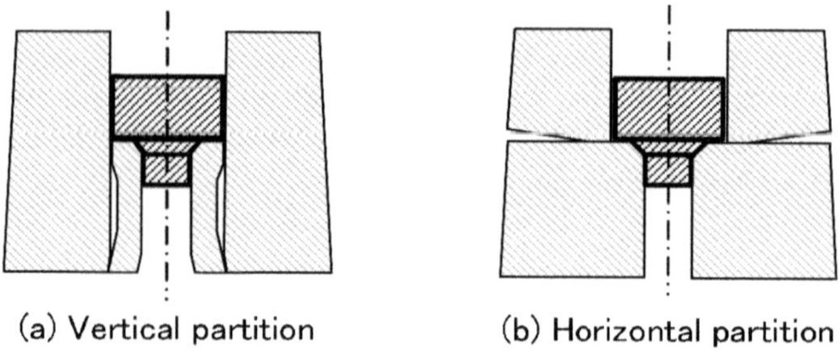

Fig. 9. Parting methods of a die insert

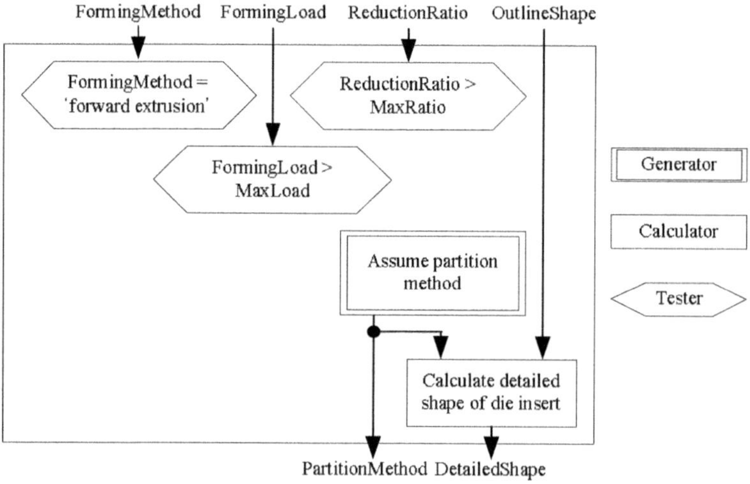

Fig. 10. Data-flow diagram for die insert partition design

6 System Implementation

The authors have been developing an integrated die design support system based on the proposed methodology. Figure 11 illustrates its overall system architecture. The knowledge base stores systematized knowledge for the forging process planning, die and die-set design, metal flow prediction, and plan evaluation. The inference engine performs reasoning, using the knowledge base, and elicits all possible solutions. The forging process planning function, die and die-set design function, metal flow prediction function, and plan evaluation function utilize the knowledge base through the inference engine, and present the solutions to the user.

The contents of the knowledge base can be classified into two: inference rules which represent processes, tasks, and procedures of design work, and engineering information, such as design constraints and design standards. The former are

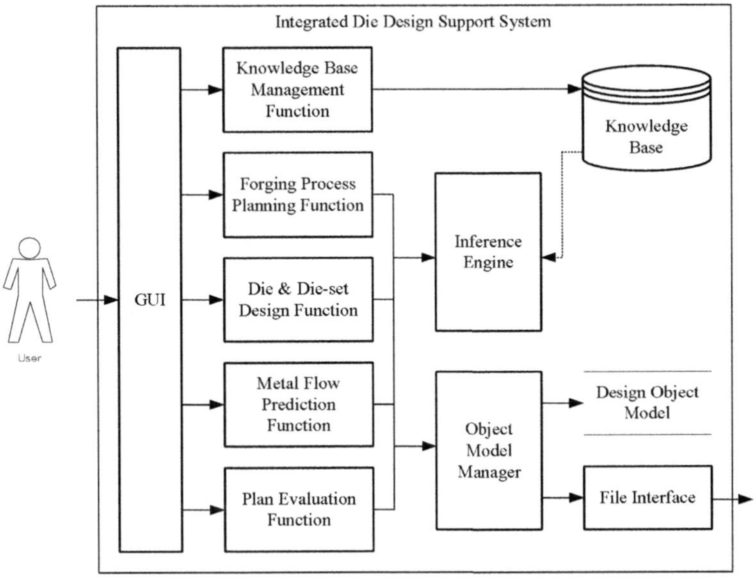

Fig. 11. System architecture of the integrated die design support system

described using a knowledge representation language named DSP [14], which is based on attribute grammars [15]. DSP is a functional programming language with search capability using the generate and test method. Because the language is capable of representing trial and error without any side-effects or loop constructs, and the knowledge descriptions using the language can be declaratively read and understood, it is suitable for representing design procedures according to systematized knowledge using the design space. The resolving method represented by data-flow diagrams can be translated into executable DSP programs with almost one-to-one correspondence. On the other hand, the engineering information is described in a knowledge representation language named PUBLIB [16], which is suitable for representing relationships between attributes, such as the dimensions of standard parts and characteristics of materials, in a structured manner. Separating the contents of the knowledge base into two, helps maintain the knowledge base and make it portable, because the latter type of knowledge is more local or individual in different organizations than the former.

All components of the system except for the knowledge base are implemented using an integrated development environment called Inside Prolog [17]. Knowledge descriptions stored in the knowledge base are translated into Prolog programs by the knowledge base management function and executed by the inference engine. Because Inside Prolog provides standard Prolog functionality and a large variety of application programming interfaces which are essential for practical application development, it is easy to integrate the inference engine and other

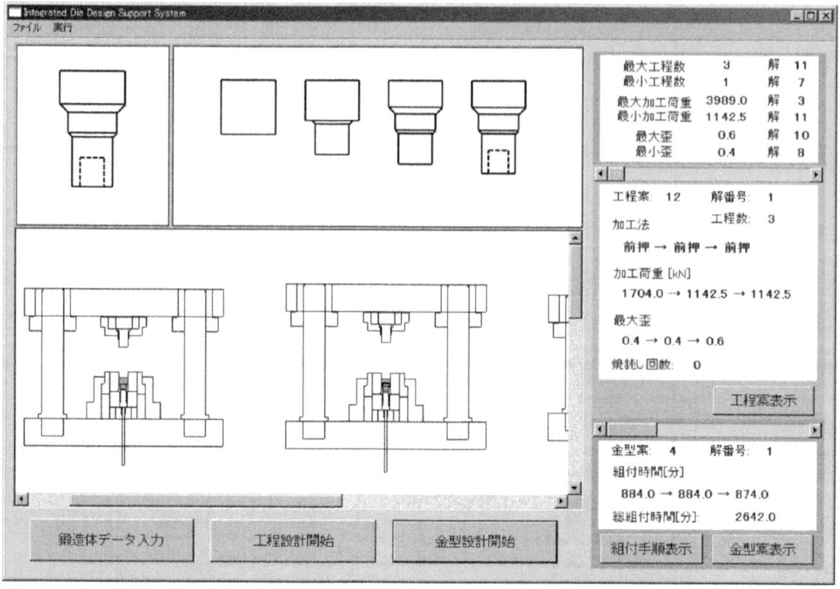

Fig. 12. Screen shot of the integrated die design support system

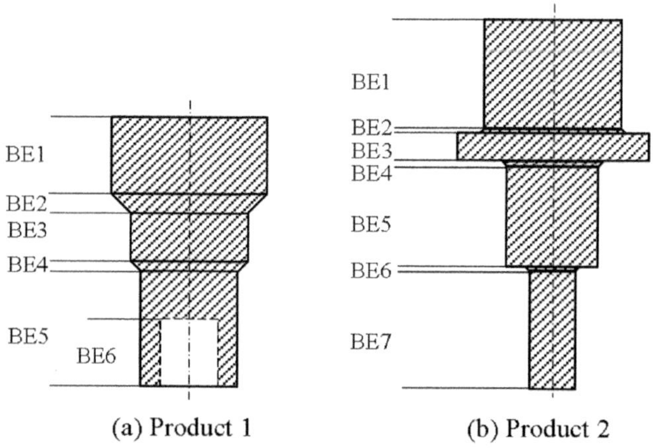

Fig. 13. Forged product examples

supporting functions in one development environment. The knowledge base and supporting functions for metal flow prediction and plan evaluation are still under development, while prototypes of the knowledge base and supporting functions for the others have been implemented. A primary user interface of the system is shown in Fig. 12.

7 Experimental Results

The integrated die design support system was applied to several examples of cold forged products. Figure 13 shows two of them, and Fig. 12 shows the results applied to Product 1. In this example, 12 forging process plans are generated within a second, and 4 solutions for the die structure are generated for all stages of one of the forging process plans also within a second. Figure 14 shows one of the process plans, and Fig. 15 shows the corresponding result of the die and die-set design. The differences between the 4 solutions of die structure come from the applied parting methods of the die inserts.

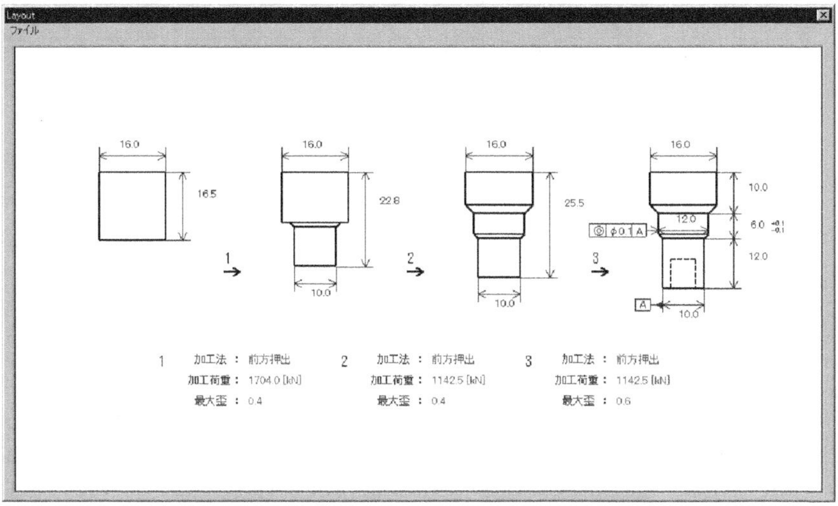

Fig. 14. Example of a forging process plan

These experiments show that the system can generate multiple forging process plans and die structures based on design knowledge, and that feasible solutions can be obtained within a practical time span. The solutions have different characteristics such as the number of stages of the forming processes, the maximum forming load, the maximum strain, the number of annealing processes, and the partition of die inserts, and an appropriate solution can be chosen from them.

8 Conclusions and Future Work

There is a great need for a framework that will enable the accumulation, utilization, and evolution of expertise for supporting process planning and the design of dies and die-sets of cold forged products, because such essential expertise tends to get scattered and lost. This paper describes the formalization and systematization methodology of forging die design knowledge to enable designers to

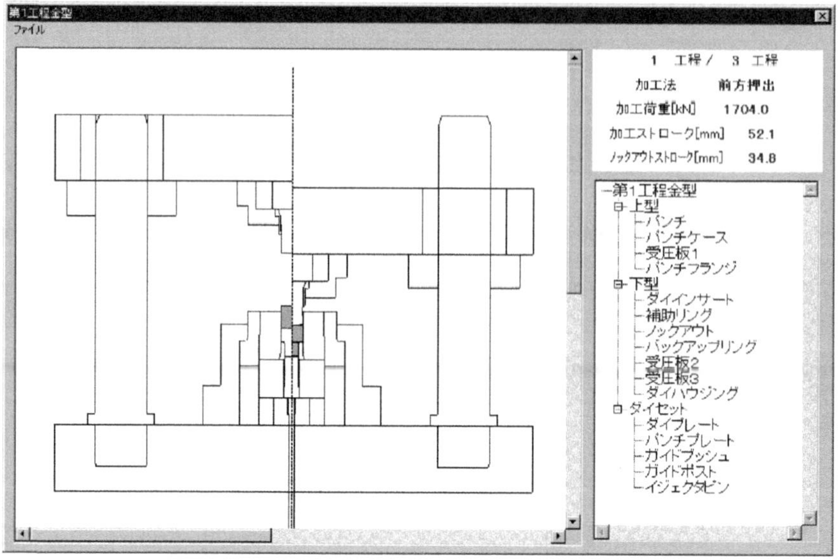

Fig. 15. Example of a die and die-set

develop, audit, maintain and extend their own knowledge base. It also describes an overview and brief implementation of an integrated die design support system based on the proposed methodology.

In this framework, the design problems of forging dies and die-sets are formally defined by using the design space, and the resolving method of the design space can be represented by a data-flow diagram based on the generate and test method. The resolving method represented by data-flow diagrams can easily be translated into executable programs with an almost one-to-one correspondence using a functional programming language based on attribute grammars.

The integrated die design support system is designed to consistently support process planning and the design of dies and die-sets. It can comprehensively enumerate all possible solutions of forging processes and die structures, and help choose an optimal solution from all of the solutions. The system was applied to examples of forged products, and it was shown that the system could generate multiple forging process plans and die structures based on the design knowledge, and that feasible solutions could be obtained within a practical time span.

As was briefly mentioned in Sect. 3, accuracy and precision management is essential in cold forging. It is essential to incorporate clearance and tolerance information of the forged products into the system and produce process plans and die structures so that the accuracy and precision of forged products are satisfied. The metal flow prediction system and plan evaluation system are still under development, and further research is necessary for its practical use.

Acknowledgment

The authors are grateful to Dr Osamu Takata, who developed the foundation of this system before he passed away in the prime of life.

References

1. Lange, K., Du, G.: A formal approach to designing forming sequences for cold forging. Trans. of the NAMRI/SME, 17–22 (1989)
2. Takata, O., Nakanishi, K., Yamazaki, T.: Forming-sequence design expert system for multistage cold forging: Forest-d. In: Proc. of Pacific Rim International Conference on Artificial Intelligence 1990, pp. 101–113 (1990)
3. Sevenler, K., Raghupathi, P.S., Altan, T.: Forming-sequence design for multistage cold forging. J. of Mechanical Working Technology 14, 121–135 (1987)
4. Mahmood, T., Lengyel, B., Husband, T.M.: Expert system for process planning in the cold forging of steel. Expert Planning Systems 322, 141–146 (1990)
5. Kim, H.S., Im, Y.T.: An expert system for cold forging process design based on a depth-first search. Journal of Materials Processing Technology 95, 262–274 (1999)
6. Kumar, S., Singh, R.: A low cost knowledge base system framework for progressive die design. Journal of Materials Processing Technology 153, 958–964 (2004)
7. Xuewen, C., Siyu, Z., Jun, C., Xueyu, R.: Research of knowledge-based hammer forging design support system. The International Journal of Advanced Manufacturing Technology 27, 25–32 (2005)
8. Kobayashi, S.: Production system. Journal of Information Processing Society of Japan 26, 1487–1496 (1985)
9. Ueno, H.: Expert systems. Journal of Information Processing Society of Japan 28, 147–157 (1987)
10. Takata, O., Mure, Y., Nakashima, Y., Ogawa, M., Umeda, M., Nagasawa, I.: A knowledge-based system for process planning in cold forging using the adjustment of stepped cylinder method. In: Umeda, M., Wolf, A., Bartenstein, O., Geske, U., Seipel, D., Takata, O. (eds.) INAP 2005. LNCS (LNAI), vol. 4369, pp. 161–174. Springer, Heidelberg (2006)
11. Umeda, M., Yamazumi, S., Mure, Y.: Development of knowledge-based metal flow prediction system in cold forging. In: The Proceedings of the 59th Japanese Joint Conference for the Technology of Plasticity, pp. 325–326 (2008)
12. Nagai, T., Nagasawa, I., Umeda, M., Higuchi, T., Nishidai, Y., Kitagawa, Y., Tsurusaki, T., Ohhashi, M., Takata, O.: A design product model for mechanism parts by injection molding. In: Umeda, M., Wolf, A., Bartenstein, O., Geske, U., Seipel, D., Takata, O. (eds.) INAP 2005. LNCS (LNAI), vol. 4369, pp. 148–160. Springer, Heidelberg (2006)
13. Yamaguchi, H., Nagasawa, I., Umeda, M., Mochizuki, M., Zhihua, Z.: Knowledge representation model for basic design of power plant equipment. Transactions of Information Processing Society of Japan 41, 3180–3192 (2000)
14. Umeda, M., Nagasawa, I., Higuchi, T.: The elements of programming style in design calculations. In: Proceedings of the Ninth International Conference on Industrial and Engineering Applications of Artificial Intelligence and Expert Systems, pp. 77–86 (1996)

15. Deransart, P., Jourdan, M. (eds.): Attribute Grammars and their Applications. LNCS, vol. 461. Springer, Heidelberg (1990)
16. Umeda, M., Nagasawa, I., Ito, M.: Knowledge representation model for engineering information circulation of standard parts. Transactions of Information Processing Society of Japan 38, 1905–1918 (1997)
17. Katamine, K., Umeda, M., Nagasawa, I., Hashimoto, M.: Integrated development environment for knowledge-based systems and its practical application. IEICE Transactions on Information and Systems E87-D, 877–885 (2004)

Searching in Protein State Space

Dietmar Seipel[1] and Jörg Schultz[2]

[1] Department of Computer Science
[2] Department of Bioinformatics, Biozentrum
University of Würzburg, Am Hubland, D–97074 Würzburg, Germany
`seipel@informatik.uni-wuerzburg.de`,
`joerg.schultz@biozentrum.uni-wuerzburg.de`

Abstract. The increasing complexity of protein interaction networks makes their manual analysis infeasible. Signal transduction processes pose a specific challenge, as each protein can perform different functions, depending on its state.

Here, we present a PROLOG and XML based system which explores the protein state space. Starting with state based information about the function of single proteins, the system searches for all biologically reasonable states that can be reached from the starting point. As facts of general molecular biology have been integrated, novel reasonable states, not encoded in the starting set, can be reached. Furthermore, the influence of modifications like mutations or additions of further proteins can be explored. Thus, the system could direct experiments and allow to predict their outcome.

1 Introduction

Current large scale projects like the sequencing of genomes and the unravelling of protein *interaction networks* produce a wealth of data and give new insights into the molecular architecture of cells. Still, it is a huge step from the data generation to the understanding of the molecular details of cellular networks. One of the primary challenges is the structured representation of a proteins function, a prerequisite for any computational analysis. Although many protein and nucleotide databases still use mainly human readable text as annotation, different approaches have been developed to structure this knowledge. These were as straightforward as defining specific keywords or as complicated as setting up an *ontology* for different aspects of protein function [Rzhetsky *et al.*, 2000]; probably, the most widely used of the latter approaches is from the Gene Ontology project [Consortium, 2008].

An additional level of complexity arises when describing not only the function of single proteins, but also their interplay within the cellular network. Here, the function of one protein has to be seen in the context of its interactions or the pathways it is involved in. In the case of metabolic networks, methods for the representation of knowledge and the computation with function have been developed [Keseler *et al.*, 2009,Karp, 2001]. Here, the function of a protein can be seen as more or less constant. This contrasts typical eukaryotic signaling pathways, where the function of a protein and therefore its influence on the cellular networks changes for different input signals. This flexibility in function is usually implemented by describing the state of a protein when performing

S. Abreu and D. Seipel (Eds.): INAP 2009, LNAI 6547, pp. 205–222, 2011.

specific actions [Duan *et al.*, 2002,Schacherer *et al.*, 2001,Ratsch *et al.*, 2003]. Systems like the π–calculus have been developed, which allow to encode signaling pathways and to explore the effects of *mutations* [Regev *et al.*, 2001]. Still, these approaches as well as Petri nets [Grafahrend–Belau *et al.*, 2008] represent rigid networks and do not allow to find states not given to the system. The Biocham system [Fages *et al.*, 2004] offers automated reasoning tools for querying the temporal properties of interaction networks under all possible behaviours using Computation Tree Logic (CTL). [Baral, 2004] uses an action–style, knowledge based approach for supporting various tasks of reasoning (including planning, hypothetical reasoning, and explanation) about signaling networks in the presence of incomplete and partial information.

Here, we describe a *simulation approach* which is based on a logical representation of protein states. Its goal is to find all possible and biological acceptable pathways which can be derived from the given starting situation. As the system is aware of general concepts of molecular biology, it can 1) generate states not known to the system and 2) simulate the outcome of modifications like mutations or addition of inhibitors.

The rest of this paper is organized as follows: In Section 2, we present the concepts and techniques for manipulating XML structures in PROLOG. Section 3 provides formal representations of protein function, general biological concepts, and then it describes the central PROLOG search algorithm for protein networks. Two practical applications are shown in Section 4. Finally, Section 5 discusses the new approach.

2 Manipulation of XML Structures in PROLOG

The logic programming language PROLOG is very useful for representing, manipulating and reasoning about *complex structures*, such as the states obtained during the simulation of biological processes [Bratko, 2001,Clocksin & Mellish, 2003]. In particular, *search algorithms* can be implemented very nicely based on PROLOG's built–in concept of backtracking, and the handling and manipulation of the relatively complex intermediate data structures obtained during the simulation can be done in a very declarative way.

XML formats have been increasingly used for representing various forms of complex, semi–structured data, and for exchanging these data between different applications. E.g., in molecular biology, XML languages such as SBML [Hucka *et al.*, 2003], MAGE–ML [Spellman *et al.*, 2002], and PSI MI [Hermjakob *et al.*, 2004] have been developed. XML data are used by many tools in different application domains, and to some extend they are human–readable.

Thus, we are using XML as the data format for the complex states of our PROLOG based search algorithm. For querying and manipulating XML elements in PROLOG, we use the XML query, transformation, and update language FNQUERY [Seipel, 2002]. This combination of XML and PROLOG facilitates knowledge representation and software engineering drastically. The elegant data access to and update of XML data by path expressions in connection with the powerful reasoning facilities and the declarative programming style of PROLOG makes our application compact, flexible, and extensible. Another PROLOG based XML query language has, e.g., been proposed in

[Alemendros–Jiménez *et al.*, 2007], without the necessary update functionality, however. Our approach is also superior to standard XML processing tools such as XQuery or XSLT, since it is fully interleaved with the declarative – and general purpose – programming language PROLOG, and since the update capabilities are better.

2.1 XML Representations and Path Expressions

There exist various PROLOG representations for XML structures. We have developed a PROLOG term representation for XML elements, which we call field notation, and a fact representation, which we call graph notation [Seipel, 2002].

We use path expressions for localizing sub–structures of an XML structure. The path language FNPATH, which we have developed, is an extension of the well–known path language XPATH, and XPATH expressions can be mapped to equivalent FNPATH expressions. Moreover, we can allow for more general path expressions, since we use PROLOG – including backtracking and unification – for their evaluation. In the following we will describe the fragment of FNPATH that is used in this paper. The path expressions in this fragment directly correspond to equivalent XPATH expressions.

A path expression $\pi = \sigma_1\sigma_2 \ldots \sigma_n$ consists of one or more steps σ_i for localizing child elements or attributes of XML elements. E.g., the path expression

```
/proteins/protein::[@name=Protein]
```

has two location steps. When this path expression is applied to an XML element `Cell`, then the first step σ_1 = `/proteins` selects the child element `Ps` of `Cell` with the tag `proteins`. Subsequently, the second step σ_2 = `/protein::[@name=Protein]` of the path expression selects a child element `P` of `Ps` with the tag `protein`, such that `P` has an attribute `name` with the value `Protein`.

In general, a location step can be of the forms $\sigma = @\,\nu$, $\sigma = /\nu$, and $\sigma = /\nu :: \tau$, where ν is a node test and τ is a list of predicates. The second form is a short hand for the third, if the list τ is empty. The predicate `@name=Protein` in the example above also contains a location step `@name`, which selects the value of the attribute `name` of the element `P`; the predicate succeeds, if this value is `Protein`.

2.2 The Query Language

The PROLOG based XML query, transformation, and update language FNQUERY is based on FNPATH, and it has three sublanguages:

- FNSELECT: selection of subelements/attributes,
- FNTRANSFORM: transformations like XSLT,
- FNUPDATE: updates (insertion, deletion) of elements/attributes.

In this paper, we have extensively used FNSELECT and FNUPDATE for computing successor states during the simulation process. For this purpose, FNUPDATE has been extended by insertion and deletion operations, which are very useful here.

Selection of Substructures. If X is an XML element in PROLOG representation and π is a path expression, then the assignment `Y := X` π selects a substructure of X and assigns it to Y. E.g., the following rule selects the location Loc of a state element for a given protein with the name Protein within a given cell Cell. The path expression π consists of 5 location steps, which are applied successively to Cell. The predicate @name=Protein in the second location step assures that the selected child has the proper value for the attribute name:

```
get_location(Protein, Cell, Loc) :-
   Loc := Cell/proteins/protein::[@name=Protein]
      /current_state/state@location.
```

Modification/Update of Substructures. If X is an XML element in PROLOG representation and π is a path expression, then the assignment `Y := X*[`π`:v]` modifies the substructure of X that is selected by π to the new value v. E.g., the assignment statement in the following rule changes the value of the attribute location to Loc.

```
set_location(Protein, Loc, Cell_1, Cell_2) :-
   Cell_2 := Cell_1 * [
      /proteins/protein::[@name=Protein]
      /current_state/state@location:Loc ].
```

Insertion and Deletion of Substructures. The following PROLOG rules are used for modifying a given cell Cell_1. The first rule adds a new interaction element with the attribute value Int for protein within the protein element with the name P. The second rule deletes such an interaction element.

```
add_interaction(P, Int, Cell_1, Cell_2) :-
   Cell_2 := Cell_1 <+> [
      /proteins/protein::[@name=P]
      /current_state/state/interactions
      /interaction:[protein:Int]:[] ].

delete_interaction(P, Int, Cell_1, Cell_2) :-
   Cell_2 := Cell_1 <-> [
      /proteins/protein::[@name=P]
      /current_state/state/interactions
      /interaction::[@protein=Int] ].
```

3 Representation and Searching

In the following, we provide formal representations of protein function and general biological concepts, and then we describe the central PROLOG search algorithm for protein networks.

3.1 Formal Representation of Protein Function

It is a fundamental feature of proteins, especially those involved in signal transduction, that their function is tightly regulated. Depending, for example, on its own phosphorylation status, a protein kinase might phosphorylate different target proteins. Therefore, any representation of a proteins function has to allow different functions for a single protein, depending on its status. This status can be described by three features, namely the localisation, modifications, and interactions [Duan *et al.*, 2002,Ratsch *et al.*, 2003].

In our approach, we combine these features with a detailed description of the function performed within this state. Currently, the *localisation* mainly describes the organelle a protein can be found in, for example the cytoplasm or the nucleus. Within the list of *modifications*, the type, but also the position in the sequence is stored. Finally, the *interactions* describe a list of bound proteins. Depending on the value of these three features, the protein might perform different functions. These are encoded in a list of actions. Each action itself consists of the type of the action, the name of the involved protein and possible parameters.

Table 1. Implemented Actions

Type	Subtypes	Parameters
moving	none	protein new location
interaction	binding dissociation	$\text{protein}_{1,2}$
modification	phosphorylation dephosphorylation	$\text{protein}_{1,2}$ position

Currently, three general types of actions are implemented, where each type can contain different subtypes and parameters (Table 1). Within this concept, it is important to note that we do not use any descriptions like *activation*, *stimulation* or *inhibition*, as these are interpretations and depend on the experiment performed. We describe the molecular details of a function a protein performs when in a given state. This might be interpreted as an activation to perform a function within a given state.

Having defined the state as the core structure, different states and their actions have to be put together with additional information to describe a proteins function. First, there are constant, that is, state independent, features which have to be represented. Second, as we aim for qualitative simulation, the actual state of a protein has to be stored. Following, all states which trigger a specific action are listed. Finally, we allow for so–called forbidden states. Especially in molecular biology, the knowledge of a proteins function frequently contains negative information like the fact that a protein will not be localised within the nucleus if bound to a defined other protein. By introducing forbidden states, we allow the handling of this information. Figure 1 shows the XML structure describing the function of a single protein.

```
<protein name="receptor" sequence="MDCQLSILLLLSCSVLD...">
   <current_state>
      <state location="transmembrane">
         <modifications/>
         <interactions>
            <interaction protein="jak"/> </interactions>
         <actions/>
      </state>
   </current_state>
   <action_states>
      <state location="transmembrane">
         <modifications/>
         <interactions mode="identical">
            <interaction protein="ligand"/>
            <interaction protein="jak"/> </interactions>
         <actions>
            <action type="interaction" subtype="binding">
               <protein name="receptor"/>
               <parameter protein="receptor"/>
               <status state="todo"/> </action> </actions>
      </state>
   </action_states>
   <forbidden_states>
      <state location="transmembrane">
         <modifications/>
         <interactions>
            <interaction protein="Grb2"/> </interactions>
      </state>
   </forbidden_states>
</protein>
```

Fig. 1. XML Representation of a Protein's Function – To represent all functions of a protein and allow simulation, the actual state of a protein (current_state) as well as all states leading to an action (action_states) have to be known. Furthermore, states not acceptable for the protein can be stored (forbidden_states). Features invariant to the protein, like the name or its sequence, are given as parameters to the protein tag.

3.2 Representation of General Biological Concepts

If one aims at qualitatively simulating signal transduction processes, it is of vital importance to take into account general biological concepts which can help to restrain the search space and keep the derived states consistent as well as biologically correct. Therefore, we have implemented the following concepts into our system.

Localisation. To describe different cellular localisations, we first have defined a set of accepted keywords describing localisations. In a second step, we have built – comparably to the GeneOntology – a hierarchy of these localisations using `subclasses/2` facts. As we are modelling changes of localisations (moves), we furthermore define between which compartments direct moves are possible using `allowed/2` facts. For example, although nucleus and mitochondrion are both organelles embedded in the cytoplasm, no direct transitions between them are possible. A protein is assigned to one localisation for each state. A special case are transmembrane proteins, which reside in up to three different localisations, for example extracellular, membrane and cytoplasmic; this is represented by a `contains/2` fact.

```
localisations([
   localisation, intra, extra,
   membrane, transmembrane,
   cytoplasma, nucleus, ... ]).

subclasses(localisation, [
   intra, extra, membrane ]).
subclasses(transmembrane, [membrane]).

allowed(intra, extra).
allowed(cytoplasma, nucleus).
allowed(X, X).

contains(transmembrane, [
   extra, membrane, cytoplasma ]).

...
```

Interaction. As protein interactions build the backbone of any signal transduction process, a substantial amount of rules was generated to assure, that the modelled interactions are biologically sound. First, only proteins not already interacting (`unbound/2`) are allowed to start a new interaction and only interacting proteins can dissociate. Second, the predicate `matching_location_/3` assures that both interacting proteins reside in the same localisation; the values of the localisations do not have to be identical. Third, reciprocity of binding as well as dissociation events is assured by `add_interaction/3`. If one of multiple interacting proteins is moving, that is, its localisation changes, then all interacting proteins have to move. This assures consistency of localisation information; furthermore a translocation will not happen if any of the interacting proteins is not allowed within the new localisation. E.g., the PROLOG module `interaction` contains the following rule for bindings:

```
binding(S1, Action, S2) :-
   P1 := Action/protein@name,
   P2 := Action/parameter@protein,
   Proteins = [P1, P2],
   unbound(S1, Proteins),
   matching_location_(S1, Proteins, SA),
```

```
    add_interaction(SA, Proteins, SB),
    !,
    \+ forbidden_state(Proteins, SB),
    add(SB, Action, Proteins, S2).
```

Based on the facts implemented for localisation, we can handle cases where the information about the localisation of one protein is more specific than the other. In an example scenario, it might be known for protein A, that it is localised within the cytoplasm whereas protein B is only known to be somewhere within the cell (intracellular). Our system does not only allow this interaction, as the cytoplasm is a specification of intracellular, it updates the localisation information for protein B. This is also done iteratively for all interacting proteins in the case of complexes. Thereby, the system can improve on current knowledge.

Modification. Currently, the only implemented modification is phosphorylation. Here, our rules assure that within the phosphorylated position resides a correct amino acid, S, T or Y. Furthermore, it is assured, that the side which becomes phosphorylated is not already phosphorylated. Complementarily, only phosphorylated sites can become de–phosphorylated. In both cases, a modification includes the interaction (predicate `interaction:unbound/2` and first call of predicate `interaction/4`), the actual modification (predicate `phosphorylation_/3`) and a dissociation (second call of predicate `interaction/4`). Therefore, only proteins which are able to interact can be involved in a phosphorylation or de–phosphorylation reaction.

```
phosphorylation(S1, Action, S2) :-
    Protein_1 := Action/protein@name,
    Protein_2 := Action/parameter@protein,
    Proteins = [Protein_1, Protein_2],
    interaction:unbound(S1, Proteins),
    interaction(S1, Proteins, binding, SA),
    phosphorylation_(SA, Action, SB),
    interaction(SB, Proteins, dissociate, S2).
```

3.3 Searching through Protein States

Thus far, we have described a static system for the representation of protein function based on states and some general rules concerning biological concepts. As it is the aim of the system to search through protein state space and to allow for qualitative simulations, the function of each protein has to be connected to and depend on the state of other proteins. This has been implemented for example by LiveDIP [Duan *et al.*, 2002] and the Molecule Pages database [Saunders *et al.*, 2008] by linking states with state transitions. Here, no state transitions are encoded. That is, no information like *protein A gets transferred from state 1 to state 2 when interacting with protein C* has to be provided. Instead, we perform actions on proteins and let the protein itself *decide* whether its new state might trigger further actions. Thereby, we allow each protein to reach states, which are not explicitly encoded in its state list, and we are able to unravel novel pathways intrinsic to the analyzed protein interaction network.

Comparing States. A fundamental concept of the presented approach is the ability to compare different states. This is, for example, of importance for deciding whether the current state of a protein *matches* a state which is connected to a new action. Obviously, the most straightforward approach would be to check for identity within all features of the state (localisation, interactions and modifications). This would lead to the same results as explicitly coding state transitions and would not allow to detect states not encoded within the system. To allow for a more explorative searching, we have defined a *subsumption* relationship for states.

```
subsumes_localisation(S, G) :-
   SLoc := S@location,
   GLoc := G@location,
   localisation:specifies(SLoc, GLoc).

subsumes_interactions(S, G) :-
   identical := G/interactions@mode,
   !,
   get_interactions(S, SInt),
   get_interactions(G, GInt),
   subset(GInt, SInt),
   subset(SInt, GInt).

subsumes_modifications(S, G) :-
   identical := G/modifications@mode,
   !,
   get_modifications(S, SMod),
   get_modifications(G, GMod),
   subset(GMod, SMod), subset(SMod, GMod).
```

In the case of localisations, the subsuming state needs to have a localisation which is either identical to or more specific than the general state. For example, a state with a cytoplasmic localisation will subsume a state with a intracellular localisation. Here, the general biological knowledge about the compartments of the cell is substantial. For the interactions and modifications, the general state has to be a subset of the subsuming state. To allow for more restrictive comparisons, both interaction and modification can be set to identical, which enforces identity between the general and the subsuming state. These rules allow to decide whether a protein is in a state which can trigger a specified action.

Search Algorithm and Implementation. Having defined a subsumption relationship between states and actions associated with given states, which are called *soups* below, the system can now be used to search through protein state space. To start the search process, an action as well as the starting states of all proteins are needed. In the first step, the system tries to perform the action, taking into account the biological background given above. If the action can be performed, at least one protein will be in a novel state. The system now compares the current state of all proteins with all action states of the protein. If no current state is found which subsumes an action state (`soup_node_subsumes/2`), then the system tries to perform the action. If successful, a new round of search is initiated (`find_next_soup/4`). In each step, applications of the general biological concepts assure, that only correct states are reached. For example, a protein A might be in a state triggering an action to bind to protein B. This action will fail, if protein B in its current state is located in a different cellular compartment than protein A. The search process iterates until no protein is in a state triggering a new action. Here, the first solution of the search process has been found.

```
protein_state_search(S, _, S).
protein_state_search(S1, Actions_1, S3) :-
   M := S1@id, not(soup_node_subsumes(_, M)),
   find_next_soup(S1, Actions_1, S2, Actions),
   find_candidate_actions(S2, Actions, Cs),
   add_candidate_actions(Cs, Actions, Actions_2).
   protein_state_search(S2, Actions_2, S3).

find_next_soup(S1, As1, S2, As2) :-
   A := As1/action::[@id=Id, /status@state=todo],
   [Type, SubType] := A-[@type, @subtype],
   once(apply(Type:SubType, [S1, A, S])),
   As2 := As1 * [
      /action::[@id=Id]/status@state:done ],
   remember_search_edge(S1, S, S2).
```

Natural numbers are assigned as identificators to Soups, and the edges between two soups are asserted in the PROLOG database:

```
remember_search_edge(S1, S, S2) :-
   M := S1@id,
   soup_to_number_(S, N),
   S2 := S * [@id:N],
   assert(soup_edge(M, N)),
   !.
```

The system finds all solutions using PROLOG's *backtracking* mechanism. In each intermediate step, the system checks whether another action than the one already performed might be triggered. If so, another search process is started, leading to further solutions of the system. Thus, a *depth first search* through the space of all possible protein states is performed.

Within the search process, care is taken to detect possible cycles, which would lead to infinite searches. Therefore, the search is stopped, if an action already performed is triggered.

```
find_candidate_actions(Soup, Actions, Candidates) :-
   findall( Action,
      ( Protein := Soup/proteins/protein,
        check_action(Protein, Action),
        \+ performed(Action, Soup),
        \+ action_already_found(Actions, Action) ),
      Candidates_2 ),
   sort(Candidates_2, Candidates).

check_action(Protein, Action) :-
   State_C := Protein/current_state/state,
   State_A := Protein/action_states/state,
   protein_state_subsumes(State_C, State_A),
   Action := State_A/actions/action.

performed(Action, Soup) :-
   Test_Action := Soup/pathway/step/action,
   action:identical(Action, Test_Action).

action_already_found(Actions, Action) :-
   Action_2 := Action * [@id:_],
   Action_2 := Actions/action.
```

Interface / Visualization. Already in comparatively small biological systems, many end states can be reached. Obviously, any two of these end states can be identical, as they can be reached by different combinations of actions. To allow for the evaluation of the results and decrease the redundancy, we have developed a visualization in SWI-PROLOG [Wielemaker, 2009], cf. Figures 2 and 3. Here, each combination of protein states, which can be reached is represented by a circle. If two states are identical, then the nodes representing these states are combined leading to a collapse of the original search tree.

For each node, not only the state of all proteins, but also all pathways leading to the node are given. As the representation is based on the same XML structure as the input, it might be used as input for other programs, e.g., for visualizing the pathways in a more detailed way.

4 Applications

To show that the proposed system is indeed able to represent signaling pathways, we have evaluated two test cases, the Jak–Stat and the MAP kinase pathway. In addition to finding novel states, it was a fundamental goal of the presented system to allow for *qualitative simulations* of modifications of the signal transduction pathways; here, the implemented general biological concepts are of major importance.

4.1 Jak–Stat Pathway

The Jak–Stat signalling pathway provides one of the fastest routes from a cell surface receptor to the nucleus [O'Shea *et al.*, 2002]. Still, all major principles of signalling pathways, dimerization, phosphorylation and translocation are implemented within this short pathway. The involved proteins are the receptor, a ligand, the Jak protein kinases, and the Stats. For each of the proteins, we have defined a starting state as well as states which lead to further actions. An example is the rule that a phosphorylated Stat can homodimerize. The state searching procedure was started with an interaction of the ligand with the receptor.

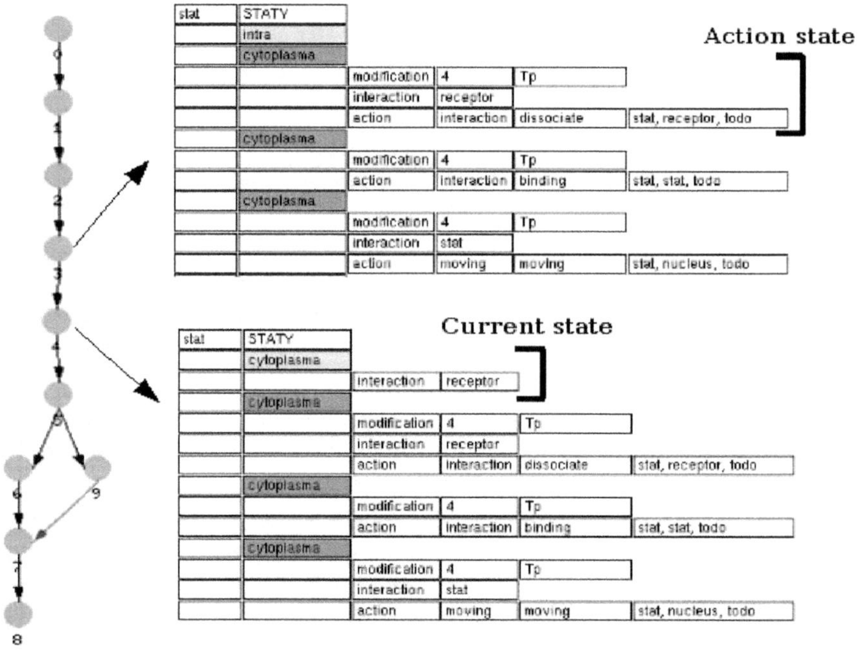

Fig. 2. Representation of the Jak–Stat Pathway

Figure 2 shows all soups (combinations of proteins states) which have been reached from this initial condition. Most interestingly, there are two ways how node 7 can be reached. Inspection of this node reveals, that the difference between the two pathways is the order in which the dissociation of Stat from the receptor and the dimerization of two Stats are handled.

- With the knowledge given to the system, two pathways have been found leading to node 7: in the first (via node 6), the phosphorylated Stat dissociates from the receptor before dimerization with another phosphorylated Stat; the second pathway via node 9 reverses these steps.
- The detailed information underlying nodes 3 and 4 is selected and shown in an HTML table. The annotation is automatically improved. After binding to the receptor, the localisation of Stat is specified from *intracellular* to *cytoplasmic* (shown in grey).

It is an important feature of our system, that states which are not explicitly given in the *knowledge base* can be generated. This happens for example at node 9, which describes a protein complex of the ligand, a dimerized receptor, Jak and Stat. Additionally, Stat itself is a dimer. The existence of such a protein complex was not given within any state described in the knowledge base.

In addition to the generation of novel states, the system can also help in refining current knowledge. At the beginning of the search process, Stats location is annotated as *intracellular*. Within node 4, Stat binds to the receptor, which is annotated as *transmembrane* protein. As in the current implementation, transmembrane proteins consist of an extracellular, a transmembrane and a cytoplasmic region, the system deduces, that Stat has to be cytoplasmic, if it binds as an intracellular protein to a transmembrane protein.

This example illustrates, that information about important states is not only sufficient to reconstruct pathways; also novel states as well as improvements of current knowledge can be automatically generated.

4.2 MAP Kinase Pathway

The MAPK pathway represents one of the oldest signalling cascades conserved between yeast and human [Bardwell, 2005,Wang & Dohlman, 2004]. Its core is a cascade of phosphorylation of protein kinases.

One of the possibly best understood MAP kinase pathways is the pheromone response in yeast. Here, after binding of a pheromone to a G–coupled receptor, leading to an activation of the protein kinase Ste20, the MEKK Ste11 gets phosphorylated. Following, this kinase phosphorylates the MEK Ste7, which can phosphorylate the MAPK Fus3 and Kss1. It is important to note that these kinases are tethered together by binding to the scaffolding protein Ste5. In the last steps of the cascade, Fus3 can phosphorylate the transcription factors Far1 and Dig1, whereas Kss1 phosphorylates only Dig1. Here, we assume that Dig1 contains only a single phosphorylation site. These transcriptions factors can – after phosphorylation – move to the nucleus. Thus, there are two branching points within this pathway: first the two phosphorylation targets of Ste7, and second the two targets of Fus3. Furthermore, Dig1 can get phosphorylated by both, Kss1 and Fus3. As there is no order defined between these steps, all possible permutations could happen. Indeed this is what was found when encoding the yeast pheromone pathway.

In total, 167 possible soups (combinations of protein states) were found. As the integration of these states and the pathways leading to them shows (Figure 3), there are many different pathways leading to identical combinations of protein states.

Between the pathways, the order of complex assembly and/or phosphorylations differs. Could this be of any biological relevance, although the end state is the same for

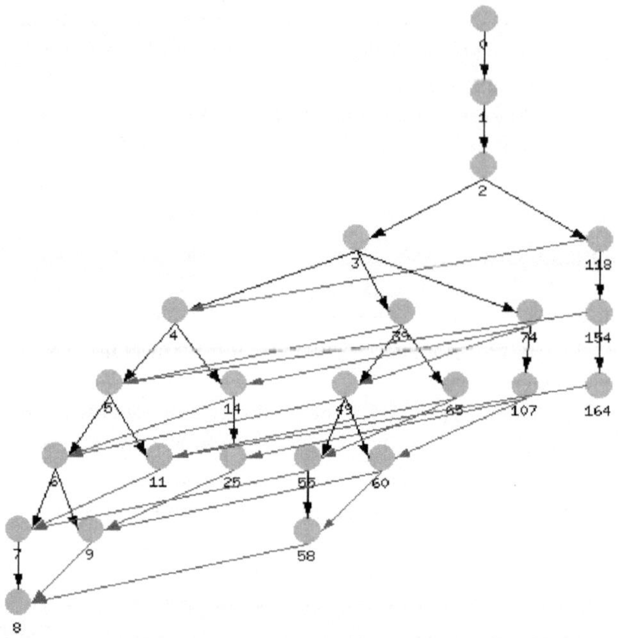

Fig. 3. Representation of the Yeast Mating Pheromone Response Pathway

all pathways? Indeed, it has been shown for other signalling pathways, that a ligand is bound with higher affinity when two receptors already have build a complex. In contrast, a slower response has been observed when first the ligand binds to a single receptor and the receptor complex is build afterwards [Heinecke *et al.*, 2009]. Thus, the route how a state is reached leads to a differing biological response. In the case of the MAPK pathway, our system identifies all possible and biologically acceptable pathways. Which of those actually happen in the cell and whether there are differences for the cell can only be analysed experimentally.

4.3 Simulation

In addition to finding novel states, it was a fundamental goal of the presented system to for allow qualitative simulations of modifications of the signal transduction pathways. Here, the implemented general biological concepts are of major importance. As a first example, we have added a mandatory cytoplasmic, Stat binding protein to the Jak–Stat pathway described above. We have used the constraint of a *forbidden state*, which does not allow any actions that would end in a non–cytoplasmic location of the added protein. As it is stated in the general biological concepts, that interacting proteins need to have the same localisation, only cytoplasmic proteins can interact with the added protein. As Figure 4 (a) shows, there were two possible end states: the first (node 46) is identical to the results of the Jak–Stat pathway above, in the second (node 8), the final state of Stat is bound to the added protein and cytoplasmic. Thus, the added protein could work as a inhibitor of the Jak–Stat pathway [Borie *et al.*, 2003]. Indeed, a similar mechanism has been described for an inhibitor of the JNK signal transduction pathway, JIP–1 [Dickens *et al.*, 1997]. As there are no additional constraints within the states of Stat and the inhibiting protein which would prohibit interaction, Figure 4 (a) furthermore reveals that there are many different pathways to reach the found end states.

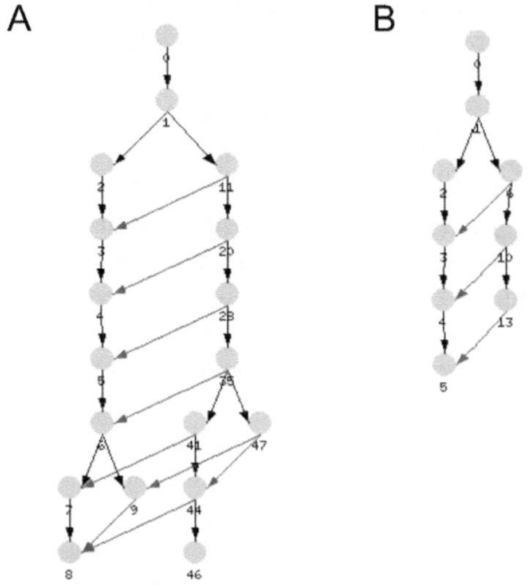

Fig. 4. Qualitative Simulation – (a) Addition of mandatory cytoplasmic, Stat binding protein. (b) mutation of Stat in the Jip containing system.

In a second experiment, the phospho–accepting site of Stat was mutated to an alanine. As it was stated in the rules describing modifications that phosphorylation are only allowed on serine, threonine or tyrosine, a phosphorylation of Stat failed. As a result, shown in Figure 4 (b), the pathway stopped after assembling of the receptor complex and the phosphorylation of the receptor.

5 Conclusions

Unravelling the molecular details of signal transduction processes is an important step towards understanding the regulation of cellular networks. Although it is the ultimate goal of systems biology to quantitatively model the whole cell, especially in signal transduction we are still far from the enumeration of all involved molecular reactions. The identification of these reactions as well as the delineation of possible pathways are therefore crucial prerequisites.

We have described a PROLOG system which, given a defined set of proteins and their functions, searches for all possible states encoded within a system and thereby finds all possible pathways using backtracking. The fundamental concept of the approach is the state of a protein, which is defined by its location, modifications and interactions. The whole system consists of three components: first an XML encoded state based representation of protein function; second, a rule based representation of general biological concepts, and third, a search algorithm implemented in PROLOG. The resulting system is not only able to search through protein state space, but furthermore to simulate the outcome of manipulations to the proteins. Declarative logic programming in PROLOG greatly simplified the system despite the *complex logic* behind the search algorithm and the complexity of the underlying *data structures*.

Contrasting other approaches [Saunders *et al.*, 2008,Zheng *et al.*, 2008], we do not encode any explicit state transitions. Instead, the protein *knows* about states which trigger further actions. If the protein is in a state that subsumes one of these states, then an action is started, which might transform other proteins, leading to further actions. Thus, it is a distinguishing feature of our system that states can be reached, which were not explicitly given to the system beforehand. In the case of the MAP kinases, the system itself revealed, that the current biological description is not sufficient. We were able to show, that there are multiple pathways to reach the given states. Thus, biological novelty was discovered, which now could guide further experimental characterisation of this well conserved signal transduction pathway. For other signalling pathways it has already been shown, that the biological response can differ depending on the choosen pathway, although the final state is the same [Heinecke *et al.*, 2009].

The result of the experiments could then be fed back into the knowlege base of the system and tested again. In general, the novel deduced states might be a good starting point for further experimental exploration of signal transduction networks.

A critical point within the approach is the collection of the functions of the involved proteins. Although manual *knowledge acquisition* will assure the highest quality, it is comparably slow. One might overcome this hindrance by adding automated function prediction for the involved proteins based for example on sequence analysis.

So far, the system has been tested only on smaller signal transduction networks. One possible challenge might be the increasing computational resources needed for larger systems. However, we see the collection of biological knowledge in the level of detail needed for the system as the biggest limitation. More on the user's point of view, the huge amount of detail might become hard to digest in the current representation. Thus, a more *graphical* and possibly *animated interface*, which might even allow to interact with the system, would be the long term goal.

References

[Alemendros–Jiménez *et al.*, 2007] Almendros–Jiménez, J.M., Becerra–Terón, A., Enciso–Baños, F.J.: Integrating XQUERY and Logic Programming. In: Proc. 17th International Conference on Applications of Declarative Programming and Knowledge Management (INAP 2007) and 21st Workshop on (Constraint) Logic Programming (WLP 2007), pp. 136–147 (2007)

[Baral, 2004] Baral, C., Chancellor, K., Tran, N., Tran, N.L., Joy, A., Berens, M.: A knowledge based approach for representing and reasoning about signaling networks. Bioinformatics 20 (suppl. 1), i15–i22 (2004)

[Bardwell, 2005] Bardwell, L.: A walk–through of the yeast mating pheromone response pathway. Peptides 26(2), 339–350 (2005)

[Borie *et al.*, 2003] Borie, D.C., Si, M.–S., Morris, R.E., Reitz, B.A., Changelian, P.S.: JAK3 inhibition as a new concept for immune suppression. Curr. Opin. Investig. Drugs 4(11), 1297–1303 (2003)

[Bratko, 2001] Bratko, I.: PROLOG– Programming for Artificial Intelligence, 3rd edn. Addison-Wesley, Reading (2001)

[Clocksin & Mellish, 2003] Clocksin, W.F., Mellish, C.S.: Programming in PROLOG, 5th edn. Springer, Heidelberg (2003)

[Consortium, 2008] Consortium, G.O.: The Gene Ontology project in 2008. Nucleic Acids Res. 36, D440–444 (2008)

[Dickens *et al.*, 1997] Dickens, M., Rogers, J.S., Cavanagh, J., Raitano, A., Xia, Z., Halpern, J.R., Greenberg, M.E., Sawyers, C.L., Davis, R.J.: A cytoplasmic inhibitor of the JNK signal transduction pathway. Science 277(5326), 693–696 (1997)

[Duan *et al.*, 2002] Duan, X.J., Xenarios, I., Eisenberg, D.: Describing biological protein interactions in terms of protein states and state transitions: the LiveDIP database. Mol. Cell Proteomics 1(2), 104–116 (2002)

[Fages *et al.*, 2004] Fages, F., Soliman, S., Chabrier, N.: Modelling and querying interaction networks in the biochemical abstract machine BIOCHAM. Journal of Biological Physics and Chemistry 4, 64–73 (2004)

[Grafahrend–Belau *et al.*, 2008] Grafahrend–Belau, E., Schreiber, F., Heiner, M., Sackmann, A., Junker, B.H., Grunwald, S., Speer, A., Winder, K., Koch, I.: Modularization of biochemical networks based on classification of Petri net t–invariants. BMC Bioinformatics 9, 90 (2008)

[Heinecke *et al.*, 2009] Heinecke, K., Seher, A., Schmitz, W., Mueller, T.D., Sebald, W., Nickel, J.: Receptor oligomerization and beyond: a case study in bone morphogenetic proteins. Journal BMC Biology 7, 59 (2009)

[Hermjakob *et al.*, 2004] Hermjakob, H., Montecchi–Palazzi, L., Bader, G., Wojcik, J., Salwinski, L., Ceol, A., Moore, S., Orchard, S., Sarkans, U., von Mering, C., Roechert, B., Poux, S., Jung, E., Mersch, H., Kersey, P., Lappe, M., Li, Y., Zeng, R., Rana, D., Nikolski, M., Husi, H., Brun, C., Shanker, K., Grant, S.G.N., Sander, C., Bork, P., Zhu, W., Pandey, A., Brazma, A., Jacq, B., Vidal, M., Sherman, D., Legrain, P., Cesareni, G., Xenarios, I., Eisenberg, D., Steipe, B., Hogue, C., Apweiler, R.: The HUPO PSI's molecular interaction format – a community standard for the representation of protein interaction data. Nat. Biotechnology 22(2), 177–183 (2004)

[Hucka *et al.*, 2003] Hucka, M., Finney, A., Sauro, H., Bolouri, H., Doyle, J., Kitano, H., Arkin, A., Bornstein, B., Bray, D., Cornish–Bowden, A., Cuellar, A., Dronov, S., Gilles, E., Ginkel, M., Gor, V., Goryanin, I., Hedley, W., Hodgman, T., Hofmeyr, J.–H., Hunter, P., Juty, N., Kasberger, J., Kremling, A., Kummer, U., NovÃÍre, N.L., Loew, L., Lucio, D., Mendes, P., Minch, E., Mjolsness, E., Nakayama, Y., Nelson, M., Nielsen, P., Sakurada, T., Schaff, J., Shapiro, B., Shimizu, T., Spence, H., Stelling, J., Takahashi, K., Tomita, M., Wagner, J., Wang, J., Forum, S.: The systems biology markup language (SBML): a medium for representation and exchange of biochemical network models. Bioinformatics 19(4), 524–531 (2003)

[Karp, 2001] Karp, P.: Pathway databases: a case study in computational symbolic theories. Science 293(5537), 2040–2044 (2001)

[Keseler *et al.*, 2009] Keseler, I.M., Bonavides–Martínez, C., Collado–Vides, J., Gama–Castro, S., Gunsalus, R.P., Johnson, D.A., Krummenacker, M., Nolan, L.M., Paley, S., Paulsen, I.T., Peralta–Gil, M., Santos–Zavaleta, A., Shearer, A.G., Karp, P.D.: EcoCyc: a comprehensive view of Escherichia coli biology. Nucleic Acids Research 37, D464–470 (2009)

[O'Shea *et al.*, 2002] O'Shea, J.J., Gadina, M., Schreiber, R.D.: Cytokine signaling in 2002: new surprises in the Jak/Stat pathway. Cell 109 suppl., S121–131 (2002)

[Ratsch *et al.*, 2003] Ratsch, E., Schultz, J., Saric, J., Lavin, P., Wittig, U., Reyle, U., Rojas, I.: Developing a protein–interactions ontology. Comparative and Functional Genomics 4, 85–89 (2003)

[Regev *et al.*, 2001] Regev, A., Silverman, W., Shapiro, E.: Representation and simulation of biochemical processes using the π–calculus process algebra. In: Pacific Symposium on Biocomputing, pp. 459–470 (2001)

[Rzhetsky *et al.*, 2000] Rzhetsky, A., Koike, T., Kalachikov, S., Gomez, S., Krauthammer, M., Kaplan, S., Kra, P., Russo, J., Friedman, C.: A knowledge model for analysis and simulation of regulatory networks. Bioinformatics 16(12), 1120–1128 (2000)

[Saunders *et al.*, 2008] Saunders, B., Lyon, S., Day, M., Riley, B., Chenette, E., Subramaniam, S., Vadivelu, I.: The Molecule Pages database. Nucleic Acids Research 36, D700–706 (2008)

[Schacherer *et al.*, 2001] Schacherer, F., Choi, C., Götze, U., Krull, M., Pistor, S., Wingender, E.: The TRANSPATH signal transduction database: a knowledge base on signal transduction networks. Bioinformatics 17(11), 1053–1057 (2001)

[Seipel, 2002] Seipel, D.: Processing XML–documents in PROLOG. In: Proc. 17th Workshop on Logic Programming, WLP 2002 (2002)

[Spellman *et al.*, 2002] Spellman, P.T., Miller, M., Stewart, J., Troup, C., Sarkans, U., Chervitz, S., Bernhart, D., Sherlock, G., Ball, C., Lepage, M., Swiatek, M., Marks, W., Goncalves, J., Markel, S., Iordan, D., Shojatalab, M., Pizarro, A., White, J., Hubley, R., Deutsch, E., Senger, M., Aronow, B.J., Robinson, A., Bassett, D., Stoeckert, C.J., Brazma, A.: Design and implementation of microarray gene expression markup language (MAGE–ML). Genome Biology 3(9) (2002); RESEARCH0046

[Wang & Dohlman, 2004] Wang, Y., Dohlman, H.G.: Pheromone signaling mechanisms in yeast: a prototypical sex machine. Science 306(5701), 1508–1509 (2004)

[Wielemaker, 2009] Wielemaker, J.: SWI–PROLOG 5.0 Reference Manual and Wielemaker, J., Anjewierden, A (2009) Programming in XPCE/PROLOG (2009), http://www.swi-prolog.org/

[Zheng *et al.*, 2008] Zheng, S., Sheng, J., Wang, C., Wang, X., Yu, Y., Li, Y., Michie, A., Dai, J., Zhong, Y., Hao, P., Liu, L., Li, Y.: MPSQ: a web tool for protein–state searching. Bioinformatics 24, 2412–2413 (2008)

Network Monitoring with Constraint Programming: Preliminary Specification and Analysis

Pedro Salgueiro and Salvador Abreu

Departamento de Informática
Universidade de Évora
{pds,spa}@di.uevora.pt

Abstract. Network Monitoring and Intrusion Detection Systems plays an important role in today's computer networks health, allowing the diagnosis and detection of anomalous situations on the network that could damage the performance and put the security of users data in risk if not detected or diagnosed in time to take any necessary measures.

In this paper we present a preliminary specification and analysis of a network monitoring and intrusion detection concept system based on constraint programming, implemented on several constraint solver systems. This concept allows to describe the desirable network situations through constraints on network entities, allowing a more expressive and clear way of describing network situations.

1 Introduction

Computer networks are composed of numerous complex and heterogeneous systems, hosts and services. Often, large numbers of users rely on such networks to perform their regular job and have to interrupt it when, for some reason, the network has a problem. In order to prevent computer network degradation or even any failure preventing users from using it, computer networks should be constantly monitored in order to diagnose its functionality as well as the security of the network and its users data.

Constraint Programming [1,2,3] is a powerful programming paradigm for modeling and problem solving and it has been widely used with success on a variety of problems such as scheduling, vehicle routing, planning and bio-informatics. Using constraint programming, the modeling of complex problems is done by asserting a number of constraints over a set of variables in a natural way, simplifying the modeling of complex problems. The constraints are then solved by a constraint solver which assigns values to each of the variables, solving the problem.

On a computer network, there are some aspects that must be verified in order to maintain the quality and integrity of the services provided by the network as well as to ensure its safety. The description of those conditions, together with a verification that they are met can be seen as network performance monitoring combined with an intrusion detection task.

S. Abreu and D. Seipel (Eds.): INAP 2009, LNAI 6547, pp. 223–238, 2011.

These two aspects are usually intertwined, from a network point view, so that it makes sense to provide a single specification for the desired system and network properties which can be used to produce network activity monitoring agents, with knowledge about conditions which must or must not be met. These conditions, specified in terms of properties of parts of the (observed) network traffic, will amount to a specification of a desired or an unwanted state of the network, such as that brought about by a system intrusion or another form of a malicious access.

It is our claim that the proper operation of a network can be described as a *constraint satisfaction problem* (CSP) [1], by using variables which represent parts of the network traffic as well as structural properties of the network itself.

1.1 Network Monitoring

System and Network Monitor Applications are designed to perform network monitoring tasks on a computer network. These applications are constantly monitoring network devices and services in order to detect possible anomalies. Besides system network monitoring, there are applications that focus on traffic monitoring trying to inspect traffic to look for anomalies or undesirable communications. This kind of applications is known as an Intrusion Detection System's(IDS) which is supposed to analyze network traffic, looking for patterns known to include intrusions or attacks passing through the network.

Well known examples of System and Network Monitor Applications include `Nagios` [4,5] while the Intrusion Detection System `Snort` [6,7] is very widely used.

1.2 Constraint Programming

Constraint Programming (CP) is a declarative programming methodology which consists in the formulation of a solution to a problem as a *constraint satisfaction problem* (CSP) [1], in which a number of variables are introduced, with well-specified domains and which describe the state of the system. A set of relations, called *constraints*, is then imposed on the variables which make up the problem. These constraints are understood to have to hold true for a particular set of bindings for the variables, resulting in a *solution* to the CSP.

Finite Domain Constraint Programming is one of the most practical and widely used approaches to Constraint Programming [1]. Many systems and libraries have been developed to perform Finite Domain Constraint Programming and rely on constraint propagation involving variables ranging over some finite set of integers to solve the problems.

Some of the more well known FD constraint programming systems include GNU Prolog [8] and SICStus Prolog [9] which extend a Prolog virtual machine with capabilities of constraint programming. Besides those systems, there are libraries which provide Constraint Programming capabilities to well known programming languages, such as Gecode [10] a constraint solver library implemented in C++. Gecode is particular, in that it is not designed to be used directly for modeling but is meant to be interfaced with other systems, such as Gecode/R [11], a Ruby interface to Gecode. CaSPER [12] (Constraint Solving Programming Environment for Research) is a new and open C++ library for generic constraint solving, that still needs to be matured.

The results presented in this paper were obtained using the previously mentioned constraint system solvers.

2 Modeling Network Monitoring with Constraint Programming

Intrusion Detection is a major monitoring task for a computer network. This task can be performed by detecting network traffic patterns that relate to known intrusions.

Our approach to intrusion detection relies on being able to describe the situation that is supposed to be identified over the network traffic and, through the use of constraints, identify the set of packets that match the target network situation.

The description of those situations is done by stating constraints over network entities, such as network packets, ip address, ports, hosts, among others. Network packet is the entity more relevant in the description of a network situation, since it is composed by most of the other entities and allows to describe all the traffic on a given network. Each network packet entity which is composed by 19 individual fields.

The problem needs to be modeled as a Constraint Satisfaction Problem (CSP) in order to use the constraint programming mechanisms. Such a CSP will be composed of a set of variables, V, representing the network packets, their associated domains, D, and a set of constraints, C that relates the variables in order to describe the network situation. On such a CSP, each network packet variable is a tuple composed of 19 [1] integer variables which represent significant fields of a network packet. The domain of the network packet variables, D, are the values actually seen on the network traffic window, which is a set of tuples of 19 integer values, each tuple representing a network packet actually observed on the traffic window and each integer value represents the fields that are relevant to network monitoring. Such a CSP can be represented in the following form, where P represents a set of network packet variables, D, a set of network packets representing the network traffic window, and $\forall P_i \in P \Rightarrow P_i \in D$ the associated domains of each variable:

$$
\begin{aligned}
&P = \{(P_{1,1}, \ldots, P_{1,19}), \ldots, (P_{n,1}, \ldots, P_{n,19})\} \\
&D = \{(V_{1,1}, \ldots, V_{1,19}), \ldots, (V_{m,1}, \ldots, P_{m,19})\} \\
&\forall P_i \in P \Rightarrow P_i \in D
\end{aligned}
$$

[1] Here, we are only considering the "interesting" fields in TCP/IP packets, from an IDS point-of-view.

The solution to the CSP described above, which describes network situations, will be a set of network packets that satisfies all the constraints that describes the network situation. If that set of packets is seen on a network traffic, then that network situation exists on that network.

Our approach to network monitoring uses a network traffic window as the network packet source, instead of using the entire network traffic, looking for the specified network situations in that traffic window. On this work we used static network traffic windows that were obtained by using the packet sniffer `tcpdump`[13].

Using constraint programming, the variables that are used to model the problem can take any value that satisfies the stated constraints. In the case of network monitoring, the domain of the packet variables is very large, since each packet is composed by 19 individual fields, each one having its own large domain. If the domain of such variables were completely free, but still respecting the constraints, the amount of valid values that could be assigned to a variable which satisfies the constraints is very large, so it makes sense that the packet variables can only be assigned with values that satisfies the stated constraints and that exists on the network traffic log. In Sect. 3 are described the several approaches that we used to force the network packet variables to only take values from a network traffic log.

3 Network Traffic Window as Variables Domain

Network monitoring based with constraint programming relies on stating rules and relations between network packets. Such network packets are composed by 19 fields, almost all of them important to describe a network situation. Such fields have a very wide domain and most of the values that can be assigned to such fields make no sense on the computer network that is being monitored. The only values that would make sense to be assigned to each field of each network packet involved in a description of a network situation would be the actual values that exist on the network traffic.

The values of such fields should be chosen from the network traffic window, not the individual fields of the packet, since those values only make sense when combined with all other fields that compose a network packet.

So, instead of each individual field of a packet be allowed to take values from its correspondent field of any packet on the traffic log, a tuple representing a network packet and composed with all the fields of a network packet can only take values from the set of tuples available on the network traffic log, this way, the network packet variables used on a network description can only take values that really exists, eliminating any unnecessary values. This can be described as follows, where P represents a network packet variable, D represents the network packet window and P should take values from D.

$$P = \{(P_{1,1}, \ldots, P_{1,19})\}$$
$$D = \{(V_{1,1}, \ldots, V_{1,19}), \ldots, (V_{m,1}, \ldots, P_{m,19})\}$$
$$P_i \in D$$

3.1 Approaches

In order to force the network packet variables to only be allowed to take values that belong to a network traffic log, several approaches were taken.

In this implementation of a network monitoring concept based on constraint programming, the network packet variables are represented as an array of integer variables, and the network traffic window were converted into an array of arrays that represents all the network packets available on the traffic window, each array representing a network packet.

Using Extensional constraints. The first approach to this problem was to use *extensional* constraints.

Extensional constraints are used to force a tuple of constraint variables of a problem to take values from a set of tuple of values, which would be appropriate to use on this problem, since we have a tuple of variables which are the network packet variables, and a set of tuples of values, which is the network traffic window, therefore, solving the problem of the domains of the network packets domain.

These constraints receives as its input a tuple of variables and a list of tuples of values or variables. In this application domain, the tuple of variables is the array representing a network variable, which is composed by several integer variables, and the list of tuples is the list with all packets found on the network traffic window. The results obtained while using this approach are described in Sect. 4.1.

The use of the *extensional* constraint can be described as follows, where P represents a network packet variable and M a set of network packets representing all possible values that packet P can take.

$$P = (P_1, \ldots, P_{19}),$$
$$M = \{(V_{(1,1)}, \ldots, V_{(1,19)}), \ldots \ , (V_{(k,1)}, \ldots, V_{(k,19)})\},$$
$$\forall P_i \in P,\ \forall M,\ extensional(P, M) \Rightarrow P \in M$$

Using Extensional and Element constraints. A second approach to the problem combines the *extensional* constraint with the *element* constraint. The *element* constraint allows to use an un-instantiated variable as an index to an array of values or variables. This allows to translate the matrix representing the network packets into a matrix of indexes to an array with all values that exists on the original matrix. By adopting this approach, one can use the *extensional* constraint on this translated matrix, composed only by indexes, with much smaller values than the original matrix, and which could improve the performance in a great scale. Using the *extensional* with the translated matrix, the values assigned to the packet variables are indexes to an array containing all the values of the original matrix, instead of the values that compose the original packets. This poses a problem, since after applying the constraints to state that the packet variables should only take values from the network traffic window, it is also necessary to state other constraints over such variables using the values of the original matrix. To solve this problem, the variables are *bonded* back to its original values by using the *element* constraint, allowing to use constraints over the original values. The results obtained by this approach are showed and described in Sect. 4.2.

The use of the extensional constraint combined with the element constraint can be can be described as follows:

$$
\begin{aligned}
&P = (P_1, \dots, P_{19}),\\
&M = \{(V_{(1,1)}, \dots, V_{(1,19)}), \dots\ , (V_{(k,1)}, \dots, V_{(k,19)})\},\\
&T = \{V_{(1,1)} \cup \dots \cup V_{(1,19)} \cup \dots \cup V_{(k,1)} \cup \dots \cup V_{(k,19)}\},\\
&N = \{(X_{(1,1)}, \dots, X_{(1,19)}) \dots\ , (X_{(k,1)}, \dots, X_{(k,19)})\},
\end{aligned}
$$

$$
\begin{aligned}
&\forall P_j \in P,\ \forall M,\ \forall X_{(k,i)}, \in N,\\
&\mathit{extensional\_element}(P, M, N) \Rightarrow\ P \in N,\ T_{X_{(k,i)}} = M_{(k,i)}
\end{aligned}
$$

where P represents a network packet variable, M a set of packets representing all possible values that packet P can take, T all the values in M and N the translated matrix M.

3.2 Modeling a Portscan Attack as a CSP

A portscan attack can be described by a set of constraints between two network packets, the packet that initiates a TCP/IP connection and the packet that closes it. In order to detect if the network is under such attack we monitor if there are how many of these sets of networks packet to appear on a network traffic in a short period of time.

A portscan attack can be modeled as a CSP in the form of $\mathcal{P} = (X, D, C)$, where X is a set with all the variables that compose the problem, D the domain of each variable and C the constraints of the CSP. The set of variables X is a set of integer variables representing all the packets described by the CSP. X can be defined as follows, where i represents the number of packets that are being looked:

$$
X = \{(P_{(1,1)}, \dots, P_{(1,19)}), \dots\ , (P_{(i,1)}, \dots, P_{(i,19)})\}
$$

Consider now the definition of the domain D: let $D_{(i,n)}$ be the domain of the corresponding variable $P_{(i,n)}$, M the set of all packets in the network traffic log and k the number of packets seen on the network traffic window. We have:

$$
\begin{aligned}
&D = \{D_{(1,1)}, \dots, D_{(1,19)}, \dots, D_{(i,1)}, \dots, D_{(i,19)}\},\\
&M = \{(V_{(1,1)}, \dots, V_{(1,19)}), \dots\ , (V_{(k,1)}, \dots, V_{(k,19)})\},\\
&\forall D_{(i,n)} \in D,\ \ \forall P_{(i,n)} \in X,\ \ P_i = (P_{(i,1)}, \dots, P_{(i,19)}) \Rightarrow P_i \in M
\end{aligned}
$$

The constraints C that compose a such a CSP are defined as follows:

$$\forall n = 2 * i, \forall n > 0, \forall P \in M \Rightarrow \quad (1)$$
$$P_{(n,14)} = 1,\ P_{(n,18)} = 0, \quad (2)$$
$$P_{(n+1,13)} = 1, \quad (3)$$

$$(((P_{(n,2)} = P_{(n+1,2)}) \wedge \ldots \wedge (P_{(n,6)} = P_{(n+1,6)}))\vee$$
$$((P_{(n,2)} = P_{(n+1,6)}) \wedge \ldots \wedge (P_{(n,6)} = P_{(n+1,11)}))), \quad (4)$$

$$((P_{(n,0)} < P_{(n+1,0)}) \vee ((P_{(n,0)} = P_{(n+1,0)}) \wedge (P_{(n,1)} < P_{(n+1,1)}))) \quad (5)$$

$$(((P_{(n,0)} = P_{(n+1,0)}) \wedge (P_{(n+1,1)} - P_{(n,1)} < 500))\vee$$
$$((P_{(n+1,0)} = P_{(n,0)} + 1) \wedge (1000000 - P_{(n,1)} + P_{(n+1,1)} < 500))), \quad (6)$$

$$\forall n = 2 * i, \forall n > 1, \forall P \in M \Rightarrow \quad (7)$$
$$((P_{(i,0)} > P_{(i-2,0)}) \vee ((P_{(i,0)} = P_{(i-2,0)}) \wedge (P_{(i,1)} > P_{(i-2,1)}))) \quad (8)$$

Some of the constraints applied to network packet variables are temporal constraints, forcing the network packets appear in the right order. Due to this fact, some of the constraints are not applied to the first set of network packets, since there is not a previous set of packets to force a correct order, so, on the listing above, the rules from (1) to (6), are applied all constraints to all network packet sets, except the ones that forces the packets to be ordered.

Rule (2) adds constraints so that the first packet of set has the SYN flag set and doesn't have the ACK flag set.

Rule (3) adds a constraint to the second packet of each set that forces them to have the RST flag set.

Rule 4 adds constraints to force the two packets of the set to be related, so that they make part of a TCP connection, the first one being the one that initiates the TCP connection, and the last one the one that closes the connection.

Rule 5 adds a set of constraints so that the second packet of the set appears after the first one, in a chronological order.

Rule 6 adds constraints to force the maximum distance between the first and the second packet of a set of two packets are less than $500ms$.

After rule (7), rule (8) adds a constraint to all network sets, except the first one, which will force them to be ordered in a chronological order.

4 Experimental Results

In this Section we present the performed experiments as well as the execution times obtained on each experiment while using each of the constraint solver as well as a description of the behavior of the performance of each experiment.

All the approaches described in this work were experimented using several constraint system solvers. The chosen constraint systems to make the experiments were Gecode 3.1.0, Gecode/R 1.1.0, GNU Prolog 1.3.0-6, SICStus Prolog 4.0.4-x86-linux-glibc2.6 and CaSPER 0.1.4. Each experiment used the same problem with the same set of data where possible.

The problem that was used to analyze the performance of each constraint system solver was the description of a portscan attack. This network situation can be detected by a set of constraints between two network packets, the packet that initiates a TCP/IP connection and the packet that closes it. In order to detect if there is a portscan attack, there is the need to decide how many sets of two of these packets have to appear on a network traffic to consider it a portscan attack. These number of sets of packets used to describe the network situation affects the performance of our approach as each set adds more constraint variables to the problem. With this fact in mind, we made several experiments with the same data sets, but using different number of sets of packets to describe the problem in order to see how the performance was affected when the size of the problem rises.

We also made some runs using different data sets in order to see the behavior of the performance when the size of the matrix varies and also when the values of the matrix varies.

On some cases we were forced to use smaller matrices with smaller values because some constraint system couldn't handle some matrices while using some constraints.

We used the same problem modeling with the same data set in all experiments in order to compare the results obtained in each of the constraint solver. The data sets we have used are composed by a set of packets, each one being composed by 19 individual values. For each constraint solver we used four sets of network packets, three of them composed by similar values, varying the number of packets, and one composed by smaller values. These were the network traffic window used in most of the constraint solvers, except in Gecode/R and on CaSPER for reasons explained above. With those constraint solvers we used network packet sets similar to the ones described above, but transformed in order to the individual fields of the network packets would be smaller values, still respecting the order and relations that existed between all the values on the original matrix.

For each experiment with each network packet set, several runs were made with similar problem modeling but with different number of variables in order to understand the behavior of the performance of each constraint solver. For each constraint solver two experiments are presented, one looking for two packet sets(four network packets variables) and the other, looking for six packet sets(twelve network packet variables), which allows to analyze the behavior of the performance of each constraint solver when the number of variables to model the problem varies.

On each of these runs, we also made several measurements of the execution time, being measured the time the system takes to build the constraints, and the time the system needs to solve the problem after it has been initialized. This network monitoring concept works with log files, so this initialization of the constraint solvers can be considered as making part of the process of the log file reading process.

On the experiments with GNU Prolog and SICStus Prolog were made two measurements of the total time to solve the problem, one using no heuristics and another using the *first_fail*[2] heuristic, where the alternative that most likely leads to a failure is selected.

All the experiments were run on a dedicated computer, an HP Proliant DL380 G4 with two Intel(R) Xeon(TM) CPU 3.40GHz and with 4 GB of memory, running Debian GNU/Linux 4.0 with Linux kernel version 2.6.18-5.

4.1 Using Extensional Constraints

This approach forces a network packet, represented by a tuple of variables, implemented as a list or array of variables to take values from a set of tuples of values that represent all the packets on a network traffic window, implemented as a matrix, an array of arrays, or list of lists.

Using Gecode. When using the extensional constraint on Gecode, the performance tend to degrade very much when the values on the network traffic window varies from very small values to very high values. The performance also tends to degrade when the number of network packet variables used to describe the network situation rises. The size of the matrix that represents the network traffic doesn't seem to affect considerably the performance, since modeling the problem with the same amount or network packet variables but varying the size of the network packet window doesn't affect its performance. Table 1 presents the execution times of the several runs using Gecode. On this experiment were made 10 runs, and the times presented are the *usertime* average of each run, in milliseconds.

Table 1. Gecode execution times using extensional constraint

Matrix	N° of Packets	2 sets (setup)	2 sets (solve)	6 sets (setup)	6 sets (solve)
pscan_small	20	441	48	1281	135
pscan	20	3735	409	10927	1100
pscan1	40	3754	395	10984	1126
pscan2	60	3748	401	11025	1082

Using GNU Prolog. Using the equivalent extensional constraint from Gecode on GNU Prolog, *fd_relation/2*, the performance is very similar to Gecode if the size of network traffic window don't have very big values. Also, similar to Gecode, the performance is affected badly when the number of packets used to model the network situation rises. The size of the network traffic window doesn't seem to affect the performance of GNU Prolog, since the execution times obtained to the same situation using matrices with different size are practically the same. One big difference to Gecode, is that GNU Prolog doesn't seem to be affected by matrices that are composed by values that varies from very low to very large values, since executing the same test using matrices of the same size, one with smaller values, and other with much grater values, presents a very similar performance. Table 2 presents the execution times of the several runs using GNU Prolog. On this experiment, 100 runs were made, and the times presented are the *usertime* average of each run, in milliseconds.

Table 2. GNU Prolog execution times using fd_relation *extensional* constraint

Matrix	N° of Packets	2 sets (setup)	2 sets (solve)	2 sets (solve ff)	6 sets setup	6 sets (solve)	6 sets (solve ff)
pscan_small	20	363.3	2.1	2.2	1075.7	226.5	225.1
pscan	20	366.0	3.0	1.3	1078.1	229.8	227.7
pscan1	40	366.9	4.3	1.6	1079.4	261.7	217.5
pscan2	60	370.08	4.5	1.7	1090.1	262.5	220.1

Using Gecode/R. The performance of using this approach in Gecode/R is very similar to the performance of Gecode, as expected, since it uses Gecode as the constraint solver, mean while Gecode/R has a big limitation, as it segfaults when the values that compose the network packets of the network traffic window are too large. Network packet windows *pscan*, *pscan1* and *pscan2* had to be transformed so the network packets were composed by smaller values in order to Gecode/R to be able to work with them. As expected, the behavior of the performance of Gecode/R using the extensional constraint is quite similar to the behavior of the performance of Gecode, when the values of the matrix rises, the performance starts to decay. The performance is also affected by the number of network packets available on the network traffic window, but in a small factor. The number of network packet variables needed to represent the problem has a large influence in the performance, degrading when the number of variables rise. Table 3 presents the execution times of the several runs using Gecode/R. On this experiment 10 runs were made, and the times presented are the *usertime* average of each run in milliseconds.

Table 3. Gecode/R execution times using the *extensional* constraint

Matrix	N° of Packets	2 sets (setup)	2 sets (solve)	6 sets (setup)	6 sets (solve)
pscan_small	20	130	492	158	1482
pscan_smaller	20	126	453	156	1380
pscan1_smaller	40	130	460	162	1399
pscan2_smaller	60	133	461	190	1395

Table 4. SICStus Prolog execution using the *extensional* constraints

Matrix	N° of Packets	2 sets (setup)	2 sets (solve)	2 sets (solve ff)	6 sets (setup)	6 sets (solve)	6 sets (solve ff)
pscan_small	20	16.1	0.2	0.2	48.0	1.5	1.6
pscan	20	16.0	0.4	0.3	48.1	1.4	1.6
pscan1	40	33.6	0.4	0.2	100.7	2.7	2.6
pscan2	60	52.3	0.4	0.4	157.4	3.6	3.0

Using SICStus Prolog. Using SICStus Prolog with the extensional constraint, *table/2*, revealed to be an interesting solution, presenting good performance numbers. The performance of SICStus Prolog didn't seem to be affected by the size of the values that compose network packets in the network traffic window. On the other hand, and opposite to the other approaches, the performance is quite affected by the number of network packets in the traffic window , getting degraded as the its size grows. Similar to all other approaches, the execution times get degrades as the size of the problem grows, getting slower when more variables are needed to model the situation. Table 4 presents the execution times of several runs using SICStus Prolog. On this experiment 100 runs were made, and the times presented are the *usertime* average of each run in milliseconds.

Using CaSPER. Using the extensional constraint, *table*, in CaSPER shows that it doesn't handle very good matrices composed by high values, degrading the performance when its values get higher. The performance of CaSPER gets worst when the number of variables needed to represent the problem gets higher, just as with all other constraint solvers experimented. It also degrades in a great scale when the size of the matrix rises. CaSPER revealed very sensitive to the size of the values that compose the network packets available on the network packet window, having problems handling big matrices composed by large values, so, in order to make some experiments, we transformed the network traffic windows used on other approaches so that the network packets that compose them be composed by smaller values. These transformed network traffic windows are the same ones that were used on the experiments with Gecode/R. The results obtained with CaSPER are presented in Table 5. On this experiment 10 runs were made, and the times presented are the *usertime* average of each run in milliseconds.

Table 5. CaSPER execution times while using the *extensional* constraint

Matrix	N° of Packets	2 sets (setup)	2 sets (solve)	6 sets (setup)	6 sets (solve)
pscan_small	20	640	52410	1910	123810
pscan_smaller	20	570	51670	1750	121420
pscan1_smaller	40	580	106470	1770	264040
pscan2_smaller	60	590	194080	1800	499440

4.2 Using Extensional Constraints with Element Constraints

The approach using *extensional* constraints described in Sect. 4.1 shows that some of the constraint solvers tested don't perform very well when using the extensional constraint when the network packets that compose the network packet window are by values that varies from very low to very high values. In order to solve this problem, the matrix with all possible values, representing the network packet window was translated into a matrix that contains indexes to an array that contains all the values of the matrix. This matrix is then used along with the extensional constraint to force the network packets variables to only take values that exist on the network packet window. These packet variables will then be composed by values that are indexes, so it is needed to create a new packet variable, and channel that variable to the values on the array with the original values, which is achieved by using the *element* constraint.

Using Gecode. Using this approach in Gecode revealed to be quite good, having an excellent performance when compared to the approach that only uses the *extensional* constraint. Although this excellent performance, it behaves much like when using only the extensional constraint, as it degrades as the number of packet variables needed to model a network situation rises. Also, the performance of this approach doesn't seem to be affected by the number of packets in the network packet window, since performing the same test using similar network traffic windows of different sizes, doesn't change the performance in a significant way. One main advantage of this approach, is that the performance is not affected by the values that compose the network packets of the network traffic window, having the same results in terms of performance when the packets are composed by large values or smaller values. Table 6 presents the execution times of the several runs using Gecode. On this experiment, 1000 runs were made, and the times presented are the average *usertime* of each run, in milliseconds.

Table 6. Gecode execution times using *extensional* and *element* constraints

Matrix	N° of Packets	2 sets (setup)	2 sets (solve)	6 sets (setup)	6 sets (solve)
pscan_small	20	4.36	0.46	7.33	1.15
pscan	20	3.86	0.49	6.14	1.24
pscan1	40	4.77	0.57	8.82	1.20
pscan2	60	5.89	0.79	12.15	1.26

Using GNU Prolog. Combining the *extensional* and *element* constraint in GNU Prolog didn't reveal to be very promising, since the performance obtained were actually slower than the version using only the *extensional* constraint. This approach tends to degrade just like the approach that used only the constraint *extensional* constraint, not being influenced by the values that compose the network packets on the traffic window or by its the size,

Table 7. GNU Prolog execution times using fd_relation *extensional* and *element* constraint

Matrix	N° of Packets	2 sets (setup)	2 sets (solve)	2 sets (solve ff)	6 sets setup	6 sets (solve)	6 sets (solve ff)
pscan_small	20	379.7	3.2	2.8	1127.1	285.6	282.6
pscan	20	381.5	3.4	3.1	1128.7	284.1	281.3
pscan1	40	381.1	3.2	3.1	1132.5	296.3	283.0
pscan2	60	389.1	3.3	3.1	1148.2	294.0	278.8

Table 8. Gecode/R execution times using the *extensional* and *element* constraints

Matrix	N° of Packets	2 sets (setup)	2 sets (solve)	6 sets (setup)	6 sets (solve)
pscan_small	20	144	88	235	267
pscan	20	148	82	238	262
pscan1	40	158	95	251	333
pscan2	60	155	121	274	382

degrading only when the number of packet variables that is being looked for gets higher. Table 7 presents the execution times of the several runs using GNU Prolog.

Using Gecode/R. Using the extensional constraint combined with the element constraint improved the performance of Gecode/R in a great factor, still, its not as good as the performance obtained by using the same approach with Gecode. Such as Gecode, the performance of Gecode/R is affected in a small factor by the size of network packet window. The size of the values that compose network packet variables in the traffic window also affects the performance in a small scale, still, more noticeable than when using Gecode, as the overall performance of Gecode/R is worse than the overall performance of Gecode. The performance of Gecode/R is affected by the number of the packet variables that is being looked for, degrading when the number of variables rises, just as in Gecode and GNU Prolog. Table 8 presents the execution times of the several runs using Gecode/R.

Using SICStus Prolog. Using SICStus Prolog with the combination of the *extensional* constraint, *table/3* and the constraint *element*, *relation/3* didn't reveal any advantage over the approach that used only the constraint *table/3* just as it happened with GNU Prolog. Table 9 presents the execution times of several runs using SICStus Prolog where can be seen the main differences between the other approaches. On this experiment, 100 runs were made, and the times presented are the average *usertime* of each run.

Using CaSPER. Using CaSPER with the *extensional* constraint combined with the *element* revealed very good results when compared to the approach using

Table 9. SICStus Prolog execution using *extensional* and *element* constraints

Matrix	N° of Packets	2 sets (setup)	2 sets (solve)	2 sets (solve ff)	6 sets (setup)	6 sets (solve)	6 sets (solve ff)
pscan_small	20	57.8	0.5	1.8	167.7	5.5	6.8
pscan	20	58.0	0.2	1.0	167.3	4.1	6.5
pscan1	40	58.1	0.4	0.6	167.4	5.1	6.8
pscan2	60	58.5	0.2	0.6	167.6	6.6	9.0

Table 10. CaSPER execution times using the *extensional* and *element* constraints

Matrix	N° of Packets	2 sets (setup)	2 sets (solve)	6 sets (setup)	6 sets (solve)
pscan_small	20	13	54	40	157
pscan_smaller	20	12	56	40	158
pscan1_smaller	40	18	118	58	343
pscan2_smaller	60	24	221	81	647

only the *extensional* constraint. This fact is due to the use of a translated matrix that represents the network traffic window, which uses much smaller values than the ones on the original values. The performance of CaSPER tends to degrade when the number of variables being looked gets higher. Also, when the size of the network packet window rises, the performance degrades. It seems not to be affected by the size of the values that compose the network packets on the traffic window. The execution times of this approach using CaSPER are presented in Table 10. On this experiment, 10 runs were made, and the times presented are the average *usertime* of each run, in milliseconds.

5 Experimental Evaluation

The results obtained in this work shows a multitude of performance figures, while some of the constraint solvers used presents quite impressive performance, mainly when using Gecode with the *Extensional* constraint combined with *Element* constraint, others, like CaSPER present poor results.

Using Gecode or Gecode/R with the combination of the *Extensional* and the *Element* constraints, there is a great improvement in terms of performance when compared to the approach using only the *Extensional* constraint, either in Gecode or Gecode/R. This solving method presents very good performance, and is affected in a very small scale, either by varying the size of the network packet window, by the size of the values that compose network packets in the network packet window, or by number of network packets being looked. As expected, the performance of Gecode/R is slightly worse than Gecode, since a new layer of modeling is being added on top of Gecode.

While Gecode and Gecode/R have a huge gain of performance when combining the *Extensional* and *Element* constraints, this approach in GNU Prolog or

SICStus Prolog actually degrades the performance. Using such constraint solvers, the performance is not affected by the values that compose the network packets of the network traffic window. Also, on GNU Prolog, an interesting fact is that the number network packets being looked for, influences the performance on a very small scale.

CaSPER, on the other end, shows a poor performance figures, either when using the *Extensional* constraint, or when combining it with the *Element* constraint, which could be explained by the early stages of development of CaSPER.

6 Conclusions and Future Work

Initial Assessment

The results obtained in this work show that it's possible to transform the description of a network situation into a Constraint Satisfaction Problem and solve it with a variety of constraint solvers, demonstrating the viability of using declarative programming technologies in network management tasks, allowing to analyze the performance of each of the constraint solvers tested.

The results obtained by Gecode shows that modeling network situations with constraints in order to perform network monitoring and intrusion detection tasks can be done in an efficient way by combining *extensional* and *element* constraints.

This work shows that the performance of each approach varies in a big scale, ranging from very good performance results when using Gecode with the *Extensional* and *Element* constraints combined, to a much lower performance when using the *Extensional* constraint with CaSPER. We haven't yet identified a valid explanation for the different performance, as the objective of this work was to experiment different approaches on several constraint solvers. An important future step will be the study in detail of the reasons that lead to such a performance difference in order to optimize the performance of this concept.

Future Work

We are currently implementing new network constraints as well as making use of new data types in order to allow for the description of more network situations. As the modeling and performance aspects progress, we will extend the application domain to include live network monitoring.

Another significant planned addition is the development of a Domain Specific Language (DSL)[14] that will use these network constraints to conveniently perform network monitoring tasks.

Besides using these constraint solvers, we are also working on using Constraint Based Local Search[15] algorithms, such as Adaptive Search[16], to solve network monitoring problems.

There is also some work being carried in our research group on using a port of Adaptive Search to the Cell/BE[17] architecture, described in[18], to solve these kind of network monitoring CSPs in a distributed environment.

References

1. Rossi, F., Van Beek, P., Walsh, T.: Handbook of constraint programming. Elsevier Science, Amsterdam (2006)
2. Apt, K.R.: Principles of constraint programming. Cambridge Univ. Pr., Cambridge (2003)
3. Schulte, C.: Programming Constraint Services. LNCS (LNAI), vol. 2302. Springer, Heidelberg (2002)
4. Harlan, R.C.: Network management with nagios. Linux J. 2003(111), 3 (2003)
5. Barth, W.: Nagios: System and network monitoring. No Starch Press, San Francisco (2006)
6. Roesch, M.: Snort - lightweight intrusion detection for networks. In: LISA 1999: Proceedings of the 13th USENIX Conference on System Administration, pp. 229–238. USENIX Association, Berkeley (1999)
7. Beale, J.: Snort 2.1 Intrusion Detection, 2nd edn. Syngress Publishing (2004)
8. Diaz, D., Codognet, P.: Design and implementation of the gnu prolog system. Journal of Functional and Logic Programming 2001(6), 542 (2001)
9. Carlsson, M., Ottosson, G., Carlson, B.: An open-ended finite domain constraint solver. LNCS, pp. 191–206 (1997)
10. Schulte, C., Stuckey, P.J.: Speeding up constraint propagation. In: Wallace, M. (ed.) CP 2004. LNCS, vol. 3258, pp. 619–633. Springer, Heidelberg (2004)
11. Gecode/R Team. Gecode/R: Constraint Programming in Ruby, `http://gecoder.org/`
12. Correia, M., Barahona, P.: Overview of the CaSPER* Constraint Solvers. In: Third International CSP Solver Competition, p. 15 (2008)
13. tcpdump web page (April 2009), `http://www.tcpdump.org/`
14. Van Deursen, A., Visser, J.: Domain-specific languages: An annotated bibliography. ACM Sigplan Notices 35(6), 26–36 (2000)
15. Van Hentenryck, P., Michel, L.: Constraint-based local search. MIT Press, Cambridge (2005)
16. Codognet, P., Díaz, D.: Yet another local search method for constraint solving. In: Steinhöfel, K. (ed.) SAGA 2001. LNCS, vol. 2264, pp. 73–90. Springer, Heidelberg (2001)
17. Kahle, J.A., Day, M.N., Hofstee, H.P., Johns, C.R., Maeurer, T.R., Shippy, D.: Introduction to the Cell multiprocessor. IBM Journal of Research and Development 49(4/5), 589–604 (2005)
18. Abreu, S., Diaz, D., Codognet, P.: Parallel local search for solving constraint problems on the cell broadband engine (preliminary results). CoRR, abs/0910.1264 (2009)

Author Index

GPSR Compliance

The European Union's (EU) General Product Safety Regulation (GPSR) is a set of rules that requires consumer products to be safe and our obligations to ensure this.

If you have any concerns about our products, you can contact us on ProductSafety@springernature.com

In case Publisher is established outside the EU, the EU authorized representative is:

Springer Nature Customer Service Center GmbH
Europaplatz 3
69115 Heidelberg, Germany

Batch number: 10844675

Printed by Printforce, the Netherlands